Entrepreneurial Finance and Accounting for High-Tech Companies

Entrepreneurial Finance and Accounting for High-Tech Companies

Frank J. Fabozzi

The MIT Press
Cambridge, Massachusetts
London, England

This book was set in Times New Roman and Syntax by Toppan Best-set Premedia Limited. Printed and bound in the United States of America.

Library of Congress Cataloging-in-Publication Data

Names: Fabozzi, Frank J., author.
Title: Entrepreneurial finance and accounting for high-tech companies / Frank J. Fabozzi.
Description: Cambridge, MA : MIT Press, 2016. | Includes bibliographical references and index.
Identifiers: LCCN 2016014528 | ISBN 9780262034982 (hardcover : alk. paper)
Subjects: LCSH: Business enterprises—Finance. | Accounting.

Classification: LCC HG4026 .F3298 2016 | DDC 658.15—dc23 LC record available at https://lccn.loc.gov/2016014528

10 9 8 7 6 5 4 3 2 1

Contents

Foreword

Mung Chiang
Arthur LeGrand Doty Professor of Electrical Engineering
Director, Keller Center for Innovation in Engineering Education
Inaugural Chair, Princeton Entrepreneurship Council
Princeton University

At Princeton University, we define entrepreneurship as "initiating transformations through risk-taking actions and value-creating organizations." To turn the mind-set of entrepreneurship into action, a wide range of capabilities must be acquired. Some of these capabilities can be taught in classrooms, while others need to come from hands-on experience in the field. Based on classroom teaching but drawing from many real-world examples, this excellent textbook provides a balanced and in-depth explanation of entrepreneurial finance: an area in which all entrepreneurs, in high tech or no tech, for-profit or nonprofit, must develop a thorough understanding.

The textbook's author, Frank Fabozzi, is an entrepreneur, educator, and highly regarded expert in the areas of financial theory and practice and the bond market. Frank was appointed the James Wei Visiting Professor in Entrepreneurship at the Keller Center for Innovation in Engineering Education at Princeton University for the 2013–14 academic year. The Spring 2014 course he taught, "Special Topics in Entrepreneurship: Entrepreneurial Finance," attracted a large enrollment of eager students. The focus of this course was on the financing of startup ventures that seek to raise external capital. The course addressed such important topics as how to develop a financial plan, including how much money to raise and when to raise it; alternative funding sources available at different stages of a new venture; alternative funding vehicles; how to negotiate the terms of a financial deal; how to value a venture; and exit strategies. The course also covered other important components that, taken collectively, lead to a successful venture: the value proposition, marketing, cost structure, key partnerships, key resources, and firm governance.

To illustrate how well received Frank's course was, here are some comments from students in his class: "Fantastic. Really helpful for my future career path as well. Meeting w Professor Fabozzi outside of class for help on my entrepreneurial ventures was very helpful, and encouraged my engagement in entrepreneurship both inside and outside the classroom." "A great speaker who knows the material well." "Professor Fabozzi is an excellent professor and mentor and is always willing to go above and beyond to help his students with in class or out of class projects."

The book you now hold contains the material of this outstanding course and should be read by all aspiring entrepreneurs.

Preface

The field of entrepreneurship encompasses several areas of study. The first is the personality of entrepreneurs with respect to their background characteristics, their behavioral patterns (particularly their attitude toward risk), and their motivation for starting a new venture. A second area of study is the link between technological innovation and entrepreneurship and the resulting impact on a country's economy in terms of economic growth, productivity, and employment. Entrepreneurial strategy is the third area of study, focusing on the unique challenges that entrepreneurs face owing to limited resources and a competitive disadvantage relative to established firms and markets. Strategies that cover marketing, production, and financing are the fourth area of study. Evaluating the relative advantages and disadvantages of corporate governance structures is the fifth area of study in the field of entrepreneurship. This area focuses on ownership control of the new venture and how alternative funding sources may have an impact on that control as the venture grows. The final area is finance, including alternative financing vehicles, sources, and strategies available to entrepreneurs at various stages of a venture's development, as well as related topics such as financial planning and accounting issues.

Several books are available that provide a good overview of each of these topics. However, in this book, *Entrepreneurial Finance and Accounting for High-Tech Companies,* the focus is on the critical financial topics associated with high-technology ventures that an entrepreneur needs to understand as a venture progresses through the various stages of its development. The book introduces the fundamentals of entrepreneurship, the legal and tax issues associated with fundraising, the various types of financing vehicles, the sources of financing, financial planning and budgeting, valuation issues, and capital budgeting decisions. The finance topics described in this book also bear on the issues associated with entrepreneurial strategy and corporate governance structure.

There are four chapters on financial accounting. Why is it necessary to cover accounting? John W. McKinley and Robert J. Ellis, in a blog post titled "Entrepreneurs Need Accounting Too: The Case for Including Financial and Managerial Accounting in an Entrepreneurship Curriculum,"[1] make a strong case for including accounting in the curriculum

---

1. John W. McKinley and Robert J. Ellis, "Entrepreneurs Need Accounting Too: The Case for Including Financial and Managerial Accounting in an Entrepreneurship Curriculum," http://blog.cengage.com/wp-content/uploads/2014/05/Winter-2014.McKinley. Ellis_.Entrepreneurs-Need-Accounting-Too.pdf.

of entrepreneurship programs. Although students might respond that accounting is unnecessary because they can retain an accountant to provide such services, McKinley and Ellis set forth the motivation as to why entrepreneurs "need accounting knowledge and understanding more than any other non-accounting major."

The reluctance of students to learn accounting results from misconceptions about what the subject matter covers and from the failure of university business schools to understand how their non-accounting undergraduate and graduate students will apply accounting in the real world. One can teach accounting in terms of the mechanics of recording business transactions that lead to the preparation of financial statements. Terms such as "debit" and "credit" dominate the discussion. To many (probably most) non-accounting majors, the mechanical aspects of accounting, although critical to would-be accountants, are neither very exciting nor viewed as useful. Students who argue that understanding this aspect of accounting is unnecessary because they can hire someone to record business transactions and create financial statements have a valid point. The aspect of accounting that is essential for an entrepreneur is how to utilize the financial statements created by accountants in order to assess a venture's economic prospects and to make critical economic decisions that will affect a venture's economic well-being, as well as to understand the limitations of financial statements. This aspect of accounting is referred to as "financial statement analysis" and is critical for entrepreneurs to understand without the need to know the debit and credit recording of business transactions. As Warren Buffet has said,

You can look at financial statements as systematic reports that inform you about the successes or failures of a company. At the end of the day, there's nothing more important to consider when you're looking to own a business—i.e., how does this company make a profit and what are they currently worth.[2]

Consequently, four chapters in this book are devoted to an understanding of financial statements that entrepreneurs should acquire and how that information is useful to understand a startup company's performance. A fifth chapter covers the fundamentals of financial statement analysis.

There are different ways to approach a book on entrepreneurial finance and accounting. One way is to assume that the reader has a background in the fundamentals of financial management, financial accounting, and managerial accounting, and then to build on that foundation. Another way is to assume that the reader has no background in any business-related course and to cover the fundamentals necessary to understand the wide range of issues discussed in the book. Based on my experience teaching a course on entrepreneurial finance at Princeton University's Keller Center for Innovation & Entrepreneurship, a course populated by engineering, economics, and social science majors, the approach I follow here is to assume no knowledge of business topics by the reader and to make the book self-contained.

---

2. Stig Brodersen and Preston Pysh, *Warren Buffett Accounting Book: Reading Financial Statements for Value Investing* (Saxonburg, PA: Pylon Publishing, 2014), 26.

OVERVIEW OF THE BOOK

The book consists of eighteen chapters and two appendices.

- *Chapter 1:* This introductory chapter covers three topics: the risks associated with a new venture, the reasons why startup companies fail, and the stages of financing.
- *Chapter 2:* The success of a new venture depends on the founding team's ability to manage costs and risks, grow the company's revenue and profits, and manage its relationship with stakeholders. Just how a company's founding team goes about executing these tasks is set forth in the business model, the first of three topics covered in chapter 2. A company's business plan, which describes how the founders plan to execute the business model, is the second topic covered in the chapter. Exit planning, the third topic covered in the chapter, consists of three activities that a founding team must go through in considering the transfer of ownership to another business or to other investors: (1) transition planning, (2) exit strategy planning, and (3) succession planning.
- *Chapter 3:* There are several forms of business organization from which the founders of a startup company may choose. The chapter begins with an overview of the different forms of business organization and then describes the non-tax factors that should be considered by founders in selecting the form of business organization and understanding how each form of business organization may either fulfill or fall short of fulfilling the different objectives. Tax factors that should be considered in deciding the form of business organization are then described. For founders who want to incorporate, the factors to consider in selecting the state in which to do so are briefly described.
- *Chapter 4:* The allocation of a company's equity among the founding team and key employees in a startup venture is a critical issue because it has an impact on both the distribution of the potential appreciation of the company's equity value and the control over the company's future direction. This chapter covers two topics: (1) the factors to be considered in allocating equity among those who are considered founders, and the issuance of what is popularly referred to as "founders' stock," and (2) the various types of equity incentive plans that a startup company can use to align the interests of founders and key employees with the interests of the company The key tax provisions that influence the type of plan the company offers are explained.
- *Chapter 5:* In raising capital, founders must comply with U.S. federal and state securities laws. In this chapter, the two principal topics related to fundraising as set forth in the U.S. federal securities laws are discussed: the rules for the solicitation of funds and the filings companies are required to make with the Securities and Exchange Commission.
- *Chapter 6:* The funding sources available to founders in the different stages of a venture's development are the subject of this chapter, including a discussion of an initial public offering. Early-stage finance includes the seed round and the first round. In the seed round, where the founders seek to finance the development of a product or

service, the financing sources are credit cards, vendors, the Small Business Administration, angel investors and angel groups, super angels, seed accelerators, incubators, and crowdfunding platforms, with the most common source of larger amounts of seed financing being angel investors. The primary source of expansion-stage financing historically has been traditional venture capital firms, corporate venture capital firms, and online venture capital funds. As explained in the chapter, the newest entrants providing expansion financing are institutional investors (mutual funds and hedge funds), which have made it possible for firms to postpone going public, merging, or being acquired in order to obtain a large infusion of capital.

- *Chapter 7:* The capital structure of company is the mix of equity and debt that the founders decide to use to finance the company. For startup companies, equity (or equity-type debt) is typically by far the largest component of the capital structure. This chapter covers the issuance of common stock prior to any initial public offering and equity dilutive securities (convertible preferred stock and convertible debt), financial instruments that lead to the issuance of common stock. As explained in the chapter, most investors in a startup company prefer equity dilutive securities to common stock. Also reviewed in the chapter are the key provisions of a term sheet used in fundraising and the computation of pre- and post-money valuation as additional equity capital is raised.

- *Chapter 8*: A company's financial statements provide a summary of the operating, financing, and investing activities of a business. The information contained in financial statements is used by current and potential suppliers of capital. There are four basic financial statements: the balance sheet, the income statement, the statement of cash flows, and the statement of shareholders' equity. This chapter, the first of four chapters on financial accounting, covers the objectives and the basic principles of financial statements.

- *Chapter 9:* In this chapter the balance sheet, also referred to as the statement of financial condition, is explained and illustrated. The balance sheet is a report of a company's assets, liabilities, and equity and is generally prepared at the end of a fiscal quarter or fiscal year.

- *Chapter 10:* The income statement or statement of income, the subject of this chapter, summarizes the operating performance of a company over a period of time—a fiscal quarter or a fiscal year. The key components of the income statement are described, as are the different measures of income: earnings available to common shareholders, comprehensive income, and earnings per share (basic and dilutive).

- *Chapter 11:* The statement of cash flows and the statement of stockholders' equity are the subjects of this chapter. The statement of cash flows provides a summary of a company's cash flows in terms of cash flow from operations, cash flow from investment activities, and cash flow from financing activities. The statement of stockholders' equity, also referred to as the statement of shareholders' equity, reports the changes in stockholders' equity between two consecutive years.

- *Chapter 12:* In this chapter the financial ratios created from the financial statements are explained. These metrics provide insight into a firm's profitability, how efficiently the founding team utilizes its resources, and the firm's reliance on debt and its ability to satisfy that debt. How all of these financial ratios link together to explain a company's earnings is discussed.

- *Chapter 13:* A component of the business plan is the financial plan, the subject of this chapter. A financial plan sets forth the company's projected financial position, cash flows, net income, and external financing needs. The starting point is projecting the revenues or sales of the company; that projection is then used to create budgets that make quantitative statements about the funding needs of a company. Since financial planning requires sales or revenue forecasting, the methods for doing so are described. The ultimate goal of a financial plan is the forecasted income statement and balance sheet for a company based on budgets, with any deviations from the budgeted amounts used to identify whether certain milestones are likely or unlikely to be achieved.

- *Chapter 14:* Profit planning, the subject of this chapter, requires the founding team to make operating decisions involving the introduction of new products, the volume of production, the pricing of products, and the selection of alternative production processes. To increase the likelihood that the best decision will be made, the founding team must understand the relationship between and among costs, revenues, and profits. The tools discussed in this chapter, break-even analysis and cost-volume-profit analysis, take this interrelationship into account and can provide the founding team with useful guidelines for decision making. The key to profit planning is understanding the cost structure of a firm; to do so, this chapter explains the nature of production costs.

- *Chapter 15:* Financial options in the form of awards granted to founders and key employees are common in startup companies. The investment attributes of financial options and the determination of their value are explained in this chapter. The concepts and principles described in this chapter are then applied in later chapters to making capital project decisions (i.e., valuing a capital project) and assessing the managerial flexibility provided by both real assets owned by the firm and real assets that are candidates for acquisition.

- *Chapter 16:* In this chapter we describe the issues and methods for the valuation of a private company. The chapter begins by introducing various definitions of the standard of value for private companies: fair market value, fair value, orderly liquidation value, intrinsic value, and investment (or strategic) value. The differences between public and private companies are then explained and the implications for alternative valuation methods that can be used and when they should be used based on the stage of a company's business development are reviewed. Typically, the most difficult valuations are those for early-stage or pre-revenue companies. The various methods suggested by practitioners (angel investors and venture capitalists) for valuing pre-revenue companies are highlighted in this chapter.

- *Chapter 17:* A venture's founding team must be able to evaluate potential investment projects to determine which projects are worth while pursuing, which projects are unattractive from an economic perspective, and which projects may potentially offer an attractive return but should be postponed to a later date. Decisions involving such acquisitions of projects are referred to as capital budgeting decisions and are the focus of this chapter. While some capital budgeting decisions may be routine decisions that do not have a major impact on the potential success of a venture, there will be some decisions that either have an impact on the company's future market position in its current offerings of goods and services or permit it to expand into new offerings in the future. A critical assessment of the methods commonly used for making capital budgeting decisions is provided.

- *Chapter 18:* When valuing a private company and potential capital projects, the founders of a company must take into account the associated risk and the value of managerial flexibility offered by existing assets or an asset that is a candidate for acquisition. Traditional valuation models do allow for the incorporation of risk into the valuation of a firm or a capital project but fail to take into account the value of managerial flexibility. The approach suggested for valuing managerial flexibility, referred to as the real options approach, is the subject of this chapter. This approach draws on the principles of options described in chapter 15. In practice, when making capital budgeting decisions, founders can use the real options approach in two general ways: (1) in a conceptual way, whereby founders use the real options approach to think about the flexibility that a capital project can provide founders without trying to quantify the value of the options that a capital project may create, and (2) by trying to quantify the value of the real options that may be created from a capital project. These two ways as to how to use the real options approach may be used are described in this chapter.

- *Appendix A:* This appendix provides a brief case study of Uber, describing its business model and its various milestones (expansion milestones, innovation milestones, and funding milestones).

- *Appendix B*: In this appendix, the income method and the market method for the valuation of a private company are applied to a real-world company, Tentex. The enterprise value and the equity value are estimated. This case study makes it clear that the application of a valuation method in practice requires a considerable number of assumptions and the use of financial models whose parameters and inputs must be estimated.

At the end of each chapter, there is list of the key points covered in the chapter.

ACKNOWLEDGMENTS

The genesis for this book was an undergraduate entrepreneurial finance course I taught at Princeton University's Keller Center for Innovation & Entrepreneurship during the Spring 2014 semester. Because of the diverse academic backgrounds of the students enrolled, I prepared material on each topic, and that material was then expanded and revised to create this book. I am grateful to the students in the course and to Changle Lin (the teaching assistant for the course), who provided me with helpful feedback on earlier drafts. Appendix A on Uber is part of the case assignment by a group of the students in the course. Those students are identified in the footnote to the appendix.

Special thanks to Professor Mung Chiang, director of the Keller Center, for hiring me to teach the course.

Chapter 16 and appendix B were co-authored with Dr. Stanley J. Feldman, chairman and cofounder of Axiom Valuation Solutions in Wakefield, Massachusetts. As chief valuation officer for that company with overall responsibility for its signed valuation reports and valuation analysis systems, Feldman brought to the task of writing valuable insights that allowed the material to be presented in a way that reflects the implementation issues involved in a valuation rather than an approach based solely on valuation theory, which would omit the difficulties in the valuation process. I thank him and his staff for their assistance.

When I first thought about expanding the course material to create a book, I discussed the project with the acquisition editor at MIT Press, Jane Macdonald. After providing feedback on various proposals for the book and drafted chapters, she offered me a contract and continued to support the work for the next eighteen months. I thank her for her patience and encouragement.

ABOUT THE AUTHOR

Frank J. Fabozzi is a professor of finance at EDHEC Business School in France and a member of the EDHEC Risk Institute. Prior to joining EDHEC, he held various professorial positions in finance at Yale University and the Massachusetts Institute of Technology. Since 2011, Frank has been a visiting fellow and a visiting professor in Princeton University's Department of Operations Research and Financial Engineering, as well as the James Wei Visiting Professor in Entrepreneurship. A trustee for the BlackRock family of closed-end funds and the equity-liquidity complexes, Frank has authored many books in financial management, including *Capital Markets: Instruments, Institutions, and Risk Management* (MIT Press, 2016), *Analysis of Financial Statements* (Wiley, 2012, third edition), *Project Finance* (Euromoney, 2012, eighth edition), *The Complete CFO Handbook: From Accounting to Accountability* (Wiley, 2008), and *Financial Management and Analysis* (Wiley, 2003). He is the 2007 recipient of the C. Stewart Sheppard Award and the 2015 recipient of the James R. Vertin Award, both given by the CFA Institute. In 2002 he was inducted into the Fixed Income Analysts Society Hall of Fame. Frank received his bachelor's and master's degrees in economics and statistics from the City College of New York and his PhD in economics from the City University of New York. He holds the professional designations of certified public accountant (CPA) and chartered financial analyst (CFA).

1

INTRODUCTION

Our focus in this book is on the various financial aspects that entrepreneurs contemplating the launching and operating of a new high-technology (high-tech) company will encounter. In this introductory chapter, the following three topics are covered: the risks associated with a new venture, the reasons why startup companies fail, and the stages of financing.

THE RISKS ASSOCIATED WITH A NEW VENTURE

By their very nature, high-tech startups are inherently risky. That is, despite the founders' confidence in the potential success of a new venture, there is a high probability of failure.

The decision to launch a high-tech venture involves rigorous analysis of the feasibility of developing and commercializing the intended products or services, referred to as the venture's "offerings." The analysis is based on identifying the risks associated with moving ahead with the new venture and the assumptions regarding how those risks will affect the viability of the new venture. A major difficulty in enumerating the risks associated with a new high-tech venture is that the would-be founders may not be sufficiently familiar with the business to be able to define the risks in advance. As former secretary of defense Donald Rumsfeld stated in a 2002 press conference at NATO headquarters in Brussels, Belgium, regarding intelligence information about terrorism:

There are no "knowns." There are things we know that we know. There are known unknowns. That is to say there are things that we now know we don't know. But there are also unknown unknowns. There are things we do not know we don't know. So when we do the best we can and we pull all this information together, and we then say well that's basically what we see as the situation, that is really only the known knowns and the known unknowns.[1]

Even if all of the relevant risks can be identified in advance, the ability to assess the likelihood of those risks occurring, as reflected in the assumptions made in the analysis of the feasibility of the planned offering and its commercial feasibility, may be lacking.

---

1. See the website http://www.defense.gov/transcripts/transcript.aspx?transcriptid=3490.

Typically for a startup in the high-tech space, either the entrepreneur or at least one member of the founding group will be a scientist or an engineer. Although many of the business issues may not lie within the expertise of a scientist or engineer, such individuals should be familiar with the principles of scientific experimentation for the purposes of identifying gaps in knowledge, formulating a hypothesis, constructing tests of the hypothesis, carrying out the experiment, and evaluating and interpreting the experimental results. The principles are the same regardless of whether the experiment is intended to yield knowledge about the feasibility of the planned offerings or to assess characteristics of the potential market for the offerings, such as consumer acceptance. The only difference between testing whether the performance of an offering will meet the expected specifications and testing whether there is a market for the offering is the use of specialized methods for conducting the experiment. In market testing, marketing specialists employ certain techniques that a scientist or engineer may be unfamiliar with.

All testing of the risks associated with a new venture should be done on a cost-effective basis. Consequently, there is a first round of testing, which is followed by additional testing if the results of the initial tests support the hypothesis. How many levels of testing are undertaken will depend on the degree of confidence obtained from earlier test results. In fact, early tests may yield insights that could materially improve the offering or suggest a major revision of the offering.

The Difficulties of Obtaining Probabilities in Risk Assessment

In assessing assumptions and their impact, one might expect that the principles of decision theory taught in every MBA program could be applied. Such application, however, requires an assessment of the probability of events that might adversely affect the viability of a new venture. Unfortunately, it is far easier to obtain probabilities in classroom exercises, where utilization of the wrong probabilities may result only in a poor grade on an assignment, than in the real world, where the demise of a new venture can affect the well-being of stakeholders.

First, although in this book the terms "risk" and "uncertainty" are used interchangeably, there is a difference between the two. The difference, and its significance, was explained by the economist Frank Knight in his 1921 book *Risk, Uncertainty and Profit*. In a constantly changing economic environment, new opportunities for profit making arise for entrepreneurs. However, such opportunities are accompanied by imperfect knowledge of future events that could or will affect the profit potential that may be realized by an entrepreneur. Knight argues that the term "risk" should be used in situations where the entrepreneur does not know the outcome of a given event but does have the information (or can obtain the information) to accurately measure the likelihood (odds or probability) of the outcome. In contrast, "uncertainty" applies when an entrepreneur encounters events for which all of the information needed to derive the likelihood of an event is unknown. As a consequence, the likelihood of such events is, in the words of Knight, "not susceptible to measurement."

Knight, in fact, linked this concept of uncertainty to the profits realized by entrepreneurs, writing:

Profit arises out of the inherent, absolute unpredictability of things, out of the sheer, brute fact that the results of human activity cannot be anticipated and then only in so far as even a probability calculation in regard to them is impossible and meaningless.[2]

Second, holding aside that Knight stated that the uncertainty of an event means that it cannot be measured, there is an entire field devoted to techniques for eliciting expert knowledge about some unknown quantity or quantities and from that information constructing a probability distribution. Elicitation techniques have been used by government agencies to assess the risk of a terrorist attack, by insurance companies to assess the risk of insuring against a new type of risk, and by regulators to assess the safety of nuclear installations. Although there is no empirical evidence about how well elicitation techniques have performed, they remain potentially useful when a decision maker faces uncertainty. However, elicitation techniques cannot help in the risk assessment of a new venture when not all of the risks have been identified.

What Is the Most Important Uncertainty?

Clark Gilbert and Matthew Eyring address the key question of what the most important uncertainty is, emphasizing that this question should be tackled early in the process of deciding whether to launch a new venture.[3] In addressing this issue, they suggest three categories of uncertainty: deal-killer risk, path-dependent risk, and high return-on-investment (ROI) risk.[4]

A risk that would undermine the launching of a new venture if left unaddressed is what Gilbert and Eyring refer to as a *deal-killer risk*. This risk tends to be identified by an entrepreneur following a catastrophic event that was unexpected either because such an event was not considered in the decision to launch or because the entrepreneur assessed the likelihood of such an event as minimal. Continuing with the quotation from Rumsfeld given above: "And each year, we discover a few more of those unknown unknowns."

When an entrepreneur pursues the wrong path in making decisions, resulting in a waste of the assets of the business, Gilbert and Eyring refer to this risk as a *path-dependent risk*. There is an extensive literature in the field of management theory on path-dependent decisions. Basically, it deals with how a decision that a manager must make today under prevailing market conditions is limited by the decisions the manager made in the past, even though past circumstances may no longer be relevant to the decision at hand. Related to

---

2. Frank H. Knight, *Risk, Uncertainty, and Profit* (Boston: Hart, Schaffner, & Marx, 1921), 311.
3. Clark G. Gilbert and Matthew J. Eyring, "Beating the Odds When You Launch a New Venture," *Harvard Business Review,* May 2010, 93–98.
4. Here we are not distinguishing between risk and uncertainty as discussed by Knight.

path-dependent risk is a topic that we discuss in chapter 18, "real options." A real option involves the selection of projects that create options or flexibility for the founding team in managing the growth of the business.

Deal-killer risk and path-dependent risk typically involve costly expenditures and considerable management time to identify the risk so that potential solutions can be considered. A risk that can be resolved without the expenditure of considerable resources (money and time) is referred to as a *high ROI risk*. With respect to these three risks, Gilbert and Eyring write:

Fail to spot a deal-killer risk, and your venture is doomed. Fail to hedge a path-dependent risk, and you dramatically raise the odds that you'll run out of funds before you ever come to market—or will get there far too late. Fail to address a high-ROI risk in an orderly way, and you may transform a temporary setback into an insurmountable obstacle.[5]

As Gilbert and Eyring note in the opening to their article, "Smart entrepreneurs aren't cowboys—they're methodical managers of risk." There are ways of dealing with the risks described above in an orderly manner without wasting a significant amount of a new venture's resources. They suggest using targeted experiments to identify a deal-killer risk or a path-dependent risk. The purpose of a targeted experiment is to test the assumptions made by the entrepreneur regarding risk, as well as to avoid confirming a bias that the entrepreneur might have. Three examples of targeted experiments given by Gilbert and Eyring are testing the battery life before starting a company to sell a new portable device, checking for the toxicity of a drug prior to performing full-scale efficacy tests, and testing concerns about bandwidth and connectivity prior to launching an online learning program at various locations across the country.[6]

A Closer Look at the Risks Faced by a New Venture: Market, Technical, Operational, and Financial

The sources of risk can be divided into four categories: market risk, technical risk, operational risk, and financial risk. On an ongoing basis, an entrepreneur must be capable of identifying risks and must have the skill set and creativity to reduce the adverse impact of those risks. As the types of risks described below are reduced or mitigated, the value of the new venture increases from the perspective of equity investors.

The risks listed under each type of risk category fall into at least one of the risk types identified by Gilbert and Eyring: deal-killer, path-dependent, and high ROI risk.

---

5. Gilbert and Eyring, "Beating the Odds When You Launch a New Venture," 95.
6. Ibid., 96.

Market Risk The market for the offering for the new venture must be clearly defined. Once the market is defined in terms of industry segment and target customers, the following market risks must be considered:

- The risk that the offering will not be accepted by the market.
- The risk that the size and projected growth of the market will not be sufficient for the new venture to grow.
- The risk that the market cannot be penetrated sufficiently so that the new venture will not be profitable.
- The risk that even if the offering is accepted by the market, it will become obsolete in the near future.
- The risk that barriers to entry will be so high as to make it difficult to compete in an established market.
- The risk for a new product that barriers to entry are low so that competition from future new ventures or established companies selling related products will erode market share before the market is inundated with "me-too" products.
- The risk that an offering subject to any regulatory approval may have sales adversely affected by unexpected changes in regulations.

The above market risks cannot be eliminated, but they can be carefully investigated. As we will see, market risk is addressed in a new venture's business model, where the founders set forth the company's value proposition. The venture's business plan serves as a blueprint for dealing with the adverse impacts that may arise from market risk. A venture's business model and business plan are discussed in chapter 2.

Technical Risk *Technical risk,* also referred to as *product development risk*, and in the case of pharmaceutical companies as *clinical risk*, is the risk that the offering that is the idea for the business or the prototype that has been developed cannot be successfully transformed into a commercial product. Technical risks include the following:

- The risk that the technology does not work.
- The risk that the technology will not perform at the standard customers were led to believe it would perform at when they purchased the product.
- The risk that the technology cannot be legally protected.
- The risk that the technology does not allow the production of a product at a reasonable cost for the targeted market segment or customers.
- The risk that the technology or components thereof might be the subject of a patent infringement.
- The risk that an offering that would be subject to regulation does not obtain regulatory approval.

Some of the technical risks listed above can be mitigated by further research, such as targeted experiments, and by obtaining legal opinion regarding protection from infringement of the technology or a claim by others that the new technology infringes on another firm's patent.

Operational Risk   *Operational risk* arises from the operation of the business and includes the following:

- The risk that production costs will be higher than expected.
- The risk that the time to delivery will be longer than expected.
- The risk that the product material will be unavailable at the expected costs necessary for a profit to be generated.
- The risk that there will be a shortage of workers with the specialized skills needed.
- For subcontracted work, the risk that the subcontractors will not perform as expected, either delivering a poor-quality or defective product or delivering a product on a schedule that impedes production.
- The risk that the distribution system will be costlier than expected.
- The risk of the loss of key employees, particularly to competitors.
- The risk that frictions among founders will arise that impede operations.

Financial Risk   *Financial risk* covers several areas:

- The risk that the entrepreneur or the founders will lose all of their investment and possibly more personal assets than are invested in the company.
- The risk that the company will have a cash shortfall because it cannot obtain short-term financing.
- The risk that customers will not have the ability to satisfy their obligations.
- The risk that the company will not be able to raise the amount of capital needed on terms that are reasonable during different periods of development.
- The risk that the company will become bankrupt.
- The risk that the company will not be able to find a satisfactory exit strategy.

WHY NEW VENTURES FAIL

It would be helpful to know about the failure rate of new ventures, particularly for high-tech start-ups. There are lots of statistics available on failure rates, some of which would make entrepreneurs excited about the prospects of launching a new venture and others that would cause entrepreneurs to be gravely concerned about launching a new venture that would be successful.

In studying failure rates, the first question is how one defines failure. Some common ways to define a failure are:

- liquidating all assets resulting in investors losing most or all their investment in the company,
- falling short of the projected return on investment, and
- falling short of declared forecasted projections or other metric that is stated in the business plan.

One might reasonably assume that a good source on failure rates for new ventures might be those entities that are involved in the financing of new ventures: venture capital firms. These firms, the subject of chapter 6, invest in early startup companies. The organization that represents the 450+ venture capital firms is the National Venture Capital Association (NVCA). According to the *Wall Street Journal*, venture capitalists suggest that a common rule of thumb is that only 30% to 40% of startups fail completely, 30% to 40% return the original investment, and 10% to 20% produce substantial returns.[7] According to NVCA estimates, only 25% to 30% of venture-backed businesses fail. In other words, 70% to 75% succeed. Not bad odds! Yet there are other studies that paint a totally different picture of the chances of a new venture failing.

Another study suggests that no matter how failure is defined, the odds are not good that a new venture will succeed. According to a study of 2,000 companies that received venture funding (generally at least $1 million from 2004 through 2010) by Shikhar Ghosh of the Harvard Business School, the failure rate for the different ways for defining failure is as follows:[8]

- the liquidation of all assets, resulting in investors losing most or all their investment in the company: 30% to 40%;
- failure to achieve the projected return on investment: 70% to 80%;
- failure to achieve declared forecasted projections: 90% to 95%.

What might explain the difference in failure rates as reported by the NVCA and in the study by Ghosh? In an interview, Ghosh proffered several reasons for the discrepancy.[9] The first reason is that venture capitalists tend to emphasize successes but avoid talking about the failures. As Ghosh points out, venture capitalists "bury their dead very quietly." Second, failure rates are biased downward because many venture-backed companies are sold at a loss, which is classified by venture capitalists as an "acquisition." Third, because venture capitalists generally provide startups with sufficient capital to survive a couple

7. Deborah Gage, "The Venture Capital Secret," *Wall Street Journal,* September 20, 2012, http://online.wsj.com/news/articles/SB10000872396390443720204578004980476429190.

8. Carmen Nobel, "Why Companies Fail—and How Their Founders Can Bounce Back," Word Knowledge, Harvard Business School, March 2011, http://hbswk.hbs.edu/item/6591.html.

9. Ghosh, quoted in Nobel, "Why Companies Fail."

of years, the companies backed by venture capitalists take several years to fail. Finally, although there are venture-capital-backed companies that go out of business, they continue to exist as legal entities, which Ghosh refers to as the "walking dead."

A study by Song, Song, and Parry investigated failure for 539 new ventures formed in the period 1991–2001. The database they used (VENSURV), developed by the Institute for Entrepreneurship and Innovation at the University of Missouri–Kansas City, combined information on venture survival and the first product launched by each of the ventures.[10] The reason for focusing on the first product launched by a new venture is because that product is critical with respect to building a new venture's reputation and ability to attract the requisite resources. The new ventures in the database studied by Song, Song, and Parry included new ventures in telephone and wireless communication equipment (49), consumer electronics (169), games and toys (110), computer and software products (107), and household-related products (104).

A "first product" was classified as successful if the performance of the product exceeded the new venture's predefined goals and objectives after two years of product commercialization. The metrics for determining success were those stated in the new venture's business plan (e.g., measures such as profitability and sales). For a new venture to be categorized as successful, it had to meet two criteria: (1) the founders and investors had to realize an acceptable return on their investment and (2) the predefined goals and objectives as set forth in the business plan had to be met. Of the 539 new ventures in the database, 176 (32.65%) were classified as successful.

Song, Song, and Parry found that fewer than half of the ventures survived more than two years. This is not a surprising finding since it is consistent with those of other studies. Another factor they investigated was whether economic downturns lead to higher failure rates. The question of the impact on failure rates of the economic environment at the time of formation has been the subject of debate. More specifically, the question is whether the failure rate for new ventures started during a recessionary period is different from that for new ventures started during an expansionary period. The argument is as follows. On the one hand, during recessionary periods, entrepreneurs might benefit from both weakened competition and lower costs of production; on the other hand, the fundraising ability during such periods might be reduced.

There were several interesting findings regarding the success of a new venture and the success of the first product that the new venture launched. First, both first-product and new venture performance are highest when a venture's first product is "based on radical innovations, serves emerging market needs, and is introduced into markets with an established industry technology standard."[11] Second, both first-product success and venture

10. Lisa Z. Song, Michael Song, and Mark E. Parry, "Perspectives on Economic Conditions, Entrepreneurship, First-Product Development, and New Venture Success," *Journal of Product Innovation and Management* 27, no. 1 (January 2010): 130–135.
11. Song, Song, and Parry, "Perspectives on Economic Conditions, Entrepreneurship, First-Product Development, and New Venture Success," 130.

performance are significantly higher when products are created based on the ideas that were generated by the founders. Finally, the attributes of first products that tend to be the most successful reflect both technology development and an analysis of customer needs.

The main reason Ghosh identifies for why startups often fail is that founders and investors carry out their business plan without taking the time to realize that key assumptions in those plans are wrong (a point we emphasized earlier in this chapter). In his experience, he finds that rather than having a balanced plan, entrepreneurs tend to be single-minded in their strategy and try to make the new venture either all about the technology or all about the sales. A market problem that leads to startup failures arises when founders simply refuse to believe that there is either no demand for the product or an insufficient demand for the product. That is, the value proposition is not compelling.

Moreover, entrepreneurs tend to pursue strategies that often do not provide them with the flexibility to maneuver the business midstream. (This risk is a form of the path-dependent risk mentioned earlier.) As Ghosh points out, "Instead of going into the venture with a broad hypothesis, they commit in ways that don't allow them to change." He gives as an example the case of Webvan (1999–2001), a company whose founder might have had a good idea but tried to grow the company too quickly. Before analyzing the demand for online grocery services, Webvan purchased warehouses all over the United States.

While many startups may fail because of the founders' inability to obtain financing, Ghosh notes that the main reason for big failures versus small failures is too much funding. Excess funding can make founders, intentionally or not, fail to identify a wide range of mistakes in conducting operations and, as a result, fail to address what led to those mistakes and correct them.

STAGES OF A VENTURE

There are various ways of describing the stages of a venture. The motivation for describing the stages of a venture is twofold. First, the sources of financing available to founders will depend on the stage of the venture. In chapter 6 we describe the alternative financing sources in terms of the stage of a venture. Second, we will be interested in valuing a venture at different stages of its life. We show how this is done in chapter 16, as well as in appendix B.

Milestones

Suppliers of capital typically look at the milestones completed by a venture. *Milestones* are the major events that suppliers of capital want to see achieved as evidence that the venture has resolved one or more of the major risks described earlier. Achieving key milestones increases the likelihood that the venture will succeed and, as a result, causes the venture's valuation to increase.

Examples of key milestones that can serve as the structure for the company's financing plan include (but are not limited to):

- assembling key management team members;
- assembling key technical staff members;
- demonstrating that technical obstacles can be overcome;
- building a prototype, with positive feedback reported by potential customers;
- obtaining customer validation through sales;
- shipping the product to customers and receiving payment;
- developing a relationship in a strategic partnership with a well-established company that can increase the likelihood of success by enhancing sales or reducing production costs;
- demonstrating that sales are beginning to ramp up;
- proving that the marketing strategy is effective in acquiring customers on a cost-effective basis;
- demonstrating that the business can be scaled;[12]
- earning sufficient revenue so that break-even operations are achieved; and
- earning a profit.

Stages of Business Development and Financing

Below we describe the stages of a privately held company in terms of the milestones achieved according to the American Institute of Certified Public Accountants (AICPA).[13] As explained in chapter 16, this classification is also useful for selecting methodologies for evaluating privately held companies. We postpone until chapter 6 a more detailed explanation of the typical sources of funding available and until chapter 7 a discussion of the types of financing arrangements available at each stage.

Using the AICPA classification, the six stages are the following:

Stage 1: In this stage, the venture is typically characterized as follows: the founders have an idea, but no product revenue has been generated; possibly product development is in the initial phase. This stage might best be described as the ***precommercialization stage*** or ***premarketing stage.*** In terms of technology, the company is in ***early-stage technology***: technology that is not yet commercialized and has not been proved beyond the drawing board (i.e., nothing beyond laboratory experiments). In fact, neither the basic research nor the commercial feasibility may have been completed or assessed. Every new high-tech product requires an extensive precommercialization stage. For some companies, the legal structure may not have been decided on by the founders because at this stage,

---

12. We explain what is meant by scaling a business in chapter 14.
13. AICPA, *Valuation of Privately-Held-Company Equity Securities Issued as Compensation* (New York: AICPA, 2004).

no decision may have been made to go ahead with the formal formation of a company. Consequently, the amount of the founders' financing needs at this stage can vary based on the costs associated with (1) conducting business feasibility studies, (2) building prototypes, (3) testing and validating the offering, (4) evaluating the market potential, and (5) filing the legal documents to protect the intellectual property developed. Financing at this stage is *seed capital financing* in the early phase of this stage and *first-round financing* or *Series A financing* in the late phase of this stage.

Stage 2: No product revenue but considerable expenses characterize this stage. Product development has begun and the founding team is identifying and managing new business challenges as they arise. It is at this stage that a second or third round of financing occurs from venture capitalists. It is also at this stage that the founders need further guidance on management strategies for growing the business so that in addition to capital, the new venture develops expertise and relationships (partnerships) that can be provided by suppliers of capital such as venture capitalists.

Stage 3: Typically, the venture is still operating at a loss because it is not generating revenue but has made significant advances in product development, such as the completion of alpha and beta testing of its offering. The venture is further increasing its value by reaching other key milestones, such as the hiring of a management team.

Stage 4: Although the venture is still operating at a loss at this stage, typically milestones have been reached regarding the product, and there is customer validation in the form of first orders and first shipments. As a result, some revenue is generated. The new venture can now be viewed as being in the expansion stage because during this stage the venture has to expand its operations, one hopes improving its production process, improving its product, and investing in more costly marketing efforts. The company has met a sufficient number of key nonfinancial milestones at this stage to consider the possibility of an initial public offering (IPO).

Stage 5: The general of product revenue at this stage has allowed the venture to reach key financial milestones such as break-even operations, operating profitability, or positive cash flows. It is possible at this stage for some type of exit event to occur—possibly an IPO or the sale of the company.

Stage 6: If an exit event has not occurred by stage 6, at this stage the company has a sufficiently strong financial and operational track record to make it a strong candidate for acquisition.

This general description of the stages of business development and financing is not carved in stone. No two ventures have the same rate of growth of revenue and product development and therefore they have different capital needs that do not fall neatly into the stages described above. The convention that is tossed about in the literature in describing the stages can vary even among venture capitalists. For example, suppose that a new venture's founders do not seek funding for what we described above as seed capital until the venture has developed a prototype for its product. A venture capitalist that provides financing for this new venture might indeed classify this investment as seed capital; however, another venture capitalist might classify it as early startup financing. What is important is not the conventions used but understanding what types of financing are needed as the business develops. In chapter 16, where we discuss the various methods for valuing private companies, we will explain which method is appropriate to use at each of these six stages.

KEY POINTS COVERED IN THIS CHAPTER

- In deciding to launch a high-tech venture, an entrepreneur should undertake rigorous analysis of the feasibility of developing and commercializing the venture's planned offerings.
- The major difficulty founders encounter is in identifying the risks associated with a new high-tech venture.
- Although the terms "risk" and "uncertainty" are often used interchangeably, there is a difference: "risk" should be used in situations where the entrepreneur does not know the outcome of a given event but does have the information to accurately measure the likelihood of the outcome, while "uncertainty" applies when an entrepreneur encounters events for which not all of the information needed to obtain the likelihood of an event is known.
- Although there are elicitation techniques for obtaining probabilities, there is no empirical evidence about how well they have performed.
- There are three categories of uncertainty: deal-killer risk, path-dependent risk, and high return-on-investment (ROI) risk.
- The sources of risk can be divided into four categories: market risk, technical risk, operational risk, and financial risk.
- In assessing failure rates for startups, it is first necessary to define what constitutes a failure. Some commonly used functional definitions include: (1) the liquidation of all assets, so that investors lose most or all of their investment in the company; (2) the company's falling short of the projected ROI; and (3) the company's falling short of declared forecasted projections or failing to achieve some other metric that is stated in the business plan.
- Empirical evidence suggests that both first-product and new venture performance are (1) highest when a venture's first product is "based on radical innovations, serves emerging market needs, and is introduced into markets with an established industry technology standard," and (2) significantly higher when products are created based on the ideas that were generated by the founders.

- Empirical evidence suggests that the attributes of first products that tend to be the most successful are those that reflect both technology development and an analysis of customer needs.

- The reasons why startups often fail are (1) the founders carry out their business plan without taking the time to realize that key assumptions in those plans are wrong and (2) the founders tend to pursue strategies that do not provide them with the flexibility to maneuver the business midstream.

- There are various ways of describing the stages of a venture.

- In assessing performance, investors look for milestones achieved, major events that suppliers of capital want to see achieved as evidence that the venture has resolved one or more of the major risks described earlier.

- Achieving key milestones increases the likelihood that the venture will succeed and, as a result, causes the venture's valuation to increase.

- Although there is no standard definition of the stages of venture, what is critical is not the definitions commonly used but understanding what types of financing are needed as the business develops.

FURTHER READINGS

Startup Failures

"135 Startup Failure Post-Mortems," *CB Insights*, August 17, 2015, https://www.cbinsights.com/blog/startup-failure-post-mortem.

"The R.I.P. Report—Startup Death Trends," *CB Insights*, January 18, 2014, https://www.cbinsights.com/blog/startup-death-data.

Ritholtz, Barry, "Postmortems for Startup Failures," *BloombergView*, June 10, 2015, http://www.bloombergview.com/articles/2015-06-10/learning-lessons-from-failures-of-tech-startups.

"Startup Business Failure Rate by Industry," Dun & Bradstreet Reports, July 5, 2015, http://www.statisticbrain.com/startup-failure-by-industry.

Yaghmaie, Bo, "A Case Study of Startup Failure," *TechCrunch*, September 16, 2015, http://techcrunch.com/2015/09/16/a-case-study-of-startup-failure.

Milestones

Espinal, Carlos Eduardo, "Setting Appropriate Milestones in an Early-Stage Startup," *Seedcamp*, November 11, 2013, http://seedcamp.com/resources/setting-appropriate-milestones-in-an-early-stage-startup.

"The 5 Most Important Milestones for New Entrepreneurs," *Internet Business Mastery*, undated, http://www.internetbusinessmastery.com/the-5-most-important-milestones-for-new-entrepreneurs.

Stages of Financing and Business Development

Benebo, Opubo G., "Founding the Business Entity: Stages of Venture Startup," *GB-Analysts Reports,* last updated August 18, 2014, http://www.gbanalysts.com/Reading%20Room/The%20Entreprenuer/newVentureDev/venstartupstgs.html.

"Equity Financing Stages for Startups," *Go4Funding*, undated, http://www.go4funding.com/articles/equity-financing-stages-for-startups.aspx.

Hofstrand, Don, "Financing Stages for Start-up Businesses," Iowa State University, April 2013, https://www.extension.iastate.edu/agdm/wholefarm/pdf/c5-91.pdf.

Lee, Terence, "Startup Stages: A Comparison of 3 Models," https://www.techinasia.com/startup-stages.

National Venture Capital Association, *National Venture Capital Association: Yearbook 2013*, appendix F (Stage Definitions).

Entrepreneurship in Europe and Asia

Gleeson, Alan, "Guest Post: Why Europe Lags the U.S. in Technology Startups," *TechCrunch*, September 17, 2010, http://techcrunch.com/2010/09/17/guest-post-why-europe-lags-the-u-s-in-technology-startups.

Shim, T. Youn-ja, ed., *Korean Entrepreneurship: The Foundation of the Korean Economy* (New York: Palgrave Macmillan, 2010).

 "Why Don't More Europeans Want to be Entrepreneurs?," January 11, 2014, http://www.debatingeurope.eu/2014/11/23/why-dont-more-europeans-want-to-be-entrepreneurs/#.VgMiosxAIT0.

"Why Startups in Europe Don't Have the Needed Support" January 29, 2015, http://businessculture.org/blog/2015/01/29/startups-in-europe.

Zhang, Marina Yue, and Mark Dodgson, *High-Tech Entrepreneurship in Asia: Innovation, Industry and Institutional Dynamics in Mobile Payments* (Cheltenham, UK; Northampton, MA: Edward Elgar, 2007).

2

THE BUSINESS MODEL, BUSINESS PLAN, AND EXIT PLANNING

The success of a new venture depends on its ability to manage its costs, grow its revenue and profits, effectively manage its risks, and manage its relationship with stakeholders (i.e., employees, customers, investors, and suppliers). How a company's founders expect to execute these tasks is set forth in the company's business model, the first of three topics covered in this chapter. The second topic is the company's business plan, which describes how the founders plan to execute the business model. Finally, we discuss exit planning.

THE BUSINESS MODEL

Despite the importance of business models, there is no definitive definition of what a business model is. Some of the proposed definitions are so abstract that they offer little insight into how to move from the definition to the formulation of a useful document that can serve as a blueprint for implementing the tasks necessary for a venture to be successful. Here we discuss some suggested definitions of a business model and then examine the components of a business model.

There is an extensive literature on what a business model is and what it is not. Alexander Osterwalder in his 2004 doctoral dissertation at the University of Lausanne, Switzerland, provides an excellent literature review and proposes the following working definition of a business model:

A business model is a conceptual tool that contains a set of elements and their relationships and allows expressing a company's logic of earning money. It is a description of the value a company offers to one or several segments of customers and the architecture of the firm and its network of partners for creating, marketing and delivering this value and relationship capital, in order to generate profitable and sustainable revenue streams.[1]

1. Alexander Osterwalder, "The Business Model Ontology: A Proposition in a Design Science Approach" (PhD diss., University of Lausanne, 2004).

Henry Chesbrough and Richard S. Rosenbloom describe a business model in terms of the functions it performs:[2]

1. It articulates the value proposition (i.e., the value created for users).

2. It identifies a market segment (i.e., the users to whom the technology is useful).

3. It specifies the mechanism by which revenue will be generated.

4. It defines the necessary value chain and what assets will be needed to support the firm's position in the value chain.[3]

5. Given the value proposition and the value chain structure, it estimates the cost structure and potential profit to be realized from producing the product or service.

6. It describes the firm's position in the value network by identifying potential complementary factors and competitors.

7. It formulates the competitive strategy by which the firm will gain and maintain an advantage over its competitors.

In their book, *Business Model Generation*, Alexander Osterwalder and Yves Pigneur state that a "business model describes the rationale of how an organization creates, delivers, and captures value."[4] They then go on to describe what they believe to be the nine basic building blocks of a business model that explains how a firm intends to generate a profit. This business model template, which they call the Business Model Canvas, provides thought-provoking questions that offer guidance in the development of an effective business model. The basic building blocks of the Business Model Canvas are the following:[5]

1. Key partners
i. Who are your key partners/suppliers?
ii. What are the motivations for the partnerships?

2. Key activities
i. What key activities does your value proposition require?
ii. What activities are important the most in distribution channels, customer relationships, revenue stream …?

---

2. Henry Chesbrough and Richard S. Rosenbloom, "The Role of the Business Model in Capturing Value from Innovation: Evidence from Xerox Corporation's Technology Spinoff Companies," *Industrial and Corporate Change* 11, no. 3 (2002): 529–555.
3. The value chain is the complete range of activities that a firm and its workers need to perform to take a product from its conception to its end use and beyond. These activities include product design, production, marketing, distribution, and post-sale customer support. In his 1988 book, *On Competition* (Harvard Business School Press, Boston MA), Michael Porter defines value in terms of the value chain in a specific industry. He argues that when a firm efficiently executes the chain of activities, more value will be added to the product than will be lost through the costs of these activities, and that this is critical for a company to gain an advantage over its competitors.
4. Alexander Osterwalder and Yves Pigneur, *Business Model Generation: A Handbook for Visionaries, Game Changers, and Challengers* (Hoboken, NJ: John Wiley & Sons, 2010).
5. This template for a business model was first proposed by Osterwalder in "The Business Model Ontology."

3. Value proposition
i. What core value do you deliver to the customer?
ii. Which customer needs are you satisfying?

4. Customer relationship
i. What relationship that the target customer expects you to establish?
ii. How can you integrate that into your business in terms of cost and format?

5. Customer segment
i. Which classes are you creating values for?
ii. Who is your most important customer?

6. Key resource
i. What key resources does your value proposition require?
ii. What resources are important the most in distribution channels, customer relationships, revenue stream …?

7. Distribution channel
i. Through which channels do your customers want to be reached?
ii. Which channels work best? How much do they cost? How can they be integrated into your and your customers' routines?

8. Cost structure
i. What are the most cost[s] in your business?
ii. Which key resources/activities are most expensive?

9. Revenue stream
i. For what value are your customers willing to pay?
ii. What and how do they recently pay? How would they prefer to pay?
iii. How much does every revenue stream contribute to the overall revenues?[6]

The Business Model Canvas template is visualized using the diagram in figure 2.1, where each box represents one of the nine building blocks.

Table 2.1 shows the nine building blocks in tabular form rather than in the Business Model Canvas template for Walmart, Google, Twitter, and LinkedIn.

Three Key Components of a Business Model
The two business model descriptions given above suggest that the three key components of a business model are the following:

1. the market: customers and customer segments;

2. the value proposition of the products or services being offered; and

3. profitability: revenue sources and cost structure.

---

6. See the website http://canvanizer.com/new/business-model-canvas.

Key partners	Key activities	Value propositions	Relationships	Customer segments
	Key resources		Channels	
Cost structure			Revenue streams	

Figure 2.1
Elements of the Business Model Canvas.
Source: Modified from http://canvanizer.com/new/business-model-canvas.

Table 2.1
Suggested Business Models Using the Canvas Building Blocks: Walmart, Google, Twitter, LinkedIn

Building Block	Walmart	Google	Twitter	LinkedIn
Key partners	1. Merchandise suppliers 2. Big consumer products companies	1. Distribution partners 2. Open handset alliance 3. OEMs (for Chrome operating system devices)	1. Search vendors 2. Device vendors 3. Media companies 4. Mobile operations	1. Equinix (for data center facilities) 2. Content providers
Key activities	1. Supply chain management 2. Brick-and-click operations	1. R&D—build new products, improve existing products 2. Manage massive IT infrastructure	Platform development	Platform development
Key resources	1. Retail and logistics infrastructure 2. Sophisticated IT infrastructure 3. Inventories	1. Datacenters 2. IPs brand	Twitter.com platform	LinkedIn platform
Value propositions	1. Everyday low prices 2. One-stop shopping 3. Strategic merchandise units—grocery, hardlines, entertainment, health and wellness, apparel, and home	1. Web search, gmail, Google+ 2. Targeted ads using Adwords (CPC) 3. Extended ad campaigns using Adsense 4. Display advertising management services 5. Operating systems and platforms— Android, Chrome 6. Hosted web-based Google apps	1. Stay connected 2. News and events 3. Targeted marketing 4. Twitter apps	1. Manage professional identity 2. Identify and reach the right talent 3. Reach the target audience 4. Access to LinkedIn database content via APIs and widgets

Table 2.1 (continued)

Building Block	Walmart	Google	Twitter	LinkedIn
Relationships	1. Store of the community 2. Clean, fast, friendly motto	1. Automation (where possible) 2. Dedicated sales for large accounts		1. Same-side network effects 2. Cross-side network effects
Channels	1. Supercenters, discount stores, neighborhood markets 2. Walmart and Sam's Club online	1. Global sales and support teams 2. Multiproduct sales force	1. Website, desktop apps, mobile apps, SMS 2. Twitter API	1. LinkedIn website 2. Field sales
Customer segments	1. Walmart U.S. 2. Walmart International 3. Sam's Club	1, Internet users 2. Advertisers, ad agencies 3. Google Network members 4. Mobile device owners 5. Developers 6. Enterprises	1. Users 2. Enterprises 3. Developers	1. Internet users 2. Recruiters 3. Advertisers and marketers 4. Developers
Cost structure	1. Labor costs 2. Inventory costs 3. Physical and IT infrastructure	1. Traffic acquisition costs 2. R&D costs (mainly personnel) 3. Data center operations 4. Subcontracting and materials costs, general and administrative expenses	1. Employees 2. Servers	1. Web hosting costs 2. Marketing and sales 3. Product development 4. General and administrative
Revenue streams	1. Merchandise sales 2. Member income	1. Ad revenues— Google websites 2. Ad revenues— Google Network websites 3. Enterprise product sales 4. Free	1. Licensing data streams 2. Promoted accounts 3. Promoted tweets 4. Promoted trends 5. Analytics	1. Free offerings and premium subscriptions 2. Hiring solutions 3. Marketing solutions

Sources: Walmart: http://api.ning.com/files/9Pd0Ofg5hVb0KIRhlZ92fMEGQ8PfvqE2i3qemPlqUtKaDva 9hMr2MX8GwqZvwLb0lA3I9PPI7TkHI2UPJMICwUDlEmnYMAA-/BusinessModelCanvasMomand PopStoresandWalmart.pdf; Google: http://bmimatters.com/2012/03/29/understanding-google-business-model; Twitter: http://bmimatters.com/2012/02/18/understanding-twitter-business-model-design; LinkedIn: http:// bmimatters.com/2012/05/16/understanding-linkedin-business-model.

Table 2.2
Example of How a Computer Manufacturer Might Segment Customers

Users or Market Segment	Features Provided to Address Needs
Family	General and educational software, basic games, DVD player, "safe" access to the Internet, email accounts for each member of the family
Small or home office	Business software, fax, broadband access to the Internet, high-quality printing, document scanning and reproduction
Specialist use	Specialist software and hardware configurations for applications such as design or digital image processing, printing, and storage
Gaming	Multimedia games, broadband Internet access, high-quality display, sound, special peripherals like joystick, powerful processor

The Market: Customers and Customer Segments   Too often in business models and in presentations to potential suppliers of capital, the firm's market for its offerings is too broadly defined. Since the firm's lifeblood is its customers, carefully dividing the entire market in terms of customer segments is crucial. There are three major benefits to market segmentation. First, it allows the identification of the least and most profitable customer segments and therefore which customer segments should be targeted. Second, customer segmentation may allow the identification of a segment of the market that may currently be overlooked by competitors, the so-called "niche market." Finally, because customers in different customer segments may have different needs, it is easier to determine whether there is a need to customize an offering for each type of customer.

At the broadest level, market segmentation begins with the type of customer: businesses and organizations or individual consumers and households. The former customer segment, referred to as the *business-to-business segment*, can be categorized according to industry sector (e.g., health care, technology, manufacturing), private versus public entities, and domestic versus foreign entities. The second customer segment, the *business-to-consumer segment*, can be segmented according to demographics such as age, gender, household income, or geographic area.

An example of how a computer manufacturer might segment customers is shown in table 2.2.[7]

Also addressed in the business model are the relationships with customer segments and the channels by which the offerings are to be delivered to each customer segment. The relationship with customers would include how the firm plans to interact with customers over time.

The different customer segments are reached by means of different channels and require different types of relationships. Each of these should be described in the business model.

---

7. The source of this table is "Segment Your Customers," InfoEntrepreneurs.org, 2009, http://www.infoentrepreneurs.org/en/guides/segment-your-customers.

By *channels* is meant the means by which the firm communicates or distributes offerings to the targeted customer segments. The *communication channel* is what makes customers (and potential suppliers of capital) aware of the company's offerings and its value proposition. *Sales channels* are the means by which customers can buy products. Also, they are the means by which the firm plans to provide customer support after the purchase of its offering is made.

The Value Proposition of the Products or Services Being Offered   After determining the targeted customer segments, the venture must describe in the business model the products and services to be offered for each customer segment This calls for more than a mere listing of the features of the offerings. This is where the value proposition must be clearly explained in a nontechnical manner for each customer segment. The *value proposition* sets forth the unique benefits that the firm will deliver to each one of its targeted customer segment by addressing the following:

- the value the firm will be delivering to the targeted customer segment;
- for the problems that a customer segment is facing, how the offerings will solve or mitigate them; and
- how the offerings are different from those provided by competitors.

The value proposition should be concise and simple. In high-tech startups, the tendency all too often is to provide a technical description of the offerings that might make sense to other scientists or engineers. However, it is not usually individuals in those professions from whom the founders of a startup will be seeking capital. So the value proposition should focus on the benefits provided by the offering and how the customer segments will benefit from utilizing the technology rather than on the unique features of the technology. For example, when the customer segment is business-to-business customers, the benefits can be cast in terms of the ability to enhance profits or return on investment through more efficient operations that will reduce manufacturing costs or provide a cheaper means of delivering products.

The value proposition will become an integral part of the business plan that we describe later in this chapter.

Profitability: Revenue Sources and Cost Structure   A firm's profit is simply the difference between its revenues and its costs. So the business model must explain the various revenues sources that are expected and the cost of producing the offerings.

Revenue sources: A firm's revenue comes from one or more of the following sources: product or service sales, usage fees, licensing fees, subscription fees, lease payments, royalties, and financing fees. The revenue sources require not only a forecast of the number of units that can be sold to each customer segment but also the price at which the products can be sold. This is clearly a simultaneous problem in that the number of units of an offering that can be sold will depend on the price that it is estimated each product can be sold at.

Cost structure: The cost structure includes the various types of costs. These include fixed costs and variables. There are further breakdowns for each type of cost. The potential for economies of scale and economies of operation should be described. The concept of *economies of scale* refers to a reduction in the average cost of producing a unit of product as output increases. The "scalability" of a product refers to the ability to achieve economies of scale. A related concept is that of *economies of scope*. Here the cost saving arises from a reduction in the average cost of producing multiple different products. For example, the sale of multiple products can reduce the average cost of marketing and servicing multiple products relative to the average cost of marketing and servicing a single product.

Related to revenue and cost are key arrangements or alliances made with noncompetitors and with competitors. These arrangements may result in improved distribution channels that will increase revenue or generate greater cost savings as a result of more efficient delivery of offerings. Special relationships with suppliers that ensure a long-term supply of a resource that may potentially be in short supply in the future or whose price volatility may jeopardize future profitability should be described. Joint ventures with other organizations in developing new products or services to reduce future research and development costs should also be explained.

The cost structure should also be thought of in terms of the value proposition. In business models where the value proposition is a low-cost product compared to competitors' offerings, the focus is on a cost structure that minimizes costs. A cost structure that is driven by a low-price value proposition is referred to as a *cost-driven structure*. At the other extreme of the business model is a cost structure dictated by the value proposition that the product is a premium value product. The cost structure in this case is called a *value-driven cost structure*. The cost structure of other business models falls between these two extremes.

Why the Business Model Has to Be Revised

A business model is not a document that is prepared once in the life of a business. For example, IBM's business model has changed many times over the company's long history. Its product and service mix has changed over time to include office equipment sales, mainframe computer sales, personal computer sales, IT services, and corporate social responsibility ("green") consulting. IBM's business model, reproduced below from the company's 2012 annual report, provides a good example of this.

The company's business model is built to support two principal goals: helping clients succeed in delivering business value by becoming more innovative, efficient and competitive through the use of business insight and IT solutions; and, providing long-term value to shareholders. The business model has been developed over time through strategic investments in capabilities and technologies that have the best long-term growth and profitability prospects based on the value they deliver to clients.

The business model is flexible, adapting to the continuously changing market and economic environment. The company has divested commoditizing businesses such as personal computers and hard disk drives and strengthened its position through strategic investments and acquisitions in higher-value segments such as business intelligence and analytics, virtualization, and green solutions. In addition, the company has transformed itself into a globally integrated enterprise, which has improved overall productivity and is driving investment and participation in the world's fastest-growing markets. As a result, the company is a higher-performing enterprise today than it was several years ago.

Failure to Revise a Business Model: The Case of Brick-and-Mortar Video Rentals

Good illustrations of the disastrous effects of failing to revise an outdated business model are provided by Blockbuster Inc. and Money Gallery, both founded in 1985. Both companies were involved in the home video business, whereby customers would visit the company's video store to select and rent a movie. Revenue was generated from the rental of DVDs, VHS movies, and video games. Failure to return the rental to the video store by the designated date resulted in the imposition of a late fee.

Both video rental companies had an initial public offering (IPO) in the 1990s (Blockbuster in 1999 and Movie Gallery in 1994). Despite the brand name developed by Blockbuster and Movie Gallery, which had become the first and second largest companies in the video rental business, respectively, their business model had flaws: it had become inconvenient for customers to pick up videos and then return them to the company's store, and customers who failed to return videos on time became dissatisfied with the imposition of a late fee. Several Internet and subscription-based services that provided video rentals emerged around 1997, the best known being Netflix (a company that Blockbuster could have purchased at one time for $50 million).

Netflix's business model provided for a service that eliminated the inconvenience of traveling to a video store and having to pay any late fee by sending DVDs by postal service, with no restrictions on the length of time that a rental could be retained by the customer. For this service, Netflix charged a monthly fee. Blockbuster eventually installed the business model used by Netflix, and also gave customers the option to return DVDs to one of its video stores. When Netflix provided an online video service, Blockbuster did so too (the Blockbuster's Total Access Program). Movie Gallery had to compete not only with Netflix but also with the revised business model of Blockbuster. In the end, the failure of both video rental companies to adapt their business model quickly enough led both to file for bankruptcy (Blockbuster in September 2011 and Movie Gallery in October 2007).

Reasons for Rethinking a Business Model

Following are some reasons why a firm is likely to rethink its business model:

- the introduction of new technology that competes with the firm's current technology;
- increased competition from new or established companies;
- changing buying habits or needs of customers;
- regulatory changes that affect the firm's offerings;
- commoditization of the firm's offerings;
- the introduction of new technology that can reduce production costs; and
- the use of new distribution channels that are more cost-effective.

For example, high-tech companies that follow the traditional model of shipping hardware products or packaged software have been forced to deal with the challenges brought about by cloud-based businesses: software-as-a-service, platform-as-a-service, or infrastructure-as-a-service cloud-based businesses. It is not always simple to assess the impact on the business model when there is a drastic change in the way businesses will deliver products, as reported in a study by Accenture.[8] Based on interviews with forty senior executives from thirty companies that operated or were building cloud-based businesses, this research firm reported that there was not a clear understanding of how the complexity of these new cloud-based business models would have an impact as well on every function of the firm.

A 2013 report by PricewaterhouseCoopers (PwC) Health Research Institute found that medical technology (medtech) companies—companies involved in diagnostics, disposable medical products, medical equipment, diversified life sciences, implantable devices, and other areas—would have to radically change their business model in order to remain competitive.[9] The study was based on interviews with more than thirty top executives as well as a survey conducted in the summer of 2013 of more than thirty-five medtech companies. In total, there were fifty firms in the study. PwC concluded that there was a need for innovation and adaption to the changing marketplace in order to defend against new market entrants. For example, the study found that at least eighteen medtech companies had entered the market and were driving technology innovation. The key message of the study for the modification of existing business models of medtech companies was that in the new health care environment, the value of a medical device lies not solely in the product or service developed but in the following, according to the study:

While clinical efficacy is a must, the true value in medtech today is a company's ability to provide information, services, and other assistance to customers to solve additional problems such as improving diagnostics, increasing operating room efficiency, reducing length of hospital stays, monitoring patients remotely, and keeping people out of the hospital.[10]

---

8. Accenture, "Where the Cloud Meets Reality: Scaling to Succeed in New Business Models," http://www.accenture.com/SiteCollectionDocuments/PDF/Accenture-Where-the-Cloud-Meets-Reality.pdf#zoom=50.

9. PwC Health Research Institute, "Medtech Companies Prepare for an Innovation Makeover," October 2013.

10. PwC Health Research Institute, "Medtech Companies Prepare for an Innovation Makeover," 2–3.

Yet the study found that only half of the firms in the study were using new social, mobile, analytic, and cloud technologies to interact with customers and patients in managing health and to monitor remotely their health condition, and only 11% of the firms were aggressively incorporating new social, mobile, analytic, and cloud technologies into their business model. Moreover, although the findings of the study stressed the need for developing partnerships, participants in the study noted that such collaborations were difficult to put in place. In fact, while the firms in the study indicated that they did work with either their customers or external partners, this was done for less than one-third of their products and services.

THE BUSINESS PLAN

How the business model is to be executed is set forth in the *business plan*, which describes the product plan, the marketing strategy, the management team, and the firm's financial condition and funding needs. That document can be short or lengthy. The length is typically dependent on the complexity of the business and the competitive environment. A business that offers a new product in effectively a new industry subsector might require a longer business plan than one offering an improved version of an existing product within an industry.

A business plan can be used solely as an internal document or it can be distributed to external parties that request it, such as potential key employees, equity investors, and lenders. A suggested template for a business plan is provided by various sources, including the U.S. Small Business Administration.

As we describe the components of the business plan in this section, the need for developing some components more than others will become clear. Some components of a business plan are so essential that without them, suppliers of capital will be reluctant to commit funds, potential customers will be reluctant to do business with a new firm for critical products that it may need in conducting its business, and suppliers of goods and services will have concerns about extending credit. For a startup, the business plan may be essential in attracting key individuals to join the company, who will likely be leaving behind well-paying positions at other firms. The amount of capital that needs to be raised at different stages of development of the new venture will be estimated in one part of the business plan.

The bare-bones components of a business plan are a description of the business concept, the marketplace in which the offerings are to be sold, and the firm's financial projections and current financial condition. Each of these components in turn has several elements that must be covered.

The *business concept* of a business plan is the vision of the company. A description of the marketplace for the company's offering includes identifying the potential customers, the marketing channels through which those customers are to be reached, and the competitive environment. The company's current financial condition and financial projections address the liquidity of the company, its current and forecasted revenue and profit potential, and its current funding and anticipated future funding needs.

A business plan begins with an *executive summary*, which highlights the key aspects of the business and the business plan. This is where the business concept is explained. When the business plan is to likely to be distributed to outsiders, then one objective of the executive summary is to be sufficiently interesting so that the supplier of capital continues reading the document. In fact, typically in screening potential investments, investors do not read the entire business plan. Rather, they are given the executive summary by an intermediary (e.g., a lawyer or accountant). Since the executive summary should be only a few pages long, preparing this part of the business plan forces the founders to streamline their thinking about the business.

The sections that follow the executive summary provide a description of the following:

- the nature of the business,
- products and services to be offered,
- the market segment or customers targeted,
- the competitive nature of the industry,
- the marketing plan,
- suppliers and service providers,
- the management team,
- the financial plan, and
- risks.

Below we explain each of these sections and what they address. Without minimizing the importance of the other sections of the business plan, we will keep the discussion of them brief. Our principal focus in this book is on the financial plan, which we cover in chapter 14. The risks have already been described in chapter 1.

Nature of the Business

A history of the business and how it has been operating is described in this section. The information contained in this section should include the following:

- how long the company has been conducting business;
- the legal form of business organization, and possibly any plans for changing that form as the business grows;
- the location of the business and whether location is important for competitive, marketing, or distribution reasons, and why;
- the accomplishments of the business to date; and
- key partnership or strategic arrangements.

In the next chapter we discuss the legal forms of business organizations from which founders may select.

Products and Services to Be Offered

A nontechnical description of the company's offerings is provided in this section. It is sometimes difficult for founders to describe offerings of a highly technical nature to outsiders. In preparing this section, the founders must realize that if the document is to be presented to potential funding sources, those entities may lack the technical skills to appreciate the significance of a product or service. A simple solution is to include an appendix to the business plan that gives technical details. In addition to a description of the offerings, this section of the business plan should include the advantages for customers (the value proposition) and the pricing strategy.

Market Segment or Customers Targeted

The market segment or customers targeted should be clearly defined. Data on how large the current and potential market are should be presented. Vague statements about the targeted market are not helpful to outsiders (potential funders and suppliers) in understanding the marketing plan (discussed shortly), the potential revenue and revenue growth, and the profit potential.

A common mistake made by founders is to describe the dollar size of the market very broadly in an attempt to make the potential revenue sound appealing should the company succeed in capturing only a small share of the market. Moreover, the sourcing of the information on market size should be reliable. Here is an example.

Suppose that in 2008 a group of scientists working on treatments for breast cancer decide to start a company based on their developments and patents. In terms of revenue, the cancer therapy market is the second largest pharmaceutical market (behind the cardiovascular drug market). In July 2008 a study by BBC Research[11] ("Cancer Therapies: Technologies and Global Markets") reported that the global market for cancer therapies was worth $47.3 billion and was forecasted to increase to more than $110.6 billion by 2013 (representing a compounded annual growth rate [CAGR] of 12.6%).[12] This information might be included as a description of the market size. However, that would be misleading for two reasons. First, the founders' targeted market may be for a specific type of cancer treatment, specifically, one of the four main types: chemotherapy, hormone therapy, targeted therapy, and immunotherapy. The market for each type is different and has different forecasted growth rates (e.g., targeted therapy: $22.9 billion in 2007, CAGR of 24.7% through 2013; chemotherapy: $13.1 billion in 2007, CAGR of 11.2% through 2013). Moreover, the founders'

---

11. BCC Research, "Cancer Therapies: Technologies and Global Markets," May 2008, http://www.bccresearch.com/market-research/healthcare/cancer-therapies-market-hlc027b.html. BBC Research is a market forecasting company.
12. This information and what follows are taken from BCC Research, "Cancer Therapies: Technologies and Global Markets."

market is not cancer therapy in general but breast cancer therapy. That market segment dominated the overall market in 2007 with a market share of 26.0% and $10.6 billion in revenue. BCC Research forecasted the market segment to increase to $12.4 billion in 2008 and $26.5 billion in 2013 (i.e., a CAGR of 16.4%). In describing the market size, it is the breast cancer therapy market that is relevant, and this market would probably have to be refined more carefully according to the type of therapy.

Competitive Nature of the Industry

The description of the industry structure for the market in which the offerings will be sold should include the competitive nature of the industry and the barriers to entry. Overly optimistic founders too often refer to competitors as if they did not exist or as if competition was minimal. Even if current competitive conditions are favorable, identifying whether there are barriers to entry is important for assessing potential newcomers to the industry as well as established firms selling related products.

Marketing Plan

Since the offerings, targeted customers or market segment, and competitors have been identified in previous parts of the business plan, the means by which the founding team plans to reach its targeted customers can now be explained. This is the marketing plan, which describes how the company plans to reach the targeted market: through advertising (e.g., direct mail, Internet blasts, periodicals), promotional campaigns (e.g., trade shows), and public relations activities. To aid in understanding the marketing plan, an explanation of the buying habits exhibited by customers who are potential buyers of the products or services should be provided. Any devices or strategies that are different from the marketing strategies used by competitors should be highlighted. How the company plans to assess the impact of its marketing plan should be mentioned.

Suppliers and Service Providers

In the production of its offerings, a company will need to acquire inputs. These inputs include generic products or services and in some instances products or services that may be in short supply. Identifying suppliers for the latter is important to avoid production bottlenecks. Consequently, alternative strategies for dealing with inputs that may temporarily be in short supply must be described. Moreover, some offerings may require that a company contract for the services of other companies, called subcontractors. For example, a product might be serviced by a subcontractor for initial assembly or for warranty work. A shortage of subcontractors will impede sales.

Management Team

The management team conducts all phases of the operation of the business. A description of the different groups within the management team should be provided, along with their experience. In the startup phase, the number of positions that need to be filled and how the company plans to identify and recruit individuals with the requisite management skills should be explained. In addition to the management team, any consultants or advisers that the firm expects to use should be identified. For example, a high-tech company may recruit a world-class expert to be a spokesperson for the company and its offerings.

Financial Plan

The financial plan covers a wide range of data. It typically includes (if available) the current financial statements, described in chapters 9, 10, and 11. The various financial ratios described in chapter 12, covering profitability, asset efficiency, return on investment, and liquidity, are explained in this part of the business plan. In addition, there will be forecasts of the financial statements. The forecasting of the income statement, for example, will require forecasts of each of its components, including revenue from each source and the different types of costs. How forecasting is done is described in chapter 14. An integrated forecasting model will also provide information about cash needs and the amount of fundraising that will be required over time.

Risks

The risks the company may encounter and how it will address those risks should be identified in this part of the business plan. We described these risks in chapter 1.

Business Model versus Business Plan

The U.S. Small Business Administration (SBA) explains the difference between a business model and a business plan as follows. The business model provides the original idea for the business and its functions. The SBA considers the business model to be a company's "foundation." The business plan, in contrast, is what the SBA describes as the "structure" of the business. It does so by elaborating on the details about the business.

We can understand the difference between the two by looking at the three components of a business model described in the chapter:

1. the market: customers and customer segments;
2. the value proposition for the products or services being offered; and
3. profitability: revenue sources and cost structure.

None of these components tells anything about how the company plans to implement the business idea set forth in the business model.

The business plan, in contrast, explains in more detail the targeted customers and how the company plans to market to those groups: the marketing plan. The value proposition in the business model tells us what value is being provided to customers. However, it does not tell us the competition in the market and barriers to entry. The profitability in the business model describes revenues and cost structure in general, but the business plan describes the revenues and cost structure in more specific terms. For example, with respect to costs, the business plan will describe the different components of costs (e.g., labor and raw materials) and the different properties of costs (e.g., fixed, variable, and semivariable). The business plan will look at the potential break-even level of operations, as well as the potential scalability of the company's offerings.

EXIT PLANNING

We conclude this chapter with a discussion of exit planning and the issues associated with such plans. One study found that about half the chief executive officers of most small private companies have an exit plan.[13]

Components of Exit Planning

Exit planning has the following three components that a founding team must go through in considering the transfer of ownership to another business or to other investors: (1) transition planning, (2) exit strategy planning, and (3) succession planning. Our primary focus is on the second component of exit planning, exit strategy planning.

Transition Planning *Transition planning* involves several activities. First and foremost is enhancing the value of the business to make it attractive to potential buyers. The strategies for doing so are described in several chapters of this book. Second, the founding team must be able to work with the intermediaries it retains (e.g., investment bankers and business brokers) to facilitate the transition process in preparing legal documents and performing due diligence. Third, it is important that the members of the founding team who may be involved in transition planning understand what financial metrics prospective buyers are looking for in a company. Thus, the financial concepts we discuss in chapters 8 through 11 should be understood.

Exit Strategy Planning Each member of the founding team has his or her exit intention.[14] By "exit intention" is meant the objective of a member of the founding team in leaving the venture at some future date. In general, the objective might be purely financial in nature, or it might be a combination of financial and legacy building. Founders' objectives in exiting may also include leaving the business to the next generation of the founding team. A considerable amount of research has looked at the strategy of passing on a private business firm to the next generation of family business members. These studies find that exiting

---

13. D. Dahl, "A New Study Says Most Small Biz CEOs Lack Succession Plans," *Inc. Magazine*, 2005, http://www.inc.com?criticalnews/articles/200502/exit.html.

14. A theory of planned behavior, developed in the field of social psychology, has been applied to entrepreneur exit strategies and predicts that intention will be a significant factor. This is supported by empirical evidence. For a review of these studies, see Teemu Kautonen, Marco van Gelderen, and Erno T. Tornikoski, "Predicting Entrepreneurial Behaviour: A Test of the Theory of Planned Behaviour," *Applied Economics* 45, no. 6 (2013): 697–707.

a business by successfully transferring it depends on nonfinancial issues, including the strength of the relationship of the entrepreneur to family members and the involvement of family members in the business before the transfer.

Exit intention is typically formulated by a member of the founding team in a company's early stages and will have an impact on the decision making by the founding team in dealing with key business decisions. The exit intention is often linked to the reason why a member of the founding team made the decision to enter into a new venture that resulted in the establishment of the firm.[15]

One empirical study found a clear link between founders' exit intentions and outcomes.[16] Comparing actual exits by entrepreneurs with their exit intentions (based on six exit paths), Dawn R. DeTienne and Melissa S. Cardon found that 70% exited according to their intended path.[17] They also found that although 9% of the founders in their study indicated that their most likely exit was an acquisition, those entrepreneurs wound up exiting as a result of either an IPO or an independent sale. The remaining 21% of entrepreneurs in the De Tienne–Cardon study liquidated their firm rather than exiting by the most likely path that they reported. These findings provide empirical support that there is a high correlation between entrepreneurs' exit intentions and actual entrepreneurial exit behavior.

Exit strategies include:

- IPO of the company,
- sale of the company/acquisition of the company,
- merger of the company, and
- liquidation of the company.

In chapter 6 we discuss IPOs, and in chapter 13 we discuss what founders consider in the acquisition of their company. As part of the exit strategy planning, founders will consider income tax consequences and estate tax consequences. This is best done through consultation with tax accountants or tax attorneys.

Succession Planning Prospective buyers of a business will want to know how the founding team plans to deal with the replacement of any team members who may decide to leave the business following the transfer or sale of the business. The departure of some members of the founding team may be welcomed by a prospective buyer, as their perceived value to the business may no longer be deemed important. However, in the case of few high-tech firms, there are typically critical members of the founding team who are viewed as

15. Dawn R. DeTienne, Alexander McKelvie, and Gaylen N. Chandler, "The Impact of Motivation, Innovation and Causation and Effectuation Approaches on Exit Strategies," paper presented at the Academy of Management Annual Meeting, Boston, August 2012.

16. Kautonen, van Gelderen, and Tornikoski, "Predicting Entrepreneurial Behaviour."

17. Dawn R. DeTienne and Melissa S. Cardon, "Impact of Founder Experience on Exit Intentions," *Small Business Economics* 38, no. 4 (2012): 352–374.

essential to the future success and growth of the firm. The process of identifying replacements for such individuals whom prospective buyers would deem critical is referred to as *succession planning*.

Issues Associated with Exit Strategies

Karl Wennberg and Dawn DeTienne identify the following critical issues associated with exit planning strategies that affect the entrepreneur's ability to successfully exit:[18]

- For entrepreneurs who have an exit strategy, how successful are they in achieving their exit?
- Do exit strategies pursued by entrepreneurs evolve or change over time?
- To what extent do exit strategies influence decisions by entrepreneurs that will have a long-term impact on the firm?

With respect to the first issue, some researchers believe that strategic exit planning will lead to a successful exit. Because of the large number of risks faced by entrepreneurs in a startup company, it is difficult for the initial exit strategy to be realized, indicating that the exit strategy will evolve over time. Accordingly, the entrepreneur should be flexible and maintain as his or her chief objective building a successful business

Entrepreneurial Exit

Entrepreneurial exit has been the focus of several studies. Two types of exits have been critically examined: the exit of the individual entrepreneur (exit from self-employment) and the exit of the new venture firm from the market (organizational exit).

Several studies have provided operational definitions of "entrepreneurial exit."[19] These include the following:

- the decision by an entrepreneur to leave the firm,[20]
- the decision to remove a firm from a particular market,[21] and
- the decision to discontinue a firm, close down a firm, or file for bankruptcy.[22]

18. Karl Wennberg and Dawn R. DeTienne, "What Do We Really Mean When We Talk about 'Exit'? A Critical Review of Research on Entrepreneurial Exit," *International Small Business Journal* 32, no. 1 (2014): 4–16.

19. See Wennberg and DeTienne, "What Do We Really Mean When We Talk about 'Exit'?," for an excellent review of the research on entrepreneurial exits.

20. See: David S. Evans and Linda S. Leighton, "Some Empirical Aspects of Entrepreneurship," *American Economic Review* 79, 3 (1989), pp. 519–535, and C. Mirjam van Praag, "Business Survival and Success of Young Small Business Owners," *Small Business Economics* 21, no. 1 (2003): 1–17.

21. Will Mitchell, "The Dynamics of Evolving Markets: The Effects of Business Sales and Age on Dissolutions and Divestitures," *Administrative Science Quarterly* 39, no. 4 (1994): 575–602; Philip Anderson and Michael Tushman, "Organizational Environments and Industry Exit: The Effects of Uncertainty, Munificence and Complexity," *Industrial and Corporate Change* 10, no. 3 (2001): 675–711.

22. Javier Gimeno, Timothy B. Folta, and Arnold C. Cooper, "Survival of the Fittest? Entrepreneurial Human Capital and the Persistence of Underperforming Firms," *Administrative Science Quarterly* 42, no. 4 (1997): 750–783.

DeTienne, for example, defines entrepreneurial exit based on the decision by the entrepreneur to leave the firm as "the process by which the founders of privately held firms leave the firm they helped to create; thereby removing themselves, in varying degree, from the primary ownership and decision-making structure of the firm."[23] Erik Stam, Roy Thurik, and Peter Van der Zwan define entrepreneurial exit as "the decision to quit an entrepreneurial career."[24]

Should Entrepreneurs Have an Exit Strategy Plan?

As explained earlier, there are three components of exit planning. Transition planning, particularly the activity of enhancing the value of the company, is critical. In the absence of transition planning the only two options for an exit available to founders are liquidation, if there are no entities willing to acquire the business, or bankruptcy, an option forced on the company by its creditors. Succession planning is necessary because of the need to ensure that the business will be ongoing should one or more critical members of the founding team, for whatever reason, leave the company. The absence of succession planning may impede execution of the transition plan.

What about the exit strategy planning component of the exit plan? Is devising an exit strategy an essential part of the exit plan? Some advisers to startups suggest that this component is important since it provides a target for the founders. Moreover, it is argued that one of the first questions that capital providers will ask of the founders is, "What is your exit strategy?"

On the flip side, some investors and observers of entrepreneurial firms believe that entrepreneurs are too focused on an exit strategy when they found a company. The view is that although it is important to harvest the benefits associated with a successful company by way of an IPO or sale, the founders' focus should be on growing the business and generating attractive returns for current investors, including the founders. Privileging exit strategies over other firm activities, it is argued, may lead to decisions that will impede the realization of that goal. For example, a policy of short-term cost cutting for the purpose of enhancing short-term profitability in anticipation of an IPO can have an adverse impact on long-term profitability and possibly on the reputation of the company, while also inviting competitors into the market. Focusing on product development and growing the business, on the other hand, will lead to a wider range of attractive opportunities when and if the founders decide to exit the business. The attention of the business should be directed toward its customers, not its investors—a problem that is faced by even accomplished companies when they become concerned more with short-term financial performance.

---

23. Dawn R. DeTienne, "Entrepreneurial Exit As a Critical Component of the Entrepreneurial Process: Theoretical Development," *Journal of Business Venturing* 25, no. 2 (2010): 203–215.

24. Erik Stam, Roy Thurik, and Peter Van der Zwan, "Entrepreneurial Exit in Real and Imagined Markets," *Industrial and Corporate Change* 19, no. 4 (2010): 1109–1139, at 1113.

Thus, if the other two components of the exit plan are executed properly, the choices for the alternatives to harvest the benefits with a successful startup will be available to the founders. The only reason to be prepared to have an "on paper" exit strategy is for the benefits of capital providers, who will invariably ask, "What is your exit strategy?" As Robert X. Cringely writes:

Were it not for demanding investors the exit question would be asked less often because it isn't even an issue with many company founders who are already doing what they like and presumably making a good living at it.[25]

While there are entrepreneurs who have an explicit exit strategy, many entrepreneurs form a new company without giving much thought to what they want to achieve in terms of an eventual exit outcome. As Cringely notes:

What's Larry Ellison's exit strategy? Larry doesn't have one.

Neither did Steve Jobs, Gordon Moore, Bob Noyce, Bill Hewlett, Dave Packard, or a thousand other company founders whose names don't happen to be household words.

What's Michael Dell's exit strategy? Dell, who is trying to take his namesake company private—to de-exit—wants to climb back inside his corporate womb.

Marc Benioff of Salesforce.com has no exit strategy. Neither does Reed Hastings of NetFlix. You know Jeff Bezos at Amazon.com has no exit strategy.

Bill Gates didn't have an exit strategy until running Microsoft stopped being fun so he found an exit. And I think the same can be said for any of these name founders, that they wanted to stay on the job as long as it remained fun.[26]

Of course, over time, as a company succeeds in realizing its goals, exit strategies become important. The reason is that control issues resulting from the types of funds raised, federal securities laws, and taxation (income taxes and estate taxes) will become important as the founders make decisions about various aspects of the business.

For example, consider the impact of federal securities law, which we discuss in chapter 5. In building Facebook, Mark Zuckerberg did not have an exit strategy. Even after Facebook's IPO in May 2012, it appears that he did not have any such strategy, though an IPO is one of the exit strategies mentioned earlier in this chapter. Zuckerberg even rejected offers of other forms of exit, such as being acquired by Google, Microsoft, or Yahoo!. It was a peculiar federal securities law that forced Facebook to make a public offering, a law that has since been changed. More specifically, as explained in chapter 5, once a company has more than a specified number of shareholders, it must comply with certain federal securities laws. Since Facebook had more than this number because of stock granted to employees, Zuckerberg had to comply with the law and have an IPO.

A fair conclusion to our discussion of exit strategy planning regarding a response to investors who ask an entrepreneur what his or her exit plan might be is the following,

25. Robert X. Cringely, "The Exit Trap," May 7, 2013, http://www.cringely.com/2013/05/07/the-exit-trap.
26. Ibid.

suggested by Hamid Shojaee in an article titled "No Exit Strategy Is Your Best Strategy": "I have no exit strategy. I plan to build an awesome company that I'd want to keep forever—a company that creates knock-your-socks-off products—and if I'm successful at doing that, I'm sure there will be buyers lining up for every share of the company."[27]

However, as startups grow and become publicly traded through an IPO, and if control of the business shifts from founders to nonfounding investors and a nonfounding chief executive officer and chief financial officer, it is the investors who will dictate the exit strategy of the business, and it is the contractual compensation and equity options made available to key officers and the board that will decide the fate of the company. The original intentions of the founders disappear and are replaced by financial metrics and targets. The permanence of the company is no longer a factor to be considered.

KEY POINTS COVERED IN THIS CHAPTER

- A business model is a conceptual tool that sets forth the key assumptions identifying how the company plans to achieve a sustainable revenue stream and earn a profit, and in doing so, it describes the value a company offers potential customers.
- The Business Model Canvas includes the following basic building blocks for a business model: key partners, key activities, the value proposition, customer relationships, customer segments, key resources, the distribution channel, the cost structure, and the revenue stream.
- Basically, the three key components that a business model should include are (1) the market (i.e., customers and customer segments), (2) the value proposition for the products or services being offered, and (3) profitability (i.e., revenue sources and cost structure).
- Because different customer segments are reached through different channels and require different types of relationships, this information should be described in the business model.
- The value proposition sets forth the unique benefits that the firm will deliver to each of its targeted customer segments by addressing each of the following: (1) the value the firm will be delivering to the targeted customer segment, (2) how the offerings will solve or mitigate the problems that a customer segment is facing, and (3) how the offerings are different from those provided by the venture's competitors.
- The value proposition not only is included in the business model, it is an integral part of the business plan.
- The business model must explain the various revenue sources that are expected and the cost of producing the offerings, thereby identifying the potential profit.

27. Hamid Shojaee, "No Exit Strategy Is Your Best Strategy," January 19, 2011, http://azdisruptors.com/blog/2011/1/19/no-exit-strategy-is-your-best-strategy.html.

- With respect to cost structure, the business model should describe the potential for economies of scale and economies of operation.
- "Economies of scale" refers to the reduction in the average cost of producing a unit of product as output increases, referred to as the "scalability" of a product.
- "Economies of scope" refers to the reduction in the average cost associated with the production of multiple different products.
- A firm's cost structure should be thought of in terms of its value proposition.
- In business models where the value proposition is a low-cost product compared to competitors' products, the focus is on a cost structure that minimizes costs. A cost structure that is driven by a low-price value proposition is referred to as a cost-driven structure.
- For a business model in which the cost structure is dictated by a value proposition that the product is a premium value product, the cost structure is called a value-driven cost structure.
- The business model is revised for one or more of the following reasons: the introduction of new technology that competes with the firm's current technology, increased competition from new or established companies, changing buying habits or needs of customers, regulatory changes that have an impact on the firm's offerings, commoditization of the firm's offerings, the introduction of new technology that can reduce production costs, and the use of new distribution channels that are more cost-effective.
- The business plan is an internal document that describes how the founders plan to implement the business model.
- The business plan describes the product plan, the marketing strategy, the management team, and the venture's financial condition and funding needs.
- The business plan is the vision of the company in which the founders describe the marketplace for the company's offerings, the marketing channels through which to reach those customers, and the competitive environment.
- The company's current financial condition and financial projections cover the liquidity of the company, its current and forecasted revenue and profit potential, and its current funding and anticipated future funding needs.
- A business plan's executive summary highlights the key aspects of the business and describes the nature of the business, the products and services to be offered, the market segment or customers targeted, the competitive nature of the industry, the marketing plan, suppliers and service providers, the management team, the financial plan, and risks.
- There are three components of exit planning that a founding team must address in considering the transfer of ownership to another business or to other investors: (1) transition planning, (2) exit strategy planning, and (3) succession planning.

- Exit strategies include an initial public offering (IPO) of the company, sale of the company or acquisition of the company, merger of the company, and liquidation of the company.

- Two types of exits include the exit of the individual founder (exit from self-employment) and the exit of the new venture firm from the market (organizational exit).

- Entrepreneurial exit includes the decision by (1) a founder to leave the firm, (2) a firm to exit from a particular market, and (3) a firm to close down or file for bankruptcy.

FURTHER READINGS

Business Models
Amit, Raphael, and Christoph Zott, "Creating Value through Business Model Innovation," *MIT Sloan Management Review* 53 (Spring 2012): 41–49.

Amit, Raphael, and Christoph Zott, "The Fit between Product Market Strategy and Business Model: Implications for Firm Performance," *Strategic Management Journal* 29 (2008): 1–26.

Casadesus-Masanell, Ramon, and Joan E. Ricart, "How to Design a Winning Business Model," *Harvard Business Review,* January–February 2011, 101–107.

Chesbrough, Henry W., "Why Companies Should Have Open Business Models," *MIT Sloan Management Review* 48 (Winter 2007): 22–28.

Eyring, Matthew J., Mark W. Johnson, and Hari Nair, "New Business Models in Emerging Markets," *Harvard Business Review,* January–February 2011, 89–95.

Gronum, Sarel, John Steen, and Martie-Louise Verreynne, "Business Model Design and Innovation: Unlocking the Performance Benefits of Innovation," *Australian Journal of Management,* 2015, doi:10.1177/0312896215587315.

Johnson, Mark W., Clayton M. Christensen, and Henning Kagermann, "Reinventing Your Business Model," *Harvard Business Review,* December 2008, 51–59.

Magretta, Joan, "Why Business Models Matter," *Harvard Business Review* 6 (May 2002): 86–92.

Sinfield, Joseph V., Edward Calder, Bernard McConnell, and Steve Colson, "How to Identify New Business Models," *MIT Sloan Management Review* 53 (Winter 2012): 85–90.

Teece, David J., "Business Models, Business Strategy and Innovation," *Long Range Planning* 43 (2010): 172–194.

Zott, Christoph, and Raphael Amit, "Business Model Design and the Performance of Entrepreneurial Firms," *Organization Science* 18 (2007): 181–199.

Zott, Christoph, Raphael Amit, and Lorenzo Massa, "The Business Model: Recent Developments and Future Research," *Journal of Management* 37 (2011): 1019–1042.

Business Plans
"Build Your Business Plan," U.S. Small Business Administration, http://www.sba.gov/tools/business-plan/1.

"Free Sample Business Plans," *Bplans,* http://www.bplans.com/sample_business_plans.php.

Parsons, Noah, "How to Write a Business Plan," *Bplans,* http://articles.bplans.com/how-to-write-a-business-plan.

Exit Strategy Planning
Alton, Larry, "5 Common Business Plan Mistakes That Torpedo Startups," *Entrepreneur,* July 29, 2015, http://www.entrepreneur.com/article/248705.

Cairns, Chris, "Planning Your Exit Strategy: Why Tech Businesses Need to Think Ahead," GrowthBusiness. co.uk, January 21, 2015, http://www.growthbusiness.co.uk/comment-and-analysis/2477662/planning-your-exit -strategy-why-tech-businesses-need-to-think-ahead.thtml#sthash.kJLavYC1.dpuf.

Corporate Exit Strategies: Selecting the Best Strategy to Generate Value, PricewaterhouseCoopers, February 2012, http://www.pwc.com/us/en/transaction-services/assets/pwc-corporate-exit-strategies.pdf.

DeTienne, Dawn R., and Karl Wennberg, eds., *Research Handbook of Entrepreneurial Exit* (Northampton, MA: Edward Elgar, 2015).

Gardner, Alison, Kara Greenblott, and Erika Joubert, "What We Know about Exit Strategies," *C-Safe,* September 2005, http://reliefweb.int/sites/reliefweb.int/files/resources/A02C7B78FB2B408B852570AB006EC7BA -What%20We%20Know%20About%20Exit%20Strategies%20-%20Sept%202005.pdf.

Jenkins, Anna, John Steen, and Martie-Louise Verreynne, "Entrepreneurial Exit: Who, What or to Where? Regional Relocation as a Form of Exit," in DeTienne and Wennberg, eds., *Research Handbook of Entrepreneurial Exit,* 246–264, doi:10.4337/9781782546979.

Osterwalder, Alexander, "3 Ways Untested Business Plans Are Worse Than a Waste of Time," *Entrepreneur,* July 22, 2015, http://www.entrepreneur.com/article/247341.

Robbins, Stever, "Exit Strategies for Your Business," *Entrepreneur*, undated, http://www.entrepreneur.com/ article/78512.

3

SELECTING A FORM OF BUSINESS ORGANIZATION

There are several forms of business organization from which the founders of a startup company may choose. In selecting the form of business organization, the founders should consider many factors. Although some forms of business organization clearly would not be prudent for founders to select, the "best" form may not exist at the particular instant in time when a decision must be made.

In this chapter we begin by providing an overview of the different forms of business organization in the United States. We then describe the non-tax factors that should be considered by founders in selecting the form of business organization and how each form of business organization may either fulfill or fall short of fulfilling the different objectives. We then turn to the tax factors that should be considered. Finally, for founders who want to incorporate, we briefly review the factors to consider in selecting the state in which to incorporate. Forms of business organization outside the United States and their tax treatment vary from country to country and are not discussed here. But the same factors considered by founders in the United States should be considered by founders in other countries.

FORMS OF BUSINESS ORGANIZATION

There are five for-profit forms of business organization in the United States:[1]

- sole proprietorship,
- general partnership,
- limited partnership,
- corporation, and
- limited liability company.

Below we briefly discuss these five forms of business organization. More details are provided in the next section when we discuss the factors to be considered in selecting a form of business organization.

---

1. The other forms of business organization are trusts and nonprofit entities.

Sole Proprietorship

The simplest form of business organization is the *sole proprietorship*. The key difference between this form of business organization and the others that we discuss below is that one person both owns and manages the company.

General Partnership

A *general partnership* is created when two or more individuals enter into an understanding to operate a business for the purpose of making a profit. There is an agreement that governs the duties and responsibilities of the partners, how they will allocate profits and losses among the partners, how the liabilities will be divided, and how the assets will be allocated should the partnership be terminated. It would be reasonable to expect a written partnership agreement. However, a general partnership agreement can be oral or written.

The Uniform Partnership Act (UPA) provides the rules that govern general partnerships. The UPA is a model law that has been adopted by the states to a great extent, but each state's partnership law can deviate in significant ways from the laws as set forth in the UPA. The guidelines set forth for a general partnership can be modified in the partnership agreement, within limits. Failure of a partnership agreement to include a provision regarding a matter that later comes into dispute is then governed by the UPA. Because the UPA may not provide for the intentions originally expressed by the partners when entering into the partnership, it is important that as many potential conflicts be addressed in a written partnership agreement. For this reason, an agreement of the partners should be written and not oral because if the agreement is oral, the UPA governs how any matter in dispute will be handled.

Limited Partnership

A *limited partnership* is a form of partnership that differs from a general partnership in certain ways and shares one critical advantage that is offered by a corporation. As with a general partnership, there are partners. However, the partners are classified as either general partners or limited partners. The *general partners* in a limited partnership face the same risk of exposure to unlimited liability, something we discuss later in the chapter. The *limited partners*, in contrast, share a similar investment feature of a corporation: they have protection against unlimited liability. Moreover, the limited partners do not participate in the business activities of the partnership.

Corporation

In all U.S. states there is a basic statute that provides for the formation of an entity called a *corporation* with the following attributes: (1) it has a legal personality; (2) it is governed by a board of directors; (3) it is co-owned by contributors of equity capital, called shareholders; (4) it provides limited liability to shareholders; and (5) it allows for transferable shares.

The laws of incorporation in every state regulate the creation, organization, and dissolution of corporations. The Model Business Corporation Act is followed by many states in establishing their statute for incorporation.

Although the basic attributes are essentially the same from state to state, there may be some attributes and duties of a corporation that differ in important ways by state. We'll discuss the last two attributes later when we describe the factors considered in selecting a form of business organization. By "legal personality" is meant that a corporation is treated as a legal "person" that can sue and be sued, distinct from its stockholders. *Corporate governance* refers to the set of systems, principles, and processes by which a corporation can be directed or controlled in order to achieve its goals and objectives. The goals and objectives are to add long-term value to the corporation so as to benefit all stockholders. The *board of directors* oversees the operation of the corporation so as to accomplish the goals and objectives.

In addition to state laws, there are federal laws governing the issuance of securities. We describe those laws in the next chapter.

State Filing Requirements   It is essential for founders seeking to incorporate to strictly follow the state laws for doing so. Failure to do so will result in a corporation being reclassified as a partnership. Typically, state statutes for the formation of a corporation require the following filings:

- A *preorganization stock subscription*, which is an agreement to purchase, at a stated price, a stated number of shares of stock of the corporation that is to be formed.
- The *articles of incorporation* (or *corporate charter*), which set forth the details of the new corporation, including the name of the corporation, the business purpose, the business location, the number of authorized shares, the classes of stock (if there is more than one class), the duration of the corporation's life (either fixed life or perpetual), and the names and addresses of the board of directors.
- The *corporate bylaws*, which define a corporation's purpose, how it will manage its business affairs, and the duties, responsibilities, and obligations of the shareholders, board of directors, and corporate officers; shareholder ownership rights; how corporate officers and board members are selected and removed; and the plan for annual meetings.

Each state may require additional filings. In addition, a state will require that an organizational meeting of the board of directors be held.

C Corporations and S Corporations   There are two types of corporations, C corporations and S corporations. The distinction between the two types of corporations is taken up later in this chapter when we discuss income tax factors to consider in selecting a form of business organization. Specifically, unless for federal income tax purposes a corporation elects to be an S corporation,[2] it is a C corporation. One can think of a C corporation as a corporation that has the disadvantage of double taxation of net income because it is taxed at the corporate level and then any portion distributed to shareholders is taxed again. When a corporation elects to be treated for tax purposes by having all its net income taxed only at the shareholder level, it becomes an S corporation. Although tax law imposes some restrictions on certain aspects of a corporation seeking to qualify for S corporation status, other attributes mentioned for corporations earlier are the same.

Limited Liability Company

States have statutes for the creation of a *limited liability company* (LLC), a business form of organization that combines the tax treatment of a partnership with the limited liability attribute of a corporation. An LLC can have one or more owners. The owners of an LLC, called "members," not shareholders or partners, have no restrictions on member involvement in managing the company.

As with a corporation, there are filings required by the state. These include the articles of incorporation and an operating agreement that is equivalent to corporate bylaws or a partnership agreement.

NON–INCOME TAX FACTORS TO CONSIDER IN SELECTING A FORM OF BUSINESS ORGANIZATION

In selecting a form of business organization, founders must consider both business and personal factors and then evaluate them, giving the proper weighting to each factor. Once the choices are weighed, founders will be in a position to identify the best alternative.

Although income tax considerations are important, in the early stages of a company there may be non-tax considerations that carry even more weight. The non-tax factors include the following:

- the cost of formation and ongoing expenses to maintain a particular form of business organization,
- protection against unlimited liability,
- continuity of the business,
- management and operational control,
- ability to raise funds, and
- ability to transfer ownership interests.

2. The name S corporation comes from the chapter of the tax code that allows the election for the corporation to be taxed as described in the next section.

Cost of Formation and Ongoing Expenses

For any form of business organization, there are costs to forming the company, and typically there are ongoing expenses required to maintain the business form selected.

For a sole proprietorship, because there are no legal formalities required to create a company, the formation costs are minimal. There is no such thing as a sole proprietary agreement that must be created by a lawyer. Any costs associated with doing business in a state and with obtaining licenses vary by state. The business can operate under the name of the owner or under a fictitious name (i.e., "doing business as …").

As with a sole proprietorship, the formation of a general partnership does not involve any legal formalities. Although there is no requirement that a written partnership agreement be prepared and then signed by the partners, it is prudent to have an attorney prepare such a document, which is a cost to the founders. Other than the cost of the partnership agreement, filing costs are minimal. There are also minimal maintenance costs.

As explained in our description of a limited partnership in the previous section, this form of business organization is created by state law. Consequently, a state will require that a certificate of limited partnership be filed, adding to the cost above that for the formation of a general partnership.

In the case of a corporation, a considerable number of documents must be filed with the state in which the business is incorporated. There are the costs associated with preparing the filing documents mandated by the state; these include but are not limited to the initial organizational documents, which set forth the corporate governance information, the size of the board of directors, the voting rights of shareholders, and the sale of securities that may be sold and the number of authorized shares. In addition to the legal fees for the preparation of these documents, there are the filing fees. If the corporation meets the asset size requirements for filing with the Securities and Exchange Commission (SEC) as explained in chapter 5, those documents must be prepared even if securities will not be issued until some future time. Preparing special agreements, such as those concerning restrictions on the sale of stock, complicated capital structure issues, or actions that must be taken should certain events occur, could add to the costs of formation.

A corporation incurs ongoing business expenses. Depending on the state of incorporation, an annual franchise fee or some other type of fee typically is required for annual renewal of the license to do business in the state. There are the legal costs of preparing each year the minutes of the corporate meetings, the minutes of the board of directors meetings, and procuring the legal advice to ensure that the corporation is complying with all the state requirements for actions that need to be taken to comply with state statutes. These are just state costs; other costs are associated with the annual SEC filings.

Protection against Unlimited Liability

With the decision to start a business, one of the foremost concerns of the founders is the potential personal liability each faces as a result of incurring debt to fund the company and its operations (e.g., the amount owed to suppliers and employees), the taxes owed to all tax authorities, and possible monetary damages from product or service failure that are not covered by insurance or other agreements. It would be naïve to think that founders would not expect to lose some amount of their personal assets. In fact, potential investors or lenders may view the amount of founders' assets at risk as a sign of the founders' confidence in the potential success of the business venture. If the providers of capital to the business venture lose money, they want to know that the founders feel at least an equal amount of economic pain.

However, the risk of possible unlimited liability concerns more than just the founders. It is a consideration in the raising of capital by outsiders as well. Potential external investors want to know whether actions by the founders in the course of managing the new venture could result in external investors losing more than their initial investment. Consequently, the form of business organization selected is critical for the founders and new investors with respect to the potential for loss of personal assets beyond those committed to the new venture.

Business organizations provide for either unlimited liability or limited liability. *Limited liability* means that typically the amount of loss that an investor will sustain is limited to the amount invested. The reason for the qualifier "typically" in describing limited liability is that management might commit certain acts that could result in the loss of some or all of the limited liability protection. The existence in the United States of business organizations that provide liability protection plays an important role in encouraging investment because it limits the risk involved in business ownership.

Sole proprietorships and general partnerships are forms of business organization characterized by unlimited liability. In contrast to a general partnership, in a limited partnership the limited partners face limited liability. The general partners in a limited partnership, however, face unlimited liability. Corporations and LLCs offer limited liability.

The general statement that corporations and LLCs have limited liability is subject to three important limitations. First, owners often have to provide outside borrowers personal guarantees for their loans if the startup company seeks to use any form of business organization that offers limited liability protection. Although the liability is not limited to the amount invested, it is capped at a known amount: the amount invested plus the amount guaranteed in any lending agreements. Second, liabilities arising from fraudulent or criminal acts in the course of business are not protected by the limited liability provision of a business organization. The third limitation on limited liability arises from what is known in corporate law as the "veil doctrine," which we discuss next.

The Veil Doctrine   There are situations in which the courts will ignore a business organization's limited liability protection and hold the shareholders or board of directors of a corporation personally liable for certain debts incurred when there is serious misconduct in the management of the business. The same is true for the actions of general partners in a limited partnership.

This setting aside of the corporate (or limited partnership) right to limited liability protection by the courts is referred to as the veil doctrine. It is governed by state law and consequently varies from state to state. There are many cases in which there is a challenge before the court as to whether to "pierce the corporate veil" involving relationships between parent and subsidiaries companies. These relationships may be relevant to founders in the later stages of a company's growth. For a small corporation, the questions the court may investigate to assess whether piercing the corporate veil is warranted involve determination of whether (1) there was undercapitalization when the corporation was started, or perhaps the corporation was nothing but a shell corporation; (2) the corporation failed to maintain the proper books and records required by state law; or (3) management abused the corporate form for its own benefit just to obtain the protection of limited liability.

With respect to the first reason above, in general, a corporation is referred to as a shell company if it has no active business and usually exists only in name as a vehicle for the business operations of another corporation. Shell corporations do have legitimate business reasons for existence. Unfortunately, all too often they are associated with fraudulent acts such as tax evasion, money laundering, fictitious businesses and billing schemes, and other scams. Even in the absence of claiming a scam, as explained in chapter 9, when a corporation is formed, there is a par value or stated value that determines the common stock value and the preferred stock value of the corporation for legal purposes. The purchasing of new equity shares at or below the par value or stated value means that there is undercapitalization, and therefore a basis exists for shareholders and others who have been harmed to petition the court to lift the limited liability protection.

As for the third reason, there are two ways in which the corporate form has been found to be abusive and used to lift the limited liability protection provided: through instrumentality (or domination) and improper purpose. The **instrumentality theory** (or **domination theory**), more commonly referred to as the **alter ego theory**, holds that if a corporation is merely an extension of the actions of an individual, then to the extent that the activities of the corporation and those of the individual are practically indistinguishable from each other, the corporation should be treated as a single individual with no limited liability. That is, in the case of a corporation, the alter ego theory considers whether there are boundaries between the corporation and its shareholders. The courts view that a corporation is the alter ego of a corporation's stockholders, corporate officers, and board of directors whenever the transactions made under the corporate name are used merely for those persons' personal business in order to obtain protection against individual liability. In some states the alter ego doctrine has been applied by courts to LLCs but not to limited partnerships. It can be argued that for an LLC that is intended to be dominated by one or a few individuals, the application of this theory may be difficult in court proceedings. ***Improper purpose*** was described earlier: a business form with limited liability cannot use that limited liability to protect against defrauding or taking advantage of other parties.

Continuity of the Business

Although there may be exceptions as a result of contractual agreements for another individual to take over the business (a family member or a key employee), in a sole proprietorship the death of the founder by law terminates the business.

The laws in each state that govern general partnerships vary; however, with respect to the continuity of the business, most state statutes specify that unless the partnership agreement states otherwise, a partnership is dissolved under certain conditions such as the death of a partner, the bankruptcy of a partner, or the voluntary withdrawal or involuntary removal of a partner. The dissolution of a partnership means only that the relationship among the partners is dissolved. The business itself may continue or may plan to go out of business. In the latter case, the partnership is wound down on the terms set forth in the partnership agreement, which involves the distribution of assets. The partnership agreement should set forth how the shares of a partner in case of death, voluntary withdrawal, or removal should be valued.

Unlike a general partnership, in a limited partnership the continuity of the company is not affected by the death or withdrawal of a limited partner. Neither is there any impact on continuity if a general partner dies or withdraws as long as at least one general partner remains.

In terms of business continuity, a corporation is the most advantageous form of business organization. Until formally dissolved, a corporation is afforded perpetual existence as set forth in the articles of incorporation, regardless of the death or withdrawal of any stockholder. A corporation can be dissolved by the shareholders in one of two ways. The first is by a vote of the shareholders and the second is by judicial dissolution. The latter method is commonly employed in situations where there are disputes regarding dissolution among the shareholders.

Management and Operational Control

Obviously, management and operational control are not issues with a sole proprietorship. In a general partnership, in the absence of a partnership agreement that states otherwise, all partners have equal rights in the management of the business. Furthermore, on business matters that require a vote, every partner has one vote unless the partnership agreement grants a different number of votes to each partner. A factor used in the granting of different votes is the relative capital contribution made by each partner. A partnership agreement can provide for different classes of partners with different voting rights when there are many different lines of business or just based on some other factor based on experience. For example, a partnership may have senior and junior partners, with only the former having voting rights. Some partners can be designated managing partners with responsibility for different lines of business. Voting matters are typically decided by a majority of the votes. There are exceptions. If the matter up for vote is one that goes beyond what might be covered in the partnership agreement, then a unanimous decision may be required.

A partnership provides operational flexibility at different stages in the growth of a business. In the initial years of operation, for example, several partners may have specialized talents but may lack sufficient capital to contribute to the partnership compared to other partners, who may have sufficient personal assets to contribute to the business but not the specialized talents needed for operation. As the business grows and begins to admit additional partners, their operational responsibilities can be limited by agreement without disrupting the objectives and goals of the founding partners. The partnership agreement should set forth the process for admitting new partners into the partnership. If a partner is permitted to sell his or her share, the partnership agreement should indicate whether the other partners have the right of first refusal before the withdrawing partner is permitted to sell to an outsider.

Because limited partnerships are managed and controlled by the general partners, it is the general partners that have the authority to manage the business. Typically the limited partners do not participate in managing the business, but they do have the right to determine who will manage the partnership.

With a corporation, daily management of the corporation is the responsibility of corporate officers. Those duties are set forth in the corporate bylaws, as well as possibly in the articles of incorporation. The selection of corporate officers and assignment of their responsibility are granted by the board of directors, who are elected by shareholder votes. As explained in chapter 9, corporate control can be maintained by founders by establishing different classes of stockholders, with each class of common stock having a different number of voting rights.

Ability to Raise Funds

In chapters 6 and 7, our focus will be on the sources of funds available and the types of financial instruments, respectively. The most limited form of business organization for fundraising is the sole proprietorship. Here the entrepreneur is constrained by personal resources and those of family members and friends, as well as the ability to obtain bank loans or other forms of credit, such as (prudently used) lines of credit available from credit cards.

Moving from a sole proprietorship to a general partnership, the same general constraints on fundraising exist except that the founder can potentially draw on more personal resources, family members, and friends for capital partners' contributions of cash or property. Some potential partners with technical capabilities may in fact have no personal resources available to contribute. Instead, for such partners, the effective partnership contribution is their intangible contributions (i.e., their specialized skills or patents or trade-marks), allowing the other partners to reduce capital needs to acquire those intangibles.

In a limited partnership, it is the limited partners that provide capital contributions. The procedure for selling limited partnership interests is similar to what we describe next for corporations. As for the general partners in a limited partnership, at one time the U.S. Department of the Treasury required that general partners contribute at least 1% of the part-nership's capital. That requirement has been removed. Limited partners may provide some contribution in the form of pledging their personal assets or providing the requisite techni-cal skills or patents. The issue of the general partners' contribution is important because limited partners want to see how much "skin in the game" the general partners have.

Subject to federal securities law, a corporate structure offers a major advantage for raising equity and debt capital as the business grows. Again, fundraising must satisfy the require-ments imposed by federal securities law, as explained in the next chapter. The selection of the type of corporation is important in terms of issuance of stock. There can only be one class of stock in an S corporation. Although there can be both voting and nonvoting shares, there cannot be a class of stock that has priority with respect to the receipt of dividends or proceeds in the case of distribution if there is a liquidation. Other restrictions imposed are the number of shareholders, which may not exceed a specified number (seventy-five or one hundred), and who may be prohibited from share ownership (e.g., foreign ownership is not always allowed).

Ability to Transfer Ownership Interests

A company's founder may want to transfer all or a part of the ownership of the company to another entity at some time in the future. The transfer of ownership interest may be as a result of bringing in new non–family member owners or one or more family mem-bers. For a sole proprietorship that wants to bring in partners but continue in the business, this involves changing the form of business to allow for a business organization that can accommodate multiple ownership interests.

In a general partnership formed by the founders of a company, a founder's ownership interest includes his or her proportionate share of the assets and liabilities. A founder's ownership interest may be assigned or transferred freely, depending on the partnership agreement.[3] As noted earlier, the remaining partners may have the right of first refusal in the sale of a partnership share. Transferring a significant portion of the ownership inter-est in a partnership may necessitate that the current partnership be terminated and a new partnership be formed.

In the absence of any restrictions on the transfer of ownership interest in the partner-ship agreement, a limited partner's interest in a limited partnership is freely transferable.

---

3. In general, an "assignment" means transferring to another the ownership of one's property (i.e., the interest and rights to the property).

However, under securities law there might be some restrictions limiting free transferability of a limited partner's interest. This will depend on the circumstances through which the limited partnership acquired the interest. As explained in the next chapter, under federal securities laws, either an ownership interest must be registered with the SEC or a registration exemption must be applied for. That exemption may restrict the transfer of ownership interest for a specified period of time (usually nine months).

In the case of a corporation (C or S corporation), a transfer of ownership can be done by the sale of equity shares to other investors. However, SEC or state registration filing requirements for the sale of securities, discussed in chapter 4, must be followed.

There may be reasons beyond complying with securities law why the founders of a company may want to restrict the transference of ownership interest of cofounders or of nonfounder investors. In such instances, this can be dealt with by using restrictive agreements (partnership agreement or shareholder agreement). The motivation may be to prevent the selling of an ownership interest to a party that the founders would find unacceptable. However, such agreements may have an adverse impact on the company's appeal to investors. Moreover, from a tax perspective, restrictions on the transfer of ownership could have an adverse impact. For example, for a corporation, a restriction on ownership transfer could have an impact on the availability of advantageous tax options, such as the election to be treated as an S corporation.

INCOME TAX CONSIDERATIONS

Now we move from non-tax factors to tax considerations. There are two primary tax structures a new business venture entity must consider: a corporation and a tax flow-through entity.

Recall that a corporation is viewed as a legal person. Consequently, a C corporation is responsible for filing income tax returns at the federal, state, and local levels, and then paying the taxes due on the reported net income. (If there is a loss due to operations, as explained later, that loss can be carried back or carried forward.) Thus there is a tax at the corporate level. However, that is not where the income tax liability ends. Any distribution of net income to shareholders is taxed again at the individual shareholder level. Hence, from an income tax perspective, a major disadvantage of a C corporation is double taxation of net income.

For most startup companies that utilize the C corporation form of business organization, in the earlier years of operation losses are generated, not net income. As a result, the likelihood of dividend payments in the earlier years that would result in double taxation of income is not a realistic concern to the founders. Even in the later stages of its corporate life, most if not all net income is likely to be retained (i.e., no income is distributed to shareholders) in order to generate internal funds needed for growth.

The double taxation of income can be avoided by using a tax flow-through entity. For a *tax flow-through entity* there is only a single layer of taxes because the net income of the business is not taxed at the business entity level but flows through to the owners, who are then taxed at the individual tax level. Obviously, a sole proprietor is taxed as an individual. For a partnership, the share of net income is allocated to each partner, who then is taxed on his or her share at the individual level. General partnerships, limited partnerships, and LLCs are tax flow-through entities.

The tax code even allows for a corporation to avoid double taxation by electing to be taxed as a flow-through entity. More specifically, founders who have formed a corporation can, if the requirements established by the tax code are satisfied, file an "S" election with the Internal Revenue Service. This election, making the corporation an S corporation, thereby makes it a tax flow-through entity for tax purposes. As a tax flow-through entity, the net income of an S corporation is not taxed at the corporate level but "flows through" to the shareholders, who are then taxed at their respective individual income tax rate. It should be noted that regardless of whether any of the net income is distributed to shareholders, income taxes are paid by shareholders on their pro rata share of net income in the case of an S corporation.

Although it might seem from a tax perspective that a tax flow-through entity is more beneficial than being taxed at the entity level, that may not always be the case. Here are two reasons. Consider first when there is a net loss rather than net income by a C corporation, as is typically the case in the early years of a new venture. The loss is referred to in the tax code as a "net operating loss" (NOL). The NOL that flows through to the individual may not have any value if the owner cannot offset NOL against income at the individual level in that year. The tax code does provide for tax relief by allowing a NOL realized by an individual or a corporation to be carried forward for up to twenty years (this is referred to as a *NOL carryforward*) so as to reduce future tax liabilities. After twenty years, a NOL cannot be used. For a C corporation that has had net income in the prior two years, the NOL can be carried back (and is referred to as a *NOL carryback*) so as to offset that net income, resulting in an immediate tax rebate.[4] Any unused NOL not carried back can be carried forward. For an individual to carry back a NOL, certain tax filings are made.[5] If the tax rate of an individual is less than that for a C corporation, then there is less benefit realized from a NOL.

Another example of why a C corporation may be more beneficial than an S corporation when there is net income is that cash has to be distributed to pay for the share of net income allocated to an owner so that the owner can pay the taxes on the allocated net income. For example, suppose that a C corporation has $1 million in net income and does not distribute

4. It may not be the best utilization of a NOL carryback to use it in the prior two years if the tax rate applied to net income was low relative to actual or anticipated future tax rates.

5. For a discussion of this, see Robert L. Venables III, "Mitigating the Results of a Failure to Carry Back an NOL," *The Tax Adviser*, August 2011, http://www.aicpa.org/publications/taxadviser/2011/august/pages/clinic-story-06.aspx?action=print.

any of that net income to stockholders. The corporate tax on the net income will be the product of the $1 million and the corporate income tax rate. Now consider instead the same scenario for an S corporation. We know that with an S corporation, the $1 million of net income will not be taxed at the corporate level but at the individual level. Suppose that a passive stockholder in this S corporation has an ownership interest such that $100,000 of the $1 million in net income is allocated as income. If there is no distribution of net income in the form of a cash dividend, the passive stockholder may find it difficult, depending on his or her financial situation, to meet the individual tax liability. Moreover, this would discourage investment in the corporation by other potential passive stockholders, who might be concerned about the same situation.

SELECTING THE STATE IN WHICH TO INCORPORATE OR FORM AN LLC

Regardless of where the founders reside or where the business is conducted, founders who elect to incorporate or form an LLC can choose any state in which to do so. Every state has its own statute for incorporation and for partnerships.

Some experts in this area have argued that the state in which the founders decide to form a corporation or partnership is likely to be the one where the business is operated (i.e., physically located), referred to as its *home state*. The reason is that the home state may provide the least complicated arrangement and may be the most cost-efficient with respect to formation costs. However, there are reasons to incorporate in states that might provide more benefits. The two states that have been most successful in attracting corporations and LLCs are Delaware and Nevada. The popularity of Delaware as a state for forming a business organization can be gauged from the fact that more than half of the companies listed on the New York Stock Exchange are incorporated in that state. Nevada has in recent years enacted laws that are pro-business. In the end, the selection of the state in which to form a business organization should be decided in consultation with an attorney who specializes in such matters.

Let's look at some of the reasons why Delaware appears to be the state of choice. First, that state has favorable corporate laws. Delaware court decisions have tended to be more favorable to corporate management and rules favorable to the indemnification of the board of directors by the corporation. Delaware has a court specifically devoted to corporate law issues, the Court of Chancery, that does not use juries, and the judges specialize in corporate law rather than in the wide range of legal issues involving nonbusiness matters. The flexibility of incorporation is important. In the formation process Delaware is the state that appears to offer the most flexible statutes dealing with incorporation. There are no minimum capital requirements, and if the speed of the process is an important consideration, it offers a speedy incorporation process.

Tax considerations are important, and those taxes go beyond just income taxes earned by a corporation within the state. For example, Delaware (1) does not impose a state corporate income tax for companies that are formed in Delaware but do not transact business in the state and (2) typically has tax requirements that are favorable to companies with complex capitalization structures and/or a large number of authorized shares of stock. Delaware does have a franchise tax. Nevada does not impose a corporate income tax and has no state annual franchise tax.

When a corporation conducts business in any state other than where it has incorporated, it is referred to as a "foreign corporation," a term that is misleading because it suggests that the corporation is a non-U.S. entity. The term "foreign" is merely a designation that a corporation is doing business in a state where it has not been incorporated. As a foreign corporation, states impose annual taxes for the privilege of doing business in their state.

Small Business Considerations

Although the above reasons may be applicable to some new ventures at a later stage of their development, the question is whether the reasons given above apply to a small business. The U.S. Small Business Administration (SBA) addresses this question in one of its publications.[6] According to the SBA, if a small business anticipates having fewer than five shareholders or members (in the case of an LLC), then it is widely considered the best strategy for such companies to be formed in the state where they have a physical presence (property, shareholders, employees). The SBA provides the following reasons as to why the "hassles outweigh the benefits" of selecting the home state (i.e., the state in which the business operates) compared to incorporating in the states of Delaware or Nevada:

*   *Even if you incorporate in tax-friendly Nevada*, if you are operating or doing business in your home state, you'll still have to pay business taxes on revenue that originates in that home state.
*   *If you don't have a physical address in the state in which you incorporate*, you'll need to hire and pay a registered agent in that state to act as your legal representative.
*   *If you are incorporated outside your home state, you'll need to file for a foreign qualification in both your home state* (if you wish to do business there) and in the state in which you are incorporated. This means double-duty paperwork, filing fees, taxes, and even penalties if you inadvertently skip this important step. You may even have an increased tax liability in your home state because you are registered as a foreign entity there. You are also subject to the same annual reporting requirements in both states.
*   *If you register out of state, you'll be subject to the laws of that foreign state of corporation.* These laws may differ from those of your own state (and state laws can vary significantly in many areas). This can have complicated ramifications and may require your presence in court in your registered state, if you run into even the simplest of legal disputes.
*   *As a "foreign" business, you may also encounter difficulties opening a business bank account* in either or both the states in which you are incorporated in and physically located.

6. Caron Beesley, "Which Is the Best State to Incorporate Your Brick and Mortar or Online Business?," blog post, April 17, 2013, http://www.sba.gov/community/blogs/which-best-state-incorporate-your-brick-and-mortar-or-online-business.

The SBA concludes:

Unless you intend to transact business in states like Nevada or Delaware, filing in these states has very few long-term advantages. Yes, the tax laws and ease of doing business may be appealing at first, but peel back the onion and you'll find that, in the long run, it is more economical and time-saving for small businesses to pursue home-state incorporation.

KEY POINTS COVERED IN THIS CHAPTER

- In the United States, the five for-profit forms of business organization are sole proprietorship, general partnership, limited partnership, corporation, and limited liability company (LLC).
- The key difference between a sole proprietorship and the other forms of business organization is that one person both owns and manages the company.
- A general partnership is a formed when two or more individuals enter into an agreement that governs the duties and responsibilities of the partners, how they will allocate profits and losses among the partners, how the liabilities will be divided, and how the assets will be allocated should the partnership be terminated.
- A limited partnership differs from a general partnership in that there are general partners who manage the entity and are exposed to unlimited liability and limited partners who have limited liability and do not manage the business.
- A corporation is an entity whose formation is governed by each state, with the following attributes: (1) it has a legal personality; (2) it is governed by a board of directors; (3) it is co-owned by contributors of equity capital, called shareholders; (4) it provides limited liability to shareholders; and (5) it allows for transferable shares.
- Corporate governance refers to the set of systems, principles, and processes by which a corporation can be directed or controlled in order to achieve its goals and objectives, with the board of directors overseeing its operation so as to accomplish the goals and objectives.
- A corporation can be either a C corporation or an S corporation. The distinction between the two is in their treatment for income tax purposes. A C corporation has the disadvantage of double taxation of net income because it is taxed at the corporate level and then any portion distributed to shareholders is taxed again, whereas all the net income of an S corporation is taxed only at the shareholder level.
- Unless for federal income tax purposes a corporation elects to be an S corporation, it is a C corporation.
- An LLC, an entity created under state statutes, combines the tax treatment of a partnership with the limited liability attribute of a corporation; it can have one or more owners.

- Non-tax factors considered by founders in selecting the form of business organization include: (1) the cost of formation and ongoing expenses to maintain the form of business organization, (2) protection against unlimited liability, (3) continuity of the business, (4) management and operational control, (5) ability to raise funds, and (6) ability to transfer ownership interests.

- Tax factors are affected by the tax structure selected: either a corporation or a tax flow-through entity.

- Because a corporation is a "legal person," the major disadvantage of a C corporation is that it is taxed at the corporate level, with any distribution of net income to shareholders taxed again at the individual shareholder level (resulting in double taxation of income).

- Because in the earlier years of startup companies that utilize the C corporation form of organization there are losses rather than net income, the probability of dividend payments resulting in double taxation of income is not a realistic concern to the founders.

- In the later stages of a corporation's life, most if not all net income is likely to be retained (i.e., no income is distributed to shareholders) in order to generate internal funds needed for growth.

- To overcome the double taxation of income, founders can under the U.S. tax code elect to be taxed as a flow-through entity.

- For a tax flow-through entity there is only a single layer of taxes because the net income of the business is not taxed at the business entity level but flows through to the owners, who are then taxed at the individual tax level.

- For a partnership, the share of net income is allocated to each partner, who then is taxed on his or her share at the individual level. General partnerships, limited partnerships, and LLCs are tax flow-through entities.

- A corporation can, if the requirements established by the tax code are satisfied, file an "S" election with the Internal Revenue Service to be taxed as a flow-through entity, where income is not taxed at the corporate level but "flows through" to the shareholders, who are then taxed at their respective individual income tax rate.

- The tax code allows losses (referred to as net operating losses, NOL) realized by an individual or a corporation to be carried forward for up to twenty years so as to reduce future tax liabilities. After twenty years, a NOL carryforward cannot be used.

- For a C corporation that has had net income in the prior two years, the NOL can be carried back so as to offset that net income, resulting in an immediate tax rebate; any unused NOL not carried back can be carried forward.

- There are reasons why a tax flow-through may not always be beneficial to founders.

- One reason why a flow-through election may not be beneficial to founders is that when a C corporation realizes a NOL, as is typically the case in the early years of a new venture, the NOL flows through to the founders, who may not have any value for it because the founder-owners cannot offset NOL against income at the individual level in that year.

- Another reason why a C corporation may be more beneficial than a S corporation when there is net income is that cash has to be distributed to pay for the share of net income allocated to an owner so that the owner can pay the taxes on the allocated net income.

- Founders who elect to incorporate or form an LLC can choose any state in which to do so, every state having its own statute for incorporation and for partnerships. The decision should be made in consultation with an attorney who specializes in such matters.

- The two states that have been most successful in attracting corporations and LLCs are Delaware and Nevada.

- Tax considerations are important in selecting a state in which to incorporate, and those taxes go beyond just the income taxes earned by a corporation within the state.

- When a corporation conducts business in any state other than where it has incorporated, it is referred to as a "foreign corporation."

FURTHER READINGS

Klein, William, John Coffee, Jr., and Frank Partnoy, *Business Organization and Finance: Legal and Economic Principles,* 11th ed. (New York: Foundation Press, 2010).

Klein, William, J. Ramseyer, and Stephen Bainbridge, *Business Associations: Agency, Partnerships, LLCs, and Corporations* (New York: Foundation Press, 2015).

Paterson, T., *Business Legal Structures: An Entrepreneur's Handbook* (CreateSpace Independent Publishing Platform, 2012).

Rosen, Cory, "A Primer on Limited Liability Companies," in *Equity Compensation for Limited Liability Companies,* 2nd ed., ed. Teresa Y. Huang, David R. Johanson, Samuel W. Krause, et al. (Oakland, CA: National Center for Employee Ownership, 2013), 1–8.

4

FOUNDERS' STOCK AND EMPLOYEE STOCK OPTIONS

The equity allocation for a startup company is a key issue because it has an impact on the distribution of the potential appreciation of the company's equity value and control over the company's future direction. There are important factors to consider in determining the allocation of equity among the founders and key employees of a startup company. However, the allocation of equity is not a one-time decision that the founders must make. As the company grows, equity is used to attract and incentivize key employees. In addition, disputes among the founders as to the fairness of the distribution of equity are not only one of the major impediments to a company's growth but also a key contributor to the likelihood of a company failing.

Our objective in this chapter is twofold. First, we describe the factors to be considered in allocating equity among those who should be considered founders. The common stock issued to the members of the founding team is popularly referred to as "founders' stock." We then turn to the various types of equity incentive plans that a startup company can use to align the interests of founders and key employees with those of the company. To appreciate the relative advantages and disadvantages of each plan, the key tax provisions for the different plan types are explained.

FOUNDERS' STOCK

Founders' stock refers to a class of common stock allotted to members of the founding team in the initial stages of the startup. Technically, there is no legal definition of founders' stock. Founders' stock is typically in the form of restricted stock, a form of equity compensation plan that we describe in more detail when we cover the various types of equity incentive plans.

There are conditions imposed on the awarding of any equity incentive plan to founders to protect other members of the founding team and investors should a founder decide to leave the company or fail to perform. The set of conditions that must be satisfied by founders is referred to as the company's *vesting requirements*. When we explain the different employee compensation plans we will describe vesting requirements in more detail.

Allocation of Stock among the Founders

Too often, in a rush to form a company, individuals agree to an equal share in the company. At the outset, when the startup has no income, such an arrangement is often satisfactory and does not lead to disputes among the founders. However, once income is generated and the value of the startup increases, disputes about the relative contributions among the founders tend to surface, causing morale problems and hindering the company's growth. For this reason, some argue that the notion of equal ownership share among founders is not optimal for sustaining growth. This is not a universal view, however, since some entrepreneurs believe that an equal ownership is appropriate.[1]

Following are factors to be considered in determining not just the amount of equity interest founders receive but whether an individual has a reasonable claim to be treated as a founder as opposed to a key employee who should receive some other form of potential appreciation in the value of the startup company rather than founders' stock.[2] It is important to bear in mind that although we will refer to the allocation of founders' stock among the founders, it is not the number of shares that is important but the percentage of equity received.

The Idea Proposer   Typically an individual who has the idea for the product or service will argue that this contribution is sufficient to warrant founders' stock. The counterargument is that an idea alone is insufficient to warrant such an award. What is far more important is the execution of the idea. That is, value is created from organizing the company, assembling the management team, gathering the resources, and commercializing the product, not merely from proposing the idea.

There is also the question of whether an idea may be new or unique. In the information technology (IT) area, for example, there are very few new ideas for products or services. Consider the case of Facebook. There were several social networking websites such as MySpace whose founders had a similar idea as Mark Zuckerberg, the founder of Facebook. Yet it was the ability of Zuckerberg to execute that brought the idea to a commercialized offering.[3]

As another example, consider electric lighting. This invention is often attributed to Thomas Edison. However, the idea behind the electric light bulb was developed in the early 1800s by Humphrey Davy, a scientist who headed the laboratory of the Pneumatic Institution, a medical research facility in England. Many scientists sought to commercialize electric lighting using Davy's ideas and discoveries. However, it was Thomas Edison who was able to do so successfully.

1. Joel Spolsky, "Equity for Startups," https://gist.github.com/isaacsanders/1653078.
2. There is no formula for determining how much founders' stock should be allocated to each founder. However, attempts have been made to do so using some formula-based allocation model. The best known is probably Alain Rayhnaud's *Co-Founder Equity Calculator,* described at http://www.sfu.ca/~mvolker/biz/equity.htm.
3. "What Every Founder Needs to Know about Equity," *Forbes,* April 5, 2012, http://www.forbes.com/sites/dailymuse/2012/04/05/what-every-founder-needs-to-know-about-equity.

Consequently, in deciding whether there should be any allocation to the "raw" idea, one might argue that there should be no allocation for the individual who seeks to be a founder. If the idea leading to an invention has been patented rather than being a raw idea, then the situation is a step beyond the pure idea stage. Yet the existence of the patent in and of itself still requires commercialization and other business efforts. The risk to investors remains considerable, even with a patent. For example, the U.S. Patent and Trademark Office reports that of the 1.5 million patents in effect and in force, only roughly 3,000 are commercially viable.[4] Rather than an allocation of ownership, a licensing arrangement can be made between the patent holder and the startup company. If the patent holder continues with the company in developing the product or service based on the patent through the launch and commercialization, then it is that contribution that might be compensated for in the form of an equity interest.

Below-Market Compensation   The founders of a startup company should be rewarded for accepting risk for the potential to generate what is hoped to be a high return on what they contribute. Individuals who work for the company in the very early stages will often draw some salary. Whether those individuals can be justified as founders might be based on the implicit cash contribution they make by receiving annual compensation that is below the fair market value that they could realize working elsewhere (i.e., their opportunity cost). For example, if a software engineer or a medical research scientist can earn $100,000 more per annum working at another IT firm or research laboratory, then effectively, that individual is contributing that amount per annum. If there is no differential, then a founder's status would not be warranted.

Some have argued that even when there is a differential between compensation received from the startup and the fair market value of services if performed elsewhere, no founders' shares should be allocated. Rather, the compensation when there is a differential should be in the form of convertible debt.

Too often the argument is made that specialized employees at the inception of the startup should receive founders' stock because their skills are highly specialized. However, the value of their contribution can only be measured by the fair market value in alternative employment. It is possible that those specialized skills may be important only to the startup company, and to no other firms. The argument for allocating founders' stock in such instances is difficult to justify. Should the specialized skill be coupled with intellectual property ownership by such individuals, then the importance of each component should be valued independently in determining whether founders' stock is warranted.

Some individuals will work for the startup full-time and others will retain their current positions and work part-time. The argument against providing founders' stock to part-time employees is that the only risk exposure of the part-time employee is the forgone wages

4. As reported in Karen E. Klein, "Avoiding the Inventor's Lament," *Business Week*, November 10, 2005.

that could have been received had the individual performed the same services elsewhere. Instead of founders' stock, convertible debt would be a fair form of remuneration for part-time service.

Some startups retain an attorney to help protect the rights of founders. To conserve cash or to avoid paying for legal services, too often the attorney retained is given some equity interest. Typically, the granting of founders' stock is unwarranted. The proper compensation to legal counsel in such instances is in the form of convertible debt, with the amount being determined by the monetary value of the services provided.

Excess Capital Contributions   Some individuals may make capital contributions to the startup that are far in excess of what is contributed by others who are treated as founders. There are two schools of thought on the treatment of capital contributions. The first is that some fair determination should be made of the contribution, and founders' stock should be granted accordingly. The second is that the additional contributions above what other founders have provided should be treated as convertible debt.

Contribution of Physical Assets   If an individual provides physical assets (e.g., equipment or real estate), the same principle as discussed above for capital contributions applies. If a physical asset is given to the startup company, then its fair market value should be determined. If the use of a physical asset at no or nominal cost is provided to the startup company, then the fair market value should be estimated and used to determine the amount of convertible debt.

Reputation Contribution   Some individuals are granted founders' stock because of their reputation in an industry. For example, a pharmaceutical startup may invite a prominent researcher or Nobel laureate in chemistry or medicine to join its board or to be a research adviser. Or a startup may invite a well-known investor to join its board. The expectation is that such individuals will add value to the startup company by giving it some form of credibility in the eyes of potential investors as well as value in seeking strategic partnerships or relationships.

Of course, it is difficult to estimate such value in determining how much ownership should be granted. It might seem that such individuals face little risk. However, that is not the case. There are two major risks for which such individuals merit compensation. The first is reputational risk. If the startup with which someone is affiliated fails for whatever reason, this could damage the individual's reputation. The second risk is litigation risk. An individual who serves on the board of a startup is exposed to legal action for a variety of reasons. For example, the startup company's product may result in damages to customers, who may then seek legal redress. The litigation risk may be mitigated by the company purchasing directors' and officers' insurance, but for most startups either this insurance does not exist or the amount of coverage is nominal.

Future Performance   A critical factor, and one difficult to measure, is the expected future contribution that an individual will make to increase the company's future value. If any of the above factors fits this criterion, then that would justify allocating founders' stock. The mechanism for controlling those granted founders' stock to meet a reasonable performance objective that is linked to increasing the company's value is the imposition of a vesting requirement that is linked or benchmarked to performance.

VESTING SCHEDULE

For each of the equity incentive plans described later in this chapter, there is an awarding or granting of the opportunity to obtain shares of common stock. The person granted that opportunity is called the *grantee*. The grantee can be a founder or an employee. The date that the opportunity to obtain shares of the common stock is granted is referred to as the *grant date*. The opportunity to obtain shares in the company can be in the form of the shares themselves or an option to purchase those shares. Restricted stock awards and restricted stock unit awards are the two types of equity incentive plans that provide the grantee the opportunity to acquire the shares directly. Stock option plans, another type of equity incentive plan, give the grantee an option to acquire the shares at a designated price.

Many equity incentive plans do not call for the immediate opportunity to acquire the shares directly or an option to acquire the shares. Instead, there is a *vesting schedule*. The vesting schedule specifies when the grantee has earned the right to the shares or the options. The vesting schedule can be based on a continuation of employment or the achievement of some performance measure or milestone or both.

For example, a vesting schedule might specify that the grantee who is awarded the right to obtain 10,000 shares of the company's common stock over the next four years will earn that right if he or she remains with the company over the next four years and if the company has achieved a certain level of sales. The vesting schedule might specify that if those conditions are satisfied, then the grantee vests 1/48th of the 10,000 shares each month. If, for example, the grantee leaves the company at the end of three years, then 7,500 shares will be vested. The remaining 2,500 share are referred to as unvested shares.

The vesting schedule will also specify how the unvested shares will be dealt with. There may be simple forfeiture of the shares, or the company's board of directors might have the option to repurchase the unvested shares at some specified price.

Vesting Requirements for Founders' Stock

The most common form of equity incentive plan for founders' stock is a restricted stock award. As explained later, with a restricted stock award, a founder is given ownership of all of the shares but the company is given the option to repurchase the unvested shares. In contrast, for other plans described later, the vesting requirements are for the right of the grantee to purchase the stock. That is, with restricted stock, the founder is granted the stock but the company is given the option to repurchase it under certain circumstances, such as the founder's departure from the company or failure to perform. Effectively, this right of repurchase by the company represents the forfeiture of a founder's unvested shares. Although the repurchase price may be agreed upon by the company, it is typically a nominal price that the founder paid for the shares.

The purpose of not providing shares outright to founders without the company having the right to repurchase the shares that have not vested is twofold. First, it aligns the interests of the founders with those of the company. This is the same motivation for providing any form of equity participation to key employees. Second, it protects members of the founding team, as well as investors, from the departure from the company of one of its members. In the absence of vesting requirements (i.e., the outright granting of stock to a founder with no repurchase option for the company), a founder who leaves the company maintains his or her equity interest in the company. Failure to satisfy vesting requirements by a departing founder means that the board at its discretion may repurchase the restricted stock that has not vested at the initial par value. For example, a founder with 10,000 unvested shares with a par value of $0.001 at the option of the company may have his or her shares repurchased for $10.

The typical vesting schedule (i.e., when the company loses the right to repurchase a certain number of shares) is as follows. A certain percentage of the shares may vest immediately. The balance of the shares will typically vest on a pro rata basis each month. For example, if the vesting is over three years, then each month 1/36th of the shares vest. At the end of the full vesting period, the founder cannot forfeit any shares (i.e., the company has no right to repurchase any shares).

There is a provision that allows for accelerated vesting of restricted stock awards under specifically defined conditions. *Accelerated vesting* means that any unvested shares become vested (i.e., the company cannot repurchase any shares that were awarded). The two most common conditions that can result in accelerated vesting are termination of the employment of a founder without cause or a change of control. By termination without cause is meant that the founder (or any employee, for that matter) is fired for reasons that are unrelated to misconduct.[5] Change of control can take the form of the sale of the business or the merger of the business with another company. If the vesting agreement calls for only one of these two events to trigger accelerated vesting, then it is said to have a "single trigger." If both events must occur for accelerated vesting to occur, then the vesting requirement is said to have a "double trigger."

It is important to note that for the founders, the vesting requirements can be altered by investors with the consent of the board of directors (which is likely to include all founders). When external funding is sought, the accelerated vesting provision may be undesirable to investors who seek protection on the departure of key members of the founding team. As

---

5. In contrast, termination with cause (or termination with just cause) means that the founder (or any employee) did something or failed to do something that irreparably damaged the relationship between the company and the founder (or employee).

part of the negotiation between the board of directors and new investors, the latter may seek to restructure any provisions in the vesting requirements, such as accelerated vesting, in exchange for providing funds. The vesting requirements do not have to be the same for each founder.

A founder may want to sell his or her shares prior to an initial public offering (IPO). This situation should be part of the founders' agreement when the company is started. Typically a founder's request for a buyback of his or her shares is made when there is a new round of financing, and the founder wants part of the funds raised from the new investors used to buy out shares. This can be done with the agreement of both the board of directors and the new investors. However, new investors are concerned about the use of their invested capital to reduce the equity interest of a founder. Nevertheless, if an agreement, referred to as the *founders' share buyback agreement*, is reached for the sale of the shares, there remains the question of the appropriate price at which the shares should be repurchased. Typically the board will retain an expert in valuation for this purpose.

TAX TREATMENT OF EQUITY INCENTIVE PLANS

There are various provisions of the U.S. tax code that are important considerations in structuring the equity incentive plan. The tax code recognizes that equity incentive plans are a form of compensation. The tax code has rules for when the person who is granted the opportunity to acquire equity in a company should recognize the income and how that income is treated. The section of the tax code that deals with these issues of compensation generated from equity incentive plans that are subject to vesting requirements is Section 83. More specifically, the three tax questions that the grantee is concerned with are:

- When will the compensation from an equity incentive plan be taxed?
- How much is the compensation that is subject to taxation?
- Will the income be taxed as ordinary income or given favorable tax treatment (i.e., a lower tax rate) because part of the income may be in the form of a capital gain?

In a startup company, if the grantee faces a large tax liability from an equity incentive, the grantee must have sufficient funds to pay that liability. Since the shares are not publicly traded, the grantee must come up with the cash without relying on the sale of the stock.

With respect to the third question above, under the tax code the tax treatment of capital gains generated from the sale of stock differs from the tax treatment of ordinary income. Specifically, short-term capital gains are taxed as ordinary income (just as compensation is taxed), while long-term capital gains are subject to a preferential tax rate (i.e., a tax rate that is less than that imposed on ordinary income). While the tax rates are subject to change, in 2015 the maximum tax rate on ordinary income and long-term capital gains was 39.6% and 20%, respectively. Consequently, a grantee would want any capital gains to be treated as a long-term capital gain. Whether a capital gain is treated as a short-term or long-term gain is determined by the length of time that the stock is held. If it is held for less than one year, it is a short-term capital gain; if it is held for one year or more, it is a long-term capital gain.

When we discuss the different equity incentive plans, we will see that to answer the three questions above, certain dates are critical. In the case of restricted stock awards and restricted stock units, those dates are the grant date, the vesting date, and the disposition date. In the case of stock option plans, there is one additional date: the exercise date

The **grant date** is the date that the opportunity to obtain the stock or a stock option is granted or awarded. The **vesting date** is the date that the stock or a stock option is earned based on the vesting schedule. In the case of stock option plans, the **exercise date** is the date that the grantee decides to exercise the option to purchase shares of the stock. The **disposition date** is the date when the grantee actually sells the shares.

Another important tax issue associated with compensation resulting from an equity incentive plan is the fair market value of the stock. Since the stock of a startup company is not publicly traded, this will require a valuation of the shares. To deal with valuation, the board of directors will engage a valuation expert to perform what is popularly referred to as a "409a valuation" of the common stock, so called because Section 409 of the U.S. tax code requires such a valuation. We discuss the issues associated with valuation in chapter 16.

EQUITY AWARD PLANS

There are two categories of incentive plans for founders and employees: equity award plans and cash award plans. **Equity award plans** include restricted stock awards, restricted stock unit awards, and stock option awards. These plans result in the potential issuance of shares of common stock. Some companies have more than one such plan. For example, IRobot Inc. has all three types of equity award plans. In this section we discuss these various plans.

In contrast, cash award plans may be based on the value of the stock but do not necessarily involve the issuance of shares of stock. Compensation is typically in the form of cash but may involve a granting of shares equivalent in value to the amount of cash that would have been awarded. The two most common form of cash incentive plans based on the value of equity are shared appreciation rights and phantom stock. Both shared appreciation rights and phantom stock are bonus plans that grant not stock but rather the right to receive cash based on the value of the company's stock.

Restricted Stock Awards

In the case of founders' stock awarded in the form of restricted stock, as explained earlier, these conditions are imposed to protect other members of the founding team and investors should a founder decide to leave the company or fail to perform. In the absence of this repurchasing option, a departing founder would be entitled to benefit from an increase in the value of the stock despite failing to contribute.

The set of conditions that must be satisfied by founders is referred to as a company's vesting requirements. When we discuss other types of employee compensation for key employees, we will refer to vesting. Technically, there is a distinction between vesting for restricted stock and other options available as a form of stock ownership provided to key employees as an incentive for performance. For these other plans, vesting involves satisfying requirements by the grantee to earn the stock.

Since the newly formed corporation is merely an idea, the fair market value per share is zero. In issuing founders' shares, however, a par value is stated. Typically it is $0.001 per share. The board can grant founders' stock to current or new key employees hired after the business has been in operation. At that later date, the early-stage company's value may no longer be worthless. Unlike the initial founders, who received founders' stock of a basically worthless company at the time, employees receiving restricted stock awards are viewed for tax purposes as receiving compensation to the extent that the stock has value.

Tax Treatment of Restricted Stock Awards   Let's look at the tax treatment of a founder who receives shares of restricted stock that are subject to vesting. As noted earlier, the relevant part of the tax code that deals with the tax issues of incentive compensation plans is Section 83. In the absence of any action taken by the founder who has restricted stock subject to vesting, the Internal Revenue Service (IRS) treats as income at the time that the stock becomes vested (i.e., the vesting date) the difference between the stock's fair market value and the price paid by the founder for the restricted stock.

One might think that no such income is generated if the founder does not sell the restricted stock once it becomes vested. However, that is not the case under Section 83 of the tax code. For example, consider a founder who is granted one million shares of restricted stock when the corporation is formed and the value of those shares on the grant date is equal to some nominal value. Assume that the restricted stock granted has a value assigned of $0.001 and that all the shares vest immediately. The compensation to the founder would be computed by the IRS as the difference between the fair market value of the shares and the amount paid at the time of vesting. The founder could argue that the one million shares have a value of zero, but the IRS would treat the fair market value as being $0.001 per share, and therefore the fair market value of all the shares is $1,000. Since the founder did not pay anything for the shares, under the tax code the founder will have to treat the $1,000 as income and be taxed accordingly in the year of the grant.[6]

Let's modify our illustration to reflect a more likely scenario for the granting of restricted stock to the founders. Suppose that on January 1 of some year one million shares of founders' stock in the form of restricted stock is awarded such that 100,000 shares vest immediately and the balance of the one million shares vests uniformly each month over three

---

6. One can see from this tax treatment why a startup company will assign a stated value that is very low. When the term "stated price" is used here, it means the price as determined by a valuation expert retained by the company's board for tax purposes.

years (thirty-six months). That is, the founder vests 1/36th of the 900,000 shares, or 25,000 shares per month. The 100,000 shares that vest immediately will be treated for tax purposes as providing a compensation of $100 (100,000 × $0.001). The entire one million shares are not treated as income because the company retains the right to repurchase the unvested shares (900,000 shares). That is, the recognition of income occurs on the vesting date, not on the grant date.

By the end of the year, the founder will have vested an additional 300,000 shares (25,000 per month × 12 months). The income realized in the absence of any provision providing otherwise will depend on the fair market value of the stock. Suppose that at the end of each month when the shares vest the fair market value is estimated as follows: for six months the company has no market value, and beginning in month 6 it is $0.05 per share because of a major milestone that is achieved in that month. Then the income for tax purposes for the first six months during which 150,000 shares have vested is equal to $150 (150,000 × $0.001), but the 150,000 shares vested in the last six months will result in an income of $7,500 (150,000 × $0.05). Thus, while the founder benefited from the appreciation in the value of the stock, the taxable income is based on the higher valuation of the stock on the vesting date, not the valuation on the grant date of the one million shares. So in the first year, the founder's income on the 400,000 shares that vested during the year (i.e., the amount that must be reported as income) is $7,750 (= $100 + $150 + $7,500).

Let's carry this calculation out further for two more years, assuming that two major milestones are realized in January of both the second and third years that substantially increase the fair market value per share. Specifically, we will assume that in January of the second year the fair market value of the stock increases to $0.30 per share and in the third year it increases to $0.50 per share. The income in the second year is $90,000 (= 300,000 shares × $0.30) and in the third year it is $150,000 (= 300,000 shares × $0.50). Note that the founder must be able to come up with sufficient funds to pay the associated tax liability in each year. This may be difficult to do since the stock will typically be illiquid and difficult to sell to generate sufficient cash to satisfy the liability. This situation arises because the founder was effectively penalized from a tax perspective for the increase in the value of the stock from the grant date of the restricted stock to the vesting date.

Fortunately, there is a provision in the tax code that allows postponing the recognition of any gain when a stock becomes vested. Instead, the recognition of income is made when the stock is sold (i.e., the disposal date). That provision of the tax code is Section 83(b), which is an election that if filed with the IRS by the founder when the grant is made allows for the taxation of income at the time the restricted stock is sold rather than at the time the stock vests (i.e., is transferred to the founder). The Section 83(b) election requires that on the grant date, the grantee must recognize the income, and furthermore the income is treated as ordinary income (i.e., as part of the founder's compensation) in the year the restricted stock is granted.

We will illustrate this treatment if the founder files a Section 83(b) election using our previous illustration of the one million shares that vest over three years. If the election is made, the one million shares awarded will be taxed in the year the award is made. The tax will be based on income of $1,000 (= 1,000,000 shares × $0.001). When the shares vest over time according to the vesting schedule, no income is recognized. Instead, any gain resulting from the actual sale of the shares at a higher price than $0.001 in our illustration will be treated as income. However, this income will be treated as a capital gain. If the shares are held for more than one year (from the time vested until sold), then the capital gain will be classified as a long-term capital gain, which is taxed at a lower tax rate than ordinary income. Moreover, the grantee will be able to use the proceeds from the sale of the shares to pay the tax liability resulting from the gain.

The election must be made within thirty days of the granting of the restricted stock. At first, it may not seem that the Section 83(b) election would be beneficial to the founder. However, that is not the case. The potential benefit arises because on the grant date, the fair market value of the restricted stock will be close to the purchase price for the stock. In that case, there would be no gain. Even if the fair market value at the time of the grant date is slightly above the purchase price, the tax liability may be small. The bet that the founder is making is that the valuation of the startup company will increase at the time the restricted stock vests and therefore at the time of vesting the capital gain resulting from the price appreciation will be postponed until the founder sells the stock.

There is a risk with a Section 83(b) election. The reason is that if the stock price does not in fact rise and if a tax was paid at the time of the grant date, then there would be a tax paid with no offsetting further benefit. To appreciate this risk, let's suppose that the restricted stock is awarded not to a founder but instead to the chief financial officer (CFO), who is hired four years after the company began operations. Suppose that the CFO is granted one million shares of restricted stock and the stated price for the restricted stock is $0.001. Suppose further that the fair market value of the stock on the grant date to the CFO is $0.10 per share. If the Section 83(b) election is made, the CFO would have to treat the fair market value of the one million shares as ordinary income and taxable in the year in which the grant date falls. Since the stock has a fair market value of $100,000 (one million shares × $0.10), a Section 83(b) election that the CFO makes would result in taxable income (ordinary income) of $100,000. Assuming for simplicity a 35% tax rate, the tax liability would be $35,000. The CFO is at risk for all or part of the $35,000, for two reasons. Suppose that for whatever reason, the CFO leaves the company's employment after one year, when the fair market value of the stock that has vested is worthless. All of the $35,000 tax payment will be lost. There is nothing in the tax law that allows a taxpayer such as the CFO to offset that loss. The same adverse tax consequence occurs if the founder decides to leave the startup and forfeits the restricted stock shares that have not vested. The second reason is that even if the CFO remains with the company and all one million shares become vested, the stock price might decline below $0.10, and therefore the actual compensation received will be less than $100,000. For example, suppose that the fair market value of the shares declines and the stock is sold for $0.01 per share. The proceeds received will be only $10,000, which is less than the amount that was taxed under the Section 83(b) election.

How does this relate to the tax treatment of restricted stock subject to vesting under Section 83? Once a founder's stock vests and the stock is purchased, the question that must be addressed is the determination of what the holding period is when the stock is eventually sold. In our earlier example, if the founder's restricted stock vests today, and the stock is then sold by the founder, what are the relevant dates for determining the holding period for the purpose of determining whether the future sale results in a capital gain that will be treated as a short-term or long-term capital gain? Of course, we know the date when the stock is sold. However, what is the date on which the stock is being treated as purchased? The answer depends on whether a Section 83(b) election is made. In the absence of a Section 83(b) election filing, the purchase date is when the stock is vested. Any gain is treated as a capital gain, and whether it is a short-term or a long-term gain depends on the disposal date. If instead there is a Section 83(b) election, the purchase date is the grant date. In our example, if the founder makes a Section 83(b) election, any initial gain is treated as ordinary income and taxed at regular tax rates; any further gains are treated as capital gains based on the holding period.

Restricted Stock Unit Awards

In our description of restricted stock awards, the founder or key employees are granted stock which they own but do not have access to until the shares are vested. Thus, common stock shares are issued. *Restricted stock unit* (RSU) awards are similar to restricted stock awards in that something is awarded (units) to a founder or key employee, but no shares are issued. Basically, an RSU represents a hypothetical share of the company's common stock. At the discretion of the company's board of directors, when the units are vested, RSUs are paid out either in shares of common stock or in cash.

Each unit of an RSU award allows the recipient to receive a specified number of shares. Typically, it is one share of common stock per unit; however, this need not be the case. Because RSUs are not actual shares of common stock, the person awarded RSUs is not entitled to receive dividends and does not have voting rights, although the board of directors may elect to pay dividends to RSU holders. This is in contrast to restricted stock awards, where dividends must be paid if they are declared by the board of directors and there are voting rights during the vesting period.

As with restricted stock awards, RSUs are subject to vesting. As an example of RSUs where the vesting schedule is contingent on performance, let's consider the performance-contingent RSUs awarded by the Human Resources and Compensation Committee of the Board of Directors of Mondelēz International, Inc., to its CEO, Irene Rosenfeld, in December 2012. As reported in its filing with the SEC, the performance-contingent restricted stock units will vest as follows when the Company's closing price maintains an average at or above the specified threshold for a minimum period of ten consecutive trading days: 25% after the stock price appreciates 20% from the Fair Market Value on the grant date; 37.5% after the stock price appreciates 30% from the Fair Market Value on the grant date; and 37.5% after the stock price appreciates 40% from the Fair Market Value on the grant date. Each restricted stock unit represents a contingent right to receive one share of the Company's common stock. In any event, the performance-contingent restricted stock units will not vest prior to the three-year anniversary of the grant date. If the stock price hurdles are not attained prior to the earlier of (i) the six-year anniversary of the grant date or (ii) one-year following Ms. Rosenfeld's retirement as an executive officer, Ms. Rosenfeld will forfeit the outstanding unvested units at that time. If the stock price hurdle for the third tranche is attained and those units vest, Ms. Rosenfeld is required to hold the resulting net shares for at least one year following her retirement as an executive officer.[7]

Taxation of Restricted Stock Unit Awards   There is a difference in the tax treatment of restricted stock awards and RSU awards for the grantee. The person who is granted a restricted stock award owns the stock, and therefore for income tax purposes the fair market value is employee compensation. The person granted a restricted stock award can file a Section 83(b) election to postpone any income realization when the stock shares vest. For RSUs the tax treatment is quite different because RSU awards are treated by the IRS as a full-value stock grant and are taxed at full value when they become vested, *not* at the grant date. Using our previous example illustrating the tax treatment for restricted stock awards, suppose that a key employee was granted one million RSUs three years ago. In the case of the restricted stock award, the exercise price and the fair value of the stock at the grant date are relevant in making the Section 83(b) election. For RSUs, it is only at the time of exercising the RSU that income is recognized, not at the time of granting of the RSUs. There is no Section 83(b) election for RSUs.

From the granting company's perspective, there are no tax implications when the RSUs are awarded. However, when the RSUs are exercised, the company is permitted to take a deduction for employee compensation equal to the fair value of the stock shares that the grantee receives.

A key factor in deciding whether to grant restricted stock or RSUs is the fair market value of the stock. For startup companies whose fair market value is nominal, the use of restricted stock awards will have minimal tax implications. In contrast, if the fair market value is high, then there is a tax advantage for recipients of RSUs. In addition to tax issues, there is the issue of control. Because with restricted stock awards the grantee owns the stock and is given voting rights, some control is sacrificed. Since the ownership of RSUs does not represent the ownership of stock, no control is given up when the RSUs become vested.

---

7. See the website http://www.sec.gov/Archives/edgar/data/1103982/000118143112066452/rrd364331.htm.

Stock Option Plans

Rather than providing grants of restricted stock or RSUs to current key employees and to attract new employees, startup companies may offer employees a common stock option plan. Depending on the type of employee stock option plan, there may be a favorable impact on the granting company's income because the compensation is not treated as an expense but rather is disclosed in a footnote to the financial statements.

A common stock option granted by a company to an employee works as follows. For a certain number of years specified by the option, the employee has the right (but not the obligation) to buy a specified number of shares of the company's common stock at a fixed price. Usually the fixed price that the employee must pay to acquire the common stock is the prevailing fair market value at the option's grant date. That price is referred to as the *grant price*. The benefit or incentive provided by the common stock option is that if the company performs well and the common share price increases above the grant price, the employee realizes a gain by exercising the option: at some future date, the employee buys the shares at the grant price and then can sell those shares on the market at a price greater than the grant price.

With an annual stock option plan, each year until the plan changes an employee is granted stock options. Typically, stock option plans are subject to a vesting schedule. That is, a plan specifies a period of time within which the grantee is not permitted to exercise the option. This time period, referred to as the vesting period, can be up to several years before the options granted become fully vested. Once the vesting period is over, the options become fully vested and the grantee can exercise the option. For a newly hired key individual, the stock options may vest immediately.

There is a difference between restricted stock vesting and vesting by way of a stock option plan. With the former, the shares are owned by the employee, but the company has the right to repurchase the shares that have not vested. With a stock option plan, the employee is awarded options that vest over time, and those options give employees the *right* to purchase the shares at different points in time. For that reason there is a difference in the tax treatment.

Vesting for stock options is based on a vesting schedule that is typically as follows. There is a period of time during which the employee does not vest any options. That period of time is referred to as the vesting "cliff." For example, the vesting cliff might be one year. After that period, vesting occurs annually on a pro rata basis. It is the options that vest, not the stock.

Incentive Stock Options versus Non-Qualified Stock Option Plans   Companies can offer different types of stock option plans. The two most popular are incentive stock options and non-qualified stock options. Each type has important tax implications for the grantee and the granting company and financial accounting implications for the granting company. Many companies have both types of stock option plans.

Incentive stock option: With an *incentive stock option* (ISO), the employee granted stock options is allowed to defer the payment of any taxes on gains that may be realized on the appreciation of the common stock above its grant price until the shares are sold. This is a benefit to the employee from a tax perspective but a drawback from a tax perspective of the granting company. This is because the value of the ISOs is not a tax-deductible expense (as employee compensation), effectively raising the cost of the company's ISO plan. The U.S. tax code sets forth rules that must be satisfied for a stock option to qualify as an ISO plan.[8]

The favorable tax treatment for the grantee if specified conditions are met is that when the options are vested, there is a postponement of any capital gain. For example, suppose that an employee is granted as part of an ISO plan 10,000 options that vest over the next four years at 25% per year. Assume also that the exercise price is $0.50 and at the time the options are granted, the fair market value of the stock is also $0.50 and the option can be exercised within six years. At the end of the next four years, suppose that the fair market value of the stock increases so that its value exceeds $0.50. The value of the 10,000 options that the grantee owns will be equal to the spread between the fair market value of the stock per share and the exercise price, multiplied by 10,000. However, for an ISO plan, this value is not recognized for tax purposes. Suppose that the grantee exercises all 10,000 options in six years, when the fair market value of the stock is $2.50 per share. There is then a gain of $2 per share (the difference between the fair market value of $2.50 and the exercise price of $0.50), or $20,000 for the 10,000 shares. However, for an ISO plan, even the exercising of an option is not recognized for tax purposes. Any gain is realized once the stock is sold by the grantee. Suppose that three years after the grantee exercises the options the stock price is $6.50 per share and sells the 10,000 shares. Then at that time, the grantee realizes a capital gain for tax purposes equal to $6 per share (the difference between the sale price of $6.50 and the exercise price of $0.50), or $60,000 for 10,000 shares. Thus, any capital gain is postponed from the vesting and exercising dates to the sale date. Moreover, the capital gain will be treated as a long-term capital gain rather than as ordinary income, and taxed at a lower tax rate.

The tax code sets forth rules that must be met for this special tax treatment to be realized. Note that in our illustration, at the grant date the exercise price and fair market value of the stock at the grant date are important. The reason is that if the exercise price is less than the fair market value, then for tax purposes the grantee is deemed to have earned income equal to the difference between the two prices multiplied by the number of shares. There is a holding period requirement. The stock must be held by the grantee for at least one year after the option is exercised and at least two years after the grant date. If these as well as other conditions are satisfied, the sale by the grantee is said to be a "qualifying disposition."

---

8. ISOs can be granted only to employees, and not to vendors or unrelated third parties.

The exercise of an option may not satisfy the two holding period requirements. In such cases, the sale by the grantee is said to be a "disqualifying disposition." The tax treatment of a disqualifying disposition is as follows. The difference between the fair market value at the exercise date and the exercise price is treated as ordinary income. When the shares are eventually sold, the difference between the sale price and the fair market value at the exercise date is treated as a capital gain and, based on the holding period, is either a long-term or a short-term capital gain.

Thus far, we have looked at the impact of an ISO plan from the tax perspective of the grantee. For the company, if a grantee satisfies the requirements for a qualifying disposition, then the company does not get a tax deduction for the cost associated with the options. In contrast, for a disqualifying disposition, the company gets a tax deduction at the time the grantee exercises the option. The deduction is the number of options granted multiplied by the difference between the exercise price and the grant price.

There are also implications for financial reporting, the subject of chapters 8–12. For an ISO plan, generally accepted accounting principles require that the company estimate the fair market value of the options and treat that amount as an expense in the income statement (see chapter 10). The key is determining what the fair market value of the option is worth.

Non-qualified stock option plan: A ***non-qualified stock option plan*** (NSO) is simply a plan whereby either the company fails to meet the tax code requirements for an ISO plan or, in the more likely case, simply elects not to create an ISO because of the drawbacks of having such a plan relative to an NSO. The advantage of an NSO plan from the company's perspective is that for tax purposes, the company may deduct as an expense when the grantee exercises the option the difference between the fair market value at the time of exercise and the exercise price. Of course, this is a disadvantage to the grantee because this difference is treated for tax purposes as ordinary income and taxed accordingly. For financial reporting purposes, the treatment is the same for an NSO plan as it is for an ISO plan.

Company-Granted Common Stock Options versus Exchange-Traded Options   There is a difference between options granted by a company and options that are traded on an exchange market. The latter, referred to as ***exchange-traded options***, are described in more detail in chapter 15, where we cover financial options. With an exchange-traded stock option, there are two parties: the option buyer and the option seller (also called the option writer). A common stock option is an agreement whereby the option seller grants the option buyer the right to enter into a transaction with the seller to either buy or sell the common stock at a specified price on or before a specified date. The specified price is called the strike price or exercise price; the specified date is called the expiration date. The price that the option buyer pays to the option seller for this right is called the option premium or option price.

An exchange-traded common stock option is typically for 100 shares. The option buyer and the option seller are free to sell their positions in the market.

The option seller can grant the option holder one of two rights. If the option grants the option buyer the right to purchase the common stock from the option seller, the option is referred to as a ***call option***. If the option grants the option buyer the right to sell the common stock to the option seller, the option is referred to as a ***put option***. Our focus here is on call options on common stock since this is the equivalent economic right that common stock options granted by companies grant to employees.

As an example of an exchange-traded common stock option, consider a call option on the common stock of Apple Inc. traded on March 26, 2015. Apple's common stock price on that day was $548. There were many call options available on that day. By "many call options" we mean options with different exercise prices and different expiration dates. For illustration purposes we will use one: a call option that expires on January 16, 2016, with an exercise price of $500. The option buyer is granted the right to buy 100 shares of Apple's common stock for $500 per share from the option seller. The option buyer has this right until January 16, 2016, when the option expires. On March 26, 2015, the buyer of the option would have had to pay the seller of the option $87 (i.e., the option price is $87). Since the option is for 100 shares, the option buyer would have had to pay $870.

Now that we understand exchange-traded options, let's look at how options granted by a company to purchase its common stock compare to them. First, exchange-traded options do not involve as a party to the transaction the company whose shares can be purchased. For an employee stock option plan, the company is the seller of the option. Second, unlike an exchange-traded option, where the option buyer pays the option seller the option price, there is no option price charged by the company when granting the option. Finally, with exchange-traded options, the two parties can sell their positions in the market. In contrast, employee stock options cannot be traded in the market, nor can the company trade its obligation in the market. Once vested, however, the employee can exercise his or her option.

EQUITY COMPENSATION AWARDS FOR PARTNERSHIPS AND LIMITED LIABILITY COMPANIES

Thus far our focus has been on equity compensation awards granted by corporations. As explained in chapter 3, there are other forms of business organization that the founders of a company may select. These include partnerships (general partnerships, limited partnerships, and limited liability partnerships) and LLCs. In discussing the federal income tax treatment of partnerships and LLCs, we explained that these forms of business organization are taxed at the investor level, not at the corporate level. That is, the income of a partnership or an LLC is passed through to the investors. Hence, partnerships and LLCs face similar tax treatment in granting equity compensation.

The types of equity awards in partnerships are partnership interests and the same three types of equity awards used for corporations discussed earlier. For a partnership, the option is an interest in a partnership, and the option can only be granted under an NSO plan (i.e., an ISO plan is not available in partnerships).

The most common form of equity award used in partnerships is the partnership interest, which includes capital interests and profit interests. Restricted stock awards and restricted stock unit awards are rarely used. Options on partnership interests receive a tax treatment that is less favorable than profit interests while, as explained below, they have a similar economic characteristic to options on partnership interests. As a result, profit interest is the preferred form of equity compensation award to options on partnership interests. As with other forms of equity compensation award plans, there is a vesting schedule.

There are two forms of partnership interests that can be used for equity compensation award plans: capital interest and profits interest. With a *capital interest* the grantee receives an allocation in the proceeds distributed when the partnership is liquidated. In contrast to the participation in liquidation proceeds given to the grantee of a capital interest, a *profits interest* limits the grantee participation in liquidation proceeds to that portion attributable to profits generated following the grant date.

As explained earlier, tax considerations in the selection of the type of equity award plan must take into consideration Section 83 of the tax code. Not only are the tax rules as they relate to equity for a compensation award plan for partnerships and LLCs much more complicated than for a corporation's equity compensation award plans, there are also legal issues that have not been completely resolved.

KEY POINTS COVERED IN THIS CHAPTER

- The equity allocation for a startup company has an impact on the distribution of the potential appreciation of the company's equity value and control over the company's future direction.

- Founders' stock, stock allocated to the founding team in the initial stages of the startup, is typically in the form of restricted stock.

- Vesting requirements are imposed on the awarding of any equity incentive plan to founders to protect other members of the founding team and investors should a founder decide to leave the company or fail to perform.

- The factors to be considered in determining the amount of equity interest for founders are (1) who proposed the idea for the company, (2) willingness to accept below-market compensation, (3) excess capital contributions, (4) contribution of physical assets, (5) reputation contribution, and (6) expected future contribution.

- With respect to the treatment of contributions of physical assets, excess contributions of capital, and acceptance of below-market compensation, there are two schools of thought once a fair valuation determination is made: either (1) grant founders' stock based on the valuation or (2) treat the valuation as convertible debt.

- Equity incentive plans call for the awarding or granting of the opportunity to obtain shares of common stock, with the individual (founder or employee) who is granted that opportunity called the grantee.

- The shares obtained by the grantee from an equity incentive plan can be in the form of shares, or the grantee may be awarded an option to purchase shares.

- Restricted stock awards and restricted stock unit (RSU) awards are the two types of equity incentive plans that provide the grantee the opportunity to acquire the shares directly.

- Stock option plans, another type of equity incentive plans, give the grantee an option to acquire the shares at a designated price.

- Many equity incentive plans impose a vesting schedule for the grantee to acquire the shares directly or an option to acquire the shares.

- The vesting schedule specifies when the grantee has earned the right to the shares or earned the right to the options.

- The vesting schedule can be based on the continuation of employment and/or on the achievement of some performance measure or milestone and will specify how to deal with any unvested shares.

- The most common form of equity incentive plan for founders' stock is a restricted stock award whereby a founder is given ownership of all the shares but the company retains the option to repurchase the unvested shares; effectively, the company's right to repurchase represents the forfeiture of a founder's unvested shares.

- The reasons for not providing shares outright to founders without reserving the company's right to repurchase the shares that have not vested are (1) it aligns the interests of the founders with those of the company and (2) it protects members of the founding team, as well as investors, from the departure from the company of one of the founding team's members.

- In the absence of vesting requirements, a founder who leaves the company maintains his or her equity interest in the company.

- There is a provision that allows for accelerated vesting of restricted stock awards under specifically defined conditions.

- The founders' shares buyback agreement sets forth the mechanism for selling a founder's shares back to the company.

- Because the U.S. tax code recognizes that equity incentive plans are a form of compensation, provisions in the tax code must be considered in structuring an equity incentive plan.

- Section 83 of the tax code addresses three tax issues faced by a grantee: (1) when compensation from an equity incentive plan is taxed, (2) how much of the compensation is subject to taxation, and (3) whether the income is taxed as ordinary income or as a capital gain.

- For tax purposes, for equity incentive plans the three important dates are the grant date, the vesting date, and the disposition date. In the case of stock option plans, another important date is the exercise date.

- Another important tax issue associated with compensation resulting from an equity incentive plan is the fair market value of the stock. The board of directors will typically engage a valuation expert to perform what is popularly referred to as a "409a valuation" of the common stock.

- If the grantee faces a large tax liability from an equity incentive award, the grantee must have sufficient funds to pay that liability without relying on the sale of the stock if it is not publicly traded.

- Incentive plans for founders and employees include equity award plans and cash award plans.

- Equity award plans—restricted stock awards, RSU awards, and stock option awards—result in the potential issuance of shares of common stock.

- Cash award plans—the two most common plans are shared appreciation rights and phantom stock—may be based on the value of the stock but do not necessarily involve the issuance of shares of stock. Compensation is typically in the form of cash but may involve a granting of shares equivalent in value to the amount of cash that would have been awarded.

- A restricted stock award either gives the grantee the right to acquire shares or gives a founder or employee shares at no cost. When the restricted stock award involves the purchase of shares, the price can be the fair market value or discounted.

- With a restricted stock award, the granting company's board of directors has the right to purchase the restricted stock if certain conditions are met.

- In the absence of any action taken by the founder who has been granted restricted stock subject to vesting, the U.S. tax code treats income at the time that the stock becomes vested as the difference between the stock's fair market value and the price paid by the founder for the restricted stock.

- Section 83(b) of the tax code, an election filed with the IRS by the founder when the grant is made, allows for the taxation of income at the time the restricted stock is sold rather than at the time the stock vests.

- The Section 83(b) election requires that at the grant date, the grantee must recognize the income, and furthermore, the income is treated as ordinary income in the year the restricted stock is granted.

- The risk with a Section 83(b) election is that if the stock price does not appreciate and if a tax was paid at the time of the grant date, then the tax would have been paid with no offsetting further benefit.
- Restricted stock units represent a hypothetical share of the company's common stock, with each unit allowing the recipient to receive a specified number of shares (typically one share of common stock per unit).
- As with restricted stock awards, RSU awards are subject to vesting.
- At the discretion of the company's board of directors, when the units are vested, RSUs are paid out either in shares of common stock or in cash.
- From the grantee's perspective, a difference in the tax treatment of restricted stock awards and RSU awards is that for the former, the grantee owns the stock, and therefore for income tax purposes the fair market value is employee compensation, and the employee can file a Section 83(b) election to postpone any income realization when the stock shares vest. RSU awards, on the other hand, are treated for tax purposes as a full-value stock grant and are taxed at full value when the RSUs become vested, not at the grant date, and there is therefore no Section 83(b) election.
- From the granting company's perspective, there are tax implications when RSUs are exercised but not when they are awarded.
- When RSUs are exercised, the company is permitted to take a deduction for employee compensation equal to the fair value of the stock shares that the grantee receives.
- For startup companies whose fair market value is nominal, the use of restricted stock awards will have minimal tax implications. If the fair market value is high, then there is a tax advantage to RSU awards.
- A stock option plan is an alternative to providing grants of restricted stock or RSUs to current key employees and to attract new employees.
- A stock option granted by a company gives the grantee the option for a specified number of years the right (but not the obligation) to buy a specified number of shares of the company's common stock at a fixed price.
- Usually in a stock option plan the grant price to acquire the common stock is the prevailing fair market value at the option's grant date.
- Although typically a stock option plan is subject to a vesting schedule, it is different from the vesting schedule for restricted stock and therefore results in a different tax treatment. In the case of restricted stock awards, the shares are owned by the employee, but the company retains the right to repurchase the shares that have not vested. In the case of a stock option plan, the grantee is awarded options that vest over time, and those options give the grantee the right to purchase the shares at different points in time.
- Vesting for stock options is based on a vesting schedule that typically involves a period of time when the grantee does not vest any options, referred to as the vesting "cliff."

- The two most popular stock option plans are incentive stock options and non-qualified stock options. Their differences have important tax implications for the grantee and the granting company and financial accounting implications for the granting company.
- With an incentive stock option plan, the grantee is allowed to defer the payment of any taxes on gains that may be realized on the appreciation of the common stock above its grant price until the shares are sold.
- With a non-qualified stock option plan, the advantage relative to an incentive stock plan from the company's perspective is that for tax purposes, the company may deduct as an expense when the grantee exercises the option the difference between the fair market value at the time of exercise and the exercise price.
- The same three types of equity awards for corporations are also used for partnerships, with the most common form being partnership interest, which includes capital interests and profit interests.
- For a partnership, the option is an interest in a partnership, and the option can only be granted under a non-qualified stock option plan.
- Restricted stock awards and RSU awards are rarely used in a partnership.
- Options on partnership interests receive a tax treatment that is less favorable than profit interests but have a similar economic characteristic to options on partnership interests, and therefore profit interest is the preferred form of equity compensation award to options on partnership interests.

FURTHER READINGS

Adams, Joseph S., and Barbara Baksa, *Equity Alternatives: Restricted Stock, Performance Awards, Phantom Stock, SARs, and More*, 13th ed. (Oakland, CA: National Center for Employee Ownership, 2015).

Johanson, David R., Rachel J. Markun, and Samuel W. Krause, "Equity Interests in Limited Liability Companies," in Teresa Y. Huang, David R. Johanson, Samuel W. Krause, et al., *Equity Compensation for Limited Liability Companies (LLCs)*, 2nd ed., 27–48 (Oakland, CA: National Center for Employee Ownership, 2013).

Johanson, David R., *Model Equity Compensation Plans* (Oakland, CA: National Center for Employee Ownership, 2008).

Rodrick, Scott, "Unrestricted Stock Grants and Stock Purchase Plans," in Corey Rosen, Pam Chernoff, Elizabeth Dodge, et al., *The Decision-Maker's Guide to Equity Compensation*, 2nd ed., 27–54 (Oakland, CA: National Center for Employee Ownership, 2011).

Rosen, Corey, "Restricted Stock Awards and Restricted Stock Units," in Rosen, Chernoff, Dodge, et al., *The Decision-Maker's Guide to Equity Compensation*, 2nd ed., 55–66.

Rosen, Corey, "Deferred Compensation Issues," in Rosen, Chernoff, Dodge, et al., *The Decision-Maker's Guide to Equity Compensation*, 2nd ed., 125–134.

Rosen, Corey, "Designing an Equity Incentive Plan," in Huang, Johanson, Krause, et al., *Equity Compensation for Limited Liability Companies (LLCs)*, 2nd ed., 9–26.

5

FUNDRAISING AND THE U.S. SECURITIES LAW

Entrepreneurs seeking to raise funds must comply with U.S. federal and state securities laws. Before we describe the different types of funds that are available to entrepreneurs, in the next chapter, and the sources of equity capital, in chapter 7, in this chapter we will look at two principal topics related to fundraising as set forth in the U.S. federal securities laws: the rules for the solicitation of funds and the filings that companies must make with the Securities and Exchange Commission (SEC).

WHAT IS A SECURITY?

Different types of financial contracts or arrangements can be used by an entrepreneur to raise funds. They include, but are not limited to, common stock, preferred stock, bonds, notes, transferable shares, partnership interests, loans, option-type arrangements that permit the acquisition of common stock, investment contracts, preorganization certificates or subscriptions, and profit-sharing agreements. We tend to think of the first three, common stock, preferred stock, and bonds, as "securities" and therefore tend to think that what is referred to as "federal securities law" deals only with those types of financial contracts. That is not the case. It has a major wider meaning and encompasses all the financial contracts or arrangements mentioned above.

The courts have used the decision in a 1946 landmark U.S. Supreme Court case (SEC v. W.J. Howey Co.) involving land sales contracts for citrus groves in Florida together with warranty deeds for the land and a contract to service the land as the basis for determining whether a transaction falls into the realm of a "securities" transaction. The court ruled the Florida transaction was an "investment contract" and therefore a security, stating that:

An investment contract for purposes of the Securities Act means a contract, transaction or scheme whereby a person invests his money in a common enterprise and is led to expect profits solely from the efforts of the promoter or a third party.

In the decision, the Supreme Court also stated that it was immaterial whether shares are evidenced by formal certificates or by nominal interests in the physical assets.

FEDERAL SECURITIES LAW

Entrepreneurs seeking to raise funds must comply with the securities laws as set forth by the federal government and the applicable states. As we focus now on federal securities law, the starting point is the Securities Act of 1933 (Securities Act), commonly referred to as the "truth in securities law," and the Securities Exchange Act of 1934 (Exchange Act). The federal government recognized the need for federal regulation of securities transactions after the Wall Street Crash in October 1929 and the Great Depression that followed. With the passage of these two acts, the position of the federal government toward securities transactions changed from what then President Franklin Roosevelt stated as a *caveat emptor* (let the buyer beware) principle to a *caveat vendor* (let the seller beware) principle. The responsibility for administrating the laws as set forth in these two acts falls to the SEC.

The Securities Act requires that an issuer of securities file a registration statement with the SEC. This act has two basic objectives with respect to an issuer's initial sale of securities. First, it requires that an entity seeking to raise funds by selling securities to the public must provide investors with financial and other significant information about the securities being offered. This is done through the issuance of a prospectus that provides "full and fair disclosure of the character of securities sold in interstate and foreign commerce and through the mails." Second, the Securities Act prohibits in the sale of securities deceit, misrepresentation, and other fraud. While the primary focus of the Securities Act is on the initial distribution[1] of securities and the registration of those securities, the Exchange Act deals with the secondary market, addressing the periodic reporting of financial information to investors and fraud and misrepresentation when securities are sold in either initial or secondary offerings.

Subsequent legislation has amended the regulations dealing with the issuance of securities to the public. Major legislation since the turn of the twenty-first century that has had an impact on fundraising includes (1) the Sarbanes-Oxley Act of 2002, which included provisions to enhance financial disclosures by issuers and combat corporate and accounting fraud, (2) the Dodd-Frank Wall Street Reform and Consumer Protection Act, signed into law in July 2010, which provides additional disclosure and transparency, and (3) the Jumpstart Our Business Startups Act (JOBS Act), enacted in April 2012, which helps businesses raise funds in public markets by minimizing regulatory requirements. We describe the JOBS Act in more detail below.

In addition to federal securities laws, there are state laws and securities laws of other countries in which an entrepreneur might seek to raise funds. With respect to state laws, also referred to as "blue sky laws," each state has a regulatory agency responsible for regulating

---

1. The Securities Act defines the "distribution" of a security not just as the initial sale of a security but as a transaction involving a large infusion of shares into the public market. More specifically, Rule 100 of the SEC's Regulation M defines distribution as "an offering of securities, whether or not subject to registration under the Securities Act, that is distinguished from ordinary trading transactions by the magnitude of the offering and the presence of special selling efforts and selling methods."

the sale of securities within the state. Every state is a member of the North American Securities Administrators Association (NASAA), which, although lacking the authority to enforce laws, formulates and recommends model securities laws. What most states use as the basis for their securities laws is the Uniform Securities Act of 1956. Because this act is written broadly and the laws can vary from state to state, no further discussion of state securities laws is provided here.

An entrepreneur must comply with these laws in soliciting funds from investors. Preventing fraud is probably one of the key objectives of federal and state securities laws in the United States. The ***antifraud provisions*** in federal securities laws are applicable to any issuer of securities regardless of whether the issuer is required to register the security sold with the SEC. Violating these antifraud provisions can result in one or more of the following by the SEC: imposition of financial penalties, criminal charges, and a prohibition against fundraising for a specified period of time. In addition, there can be private litigation that results in financial compensation to investors who can demonstrate fraud. What an entrepreneur might think is an innocent statement to a reporter, a statement at an industry conference, or a posting on the Internet could be viewed by the SEC as a violation of an antifraud provision. Moreover, it is not always easy for an entrepreneur to identify what matters are important to disclose in a new offering of securities and in periodic reporting.

An entrepreneur who seeks to raise funds by means of a transaction that involves a security must register the security offered with the SEC or rely on an exemption from registration. Most of the exemptions from registration prohibit companies from engaging in what the SEC refers to as general solicitation or general advertising in connection with the offering of securities. This prohibition covers advertising in newspapers or over the Internet.

Although our discussion here focuses on securities law requirements for the issuance of securities, an entrepreneur may still have to become an SEC reporting company and file a registration of certain securities under the Exchange Act if a security is listed on an exchange or if the company has more than $10 million in total assets and a class of equity securities is held by either (1) 2,000 or more persons or (2) 500 or more persons who are not accredited investors. (We define accredited investors later in this chapter.) For startup companies whose employees are granted the right to acquire common stock or who hold common stock based on previous employment, there is a concern with the quantitative measure involving the number of persons holding securities. However, the SEC excludes person who acquired securities as part of a compensation plan where the transaction was exempt from registration under the Securities Act. A company that is classified as an SEC reporting company must comply with the reporting requirements.

RULES ON GENERAL SOLICITATION AND ADVERTISING

Prior to 2013, there was a ban on general solicitation or advertising in connection with the offering of securities. Guidance on what types of activity constitute general solicitation and advertising is provided by SEC Rule 502(c), which offers some general examples of activity that the SEC has historically viewed to be general solicitation, including advertising in newspapers and magazines, through television and radio broadcasts, and by offering seminars to which attendees are invited by general solicitation.

In addition, the SEC provides prior interpretive guidance confirming that other uses of publicly available media, such as unrestricted websites, may also constitute general solicitation. Despite this general guidance, what constitutes general solicitation and advertising is still tricky because it is a matter of judgment and may come down to the responses to any SEC investigation. In fact, it has been consistently stated by the SEC that its position on what is general solicitation is a matter of particular facts and circumstances.

However, there are relatively recent market practices in which startups communicate regarding their business and products or services with others. These practices and forums include startup competitions, sharing information on social media, holding demonstration days, attending screening sessions at angel group meetings, and holding pitch events. Some would argue that these practices are simply communication and not fundraising, and so should not be viewed as general solicitation. Whether any practice does or does not constitute general solicitation is up to the SEC (and possibly the courts) to determine.

The focus of the SEC with respect to avoiding an action becoming a general solicitation has been what it refers to as the existence of a "pre-existing substantive relationship" between an issuer or its agent or representative (e.g., a broker or placement agent) and the potential buyer. The reason why the SEC has looked carefully at a preexisting substantive relationship is to ensure that even before an offer is made, the potential buyer has enough knowledge and experience in financial and business matters to be capable of evaluating the merits and risks of the prospective investment. It seems that the belief of the SEC is that such a relationship should be based on the issuer's actual knowledge of or familiarity with the potential buyer's current situation, and not just on the potential buyer's general characteristics (e.g., well-compensated professional worker or a person with a high net worth).

Although there were exemptions to this ban on general solicitation and advertising, the SEC rules severely handicapped the fundraising ability of entrepreneurs. The most commonly used exemption that could be used by a qualifying company to avoid the ban on general soliciting and advertising is Rule 506 of Regulation D. This rule allows an issuer to raise an unlimited amount of capital from an unlimited number of what the SEC defines (and we explain later) as "accredited investors" and up to thirty-five nonaccredited investors.

However, it was not until July 2013 that the SEC adopted a new set of rules (described below) removing the ban on general solicitation and advertising under certain circumstances but introducing some rules that may impede fundraising from certain types of investors.

The rules lifting the ban on general solicitation and advertising were the result of the JOBS Act, which was passed in April 2012 to stimulate economic recovery in the United

States by making it easier for a company to find investors and, as a result, stimulate the economy by expanding employment opportunities. A section of the JOBS Act directed that the SEC remove the ban on general solicitation and advertising for securities offerings relying on Rule 506, provided that (1) the securities that are sold are limited to accredited investors and (2) the issuer of the security takes "reasonable steps" to verify that all buyers of the securities are accredited investors. Rule 506 was part of the original Securities Act, but the new rule that provides for the ban on general solicitation and advertising is Rule 506(c). What this provision in the JOBS Act did was to make the formulation of the rules for an issuer to take reasonable steps regarding the verification of buyers of the security the responsibility of the SEC, thereby providing guidance to entrepreneurs as to how they should act to reasonably verify that they are soliciting accredited investors. Consequently, what the JOBS Act specified is that while there is no restriction imposed on whom a company can solicit to purchase its securities, there are restrictions on who is allowed to purchase its securities.

If a startup company wants to do a filing with the SEC based on Rule 506(c), there is a complicated set of principles set forth by the SEC regarding what constitutes "reasonable steps" to ensure that the firm is soliciting an accredited investor. However, the SEC did provide the following nonexclusive list of methods that would satisfy the requirement of reasonable steps to verify that a potential investor solicited is an accredited investor:

- Reviewing copies of any IRS form that reports the income of the purchaser and obtaining a written representation that the purchaser will likely continue to earn the necessary income in the current year.
- Receiving a written confirmation from a registered broker-dealer, SEC-registered investment adviser, licensed attorney, or certified public accountant that such entity or person has taken reasonable steps to verify the purchaser's accredited status.[2]

The second method basically requires that accreditation be verified by a third party. Moreover, investors must be recertified periodically (e.g., every quarter). Third parties that could perform the accreditation function are lawyers, accountants, and financial advisers. However, this adds a cost for a startup company. As David Verrill, president of the Angel Capital Association (the largest organization of accredited investors), notes, this method adds unnecessary costs to the fundraising process because angel investors' knowledge of startups makes the need for lawyers, accountants, or financial advisers unnecessary. As he correctly points out, the angel investor is typically more knowledgeable about the issues than those third parties. Regarding third-party verifiers, Verrill said, "We don't need them, don't want to pay for them, and don't want to introduce unnecessary third parties into an ecosystem where there is virtually no fraud. We want every penny going to the startup—not some unnecessary third party." In an op-ed piece appearing in the July 24, 2013, *Wall*

---

2. See the website http://www.sec.gov/news/press/2013/2013-124-item1.htm.

Street Journal carrying the subtitle "How many people would buy stock if they had to give the company copies of their tax returns?," Verrill describes the issues.[3]

The JOBS Act also directed the SEC to amend Rule 144A under the Securities Act. As explained later, there is a private offering exemption for SEC registration for nonpublic offering of securities. This exemption from registration applies to the resale of securities to larger institutional investors known as *qualified institutional buyers* (QIBs). Prior to the passage of the JOBS Act, Rule 144A set forth that the offering of securities be made only to QIBs. Under the new Rule 506(c), Rule 144A was amended so that offers of securities can be made to investors who are not QIBs as long as the securities are sold only to persons who the seller reasonably believes are QIBs.

Whether or not Rule 506(c) will help startups in their fundraising is yet to be seen. The concern, which is one we return to when we discuss the different forms of exemption from SEC registrations, is that although at the time of the sale of a security, the conditions for exemption may be satisfied, subsequent action by a single buyer (such as the resale of a security before a specified time period) or the determination that an investor does not satisfy the conditions for exemption can result in the exemption being voided and the issuer in violation of the Securities Act (i.e., the issuer has not properly registered the security). Since the security was not registered, it is possible the issuer could be ordered by the SEC to offer to repurchase the security from all investors. For this reason, early-stage companies should be concerned about a filing under Rule 506(c).

What Are Accredited Investors and QIBs?

As can be seen from the discussion above (and further below), security offerings to what the SEC classifies as accredited investors and QIBs are potential exemptions to certain securities laws. Below we provide a nonlegal definition of such investors. The SEC provides a more extensive list of criteria for determining these two investor types.

There are individual accredited investors and institutional accredited investors. Under Regulation D of the Securities Act, an *individual accredited investor* is an individual who meets certain annual income or net worth thresholds. As of this writing, an accredited investor is an individual whose annual income exceeds $200,000 (or $300,000 combined annual income with a spouse) *or* who has at least $1 million of personal net worth, with the investor's primary residence excluded in the determination of net worth. Some individual accredited investors, called angel investors, invest in early-stage startup companies. An *institutional accredited investor* includes entities such as banks, insurance companies,

---

3. David Verrill, "SEC Rules Will Clip the Wings of Angel Investors," *Wall Street Journal*, July 24, 2013. This piece was also posted on a blog by David Verrill on the website of the Angel Capital Association under the title, "Why Is the ACA Making a Big Deal about the SEC Ruling on General Solicitation?," http://www.angelcapitalassociation.org/blog/why-is-the-aca-making-a-big-deal-about-the-sec-ruling-on-general-solicitation. See also the following article by Dan Rosen, a board member of the Angel Capital Association and chairman of the Alliance of Angels: "Why Angels Are Making a Big Deal about the SEC's New Rules on Advertising Investment Opportunities," *Venture Beat,* July 28, 2013, http://venturebeat.com/2013/07/28/why-angels-are-making-a-big-deal-about-the-secs-new-rules-on-advertising-investment-opportunities.

mutual funds, and venture capital funds, the last being major investors in startups at later stages of development.

The accredited investor standard is not determined by the SEC. Instead, Congress has delegated to the U.S. General Accounting Office (GAO) the responsibility for determining the rules for individuals to qualify as accredited investors. In July 2013 the GAO published a report on alternative criteria for investors to be classified as accredited investors.[4] In that report, the GAO recommended that the SEC consider alternative criteria, including those suggested in the report, which could help in determining an individual's ability both to bear the risk and to assess the risks associated with investing in private placements. For example, in the survey conducted by the GAO, market participants suggested adding a liquid investment requirement or the use of an investment adviser as an alternative criterion.

A *qualified institutional buyer* is a large sophisticated organization with the primary responsibility of managing large investment portfolios with at least $100 million in securities; they are recognized by regulators of securities market as needing less protection from issuers than the typical public investor. QIBs include a wide range of entities, among them banks, insurance companies, mutual funds, employee benefit plans, and entities owned entirely by accredited investors.

Reasons for Exemptions

Basically, there are five common exemptions that can be used to avoid SEC registration:

- an intrastate offering exemption,
- a private offering exemption,
- Regulation A,
- Regulation D (Rules 504, 505, 506), and
- an Accredited Investor Exemption.

But it is important to repeat that even if an entrepreneur qualifies for one of the exemptions, the antifraud provisions under the federal securities law still apply. Moreover, the entrepreneur almost always is required to make available to prospective investors certain information. The amount of detail and the content of such disclosures vary depending on the particular requirements for registration or exemption set forth by the applicable securities authority.

Intrastate Offering Exemption   As Congress recognized the need for small local businesses to obtain financing but still wanted to protect investors against fraud, there is a section in the Securities Act that allows for an exemption for securities sold within a state (i.e.,

---

4. General Accounting Office, "Securities and Exchange Commission: Alternative Criteria for Qualifying as an Accredited Investor Should be Considered," GAO-13–640, July 18, 2013.

intrastate). This exemption is accordingly referred to as the ***intrastate offering exemption***. There are no restrictions imposed on the amount that can be raised or on the number of investors.

Exemptions in general can be categorized based on the security itself being exempt from registration (i.e., an "exempt security") and a transaction involving the sale of a security being exempt. The intrastate offering exemption, unlike the other exemptions described later, is an example of exemption because it is an exempt security.

To qualify under this exemption, the following three conditions must be satisfied:

- The issuer must be incorporated in the state where the securities are to be offered.
- The issuer must be doing a significant amount of its business in the state where the securities are to be offered.
- The offer and ultimate sale of the securities are only to bona fide residents of the state.

The first condition seems simple enough. The last two conditions may not be easily satisfied but also hamper the operations and decisions of an entrepreneur seeking to operate on a regional, national, or international level and seeking the widest range of potential investors. The second condition, regarding doing significant business within the state, may have to be satisfied by numerical measures when a company has significant out-of-state revenues. The third condition, that all sales be limited to bona fide state residents and not be made to out-of-state investors, is one that might be satisfied at the time of issuance but might ultimately be violated by buyers of securities in subsequent transactions resulting in the security losing its exempt status. More specifically, if the buyer of the exempt security resells it to an out-of-state person within a short period of time after the offering, the entrepreneur might be in violation of the Securities Act because of failure to register the security. The SEC uses nine months as the period of time during which a security cannot be resold to an out-of-state person. There are ways in which an entrepreneur can reduce the likelihood of resale of a security to an out-of-state person by setting forth in the original sale contractual arrangements that prohibit such a sale.

To make it easier for an entrepreneur to ensure that it is covered by the intrastate offering exemption, the SEC has adopted a "safe harbor rule" (Rule 147). In general, a safe harbor rule refers to a set of requirements that, if complied with, ensure eligibility under some standard. However, the failure to comply with safe harbor rules does not mean ineligibility. In the case of Rule 417, if the requirements are satisfied, the security will qualify for the intrastate offering exemption; failure to satisfy the rule does not mean the entrepreneur cannot obtain an intrastate offering exemption.

An entrepreneur seeking to use the intrastate offering exemption must be familiar with the registration and regulatory requirements of the state in which the securities will be offered.

Private Offering Exemption   Under the Securities Act, the *private offering exemption*, also referred to as the *nonpublic offering exemption* and the *private placement exemption*, exempts from registration "transactions by an issuer not involving any public offering." To qualify for this exemption, the buyers of the security must satisfy all of the following three requirements:

- They must either (1) be capable of evaluating the investment risks and attributes of the security (i.e., be "sophisticated investors" based on their finance and business experience) or (2) be able to bear the economic risks associated with the security.
- They must have access to the type of information typically provided in a prospectus for a registered security.
- They must agree not to resell or distribute the security to the public.

An entrepreneur seeking exemption under the private offering exemption must realize that there can be no general, public advertising of the offering or general solicitation of investors. Also, as noted for the intrastate offering exemption, if the security is offered to even one person who does not meet the first condition above and who, post issuance, resells the security, the entrepreneur would be in violation of the Securities Act.

There are objective standards that can be relied on that, if satisfied, meet the conditions for a private offering exemption. These objective standards are set forth in SEC Rule 506(b), which is part of Regulation D.

REQUIRED FILINGS WITH THE SEC

In the United States, an entrepreneur seeking to raise funds through the sale of securities must either (1) register the securities offering with the SEC or (2) rely on an exemption from registration. The SEC mandates that any company, domestic or foreign, must file certain statements unless an exemption can be identified. The filings include:

- Registration Statement,
- 10-K Report,
- 10-Q Report,
- 8-K Report,
- Proxy Statement,
- Forms 3, 4, and 5, and
- Schedule 13D and Schedule 13G.

The SEC has adopted special rules for companies that it refers to as "smaller reporting companies."⁵ SEC Rule 405 sets forth the following criteria for a company to qualify as a smaller reporting company:

- For a company whose common stock is being publicly traded, the float must be less than $75 million as of the last business day of its most recently completed second fiscal quarter.

- For a company whose common stock is not publicly traded, the float must be less than $75 million as of a date within thirty days of the date of the filing of the registration statement.

- For a company with a public float greater than zero, the annual revenues must be less than $50 million during the most recently completed fiscal year for which audited financial statements are available.

Companies that qualify as a smaller reporting company must use the same forms as other domestic companies that are required to report to the SEC. However, the information contained in the registration statement and the periodic reports may differ. That is, the information is scaled to reflect the characteristics and needs of smaller companies and their investors.

Registration Statement

Form S-1 is an initial registration filing by a company planning to issue new securities. This filing, also referred to as the "Registration Statement Under the Securities Exchange Act of 1933," requires that the following information be included:⁶

- Front Cover Page and Summary Information
- Risk Factors
- Use of Proceeds
- Determination of Offering Price and Dilution
- Selling Shareholders and Insiders
- Plan of Distribution
- Legal Proceedings and Indemnification
- Directors, Executive Officers, Promoters, and Control Persons
- Description of Securities
- Description of Business
- Description of Property and Financial Statements

---

5. At one time the SEC referred to "small business issuers" and had special rules for those companies that fell into this group. New rules have been adopted for a larger group of companies that the SEC now refers to as "smaller reporting companies." Companies that fall into the "smaller reporting company" category are those that qualified as "small business issuers" prior to the new rules, as well as most companies that qualify as what the SEC refers to as "non-accelerated filers."
6. These reporting requirements are set forth in SEC Regulation S-K.

- Management's Discussion and Analysis of Financial Condition and Results of Operations
- Certain Relationships and Related Transactions
- Market for Common Equity and Related Stockholder Matters
- Executive Compensation, Indemnification of Officers and Directors, and Other Expenses of Issuance and Distribution
- Expenses of Issuance and Distributions
- Recent Sales of unregistered Securities

The financial statements that are required to be included in the S-1 are:

- Audited balance sheets for each of the two most recent fiscal years. (In the case of a company that has been in existence for less than one fiscal year, an audited balance sheet as of a date within 135 days of the date of filing the registration statement is acceptable.)
- Audited statements of income and cash flows for each of the three fiscal years preceding the date of the most recent audited balance sheet being filed or such shorter period as the company has been in existence.
- Interim financial statements for the current period if the filing is more than 135 days after the end of the company's fiscal year.[7]

10-K Report

Under the federal securities laws, publicly traded companies are required to disclose information on a periodic basis. One such report, Form 10-K, or simply the *10-K*, must be filed by domestic issuers, other than small business issuers, on an annual basis. (We discuss other reports that must be filed periodically below.) The 10-K has to be filed with the SEC within ninety days after the end of the company's fiscal year.

The 10-K consists of the following sections:

- *Business Summary*: Comprehensive overview of the company's operations (including those that are international), business segments, history, marketing, research and development, competition, and employees.
- *Management Discussion and Analysis* (MDA): Provides a discussion by management of (1) significant components of revenues and expenses that are important in understanding the company's results of operations, (2) the financial outlook for the company, (3) information that may help reconcile previous years' financial results with the current year's results, and (4) additional information about off-balance sheet arrangements, as well as a table that discloses contractual obligations.

---

7. As explained in chapter 8, these statements have a limited review and are not audited.

- *Financial Statements*: Includes the four major financial statements (balance sheet, income statement, statement of cash flow, and statement of changes in stockholders' equity) prepared according to GAAP and audited by an independent certified public accountant.

In addition, there are other sections that discuss the company's management team and any legal proceedings that the company faces.

It should be noted that there is often confusion between the "annual report on Form 10-K" and the "annual report to shareholders." The former differs from the latter in that the annual report to shareholders is a report that must be sent to a company's shareholders when the company holds an annual meeting to elect directors.

10-Q Report

Form 10-Q, or simply *10-Q*, is another ongoing filing required by the SEC. It must be filed within thirty-five days after the close of a corporation's fiscal quarter. Although the 10-Q is similar to the 10-K, much less detailed information is required, and the financial statements are unaudited but subject to a review. The information that is required includes (1) financial statements, (2) the MDA, (3) quantitative and qualitative disclosures about market risk, (4) legal proceedings, and (5) controls and procedures.

8-K Report

Form 8-K is an occasional filing that provides information about the company that is not generally found in the financial statements if a certain event occurs. These events include:

- bankruptcy or receivership,
- completion of an acquisition or disposition of assets,
- changes in the registrant's certifying accountant,
- changes in the control of the registrant,
- change in fiscal year,
- temporary suspension of trading under the registrant's employee benefit plans,
- amendments to the registrant's code of ethics or the waiver of a provision of the code of ethics,
- Regulation FD disclosure,
- departure of directors or principal officers, election of directors, or appointment of principal officers,
- unregistered sales of equity securities,
- material modifications to the rights of security holders,
- amendments to articles of incorporation or bylaws,
- entry into a material definitive agreement,
- termination of a material definitive agreement,

- the creation of a direct financial obligation or an obligation under an off-balance sheet arrangement,
- events that accelerate or increase a direct financial obligation or an obligation under an off-balance sheet arrangement,
- costs associated with exit or disposal activities,
- material impairments,
- notice of delisting or failure to satisfy a continued listing rule or standard, or a transfer of listing,
- unregistered sales of equity securities, and
- nonreliance on previous issued financial statements or a related audit report or completed interim review.

Form 8-K must be filed within four business days of the event.

Here are a few examples of 8-K filings.

- Twitter, Inc., filed Form 8-K after acquiring MoPub (a mobile ad startup) in September 2013. The acquisition was a few days prior to Twitter's announcement that the company was going public. As a result, Twitter had to report via the 8-K the financial statements and exhibits as a result of the acquisition.
- In June 2013, Apple Inc. filed Form 8-K to disclose the following five items: (1) "Departure of Directors or Certain Officers; Election of Directors; Appointment of Certain Officers; Compensatory Arrangements of Certain Officers," (2) "Move to Performance-Based Equity," (3) "CEO Leadership by Example," (4) "Performance Measurement and Shareholder Alignment," and (5) "2011 CEO Equity Award Modification."
- In March 2014, Global Digital Solutions, Inc., filed Form 8-K providing information regarding three proposed transactions, including an unsolicited letter of intent to acquire Remington Outdoor Company, Inc.
- In March 2014, Zayo Group, LLC, filed Form 8-K after it announced the acquisition of CoreXchange, Inc., a data center, bandwidth, and managed services provider. The revised financial statements and exhibits were provided in the 8-K.
- In March 2014, Ekso Bionics Holdings, Inc., a robotic exoskeleton pioneer, filed Form 8-K to disclose the joining of the firm of two individual to amplify its sales and marketing strategies.

Proxy Statement

A *proxy statement* issued by the company provides information about the issues to be voted on by shareholders[8] and management's recommendation. These issues include compensation of senior management and shareholdings of officers and directors.

---

8. State law determines the circumstances that are required for a vote.

For example, the following was included in Facebook, Inc.,'s April 26, 2013, proxy statement:

5. *What items of business will be voted on at the Annual Meeting?*
The items of business scheduled to be voted on at the Annual Meeting are:

- Proposal One: the election of eight directors;
- Proposal Two: a non-binding advisory vote on the compensation program of our named executive officers as disclosed in this proxy statement;
- Proposal Three: a non-binding advisory vote on the frequency with which we will conduct a non-binding advisory vote on the compensation program for our named executive officers; and
- Proposal Four: the ratification of the selection of Ernst & Young LLP as our independent registered public accounting firm for the fiscal year ending December 31, 2013.

6. *How does the board of directors recommend I vote on these proposals?*
- "FOR" the election of each nominee;
- "FOR" the approval of the compensation program of our named executive officers;
- "FOR" a frequency of EVERY THREE YEARS regarding how frequently we should seek an advisory vote on the compensation program for our named executive officers; and
- "FOR" the ratification of the selection of Ernst & Young LLP as our independent registered public accounting firm for the fiscal year ending December 31, 2013.

Forms 3, 4, and 5

Information about the ownership of securities by corporate insiders (i.e., officers and directors) and any beneficial owners (i.e., owners of more than 10% of the company's equity securities) and how that ownership changes over time is provided on Forms 3, 4, and 5.

Form 3 is the initial report to be filed with the SEC by a person such as director, officer, or senior executive either (1) within ten days after assuming his or her position or (2) no later than the effective date of the registration statement. The information reported on Form 3 is how much company stock is owned by the filer and in what form it was held on the date this filer assumed the position with the company or as of the date of the IPO. In addition, there must be a Form 3 filing by a person whose holdings exceed 10% of any class of the company's registered equity securities. This filing is required within ten days.

The reporting of the changes in stock ownership is done by filing Form 4 before the end of the second business day after the day on which the relevant transaction took place. It is on Form 5 that a person that had not yet reported a transaction on Form 4 during the year must report any such transactions.

Schedule 13D and Schedule 13G Reports

The SEC defines the "beneficial owner" of a company as any person who directly or indirectly shares voting power or investment power (the power to sell the security). Schedule 13D, commonly referred to as the "beneficial ownership report," must be filed when a person or group of persons acquires beneficial ownership of more than 5% (viewed to be a significant ownership) of a voting class of a company's equity registered within ten days after the purchase. Schedule 13G is similar to Schedule 13D but requires less information, and the party acquiring the shares needs be only a passive investor with any purpose, or with the effect of altering or influencing the control of the issuer.

KEY POINTS COVERED IN THIS CHAPTER

- A founding team seeking raise funds must comply with U.S. federal and state securities laws.

- Each state has its own laws, referred to as blue sky laws, to regulate the sale of securities within the state.

- At the federal level, the key legislation dealing with fundraising is the Securities Act of 1933 (Securities Act).

- The Securities Act has two basic objectives: (1) it requires an entity seeking to raise funds by selling securities to the public to provide investors with financial and other significant information about the securities being offered and (2) it prohibits in the sale of securities deceit, misrepresentation, and other fraud.

- The other major federal legislation is the Securities Exchange Act of 1934 (Exchange Act), which deals with the secondary market, addressing the periodic reporting of financial information to investors and fraud and misrepresentation when securities are sold in either initial or secondary offerings.

- Amendments to the Securities Act related to fundraising are (1) the Sarbanes-Oxley Act of 2002, which included provisions to enhance financial disclosures by issuers and to combat corporate and accounting fraud, (2) the Dodd-Frank Wall Street Reform and Consumer Protection Act, which provides additional disclosure and transparency, and (3) the Jumpstart Our Business Startups Act (JOBS Act), which assists businesses in raising funds in public markets by minimizing regulatory requirements.

- The antifraud provisions in federal securities laws apply to any issuer of securities regardless of whether the issuer is required to register the security sold with the SEC.

- Violation of antifraud provisions can result in one or more of the following by the SEC: imposition of financial penalties, criminal charges, and a prohibition against fundraising for a specified period of time.

- Founders must be sensitive to what they may perceive as an innocent statement to a reporter, a statement at an industry conference, or an Internet posting, which could be viewed by the SEC as a violation of an antifraud provision.

- Although a security must be registered with the SEC, there are exemptions from SEC registration if certain requirements are met.

- Most of the exemptions from registration prohibit companies from engaging in what the SEC refers to as general solicitation or general advertising in connection with the offering of securities.
- At one time, Rule 506 of Regulation D of the securities law was the most commonly used exemption by a qualifying company to avoid the ban on general soliciting and advertising, allowing an issuer to raise an unlimited amount of capital from an unlimited number of "accredited investors" and up to thirty-five nonaccredited investors.
- In July 2013 the SEC adopted a new set of rules that removed the ban on general solicitation and advertising under certain circumstances but also introduced some rules that may impede fundraising from certain types of investors.
- The JOBS Act of 2012 made it easier for founders to find investors by requiring that the SEC remove the ban on general solicitation and advertising for securities offerings relying on Rule 506, provided that (1) the sale of the securities is limited to accredited investors and (2) the issuer of the security takes "reasonable steps" to verify that all buyers of the securities are accredited investors.
- Because of the JOBS Act, although there is no restriction imposed on whom a company may solicit to purchase its securities, there are restrictions on who is allowed to purchase its securities, and this restriction may impede entrepreneurial fundraising.
- The JOBS Act also directed the SEC to amend rules for the private offering exemption for SEC registration for the nonpublic offering of securities.
- In understanding federal securities laws regarding fundraising by entrepreneurs, it is important to understand the difference between accredited investors and qualified institutional investors.
- Under the Securities Act, an individual accredited investor is an individual who meets certain annual income or net worth thresholds. An institutional accredited investor includes entities such as banks, insurance companies, mutual funds, and venture capital funds.
- A qualified institutional buyer (QIB) is a large sophisticated organization with the primary responsibility of managing large investment portfolios with at least $100 million in securities and recognized by regulators of securities market as needing less protection from issuers than the typical public investor.
- Exemptions that can be used to avoid SEC registration (but still subject to the antifraud provisions) include the intrastate offering exemption, the private offering exemption, Regulation A, Regulation D, and the accredited investor exemption.
- The filings with the SEC that are required if there is no exemption include the Registration Statement, 10-K Report, 10-Q Report, 8-K Report, Proxy Statement, Forms 3, 4, and 5, and Schedule 13D and Schedule 13G.
- There are special filing rules for companies classified as smaller reporting companies.

FURTHER READINGS

Casey, Neil P., Lori S. Smith and Merritt A. Cole, "General Solicitation and (Public) Private Placements: Navigating the Minefield Planted by New and Proposed SEC Rules," *White and Williams Securities Alert,* September 11, 2013.

Cunningham, Michael M., *The JOBS Act: Crowdfunding for Small Businesses and Startups* (New York: Apress, 2012).

Palmiter, Alan R., *Examples & Explanations: Securities Regulation,* 6th ed. (New York: Walters Kluwer Law & Business, 2014).

Rapp, Robert N., "How to Apply Blue Sky Laws to Securities Offerings," *Law 360* (November 14, 2013), http://www.law360.com/articles/488533/how-to-apply-blue-sky-laws-to-securities-offerings.

6

SOURCES OF FINANCING

Now that we know the applicable federal rules for raising funds for a startup that founders must follow, in this chapter we describe the sources of financing. Before we do so, we provide a brief description of the stages or rounds of financing, including an initial public offering (IPO).

PRELIQUIDATION STAGES OF FINANCING

In chapter 1, the six stages of business development and financing were described. For purposes of describing the various funding sources prior to the anticipated liquidation of a company resulting from either an acquisition, a merger, or an IPO, we can simplify those six stages into two broader stages of financing: early-stage financing and expansion-stage financing.

Early-stage financing includes stage 1 of the six stages described in chapter 1. Early-stage financing can be divided into two phases, the seed round and the first round. In the *seed round*, the founders seek to finance the development of a product or service (i.e., the venture's offerings). Typically, no commercialization of the intended offerings has occurred, and hence this stage of financing is sometimes referred to as the *precommercialization financing stage*. In addition to administrative costs, the major costs incurred are for developing a customer base, developing a prototype of the offering, and market testing. For high-tech startup companies, there may be the need to hire technical staff such as engineers, scientists, and software developers. For investors, this is the stage of a startup that has the greatest risks and therefore should offer the greatest rewards.

Funding in the very early stages usually comes primarily through the founders' utilization of whatever cash they can obtain from personal savings, by refinancing a home that may have appreciated in value in order to withdraw equity, by using a home as collateral for a second mortgage, by cashing out a life insurance policy, and by obtaining a personal bank loan (as opposed to a business bank loan). Some founders will start a business while still employed by another organization and use their salary to help fund the new business. Founders' use of these sources of funding is referred to as *bootstrap financing*. Other sources of funding at this stage may be the personal assets of the family members and friends.

After those sources are exhausted, the sources of seed finance are one or more of the following:

- credit cards,
- vendors,
- Small Business Administration loans,
- angel investors and angel groups,
- super angels,
- seed accelerators,
- incubators, and
- crowdfunding platforms.

The most common source of larger amounts of seed financing is angel investors. We describe each of these sources in the next section.

First-round financing is commonly referred to as the *Series A round* or simply *A financing*. The milestone that has been reached at this stage is the generation of revenue. Neither break-even operations nor profits are typical of this stage. Although the risk of first-round investors is still considerable, it is less than that for investors in the seed round. The most common source of funding during the Series A round is venture capitalists, as we describe later in this chapter.

In the seed stage, it is difficult for founders to obtain debt financing from banks in the form of loans except in instances where the founders have sufficient collateral or have sufficient assets to provide personal guarantees. Nor has the startup generated sufficient cash flow to justify a business loan. However, once first-rounding financing is obtained from venture capitalists, there are specialty banks and nonbank entities that are willing to provide such loans. These loans are referred to as *venture debt* and contain an equity kicker for the lender in the form of warrants.

Expansion-stage financing includes the last five stages of business development and financing described in chapter 1. It is funding for the purpose of expanding the company's business by expanding production and acquiring customers based on the venture's market-ing strategy. Financing here includes bridge loans, second-round financing (also called Series B round financing), third-round financing (also called Series C round financing), and so on. Additional rounds of financing may be necessary if the company does not have a liquidating event after several rounds of financing. As explained later in this chapter, the entry of a new investor group, institutional investors, has allowed ventures to raise funds through an IPO by providing substantial funds for a company to expand without the need to go public.

DUE DILIGENCE PROCESS

When considering a request for funding by a startup company, potential investors will go through a *due diligence process*. This process involves potential investors assessing both the responses by founders to questions raised about the company during presentations and evaluating the written information supplied by the founders. When an investor is part of an investor group, the information and assessment of the venture as a candidate for funding are shared with others in the investor group.

During the due diligence process founders will be asked questions regarding the business and legal matters related to the business. With respect to the business, investors will want the following information:

- *Background of the founders:* Investors will want to know the founders' educational training, experiences related to the management of the startup, and track record in other businesses that the founders may have been associated with at the senior level.

- *Business model:* Investors will want to know whether the business is scalable, the channels of distribution, the value proposition, and the founders' exit strategy.

- *Historical performance:* Although it may be limited in terms of number of years of operation so that revenue and expenses may not be indicative of future operations, the historical performance of the business since inception must be supplied. This history includes financial accounting information. Depending on the investor, the financial accounting information need not be prepared in accordance with generally accepted accounting principles (GAAP). Other acceptable accounting methods may satisfy investors.[1]

- *Management team:* Investors will look at the organizational structure and, in particular, the management team (founders plus key employees).

- *Targeted market:* Investors will want to know the startup's targeted market, the expected market growth, and the degree of competition. With respect to information about expected market growth and competition, investors will realize that the information presented may be optimistic in an attempt to make the startup a more appealing investment opportunity.

The legal information is particularly important for investors in high-tech startups because the business may depend on intellectual property (patents, copyrights, trademarks, domain names, and other proprietary rights). Related to legal matters, the information sought by investors would include, for example, any threatened, pending, or current lawsuits, or any licensing or patent violations. In the case of startups that will be regulated by some government entity, investors will want to know about any current or pending regulatory

---

1. Other accounting methods that may be acceptable are described in chapter 8.

investigations or government actions. Investors will also want to know if there are any important federal or state tax matters pending. The legal review part of the due diligence process is conducted by the investor's lawyers.

SOURCES OF SEED STAGE FINANCING

Earlier we listed the sources of seed stage financing. In this section, we describe each of these sources.

Credit Card Financing

Credit cards, used prudently, appear to be a particularly important source of funding at this stage. Timothy Faley, managing director of the Samuel Zell & Robert H. Lurie Institute for Entrepreneurial Studies at the University of Michigan's Ross School of Business, suggests that perhaps half of all startups are funded by credit cards.[2] This view appears to be supported by others. For example, according to Sam Thacker, owner of Business Finance Solutions, although at one time bankers viewed credit card financing as a negative credit event for a business, by the late 1990s this source of financing had become popular for growing a business. By 2007 it was the norm.[3]

Probably the best-known use of credit card financing was by the founders of Google. While doctoral students in the Computer Science Department at Stanford University in the mid-1990s, the founders of Google, Larry Page and Sergey Brin, financed the company in the first two years of operation with the prudent use of credit cards. Carefully watching spending limits, they used credit cards to purchase used computers and open-source software.[4] Another example is Charles Huang, the designer of the game Guitar Hero III: Legends of Rock, who in 2007 used credit cards to finance his company, RedOctane.[5]

Credit card financing is a form of debt financing and carries the risks of using debt. The advantage of credit card financing is the ease with which founders with a good credit rating can obtain multiple credit cards with good-sized lines of credit. Unlike a loan that must be repaid on a scheduled basis, the periodic obligation for the credit card holder is the minimum payment due, which is based on the outstanding loan balance. In selecting a credit card, individuals should consider not only the interest rate that is charged but also how the minimum payment due is determined by the credit card issuer. For example, some banks may compute the amount as 1% of the new balance, plus finance charges and any late fees. Other banks may charge the greater of 2% of the balance or 1% plus all interest

2. Timothy Faley, quoted in Anne Field, "7 Ways to Finance a Startup," *FSB Magazine*, October 18, 2007, http://money.cnn.com/2007/05/03/magazines/fsb/raising.money.fsb.

3. "Finance Your Start-up with Credit Cards? Google Did," CreditCards.com, April 27, 2011, http://smallbusiness.foxbusiness.com/finance-accounting/2011/04/26/finance-start-credit-cards-google-did.

4. Tom Ehrenfeld, *The Startup Garden: How Growing a Business Grows You* (New York: McGraw-Hill, 2002).

5. "Finance Your Start-up with Credit Cards? Google Did."

and any fees.[6] Since a line of credit is being obtained, interest is charged only on the amount drawn down.

Vendor Financing

The use of suppliers to provide funding for the purchase of equipment, material needed for production, and services needed for production is known as *vendor financing* or *trade credit*. The potential benefit to vendors of offering attractive trade credit terms is that it may stimulate sales, and vendors do compete on the trade credit terms that they provide. Trade credit works as follows. Suppose the founders of a company make a purchase from a vendor. The vendor might give the founders a specified time period to make the payment, and if payment is made within the designated time period, the founders are permitted to take a discount from the invoice price. The time period in which the founders are entitled to take the discount is called the ***discount period***. Once the discount period passes, the company must pay the full invoice price.

The terms of trade credit are conventionally expressed as "x/y, net z," where x is the discount percentage, y is the number of days in the discount period, and z is the number of days when the full payment is due. For example, if a company makes a purchase from a vendor of $100,000 based on trade credit terms of 2/15, net 45, this means that if by the fifteenth day a payment is made, the founders can take a discount of 2% of the $100,000, or $2,000. Thus the payment to the vendor would be $98,000. If the payment is made any time after the fifteenth day, the full amount of the payment must be made and it must be made by the forty-fifth day.

If the discount is not taken, vendor financing becomes another form of debt financing and it too comes with a cost, although there is no stated interest rate. Instead, there is an implicit interest rate that should be estimated before this form of debt financing is used, and it should be compared to alternative forms of debt financing. The implicit interest rate can be determined as follows using the previous illustration. By not taking the $2,000 discount, the founders are effectively borrowing $98,000 for thirty days. (Note that the firm is not borrowing $100,000.) The cost of borrowing for thirty days is therefore $2,000/$98,000, or 2.04%. Although there are different methods for annualizing a thirty-day interest rate, to keep it simple, we can multiply by twelve. Thus the implicit interest cost is 24.48%.

Bear in mind that trade credit is an important competitive tool for a vendor. Some vendors, to encourage business, may be willing to work with startup companies to provide more accommodating trade credit terms.

Small Business Administration Loans

The U.S. Small Business Administration (SBA) is an independent agency of the U.S. government created by the Small Business Act of 1953. Its mission is to "aid, counsel, assist

---

6. See Analisa Nazareno, "Understanding How Credit Card Minimum Payments Are Set," CreditCards.com, December 17, 2008, http://www.creditcards.com/credit-card-news/minimum-credit-card-payments-1267.php.

and protect the interests of small business concerns, to preserve free competitive enterprise and to maintain and strengthen the overall economy of our nation."[7]

Although the term "SBA loan" may suggest that the SBA is the lender, that is not the case. Participating banks and other lenders make the loans. It is through these lending entities that an entrepreneur must obtain a loan. A majority of the loan is then guaranteed by the SBA.

The SBA has loan programs for a wide range of purposes: (1) starting and expanding businesses, (2) disaster loans, (3) export assistance loans, (4) veteran and military community loans, and (5) special-purpose loans. The relevant loan program for entrepreneurs of high-tech startups is the first loan program, that for starting and expanding businesses. Within this category there are three loan programs:

- Basic 7(a) Loan Program
- Certified Development Company 504 Loan Program
- Microloan Program

Basic 7(a) Loan Program   The Basic 7(a) Loan Program (hereafter referred to simply as a 7(a) loan) is the program most often used for starting, acquiring, or expanding a business.[8] The loan is made not to the entrepreneur but to his or her business. Consequently, eligibility for a loan is based on the business rather than on the entrepreneur. The maximum amount available for a 7(a) loan is $5 million.

Although the SBA does not specify what types of businesses are eligible, it does identify certain characteristics of those that are eligible. They must:

- Operate for profit
- Be small, as defined by SBA
- Be engaged in, or propose to do business in, the United States or its possessions
- Have reasonable invested equity
- Use alternative financial resources, including personal assets, before seeking financial assistance
- Be able to demonstrate a need for the loan proceeds
- Use the funds for a sound business purpose
- Not be delinquent on any existing debt obligations to the U.S. government.[9]

The SBA also specifies the types of businesses that are not eligible for a loan.

The maturity of 7(a) loans is based on three factors: the ability of the business to repay the loan, the purpose of the loan proceeds, and the useful life of the assets financed by the loan. The maturity for loans to purchase equipment is a maximum of ten years and for real estate it is twenty-five years. When the proceeds are used for working capital, the maturity

---

7. See the website http://www.sba.gov/about-sba/what_we_do/mission.
8. Information about the Basic 7(a) Loan Program was obtained from several articles posted on the SBA website.
9. See the website http://www.sba.gov/content/7a-loan-program-eligibility.

cannot exceed seven years. Lines of credit and short-term loans are available for seasonal working capital needs.

Loans can carry a fixed or variable (i.e., floating) interest rate. Although the interest rate that the lender may charge is subject to a maximum rate imposed by the SBA, the interest rate for a 7(a) loan is the result of the negotiation between the borrower and the SBA-approved lender. There are also fees that relate to the guarantee provided by the SBA (i.e., guarantee fee). The fee is based not on the amount of the loan but on the amount that the SBA guarantees. That fee is paid by the lender, with the lender having the option to pass it along to the borrower.

The maximum guarantee that the SBA will provide is 85% of the loan amount up to $150,000 and drops to 75% on loans of more than that amount. Since the maximum 7(a) loan is $5 million, this means that the maximum guarantee is $3.75 million.

The repayment of the principal and interest on a fixed-rate loan is on a monthly basis with the payment set so as to fully amortize the loan. This means that each month the borrower pays principal and interest, with the principal repayment being sufficient to repay the full amount borrowed by the loan's maturity date. Because the interest rate changes for variable-rate loans, a different type of repayment schedule has to be set up. There is the possibility of establishing monthly payments whereby for a specified period of time only interest is paid, and after that period the monthly payments include interest plus principal repayment. A 7(a) loan may not be a balloon loan (i.e., carrying only monthly interest payments and no principal repayment), with the amount borrowed being paid at the maturity date.

Typically loans by banks that an entrepreneur may seek are loans that are secured by some asset (referred to as collateral) and a personal guarantee. Every 7(a) loan is expected to be fully secured. However, failure to provide sufficient collateral is not the basis for SBA rejecting an application for a loan if that is the only unfavorable factor, for all owners of 20% or more of the equity of the business must provide a personal guarantee. SBA participating lenders can require personal guarantees by owners with less than 20% ownership, and they may require liens on the personal assets of the owners.

Certified Development Company 504 Loan Program   The Certified Development Company 504 Loan Program (or, more simply, 504 loan) provides loans solely for the acquisition of fixed assets (equipment and real estate). Entrepreneurs can use this type of loan for "bricks-and-mortar" financing. The interest rate for the loan is fixed. There are three parts to the loan: (1) 10%, put up by the borrower; (2) 50%, supplied by a banking partner; and (3) 40%, supplied by a Certified Development Company (CDC). The CDC provider, a unique entity involved in a 504 loan, is a nonprofit corporation that provides loans for the purpose of fostering the growth of small businesses in the CDC's local community.

Microloan Program   The Microloan Program provides short-term loans to businesses for working capital and the financing of inventory, supplies, furniture, fixtures, and machinery or equipment. The amount of the loan cannot exceed $35,000.

Angel Investors and Angel Groups

Between the time that founders have exhausted funding sources from their personal assets and those of family and friends and before venture capitalists have stepped up to provide funding, the primary source of early-stage funding is so-called ***angel investors***.[10] Angel investing is available to individuals who qualify under the SEC's definition of "accredited investors," as explained in the previous chapter. Angel investors are wealthy individuals who typically invest between $150,000 and $2 million. The funding vehicle used is convertible notes, which we describe in the next chapter.

In addition to providing funding, angel investors provide strategic planning advice, assist in team building, and provide contacts for developing key partnerships and further fundraising. There are approximately 270,000 active angel investors in the United States.[11] It is estimated that in 2012, angel investors invested about $23 billion in more than 67,000 startup companies, representing nearly 90% of the outside capital for these ventures. Compared to the number of startup companies that venture capital (VC) firms invested in, angel investors provided funding for roughly twenty times more, even though VC firms invested $27 billion.[12] Although venture capitalists are credited with success stories such as assisting Apple, AOL, Amazon.com, Facebook, and Google in early-stage financing, for seed stage financing these companies all relied on angel financing.

Angel Groups   Since the mid-1990s, angel investors typically have invested through groups or networks. Some of the groups specialize in particular industries and may restrict their investments to particular regions of the country. Business schools that have entrepreneurship programs have formed angel groups of alumni, who typically invest a minimum of $25,000.[13]

The Angel Capital Association, a trade association that supports the American professional angel community and provides a directory of angel investors, reports that within the United States and Canada there are 330 angel groups active in the startup business.[14] According to the first quarter 2013 Halo Report, a report on angel group investment activity

10. The term "angel investor" originally referred to wealthy individuals who provided funding for Broadway theatrical productions.
11. See the website http://www.angelcapitalassociation.org/blog/why-is-the-aca-making-a-big-deal-about-the-sec-ruling-on-general-solicitation.
12. Ibid.
13. The Angel Capital Association estimated there are approximately forty angel groups affiliated with universities: http://www.businessweek.com/articles/2012-07-02/mba-startups-find-alumni-angels-with-money-to-burn.
14. See the website http://www.angelcapitalassociation.org.

published each quarter by the Angel Resource Institute in collaboration with Silicon Valley Bank and CB Insights, 72% of angel group deals were concentrated in three sectors, the Internet, health care, and mobile companies, with those three sectors receiving 64% of the dollar amount invested by angel groups.[15] The Halo Report also provided the following data: (1) the median round size was $680,000, but when angel groups coinvested with other types of investors, the median round size was $1.5 million; (2) the pre-money valuations (i.e., valuation prior to the angel financing) was $2.5 million; and (3) about 81% of the deals were completed in the home state of the angel group.

There are four benefits for angel investors to forming an angel group to collectively evaluate and invest in startups. First, pooling funds allows investing in more startups, which in theory reduces risk through diversification. Second, the cost of information gathering and contracting can be shared by members of the group. Third, the diverse expertise among members of the angel group reduces the risk of not taking into account key factors that may lead to a potentially good venture being overlooked. Finally, the greater name recognition of a group of wealthy individuals, as opposed to a single individual, is likely to result in more deals being shown.

From an angel investor's perspective, a disadvantage of participating in (i.e., becoming a member of) an angel group is the time commitment required. Members must attend events, particularly participation in the screening of deals.

Let's illustrate the mission, composition, and review process of the Band of Angels, Silicon Valley's oldest seed funding organization. Founded in 1994, the group has more than 150 members.[16] Members include former and current executives of high-tech companies, including founders of such companies as Symantec, Logitech, and National Semiconductor. Reflecting the diverse expertise of its members in the high-tech sector, the Band of Angels has invested about $225 million since 1994 in 254 companies across the high-tech sector: Internet/web services, software, network/telecommunications, life sciences/biotechnology, semiconductor, and electronics/industry. No investments are generally made in non-high-tech startups. Of the 254 companies for which Band of Angels has provided seed funding, ten resulted in IPOs and fifty-four were acquired.

The deal criteria statement for this angel group is as follows:

The Band is primarily focused on seed stage high technology companies with strong teams, proprietary technology, and big markets. We invest in the range of $300k to $750k, but often lead a syndication of $2–3M. The largest investment ever made by the Band was $3.3M. Valuation depends on many things but few companies successfully raise financing from the Band at valuations greater than $5M.

---

15. See the website http://www.angelresource.org/en/Research/Halo-Report.aspx.
16. The information and quotations here are from the website of the Band of Angels as of September 2013: http://www.bandangels.com.

The formal process for reviewing startup investment candidates is as follows. Every month, the Band of Angels considers three startups selected by the Deal Screening Committee, which screens more than fifty startups each month. The seven members on the committee serve for twelve months. The members are selected so as to represent each of the high-tech categories of semiconductors, software, Internet, life sciences, and networking/telecommunications.

The review and selection process, as per the website, is:

If you submit a plan for review to the Band it will be forwarded to a prescreen committee for review. This committee is made up of experts from every high tech category including life science, semiconductor, software, and internet. This committee reviews close to 50 plans a month and selects 6 for an invitation to the Deal Screening Committee. If your plan makes it this far you will be asked to place it in a standard format and come to a meeting held the last Wednesday of each month. There, six Band members (one from each major discipline) will ask you questions about the company for 15 minutes to better understand the printed material. This Committee then selects three companies and one runner up, for presentation to the full Band of Angels.

Once the three companies are selected, the process is as follows:

The three selected companies will present to the full Band of Angels at the monthly dinner meeting held the second or third Wednesday of each month. In the two weeks between selection and presentation the Band provides value-added preparatory services to the companies. In concert with selected service providers the Band will help the companies refine both their written and oral presentations in preparation for the Band dinners. These dinners are held the second or third Wednesday of the following month; typically 40 people attend a dinner. Each company has 10 minutes to present followed by a five minute Q/A session.

The follow-up process is then as follows:

Band members invest directly; there is no legal pooling of resources. However, within two weeks of the dinner most companies that present to the Band will have scheduled a follow up meeting with interested members who may ask additional questions for the company. This also provides an opportunity for an organized syndicate of individual angels to be formed for the purpose of evaluating the company, negotiating a set of terms, and executing an investment.

To see how competitive the process is, more than 700 deals are considered each year. In 2012, only thirteen startups were selected for funding.

Angel Investors and Performance of Startups   One study investigated the role of funding for high-growth startup firms by angel investors in terms of the growth, survival, and access to follow-up funding.[17] The four key findings of the study were the following:

---

17. William R. Kerr, Josh Lerner, and Antoinette Schoar, "The Consequences of Entrepreneurial Finance: A Regression Discontinuity Analysis," Harvard Business School Working Paper 10–086, 2010.

- The success of a startup is highly predicted by the level of interest that angel investors exhibit during the initial presentation and by the follow-up due diligence performed by angel investors.

- Startups are more likely to survive at least four years if they have angel funding.

- Startups are more likely to raise follow-up funding outside the angel group if they obtain funding from angel investors.

- There is more likely to be an improvement in startup performance and growth if there is angel investor funding.

Moreover, the study found that access to capital per say may not be the most important thing that angel groups provide entrepreneurs of startup firms. Instead, it may be the benefits of advising and the furnishing of business contacts that provide the greatest value.

Returns Earned by Angel Investors   There is disagreement as to whether angel investors earn attractive returns from the ventures in which they invest.[18] As Robert Wiltbank of Willamette University writes:

The investing world seemed certain that angel investors were rubes. Conventional wisdom dictated that they made reckless investments in very early-stage ventures mostly doomed to fail. And whenever they might come close to succeeding, savvy "professional" investors would just swoop in, cram them down, and win the real returns. In addition, angels were up against a selection problem: All the best entrepreneurs and opportunities would naturally gravitate to the best venture capital funds, leaving only the "scraps" for angel investors.[19]

Wiltbank and Warren Boeker studied the returns on angel investments that were completed by 2007 using the most comprehensive data available.[20] Their findings for returns on group-affiliated angel investments were as follows:

- The average was 2.6 times the return on investment after 3.5 years.

- Almost 48% of exited investments provided a return that was greater than the amount invested by the angel group, or equivalently, 52% resulted in a loss.

- There were returns of more than ten times the amount invested for 7% of the exited investments.

The above findings are the returns for individual ventures. When looking at angel investor portfolios, Wiltbank and Boeker found that only 39% of the portfolios realized a loss

18. For arguments suggesting why angel investors do not make money, see Andy Racheff, "Why Angel Investors Don't Make Money … And Advice for People Who Are Going to Become Angels Anyway," *TechCrunch,* September 20, 2012, http://techcrunch.com/2012/09/30/why-angel-investors-dont-make-money-and-advice-for-people-who-are-going-to-become-angels-anyway.

19. Robert Wiltbank, "Angel Investors Do Make Money: Data Shows 2.5× Returns Overall," *TechCrunch,* October 13, 2012, http://techcrunch.com/2012/10/13/angel-investors-make-2-5x-returns-overall.

20. Robert Wiltbank and Warren Boeker, "Returns to Angel Investors in Groups," November 1, 2007, http://ssrn.com/abstract=1028592.

(in contrast to 52% of individual investments). Overall, the findings appear to be comparable to those of the venture capitalists we describe in this chapter.

Instead of studying actual returns on angel investments, Ramon P. DeGennaro and Gerlad P. Dwyer in a study conducted under the auspices of the Federal Reserve Bank of Atlanta investigated the expected returns driving investments.[21] For their sample of 588 angel investments over the period 1972–2007, which included 419 investments that were completed by the end of 2007 (i.e., exited investments),[22] they found that angel investors could expect to earn net returns[23] of 70% in excess of the risk-free rate of return available in the market for an average holding period of 3.67 years. This is roughly the same profile that has been found for venture capitalists.[24]

Super Angels

Although venture capitalists invest primarily in first-round financing, there are VC firms that do provide seed financing. These firms, referred to as **super angels**, are set up as private equity firms. (A description of private equity firms is provided when we describe VC firms later in this chapter.) They differ from traditional VC firms in that the amount that can be raised from super angels is less.

Equity Crowdfunding Platforms

Crowdfunding is the practice of raising funds for a startup from a large number of investors who invest small sums. Typically the funds are raised via the Internet. There are two types of crowdfunding: reward (donation) crowdfunding and equity crowdfunding.[25] Our focus here is on **equity crowdfunding**, which allows investors to obtain an equity interest in a startup company.

Any startup that is interested in raising equity capital has to comply with the federal securities rules dealing with general solicitation and advertising as set forth by the SEC and states, as explained in chapter 5. Prior to April 5, 2012, the way equity crowdfunding operates would have prevented the raising of funds in this way. However, provisions in the Jumpstart Our Business Startups Act (JOBS Act) made possible the soliciting of funds by startups, allowing for equity crowdfunding. Since that time, numerous equity crowdfunding platforms have been started.

There are several estimates of the potential growth of equity crowdfunding as a source of seed funding. One estimate by Massolution, a firm that provides crowdfunding industry

21. Ramon P. DeGennaro and Gerald P. Dwyer, "Expected Returns to Stock Investments by Angel Investors in Groups," Working Paper 2010–14, Federal Reserve Bank of Atlanta, August 2010, https://www.frbatlanta.org/research/publications/wp/2010/14.aspx.
22. The data used were from the Angel Investor Performance Project.
23. The net return is the internal rate of return, a profitability measure that we discuss in chapter 17 when we cover valuation.
24. John H. Campbell, "The Risk and Return of Venture Capital," *Journal of Financial Economics* 75 (January 2006): 3–52.
25. Tanya Prive, "Crowdfunding: It's Not Just for Startups," *Forbes,* February 6, 2013, http://www.forbes.com/sites/tanyaprive/2013/02/06/crowdfunding-its-not-just-for-startups.

reports, was that the global crowdfunding market would reach $34.4 billion in 2015. The estimate was based on 1,250 crowdfunding platforms throughout the world. To appreciate the growth in the global crowdfunding market, consider that Massolution's 2013 forecast was only $5.1 billion, a forecast that was realized.[26]

Seed Accelerators

Seed accelerators provide a vehicle for founders to launch a company in a high-tech industry. They do so by providing seed stage financing in exchange for a small equity stake in the startup. The amount of funding available from accelerators ranges from $20,000 to $100,000 in exchange for 2% to 10% equity in the company. Funding is in the form of a convertible note, the same instrument used by angel investors and described in the next chapter.

What is key for founders who are considering seed accelerators is the opportunity to gain access not just to needed funding but to other potential investors, training in a short period of time, temporary office space, and a team of experts. By providing mentoring for founders, seed accelerators prepare founders to present their ideas for a product or service to potential venture capitalists. At the conclusion of the program (i.e., on graduation from the program), there is a "demo day" at which founders can do so before potential investors and the press.

Reports by Yael Hochberg and Kristen Kamath of Northwestern University, who are the co-administrators of the National Seed Accelerator Rankings, provide helpful information to founders in selecting seed accelerators. Hochberg and Kamath rank seed accelerators that offer a small stipend in exchange for equity, mentorship, office space, and training sessions of less than one year, and that end with a demo day. The six criteria that they use for ranking include:

- *Qualified financing activity*: Qualified financing occurs within twelve months after the founders graduate from the program; founders must have raised at least $350,000.

- *Qualified exits*: There is an IPO or an acquisition in the amount of at least $1 million for the founders.

- *Reputation with leading venture capitalists*: This metric is based on responses from interviews with VC firms.

- *Alumni network*: The network is measured by the number of startups whose founders have graduated from the program.

- *Equity taken*: This is measured by the percentage of the startup's equity that the founders must grant to the accelerator in order to obtain the stipend and participate in the program.

---

26. "Global Crowdfunding Market to Reach $34.4B in 2015, Predicts Massolution's 2015CF Industry Report," Research report by Massolution.

- *Stipend*: Funds are provided to the founders to support the support the startup's activities and the living expenses of the founder during the program.

Based on these criteria and the eligible accelerators at the time of the study, the U.S. Seed Accelerator Rankings in 2013 (released in March 10, 2014), the third year for which rankings are available, were as follows:[27]

1. Y Combinator	6. Alpha Lab (tie)	11. BetaSpring
2. Techstars	6. Capital Innovators (tie)	12. BoomStartup (tie)
3. Angelpad	8. Tech Wildcatters	12. ERA (tie)
4. Mucker Lab	9. Surge	12. JumpStart Foundery (tie)
5. Launchpad LA	10. Brandery	15. Dreamit

The report by Hochberg and Kamath provides two further insights into the future developments in the industry. The first is the trend toward specialization in specific industries such as health care, energy, and big data and cloud-based computing and services. The second is the partnering of accelerator programs with established firms. The example they cite is the partnering of Microsoft with TechStars to mentor the founders of startups for the purpose of developing applications using the Kinect for Windows platform.

Incubators

Another type of program that mentors entrepreneurs and provides other similar services as a seed accelerator is an incubator. Entrepreneurs use incubator programs to develop their ideas and businesses. Because incubators provide similar support for entrepreneurs as seed accelerators, often the terms seed accelerator and incubator are used interchangeably. However, there are several differences between the two.

Incubator programs typically take three to five years to complete, in contrast to the programs offered by seed accelerators, which typically last less than twelve months. As a result, seed accelerators typically get a startup going faster than an incubator does, and this acceleration of business development is important for the financial objective of a seed accelerator: help the startup get angel or VC financing so that a return can be realized on the accelerator's investment. To accomplish this, seed accelerators, unlike incubators, provide better media exposure for the startups in their program.

The mentoring for startups in an incubator program is typically less important than another important resource an incubator can provide: a working space for the founders. This is particularly important for startups in the life sciences industry. Several companies

---

27. The 2013 rankings are taken from http://yael-hochberg.com/rankings.htm. The 2012 rankings were as follows: 1—Y Combinator; 2—TechStars Boulder; 3—KickLabs; 4—i/o Ventures; 5—Excelerate Labs; 6—AngelPad; 7—TechStars NYC; 8—TechStars Boston; 9—Launchpad LA; 10—500 Startups; 11—DreamIt Ventures; 12—TechStars Seattle; 13—NYC SeedStart; 14—Entrepreneurs Roundtable Accelerator; 15—The Brandery. See http://yael-hochberg.com/Accelerator%20Companion%20FINAL.pdf.

may share the same working space, giving entrepreneurs the opportunity to interact and potentially build relationships with other entrepreneurs.

Finally, as explained earlier, seed accelerators extract a small amount of equity from the startups that are part of their program. Incubators typically charge rent for the facilities or a monthly fee or membership charge in lieu of an equity share.

An example of this is Janssen Labs in San Diego, which is part of Johnson & Johnson's external research and development engine that was opened in early 2012, a 40,000 square foot facility for independent startups for health care companies. As stated on its website:

Janssen Labs offers a variety of offerings between the flagship and satellite facilities including singular bench tops, modular wet lab units and office space on a short-term basis, allowing companies to pay only for the space they need, with an option to quickly expand when they have the resources to do so. Companies residing at Janssen Labs sites also have access to core research labs hosting specialized capital equipment and shared administrative areas. Additionally, Janssen Labs produces a year-round curriculum designed to assist innovators along the commercialization continuum. Janssen Labs is an open innovation model, and the agreement for space does not grant Janssen any stake in the companies, nor will the companies have a guaranteed future affiliation with Janssen; but the model is designed to initiate a dialogue early and foster long term relationships with innovators in healthcare.[28]

PRE-IPO EXPANSION FINANCING

Until about 2010, the primary sources for expansion financing were traditional VC firms, corporate VC firms, and online VC funds. The most recent entrants providing financing for startup companies in the very late stages are institutional investors such as mutual funds and hedge funds.

Venture Capitalists

According to the National Venture Capital Association (NVCA), VC firms are "professional, institutional managers of risk capital that enables and supports the most innovative and promising companies."[29] The funds invested in a startup business are in the form of equity. The investments are typically made in a series or rounds that typically occur every two years, based on predetermined milestones being reaching by the startup company. The equity investments are typically highly illiquid and have little value until the company matures, which is expected to take from five to eight years after the company is launched.

---

28. See the website https://www.janssenlabs.com/about/overview.

29. National Venture Capital Association, "Venture Capital: 101: What Is Venture Capital?," http://www.nvca.org/index.php?option=com_docman&task. From a regulatory perspective, there was a concern that under the Dodd-Frank Act, VC funds, hedge funds, and private equity firms would need to provide certain information to the SEC. Fortunately for VC firms, the SEC in 2011 provided a definition of a VC fund that avoided this requirement. The SEC defined a VC fund as one that invests in "qualifying investments." A qualifying investment is mainly in shares of private companies. A VC fund, however, is permitted to invest 20% in nonqualifying investments. It may not use significant leverage.

Because VC firms take equity positions in typically private companies, how do they differ from private equity firms that invest in private companies? VC firms are often said to be a special type of private equity firm that invests in startup companies.[30] In contrast, the typical private equity firm invests in mature companies that are seeking to go private or are viewed to be underperforming and have the potential for highly attractive returns. One important difference in how returns are generated between the investments made by VC firms and those made by private equity firms is the use of leverage by the latter.

In 2015, VC investments were approximately $59.1 billion and were used to finance the following stages, as categorized by the NCVA: seeding stage, 2%; early stage, 34%; late stage, 27%; and expansion stage, 37%. Of the $59.1 billion, $42.1 billion was invested in 2,620 information technology companies, $10.9 billion in 664 medical/health/life sciences companies, and the balance, $6.1 billion, in 420 non-high-tech companies. Of the nine industry sectors in which investments were made by VC firms in 2015, half were in two industry sectors: the software sector (40%) and biotechnology sector (13%).[31]

According to the NCVA, usually only 10% of the business plans that are submitted to a VC firm for funding are given serious consideration and only 1% of the submitted business plans are eventually funded.

Because of the long-term investment in a startup company, the partners of a VC firm actively engage in various aspects of the company in which they invest. At a minimum, this takes the form of participation in corporate governance by obtaining one or more seats on the board of directors.

The portfolio of ventures created by a VC firm is referred to as the "VC fund," and the process for forming it is as follows. Typically a limited partnership[32] is formed by the VC firm. In a limited partnership there are general partners and limited partners. The former manage the investment portfolio of ventures and have unlimited liability, while the latter do not participate in the selection of ventures to be included in the investment portfolio and have limited liability. For a VC fund, the VC firm is the general partner and the limited partners are the outside investors from whom the VC firm obtains commitments to invest in the VC fund. Thus, an investor does not invest in the capital venture firm or in an individual venture but rather in a particular VC fund (i.e., portfolio of ventures).

The investors in the VC funds created by VC firms are institutional investors, family offices, and high-net-worth individuals. Institutional investors include pension funds, insurance companies, endowments, and foundations. Family offices are entities that manage the financial and personal affairs of a wealthy family.

---

30. Each year *Forbes* publishes a list of the top ten VC firms in the world and the top ten VC investors in the world. Forbes refers to this as the "Midas List."

31. The data in this paragraph were taken from figures 5.0, 6.0, and 7.0 in *National Venture Capital Association Yearbook 2016*, prepared by Thomas Reuters.

32. The limited partnership form of business organization is explained in chapter 3.

A VC fund is created when the VC firm gets sufficient commitments from investors. As investors provide cash to the VC firm, the VC fund's general partners make the investments in ventures that are identified by the firm's analysts. Because there are multiple rounds of financing, a certain amount in reserves is set aside for those future rounds. The VC fund's return is realized when the venture either goes public by way of an IPO, is acquired by another company, or merges with another company.

An article published in the May 2013 issue of the *Harvard Business Review* and authored by Diane Mulcahy,[33] a former venture capitalist and a director of private equity for the Ewing Marion Kauffman Foundation,[34] explains myths that she believes exist about venture capitalists. Her motivation for busting the six myths was "to help company founders develop a more realistic sense of the industry and what it offers." Mulcahy's six myths are:

Myth 1: The primary source of funding for startup companies is venture capitalists.

Myth 2: There is a big risk that a venture capitalist takes when investing in a startup.

Myth 3: Valuable advice and mentoring is provided by most venture capitalists.

Myth 4: The returns generated by VC firms are spectacular.

Myth 5: The larger the VC fund, the better.

Myth 6: Venture capitalists are innovators.

In disputing myth 1, Mulcahy notes that (1) VC funds have provided capital for fewer than 1% of U.S. companies and (2) in contrast to angel investors, whose numbers are growing, the VC industry is contracting. Myth 2 is clear: it is the investors in VC funds who are accepting the risks associated with investing in startups, not the VC firm that is the general partner of a VC fund. Not all VC firms commit the same amount of time to advising and mentoring a startup company (myth 3). This means that founders must perform due diligence in selecting a VC firm so that the anticipated involvement sought will be provided by the firm selected. As for myth 4, regarding returns performance, we discuss that further below. Suffice it to say that the empirical evidence does not support the view that VC funds have generated anything near spectacular returns. Empirical evidence also fails to support the view that the larger the VC fund, the better (myth 5). In particular, the evidence shows that as a VC fund's size increases above $250 million, performance declines. Finally, while venture capitalists may provide funding for founders with innovative ideas that need to be commercialized, management of VC firms has not been innovative over the past two decades, according to Mulcahy (myth 6). She concludes by saying that although venture capitalists will play a significant role in funding startups in the future, it will be less than in the past because the VC industry is contracting as new funding sources become available.

33. Diane Mulcahy, "Six Myths about Venture Capitalists," *Harvard Business Review,* May 2013, https://hbr.org/2013/05/six-myths-about-venture-capitalists.

34. This foundation is one of the largest private foundations in the United States, with assets of approximately $2 billion.

Venture Capital outside the United States   In 2014, $86.7 billion was invested by VC funds in 6,507 deals throughout the world, according to a study by Ernst & Young, with the average deal size being $16.7 million. According to the study, the amount of funding by VC firms was highest in the United States, China, and Europe.

In Europe, the European Union (EU) has addressed the issue of the importance of VC funding as an alternative to bank financing for startup and small companies. The European Commission (EC) in its publications and regulatory plans has stressed the important role of VC funds not only in providing an alternative to bank financing but also for the nonfinancial support provided by VC investors. In its assessment of the impact of venture capitalists on small and medium-sized enterprises (SMEs), the EC concluded that "SMEs that rely on venture capital financing fare better than those that receive no venture capital backing."

Although VC funds have participated in the European market, outside Europe nonbank financing for startups, such as VC funding, is used to a greater extent. The problem has been that the relatively small size of European VC funds has been an obstacle to achieving economies of scale and has, as a result, prevented the development of specialized VC funds for high-tech companies. To overcome the impediments to the growth of the European VC market, the EU approved an action plan in September 2015 for instituting measures that allow VC firms to market their funds across the EU member countries using a single set of regulations. The funds, called "European Venture Capital Funds," require that certain provisions be met before VC firms can use that label in marketing their funds. More specifically, the fund manager must prove that a high percentage of investments (70% of the capital received from investors) is invested in young and innovative companies. The expectation is that investment funds that can be obtained by VC funds will grow by making those funds more attractive to investors. In turn, it is expected that larger VC funds will translate into more capital for specialized industries, such as those in the high-tech area.

In Southeast Asia, the VC industry is in its infancy. Singapore is seeking to be the Silicon Valley of Southeast Asia. In 2013, for example, VC funding in high-tech companies in Singapore was $1.71 billion, exceeding that of other Southeast Asian countries except China ($3.46 billion). In Israel, VC funding was about $1 billion, ranking Israel ninth out of 148 economies for VC funding availability, according to *The World Economic Forum Global Competitiveness Yearbook 2014–2015*, and third according to the World Competitiveness Scoreboard 2014.

Corporate Venture Capitalists

Corporate venture capitalists are corporations that invest in startups that have the potential for providing a good strategic fit with their company's offerings. Although we have described VC funds as sources for expansion financing, they are also involved in the seed phases of early-stage financing.

Examples of corporate venture funds include Dell Venture, Google Ventures, Cisco Investments, Lilly Ventures, Johnson & Johnson Development Corporation, Microsoft Ventures, Intel Capital, and Samsung Ventures. The most active corporate venture funds in the third quarter of 2013 according to *Corporate Venture Capital Report,* authored by CB Insights, was Google Ventures, followed by Intel Capital.[35] Tied for third place were Samsung Ventures, SAP Ventures, and Cisco Investments. A benefit of obtaining funding from corporate venture capitalists is that they provide the founders with access to corporate distribution channels and infrastructure, as well as potential strategic partners.

Corporate venture funds were an important source of startup funding during the first half of 2011, a time when traditional VC firms were finding it difficult to raise investment funds because of the global financial crisis. At that time, corporate venture funds provided 11% of VC financing.[36] According to the *Corporate Venture Capital Report*, in the third quarter of 2013, investments by corporate venture funds reached their highest level since 2011, with $2.1 billion spread over 140 investments. In terms of all VC financing, corporate VC funds accounted for 30%. This trend may be expected to continue as the cash build-up on corporate balance sheets increases and traditional VC firms continue to find it difficult to raise funds.

The dollar investment that is available from corporate venture funds is greater than that provided by traditional VC firms. The average deal size for corporate VC funds in the third quarter of 2013, according to the *Corporate Venture Capital Report,* was $17 million; the average for overall VC funding was $9.3 million.

The potential benefits to the corporate venture fund's parent company are threefold.[37] First, it may help the parent company respond to technological changes faster than traditional research and development programs. Josh Lerner of the Harvard Business School cites Lilly Ventures as an example of a corporate venture fund that helped its parent company, the pharmaceutical company Eli Lilly, "catch up with the rapid advances in bioscience that were threatening to render their chemistry-based expertise irrelevant."[38] Second, there are potentially attractive financial returns that can be realized. Finally, there is the potential for a corporate venture fund to provide a boost to the parent company's product or services as a result of technological spillover.

Empirical evidence reported by Hyunsung Daniel Kang and Vikram Nanda based on an analysis of technological and financial returns generated by investments by 796 corporate venture funds in the biopharmaceutical industry between 1985 and 2006 supports this third benefit. They found that the technological advances attributable to investments made by corporate venture funds did increase the parent corporation's value. However, in contrast to the positive spillover effect generated by technology on corporate value, they found only a negligible effect on financial returns.[39]

35. *Q3 2013 Corporate Venture Capital Report,* CBInsights, October 24, 2013, http://www.cbinsights.com/blog/corporate-venture-capital-q3-2013.

36. Josh Lerner, "Corporate Venturing," *Harvard Business Review*, October 2013, 86–94.

37. These potential benefits were identified in Lerner, "Corporate Venturing."

38. Lerner, "Corporate Venturing," 86.

39. Hyunsung D. Kang and Vikram K. Nanda, "Technological Spillovers and Financial Returns in Corporate Venture Capital," Working Paper, Georgia Institute of Technology, March 2011, http://www.researchgate.net/publication/256016429_Technological_Spillovers_and_Financial_Returns_in_Corporate_Venture_Capital.

Online Venture Capital Funds

In May 2012, a platform was launched by FundersClub to allow accredited investors to become equity holders in startup ventures by selecting ventures online.[40] At the time of launch, FundersClub had 5,000 members (i.e., accredited investors). There are two types of funds offered to its members: single-company funds and multicompany funds that are managed by FundersClub. For a single-company fund, the member selects from a pre-screened list of startup companies whose investment profile is provided. In contrast, for a multicompany fund, an investor is investing in a portfolio of yet to be determined startup companies where selection of the companies is based on an investment strategy formulated and then executed by the FundersClub Investment Committee.[41]

Although at the time of launch, 500 of the 5,000 members of the FundersClub invested approximately $2.5 million in nine different funds, the typical investment made by investors ranges from $2,500 to $250,000. The startup companies available to invest in, which are early-, mid-, and late-stage private U.S. technology companies, are prescreened by the FundersClub Investment Committee and the FundersClub Panel each week. The startup companies that are screened typically are identified from the FundersClub network and partners. According to FundersClub, fewer than 5% of the ventures vetted are selected to be listed on its website for members to review. Using a web-based platform, members can browse the prescreened startup companies, review their investment profile (which includes a pitch video by the founders), and sign the legal documents. Members also have the opportunity to query a startup company's founder on a moderated question-and-answer forum. To keep investors up-to-date after they invest in a startup company, as well as potentially to get them involved further, the startup company identifies in its profile the manner in which it will communicate with its investors. There are several methods of communication, such as quarterly email updates or inclusion in an "insider investor distribution list," to inform investors of significant milestones, developments that have been achieved, and video messages from the startup company's founders.

The FundersClub platform might seem like crowdfunding as described earlier in this chapter. However, it is not, because investors in crowdfunding each invest a sum in one company on an individual basis. FundersClub instead pools the amount invested by individuals and then creates a VC fund to invest either in a single startup company or in a portfolio of startup companies. Hence this investment approach is no different from what traditional venture capitalists do in creating VC funds and can be correctly described as an "online VC fund." To avoid potential conflicts in the selection of startups included in one of the funds, FundersClub does not charge startup companies to be included on its platform.

---

40. There was a regulatory issue as to whether FundersClub was a registered broker-dealer and therefore had to be registered with the SEC as such. FundersClub refuted this position taken by the SEC, arguing that it was a VC adviser that was working online instead of offline. In May 2012, FundersClub received from the SEC a "no-action letter," indicating that the SEC would not recommend enforcement action.
41. The shareholder of record for both types of funds is FundersClub.

Institutional Investors: Mutual Funds and Hedge Funds

The latest entrants providing expansion financing for new ventures prior to an IPO, acquisition, or merger are institutional investors. These investors include mutual funds[42] and hedge funds.

Like VC funds, these institutional investors are collective investment vehicles. Investors in these collective investment vehicles own a pro rata share of the fund's portfolio, which is managed by the fund's manager, who buys and sells securities. The value or price of each share of the portfolio, called the net asset value (NAV), equals the market value of the portfolio minus the liabilities divided by the number of shares owned by the fund's investors.

Several of the sponsors of mutual fund families, such as BlackRock Financial Management, Fidelity Investments, T. Rowe Price, Janus Capital Group, and Wellington Management, have invested in startup technology companies for certain of their funds. According to *CB Insight*, mutual funds and hedge funds invested $628 million in eleven startup technology companies in 2010. In the following three years they invested in more than thirty-one deals. In 2013, $2.5 billion was invested.[43] As of the first quarter of 2014, four of the fund sponsors had invested in thirteen deals.[44]

Since investments in startup companies are referred to as alternative investments or alt investments, mutual funds that invest a significant portion of the fund's assets in startup companies are referred to as a "alternative" or "alt" mutual funds. An example is New Horizons Fund, Inc. According to the fund's prospectus, the fund is an "aggressive stock fund seeking long-term capital growth primarily through investments in small, rapidly growing companies." The fund is permitted to invest in privately held companies. This fund's 2013 annual report indicated that early-stage companies accounted for about a third of the portfolio's holdings. An example of this fund's holdings in a startup company is its 2009 investment in Twitter.

An example of a startup company with mutual fund participation is Apptio. Founded in 2007, Apptio develops on-demand, cloud-based business software applications that "help companies align technology spending to business outcomes and automate IT processes like cost transparency, benchmarking, showback/chargeback, operational efficiency, and planning." The company's Series A financing of $7 million was obtained in the summer of 2007 from two VC firms and an angel investor. Following two additional rounds of financing,

---

42. Technically, there are mutual funds and closed-end funds. The former are open-end funds. There are differences in the structure of an open-end fund and a closed-end fund. For open-end funds the number of fund shares outstanding may change each day because the fund agrees to sell and redeem shares once each trading day. The price at which shares are sold or redeemed is determined at the close of the trading day at the NAV. For closed-end funds, the number of shares issued is fixed at the time of issuance. The price of a closed-end fund is determined by the market, just as that of any stock. The price of a closed-end fund can therefore sell at the NAV or at a price different from the NAV. Despite this technical difference in structure, it is common to refer to both open-end and closed-end funds as mutual funds, and we shall do so in our discussion.

43. "Hedge Funds and Mutual Funds Increase Investment Pace to Private Tech Companies," *CB Insights*, January 7, 2014.

44. Kristen Grind, "Mutual Funds Moonlight as Venture Capitalists: Firms Are Pushing into Silicon Valley at a Record Pace," *Wall Street Journal*, April 20, 2014, http://www.wsj.com/articles/SB10001424052702304626304579509494155922018.

Apptio's existing investors by May 2012 included four VC firms. In May 2012, Apptio obtained its fourth round of financing (Series D financing) of $50 million not only from its existing VC firms but also from T. Rowe Price, which acquired shares for several of the mutual funds it sponsors. One year later, in May 2013, Apptio added to its existing investors another mutual fund, Janus Capital, as well as another unnamed institutional investor, in a $45 million Series E round financing.

Late-stage expansion financing rounds prior to an IPO typically have not involved the megadeals or rounds that are now possible with institutional investors, involving amounts that can run into the hundreds of millions of dollars. The advantage to the founding teams of high-tech startup companies is that they can postpone going public (i.e., doing an IPO) so that when they do go public, they will have a better track record regarding growth and brand name. The motivation for these institutional investors is to get in on the pre-IPO valuation. For example, in the first quarter of 2014, Airbnb, Inc., was said to have raised about $450 million with institutional investor participation. To put this amount in perspective, with the exception of the Twitter IPO, no technology startup company had raised more than that amount when it went public.

INITIAL PUBLIC OFFERING

As the need for financing of a private company grows, the founders can turn to the general public to meet their equity needs. Public funding is obtained via an IPO. An IPO was long viewed as the golden grail of exit strategies. However, as explained in chapter 2, not all founders have as their exit plan strategy an IPO. For some founders, an IPO is a necessary evil to obtain adequate funding that was unavailable from traditional sources, including angel and VC financing. However, as explained above, new players in the market, institutional investors, have made the need for a quick rush to an IPO unnecessary for some firms. Instititutional investors can provide a large injection of funds to allow founders to expand without the need for public funding, and as a result, companies have delayed going public by several years.

The decision to go public begins with discussions with the company's financial adviser to determine whether the company is a suitable candidate to go public and whether market conditions are right for an IPO. Financial advisers know what investors will consider in acquiring the shares in an IPO. For example, in some industries a company may only be able to go public by exhibiting a long history of strong financial performance, including revenue and earnings growth. However, a short history of potential performance may be acceptable for going public for companies in certain high-tech industries. In addition, the founders must determine the trading location for their shares (i.e., an exchange or over-the-counter market). In the case of a company whose stock is listed on an exchange, there are listing requirements that the exchange specifies. With respect to timing, market conditions may be such that IPOs coming to market face a low stock valuation. Such unfavorable conditions would encourage postponement of an IPO until market conditions improve.

The rules for raising funds from the public through a common stock offering were explained in chapter 5 and will not be reviewed here.

Advantages of Going Public

There are two principal advantages of a company going public. First, publicly traded common stock provides liquidity for the shares owned by founders as well as by investors and employees who are shareholders. For some founders who desire to harvest or cash out on the value they created by building the company, an IPO allows them to do so.

Second, founders can use shares as a form of currency, allowing them to make acquisitions needed to expand their business as well as to attract key executives by offering stock options. The shares are a form of currency because the shares have a market price, making it unnecessary in transactions involving an acquisition or the hiring of a key officer to negotiate the value of the shares that are used in an exchange. The management of targeted companies that the founders seek to acquire and the key officers the founders seek to attract have a clearly defined idea of what is being offered by looking at the market value of the shares.

There are two other alleged advantages of going public. The first is that publicly traded companies have greater access to alternative financing sources such as bank loans and bond financing. The second is that a publicly traded company is viewed as more prestigious than a private company, providing greater exposure of its offerings to the public and suppliers, as well as greater exposure of the company to the public investing community.

Disadvantages of Going Public

Certain factors make going public less appealing to founders. First, a publicly traded company must comply with the SEC regulatory requirements explained in chapter 2 for reporting companies. There are ongoing costs beyond the initial costs (legal, accounting, and banker fees) associated with an IPO, as well as listing fees charged by an exchange, if that is the trading venue selected. The costs of being a public company have increased as a result of the Sarbanes-Oxley Act of 2002, such as the Section 404 provision mandating that a company have certain internal controls for financial reporting in place. Second, there are implicit costs in the time involved for founders to prepare the information that a reporting company must provide on a periodic basis to public investors.

Loss of confidentiality is often cited as a third disadvantage of taking a private company public. A reporting company in its prospectus, its IPO, and its Form 10-K is required to disclose information that founders might view as highly sensitive about its operations and business strategy. The information that is not required of private companies but is required of reporting companies includes information about products, customers, research and development, and management strategies.

The potential loss of control and flexibility in making business decisions as a result of going public is a fourth disadvantage of going public. When the founders lose controlling interest, major decisions (and even minor ones) may necessitate shareholder approval, which may require costly proxy voting, as well as a considerable time delay while approval is sought from shareholders. The board of directors may no longer be controlled by the founders but by major shareholder groups should more than a majority of the shares be sold to the public. Of course, as explained in the next chapter, common stock with limited voting rights can be sold, but this may make the common stock less appealing to investors, resulting in a lower share valuation. Moreover, not all founders will be in a position to issue shares with limited voting rights.

Finally, there is pressure on founders who remain with the company after the IPO to perform as expected by shareholders and the financial community to achieve targeted financial metrics, such as earnings per share and earnings per share growth. This expectation often means that founders must shift their focus from building a stronger company to achieving short-term financial targets at the expense of long-term performance.

Issuance Method

A decision that the founders must make in consultation with their financial adviser is the manner in which the shares should be issued to the public. There is the traditional underwriting arrangement and there is an auction process.

Traditional Underwriting Process   The traditional process of issuing shares in an IPO involves using an investment bank to distribute shares to the public. The investment bank can act as a distributor in one of two ways. The first is by buying the common stock of the company and then distributing it to investors. This is referred to as underwriting the shares, with the investment bank referred to as the *underwriter.* When the investment bank agrees to buy the shares from the issuer at a set price, the underwriting arrangement is referred to as a *firm commitment.* The risk that the investment bank accepts in a firm commitment underwriting arrangement is that the price it pays to purchase the shares from the company may be less than the price it receives when it reoffers the shares to the public. In contrast, in a *best-efforts underwriting arrangement*, the investment bank agrees only to use its expertise to sell the shares; it does not buy the issue from the company.

The fee earned from common stock underwriting is the difference between the price at which the investment bank offers the shares to the public and the price the investment bank pays to the company. This difference is called the *gross spread.* Numerous factors affect the size of the gross spread.

Several studies have looked at the size of the gross spread for IPOs. A study by Hsuan-Chi Chen and Jay Ritter of moderate-sized IPOs during the period 1995–1998 found that the gross spread was consistently 7%.[45] Follow-up research by Ritter on IPOs from 1999

---

45. Hsuan-Chi Chen and Jay R. Ritter, "The Seven Percent Solution," *Journal of Finance* 55, no. 3 (2000): 1106–1132.

to 2013 found that although there were a few exceptions, gross spreads for moderate-sized IPOs remained at 7%.[46] Megadeals had gross spreads of far less than 7%:[47] Facebook had a 1.1% gross spread on a $16 billion IPO in 2012, Twitter had a 3.25% gross spread on a $10 billion IPO in 2013, and Visa had a gross spread of 2.8% on a $17.9 billion IPO in 2008.

The typical underwritten transaction involves so much risk of capital loss that for a single investment bank to undertake it alone would expose the bank to the danger of losing a significant portion of its capital. To share this risk, the investment bank selected by the founders puts together a group of firms to underwrite the issue, referred to as the *underwriting syndicate*. The gross spread is then divided among the lead underwriter(s) and the other firms in the underwriting syndicate. The lead underwriter manages the deal ("runs the books" for the deal). In many cases, more than one underwriter may act as lead underwriter, in which case the lead underwriters are said to "colead" or "comanage" the deal.

To realize the gross spread, all the shares must be sold to the public at the planned reoffering price, which usually requires a great deal of marketing muscle. The underwriting investment banks attempt to sell the shares to their investor client base. To increase the potential investor base, the lead underwriter puts together a *selling group* that includes the underwriting syndicate plus other firms not in the syndicate.

Auction Process   Several companies have selected an alternative manner in which to distribute IPO shares to the investing public. In an *auction process,* the company announces its share offering and interested parties submit sealed bids to receive an allotment of the shares auctioned. Starting in the mid-1990s, several firms in the technology sector used this form of IPO issuance, among them Yahoo!, Overstock.com, and Google Inc.

Let's first discuss the mechanics of an auction and how the price that winning bidders must pay is determined. Then we will look at the relative merits of a traditional issuance of an IPO versus that of an auction.

Suppose there are 30 million shares to be issued for an IPO and that the bids and the number of shares are as shown in table 6.1.

The first column in the table shows all the bids from those who bid at the price shown in the second column. So "A" represents all investors who bid $50.00, and the number of shares that they bid for in the aggregate was three million. Since there were 30 million shares to be allotted, this means that the remaining number of shares (shown in the last column) is 27 million. For Investors "I," at the bid price of $34.00, only two million shares remain to be allocated. Investors "J" bid at $32.00 for the three million of the remaining

46. Table 10 in Jay R. Ritter, "Initial Public Offerings: Updated Statistics," December 4, 2014, http://bear.warrington.ufl.edu/ritter/IPOs2013Statistics.pdf.
47. All of the IPO gross spreads with the exception of Twitter were obtained from table 10 in Ritter, "Initial Public Offerings: Updated Statistics." The Twitter gross spread was reported by Telis Demos, "Twitter Squeezes Banks on IPO," *Wall Street Journal,* October 13, 2013.

Table 6.1
Illustration of an Auction Process

Investors	Bid Price per Share	Aggregate Number of Shares Bid	Remaining Shares to Be Allocated
A	$50.00	3,000,000	27,000,000
B	48.00	3,000,000	24,000,000
C	46.00	7,000,000	17,000,000
D	44.00	5,000,000	12,000,000
E	42.00	2,000,000	10,000,000
F	40.00	2,000,000	8,000,000
G	38.00	2,000,000	6,000,000
H	36.00	2,000,000	4,000,000
I	34.00	2,000,000	2,000,000
J	32.00	3,000,000	0
K	30.00	4,000,000	0
L	28.00	3,000,000	0
M	26.00	4,000,000	0
N	24.00	5,000,000	0

two million shares. So at a price of $32.00, the market has cleared (i.e., the total number of shares will be sold).

The question then is what price the winning bidders (Investors "A" through "J") will pay. The price will be that of the lowest winning bidder, $32.00. That is, there is a single price paid by all bidders. This type of auction is called a ***Dutch auction***. So, while Investors "A" bid for three million shares at $50.00 per share, they will pay only $32.00 per share. Investors "K" through "N" will receive no shares. How much will be allocated to Investors "J," who bid for three million of the two million remaining shares? All those who bid $32.00 will receive a proportionate allocation. For example, if an investor bid for 3,000 shares at $32.00, that investor will be allocated only 2,000 shares. For our hypothetical IPO issuer, the amount that will be raised before any fees is $960 million.

In August 2004, Google Inc. used a Dutch auction for its IPO, raising $2.7 billion. The question that arises is what is the best method for an IPO: traditional issuance using the underwriting process with investment bankers or a Dutch auction? Let's consider the Twitter IPO on November 7, 2013, priced at $26 per share, as determined by the firm's investment bankers. The valuation for the firm based on $26 per share was $15.2 billion. The opening price at which it traded on the New York Stock Exchange was $45.00 per share and its closing price was $44.90 per share. At a price per share of $45.00, the valuation of the company was $31.8 billion. Think about those numbers: the investment bankers felt the company was worth $15.2 billion and the market thought it was worth $31.8 billion. Somebody's valuation model was off!

Traditional IPO Offering versus an Auction   Of course, investment bankers argue that their direct purchase of the stock in an IPO offering as intermediaries adds value because they search their institutional client base, making it likely that the issuer will get the highest price (proceeds) after adjusting for the underwriting fees. However, since the 1990s it seems that the measure of a good underwriting is not the amount of proceeds received by the company in its IPO but rather the jump in the stock price at the time of issuance. For example, in the Twitter case, the pricing considerably below what the market suggested on the opening day (about $45) resulted in substantially less proceeds to Twitter. The beneficiaries were those who were fortunate enough to get an allocation of the shares from their broker, primarily institutional investors. One of the reasons Google Inc. selected the Dutch auction was because it was viewed as more "democratic," in that it allowed retail investors to participate in the IPO offering.

One argument put forth by investment bankers as to the advantage of the traditional underwriting process is that the syndicate involved in the underwriting process can support the market price for a period of time after issuance. This is because in most such underwritings, the investment bank agrees to stabilize the price in the secondary market to keep it from falling below the price at which it was sold to the public.[48]

KEY POINTS COVERED IN THIS CHAPTER

- Early-stage financing includes the seed round and the first round.
- In the seed round, sometimes referred to as the precommercialization financing stage, the founders seek to finance the development of a product or service.
- In very early-stage financing, typically the major source of funding is the personal assets of the founders. Such financing is referred to as bootstrap financing.
- In first-round financing (or Series A round financing), the milestone that has been reached is the generation of revenue, even though neither break-even operations nor profits are typically reached at this stage.
- It is typically difficult for founders to obtain bank financing in the seed stage (except in instances in which the founders have sufficient collateral or sufficient assets to provide personal guarantees), but once first-round financing is obtained, there are specialty banks and nonbank entities that are willing to provide venture debt that contains an equity kicker for the lender in the form of warrants.

48. One might think that this constitutes market manipulation. However, it is permitted by SEC Rule 10b-7, where the SEC sets forth the activities it considers market stabilization of a new issue and what it considers market manipulation.

- Sources for seed-round financing are credit cards, vendors, Small Business Administration loans, angel investors and angel groups, super angels, seed accelerators, incubators, and crowdfunding platforms, with the most common source of larger amounts of seed financing being angel investors.
- Expansion-stage financing is undertaken to expand the company's business by expanding production and acquiring customers through marketing.
- Expansion-stage financing includes bridge loans, second-round financing (Series B round financing), third-round financing (also called Series C round financing), and so on.
- Additional rounds of financing may be necessary if the company does not have a liquidating event after several rounds of financing. The entry of a new investor group, institutional investors, has allowed ventures to raise substantial funds to expand without the need to go public.
- When considering a request for funding by a startup company, potential investors go through a due diligence process that involves assessing the responses by founders to questions raised about the company during presentations regarding business and legal matters related to the venture.
- The business questions that will be asked by potential investors relate to (1) the background of the founders, (2) the business model, (3) the company's historical performance, (4) the management team, and (5) the targeted market.
- The legal matters include, for example, any threatened, pending, or current lawsuits, or any licensing or patent violations.
- The primary source of early-stage funding is angel investors, wealthy individuals who typically invest between $150,000 and $2 million and who qualify under the SEC's definition of "accredited investors."
- In addition to providing funding, angel investors provide strategic planning advice, assist in team building, and provide contacts for developing key partnerships and further fundraising.
- Angel investors typically invest through groups or networks for four reasons: (1) such groups provide for pooling of funds, thereby allowing investing in more startups, which theoretically affords risk reduction through diversification; (2) they reduce the cost of information gathering and contracting; (3) such groups can call on the diverse expertise and experience of group members to evaluate startups; and (4) the greater name recognition of a group of wealthy individuals as opposed to a single individual is likely to attract more deals.
- Although venture capitalists invest primarily in first-round financing, VC firms that do provide seed financing are referred to as super angels and are set up as private equity firms.

- Crowdfunding is the practice of raising funds for a startup from a large number of investors who invest small sums, typically over the Internet.
- Equity crowdfunding, one form of crowdfunding, allows investors to obtain an equity interest in a startup company.
- Provisions in the Jumpstart Our Business Startups Act (JOBS Act) made possible the soliciting of funds by startups, allowing for equity crowdfunding.
- Seed accelerators offer the opportunity for founders to gain access not only to early-stage financing in exchange for equity but also to other potential investors, training in a short period of time, temporary office space, and a team of experts.
- An incubator is another type of program that mentors entrepreneurs and other similar services as a seed accelerator, with the following differences between the two: (1) incubator programs typically take three to five years to complete, whereas seed accelerators typically last less than twelve months; (2) the mentoring for startups in an incubator program is typically less important than another important resource that an incubator can provide: a working space for the founders; and (3) seed accelerators extract a small amount of equity from the startups, whereas incubators typically charge rent for the facilities or a monthly fee or membership fee in lieu of an equity share.
- The primary sources for expansion financing have historically been traditional VC firms, corporate VC firms, and online VC funds.
- VC firms invest in a startup business in the form of equity, with the investments typically made in a series or rounds that typically occur every two years, based on predetermined milestones being achieved.
- VC firms are often said to be a special type of private equity firm that invests in startup companies, in contrast to a typical private equity firm, which invests in mature companies seeking to go private or that are viewed to be underperforming and have the potential for highly attractive returns.
- Corporate venture capitalists are corporations that invest in startups that have the potential for providing a good strategic fit with their company's offerings.
- Institutional investors such as mutual funds and hedge fund are the latest entrants providing expansion financing for new ventures prior to an IPO, acquisition, or merger.
- The provision of funding in large sums for expansion by institutional investors has resulted in new ventures postponing going to the public to raise funds through an IPO or being acquired.
- The founders of a company can turn to the general public to meet the company's needs through an IPO of its shares.
- An IPO is governed by securities regulations.
- The two principal advantages of an IPO are (1) publicly traded common stock provides liquidity for the shares owned by founders, as well as by investors and employees who

are shareholders, and (2) founders can use shares as a form of currency, allowing them to make the acquisitions necessary to expand their business and to attract key executives by offering stock options.

- The disadvantages of an IPO are (1) the company must comply with and incur the costs associated with SEC regulatory filing requirements; (2) the company faces implicit costs in the form of the time devoted by founders to preparing the information that a reporting company must provide on a periodic basis to public investors; (3) the company faces loss of confidentiality because of required disclosures; and (4) management experiences pressures to perform as expected by shareholders and the financial community to achieve targeted financial metrics, resulting in the founders shifting their focus from building a stronger company to achieving short-term financial targets at the expense of long-term performance.

- The issuance of common stock to the public can be done by a traditional underwriting process or an auction process.

FURTHER READINGS

Angel Investors
Bryant, Tarvy, *The Entrepreneur's Guide to Raising Capital from Angel Investors* (Athens, GA: Deeds Publishing, 2014).

Ramdev, Vinil, *Insider Secrets to Raising Capital from Angel Investors* (Bangalore, India: Zaang Entertainment, 2012).

Venture Capital Firms
Dotzler, Fred, "Raising the First Round of Venture Capital: What Founding Teams Should Understand," *Journal of Private Equity,* Winter 2012, 9–12.

Lerner, Josh, Ann Leamon, and Felda Hardymon, *Venture Capital, Private Equity, and the Financing of Entrepreneurship* (Hoboken, NJ: John Wiley & Sons, 2012).

Metrick, Andrew, and Ayako Yasuda, *Venture Capital and the Finance of Innovation,* 2nd ed. (Hoboken, NJ: John Wiley & Sons, 2010).

Ramsinghani, Mahendra, *The Business of Venture Capital: Insights from Leading Practitioners on the Art of Raising a Fund, Deal Structuring, Value Creation, and Exit Strategies,* 2nd ed. (Hoboken, NJ: John Wiley & Sons, 2014).

Initial Public Offerings
Draho, Jason, *The IPO Decision: Why and How Companies Go Public* (Cheltenham, UK: Edward Elgar Publishing, 2006).

Westenberg, David, *Initial Public Offerings: A Practical Guide to Going Public,* 2nd ed. (New York: Practising Law Institute, 2014).

7

FINANCING VIA EQUITY AND EQUITY DILUTIVE SECURITIES

The financial instruments that can be issued to raise funds are classified as either equity or debt. The mix of equity and debt that founders decide to use to finance the company is referred to as its ***capital structure***. For most publicly traded nonfinancial corporations, equity is the larger component of the capital structure. For startup companies, equity (or equity-type debt) is typically a larger component of the capital structure, particularly in the early stages of financing, than it is for publicly traded nonfinancial corporations. This decision about a startup's capital structure (i.e., how much should be financed by equity versus debt) is typically forced on the founders because of the limited sources of pure debt financing available. By "pure debt financing" is meant debt that cannot be converted by the creditors to equity. As a startup enters its later stages, there are opportunities to issue pure debt.

In this chapter, we cover the issuance of common stock prior to any initial public offering (IPO) and other securities that lead to the issuance of common stock, referred to as ***equity dilutive securities***. These securities include convertible preferred stock and convertible debt. Most investors in startup companies prefer equity dilutive securities to common stock for the reasons described in this chapter. We also review the key provisions of a term sheet used in fundraising and the computation of pre- and post-money valuation as the result of a round of financing.

COMMON STOCK

Equity securities represent an ownership interest in a company. Equity securities can be classified into two general categories, common stock and preferred stock. Our focus in this section is on common stock. In the next section we discuss preferred stock.

Holders of the common stock of a company are entitled to receive a pro rata share of the company's earnings. The company, or more specifically the company's board of directors, decides how much of the earnings to distribute to common shareholders. When earnings are distributed to common shareholders, the payments are referred to as ***dividends***. Startup companies typically do not pay dividends because of the need to conserve cash to grow the business. Typically, common stock investors in startup companies do not expect to receive dividends as a form of income when investing in a startup company but instead expect to benefit from the price appreciation of the shares owned.

Common shareholders are referred to as the "residual" owners of the company. This is because in the case of a bankruptcy, when the company is dissolved and the assets are distributed to all the company's investors, this class of stockholder receives a distribution only after all other security holders are paid the amount due to them.

Common stock issuance can be done through the sale of the securities to the public, as explained in chapter 6, or by a private placement. Common stock is also issued as awards and options granted by a startup company to founders and other key employees, as explained in chapter 4. Issuing common stock by means of such mechanisms is done to compensate founders and other key employees rather than to raise funds. Of course, a startup is also conserving cash when it issues common stock for this purpose.

Ownership and Control Issues

Of importance to the founders when common stock shares are issued to obtain financing is the impact on ownership and control of the company. With respect to ownership, founders will look at how their ownership percentage changes following a round of financing. Control means the flexibility afforded the founders in managing the company with respect to strategic planning and directing the future of the company. The document that provides for corporate governance is the shareholders' agreement.

The provisions in this legal document, as well as in the company's organizational documents, that have an impact on control are (1) voting thresholds and (2) board of director composition. Voting thresholds specify the percentage of shareholders needed to obtain approval of certain types of action that the founders desire to undertake. However, it may not be just the percentage ownership but the voting percentage if a company is able to issue common stock with dual voting rights. Many startup companies have been moving away from the "one share, one vote" common structure and toward a dual-class stock structure where each class of stock has a different number of voting rights. The motivation for creating different classes with different voting rights is that it allows the company's founders to retain control of the company by controlling the class of common stock with the largest number of voting rights. Typically in a dual-class structure the two classes of common stock are referred to as Class A stock and Class B stock. One cannot simply tell which class has the larger number of voting rights from the label. That is, there is no industry rule that says A or B will have the larger number of voting rights.

With respect to the board of directors, control is affected by the composition of the board since it is this group of individuals that will approve major decisions that are not voted on by shareholders. The founders will typically each seek a board seat, and investors who provide funding will seek a certain number of board seats as independent directors. Loss of control of the board will reduce the flexibility of founders in managing the company. These provisions are described later when we discuss the term sheet for a security offering.

Historically, founding members of companies have been able to maintain control by owning less than a majority of the shares but controlling the voting shares. For example, Robert Murdock, CEO of News Corp., owns less than 1% of the nonvoting stock (which is traded in the market) but controls 40% of the voting stock. In 2004, Google adopted a dual-class structure—Class A and Class B common stock. Each share of Class A common stock has one vote per share, while Class B has ten votes per share. The two founders, Larry Page and Sergey Brin, as well as the then CEO, held the Class B shares. When Google went public, its Class A shares were sold by a Dutch auction. The dual-class structure gave the founders and CEO control over two-thirds of the voting shares. More recently, Google sought to provide another class of stock, Class C, which had no voting rights. Litigation followed, with opponents of the issuance of a new class of stock arguing that it would further entrench the founders' control over Google while at the same time allowing the company to obtain additional proceeds.

Facebook has a dual-class structure with the same number of votes as Google for its Class A and Class B stock. The CEO and cofounder, Mark Zuckerberg, owned shares of Class B stock that allowed the retention of control after the Class A stock was sold through its IPO in 2012. (Facebook adopted the dual-class structure in 2009.) In its filing with the SEC (S-1 filing) before its IPO, Facebook estimated that the Class B shareholders would have 70% of the voting power prior to the offering and warned, "This concentrated control will limit your ability to influence corporate matters for the foreseeable future." (After the IPO Zuckerberg owned 57% of the voting shares but had only a 28% ownership of the company.)

While several technology companies have adopted the dual-class structure, the cofounders of Twitter, Dick Costolo and Evan Williams, did not. Each share acquired by investors has the same number of votes as the cofounders. Twitter's board of directors does have the right to issue preferred stock with special voting rights.

CONVERTIBLE PREFERRED STOCK

Preferred stock is a hybrid security that combines the features of common stock and a debt obligation such as a bond. Despite its debtlike feature, it is considered a form of equity security and on the balance sheet it appears as part of stockholders' equity. Unlike common stockholders, preferred stockholders typically do not have voting rights except under certain circumstances, described later. In the early stages of a startup company, preferred stock that allows for investors such as angel investors and venture capitalists to convert the preferred stock into common stock is the vehicle of choice for investors who seek to benefit from the price appreciation potential of the common stock.

Preferred stock comes with provisions that convey rights, preferences, and privileges to the investors. The holders of a company's preferred stock have a claim on the dividends declared by a corporation's board of directors, and that claim is senior to that of the holders of the company's common stock. Preferred stock has a par value and a dividend rate. However, as with common stock issued by a startup company, investors in preferred stock typically are not paid a dividend, owing to the firm's need to conserve cash. Unlike the par value of common stock, which has little meaning except for legal purposes, as explained in chapter 9, the par value of preferred stock is important.

Below we describe the different features of preferred stock.

Dividends

The par value, along with the preferred stock dividend rate, determines the dollar amount of the dividends that will be paid if there are sufficient earnings to pay preferred stockholders. For example, suppose that a company's preferred stock has a par value of $100 per share and a dividend rate of 6%. Multiplying the par value of $100 by the 6% dividend rate gives the annual dividend amount ($6 in our example) that the company agrees to pay preferred stockholders before common stockholders are paid any dividends.

Suppose that a company that has issued preferred stock with a total par value of $10 million and a dividend rate of 6% has earnings after taxes (i.e., after paying interest to the debtholders and its taxes) of $1 million. This means that when and if the company's board of directors declares dividends, the company must pay to preferred stockholders dividends of $600,000 ($10 million × 6%) before common stockholders can receive one penny of dividends. Typically payments are made quarterly, so in our example this means a quarterly dividend payment of $150,000 to preferred stockholders. Suppose that the board of directors decides to distribute $800,000 in dividends. Then the preferred stockholders will receive $600,000 and the common stockholders will receive $200,000.

A company is under no legal obligation to pay preferred stockholders any dividends. However, in such instances there is typically a provision that imposes restrictions on management when dividends are not paid. One such provision activates preferred stockholders' voting rights to elect some members to the issuer's board of directors. This feature is called **contingent voting rights** because the voting rights are contingent on a missed dividend payment. Despite this adverse impact, failure to make a preferred stock dividend payment does not have legal consequences as dire as when a company fails to pay creditors the interest payment due to them. In that case, the company is legally obligated to repay the principal immediately (i.e., pay off the debt obligation), and failure to do so may result in bankruptcy.

Should there be a shortfall in the quarterly dividend payment to preferred stockholders, is the company required to make up the shortfall in future quarters? The answer depends on how this situation is provided for in the preferred stock agreement. Preferred stock can be either cumulative or noncumulative preferred stock. For **cumulative preferred stock**, the dividend payment accrues until it is fully paid, and therefore common stockholders cannot receive any dividends until that is done. In the case of **noncumulative preferred stock**, any shortfall in a quarterly dividend payment is lost. As noted earlier, startups typically do not pay dividends. Consequently, typically preferred stock issued by a startup company will be cumulative preferred stock and the unpaid dividends are added to the preferred stock's par value.

Liquidation Preferences

If there is a liquidating event, the par value is the amount that the holder is entitled to receive before common stockholders can receive any amount of the liquidation proceeds. A *liquidating event* is defined in the term sheet (see below). Typically it is broadly defined. That is, it is not limited to the actual liquidation of the company as a result of bankruptcy or dissolution. Rather, it typically includes sale of the company or a change of control. In practice, startups typically will not have much in proceeds if there is a liquidation event that results in the bankruptcy of the company. Moreover, as explained later, the type of preferred stock that is typically required by investor is one that gives the investor the right to convert to common stock and thereby terminate the preferred stock if the company is successful.

It is critical for founders to understand the preference granted to preferred stockholders should a liquidating event occur as set forth in the term sheet since it affects the amount the founders will receive upon the sale of the company or a change in control. Indeed, the preference granted to preferred stockholders is considered the most important provision in the term sheet, following that of the negotiation of the company's pre-money valuation (see below). Moreover, it has an impact on subsequent rounds of financing.

To illustrate, let's consider the case in which a company is sold (a liquidating event) for $22 million (net of all costs associated with the sale), and assume the following for pre-sale capital structure:

Par value of preferred stock	$5 million
Debt	$2 million

Once creditors are paid their $2 million, the amount available to all equity investors (preferred stockholders and common stockholders) is $20 million. Now the question is how the $20 million is allocated between the preferred stockholders and the common stockholders. If the preferred stockholders are not permitted to participate in any proceeds above the amount of their par value when there is a liquidation event, then the preferred stock is said to be *nonparticipating preferred stock* (or "1× liquidation preference"). (We will ignore for simplicity that the amount due to preferred stockholders would reflect the dividends that may have accumulated since the issuance of the preferred stock.) In our illustration, the distribution of proceeds resulting from the sale would be as follows:

Proceeds to preferred stockholders:	$5 million
Proceeds to common stockholders:	$15 million

Founders seek to negotiate terms such that the preferred stock is nonparticipating. In contrast, preferred stockholders in new ventures will seek to participate in the liquidation proceeds beyond the par value of the preferred stock. If preferred stockholders are entitled to share along with common stockholders any remaining liquidation proceeds, then the preferred stock is said to be ***participating preferred stock***. Preferred stock that conveys a participating right can have different forms of participation, referred to in terms of a multiple of the preferred stock's par value. For example, if preferred stockholders are entitled to receive twice or triple their par value, referred to as "2× liquidation preference" and "3× liquidation preference," respectively, then the distribution would be as follows:

Distribution to:	2 × Liquidation preference	3 × Liquidation preference
Proceeds to preferred stockholders:	$10 million	$12 million
Proceeds to common stockholders:	$10 million	$8 million

A hybrid of the two types of preferred stock just described is one in which there is participation, but it is capped at a specified amount. This form of preferred stock is referred to as ***capped participating preferred stock*** or ***partially participating preferred stock***. For example, suppose that in our previous illustration the preferred stockholders are entitled to share equally in liquidation proceeds up to $8 million. This means that the preferred stockholders would receive $8 million and the common stockholders would receive the balance of $12 million.

Once the amount of the proceeds to be paid to common stockholders is determined, then the distribution to founders and nonfounders must be determined. For example, if preferred stockholders in our example paid $5 million to obtain 30% of the company, then they would be entitled to 30% of the proceeds available to common stockholders. Table 7.1 shows the proceeds to be received by the founders and the investors who purchased the preferred stock (assuming no other equity investors). Notice the considerable variation in the amount paid to founders based on the liquidation preference granted to preferred stockholders.

Conversion Provision

The optional conversion feature in a preferred stock offering often granted to investors in a startup company typically grants the investor the right to convert preferred shares into the company's common shares. There may be restrictions imposed on when the conversion may or must occur. Typically, conversion is mandatory if certain events occur, such as an IPO. Provisions to protect investors against dilution of their potential equity position are included and described later when we cover term sheets.

Table 7.1
Distribution of $20 Million of Proceeds (in $ millions)

Paid to	Liquidation Proceeds			
	Nonparticipating	2× Preference	3× Preference	Capped at $8 Million
Preferred stockholders	$ 5.0	$10.0	$12.0	$ 8.0
Common stockholders	15.0	10.0	8.0	12.0
Investors (Preferred stockholders)*	4.5	3.0	2.4	3.6
Total to preferred stockholders	9.5	13.0	14.4	11.6
Founders	10.5	7.0	5.6	8.4

Note: *This is the share preferred stockholders receive as investors for 30% ownership of the company.

CONVERTIBLE NOTE

A *convertible note* is typically issued to investors in the early state of the financing of a startup, prior to a Series A round of financing. Unlike convertible preferred stock, which is a form of equity, a convertible note is a form of debt. The holder of the convertible note either (1) has the option to exchange the note for an equity position or (2) has the position automatically converted into an equity position if there is a Series A round of financing. The equity position received by the holder of a convertible note typically is preferred stock.

Conversion Terms

Let's first look at a traditional convertible note issued by a mature corporation. The traditional convertible note gives the investor the right to convert the note into the issuer's common stock. The number of common stock shares into which the convertible note can be converted is called the *conversion ratio*. Typically, the conversion ratio is fixed over the life of the convertible note. If the par value of the convertible note is $1,000 and the conversion ratio is 20:1, this means that the investor is entitled to convert the note into twenty shares of common stock. Effectively the price that the investor would be paying for each share of common stock by exercising the conversion privilege, called the *conversion price*, would be $50 per share.

The convertible note when used for seed financing by a startup is different in two ways. First, the conversion is typically into preferred stock and not into common stock as in the case of a traditional convertible note. Moreover, the preferred stock is convertible preferred stock. So the exercise of the conversion privilege gives the investor the right to convert into a security that, in turn, the investor has the right to eventually convert into common stock. Because a convertible note (debt) can ultimately result in the issuance of more common stock, it is a form of equity dilutive security.

The second difference is the price paid for the preferred stock when conversion occurs. The price that an investor will have to pay for the preferred stock shares if conversion occurs is based on a provision set forth in the convertible note offering. There could be a conversion discount or a conversion valuation cap. As explained below, both of these provisions are included for the benefit of convertible note investors to compensate them for the substantial risks that they accepted by being early investors.

Conversion Discount   Early investors in a startup who purchase the convertible note do so in anticipation of generating an attractive return should the startup perform well and its common stock price increase. Consequently, there must be provisions in the convertible note offering that allows investors to be compensated for accepting this risk exposure in the early stages of the startup, and that reward should be potentially greater than for later investors who invest in later financing rounds of the startup. Simply put, when later investors such as venture capitalists make a determination of the value of the startup to purchase the shares of the preferred stock, investors in the convertible note want to be able to purchase the preferred shares at a lower price since they were the initial bearers of the high risks associated with a startup company.

The provision that allows convertible note investors to do just that is the *conversion discount*, which specifies by how much less the convertible note investors can buy the preferred stock shares below what Series A investors pay for the preferred stock shares. Here is how it works, assuming a 25% conversion discount.

Suppose that the convertible note funding is $300,000 with an interest rate of 10%. Two years later, there is a Series A financing by a venture capital (VC) fund and the terms obtained are such that preferred stock could be purchased for $1 per share. The 25% conversion discount means that the convertible note investors would pay $0.75 per share of preferred stock, or what we referred to earlier as the conversion price. How many shares of preferred stock would the convertible note investors receive? Since the convertible note investor is entitled to convert both the par value ($300,000) plus the accrued interest ($60,000),[1] the amount converted is based on $360,000. Since the convertible note's amount to be converted is $360,000 and each preferred share can be purchased for $0.75 per share, the number of preferred shares would be 480,000 shares ($360,000/$0.75).

The conversion discount need not be fixed over the life of the security. Rather, it can be structured so that it increases over time until Series A financing is obtained. One might expect that the longer it takes to obtain Series A financing, the greater the risk exposure of the convertible note investor and therefore the higher the conversion discount that is warranted. This is also an incentive for the founders to seek Series A financing as soon as is reasonably possible to avoid further dilution.

---

1. Two years of interest at 10% on $300,000 is $60,000, ignoring the compounding of interest.

A startup company may not necessarily raise all funds by means of convertible notes at one time. There may be several issues of convertible notes offered at different times. The conversion discount can be different for each offering, depending on what is needed to attract investors at different times. For example, a conversion discount may be higher for very early investors interested in purchasing convertible notes than for later investors in convertible notes.

It is interesting to note that unlike investors in a traditional convertible note, who benefit from a rise in the value of the company, investors in a startup's convertible note, though they also benefit from an increase in valuation, do not want to see it rise that much by the Series A round of financing. The higher the valuation placed by the Series A investors, the fewer shares of preferred stock will be received.

Conversion Valuation Cap   A *conversion valuation cap* is the maximum dollar amount that can be used for determining the conversion price the holder of the convertible note has to pay for the right to convert to the preferred stock. The reason why this provision benefits the investor is that a lower price can be paid for the preferred stock than Series A investors pay.

To illustrate, suppose that an investor owns $300,000 par value of a convertible note with a conversion valuation cap of $6 million and the company is raising funds in a Series A financing. Suppose further that the pre-money valuation, a measure discussed later in this chapter, is $8 million in this financing for preferred stock with a par value of $1. At the time of financing, assume that the accrued interest for the convertible note is $60,000. The conversion valuation cap of $6 million means that the conversion price for the convertible noteholders to purchase the preferred stock is adjusted below that paid by the Series A investors. The procedure to obtain the adjustment is found by dividing the conversion valuation cap ($6 million in our example) by the pre-money valuation ($8 million in our illustration). In our illustration it is 75%. This means that the convertible note investors will pay 75% of the price paid by the Series A investors to buy the preferred stock. Since Series A investors pay $1 per share of preferred stock, the convertible note investors pay only $0.75. Since convertible note investors are converting $360,000 (principal plus accrued interest), they will receive 480,000 preferred stock shares ($360,000/$0.75).

Note that with a convertible note, there is no need for a valuation of common stock because a debt obligation is nothing more than a loan and as such, requires no valuation. Hence at the time of issuance a valuation is not needed because the conversion value will be determined in the next round of financing (Series A).

DEBT WITH WARRANTS

Another form of debt that is an equity dilutive security is debt with warrants to purchase the company's common stock. A *warrant* is a form of option that grants the warrant holder the right to exercise it and receive a specified security. Often this type of financing is used in the later stages of a company to obtain financing between rounds of financing (i.e., bridge financing).

For example, a company might issue convertible debt with warrants to purchase up to 15% of the common stock. This is referred to as "convertible debt with 15% warrant coverage." Suppose that the par value of this convertible debt is $5 million. This means that investors in this convertible debt with warrants have the right to purchase $750,000 (15% of $5 million) of the issuer's common stock. The exercise price for the warrants is determined by what investors in the next round of financing agree to pay for the common stock. Thus, what is important is that investors are confident that there will be another round of financing to determine the conversion price. This is why such financing is used less often in the very early stages of financing but later on in bridge financing, when the company has already gone through several rounds of financing. However, there have been suggestions for tweaking the convertible debt with warrant structure to increase its use in certain early-stage financing situations.[2]

TERM SHEETS

The terms on which a company raises funds for any type of funding vehicle (common stock, preferred stock, and debt obligations) are negotiated between the founders and investors and are set forth in a *letter of intent*. In the parlance of the finance industry, the letter of intent is referred to as a *term sheet*. The term sheet is written by lawyers, typically to be read by other lawyers. Most founders will therefore be highly dependent on legal counsel for guidance and interpretation. Term sheet templates are available on the Internet.

The term sheet provides the terms agreed upon by the two parties, setting forth the groundwork for making sure that the parties (the founders and the suppliers of capital or investors) are in agreement with respect to the major terms of the transaction. There are two views about the amount of detail to include in a term sheet. On the one hand, some parties believe that the terms specified as a result of the negotiation should result in a detailed term sheet; on the other hand, there are parties who believe that the terms should be more of a generalized understanding, with details to follow in the final stages of the transaction when the legal documents are drafted.

Regardless of the details provided, one or more terms may have to be modified slightly or renegotiated completely as the new investor performs its due diligence with respect to the company. Consequently, since the major terms are outlined in terms of broad parameters no matter how much detail is provided, a term sheet is not a legal document and therefore is not legally enforceable. However, there are typically two elements of the term

2. See Paul A. Jones, "Seed Financing Option: Convertible Debt with Warrants," *WTB News,* December 7, 2009, http://wtnnews.com/articles/6889.

sheet that are intended to be legally binding on both parties: the confidentiality provision and what is known as the "no-shopping" provision.

Binding Provisions in a Term Sheet

The *confidentiality agreement* is needed by a founder because sensitive information about a company's strategies or plans that is not publicly available is furnished to the potential new investor. The founders may not want this information disclosed to third parties such as competitors who may be able to capitalize on such information. On the flip side, investors such as venture capitalists and bankers may be concerned about executing a term sheet that contains an overly restrictive confidentiality provision because the nature of their business may at some future date result in a relationship with the company's competitors seeking to raise funds.

Transactions involving the funding of startup companies are costly for the investor. There are legal fees and other fees associated with the due diligence process that the potential investor performs. Consequently, an investor wants to be assured that the founders are not shopping the transaction around to other potential investors with the hope of getting better terms than the investor might offer. The *no-shopping provision* in the term sheet requires that the founders not seek funding arrangements from other investors over some designated period of time. Although it might be difficult for founders to get an investor to exclude a no-shopping provision from the term sheet, founders should negotiate for as short a period of time as possible before they can seek out other investors for funding. Founders who are in need of funds quickly should be particularly keen on negotiating a less restrictive no-shopping provision.

Basic Elements of a Term Sheet

Here we briefly describe the components of a term sheet. A term sheet for any security or funding instrument is basically divided into three sections:

1. a description of the funding,
2. the terms of the funding, and
3. investor protective provisions.

Description of the Funding In describing the funding, the following information is included:

- the issuer,
- the security type,
- the pre-money valuation,
- the amount of the offering,
- the number of shares, and
- the price per share.

When the offering is for convertible preferred stock, the term sheet will specify the pre-money valuation (explained later). However, as explained earlier, for convertible notes it will not.

The valuation process is complicated, as explained in chapter 16. Investors will determine the valuation based on the method they employ. In the case of funding where the company is preparing a term sheet to solicit investors in later stages of financing, the company will provide its own estimate of the company's value.

Terms of the Funding   The specific terms of the funding cover the following:

- payment of dividends in the case of convertible preferred stock and interest in the case of convertible debt, and
- liquidation preference in allocating liquidation proceeds.

For convertible preferred stock there is a dividend rate that the investor and the founders will negotiate, while for convertible debt there is an interest rate. Unlike the standard convertible preferred stock and convertible debt issued by mature companies, the payments of dividends and interest are quite different when the investor is an angel or a venture capitalist. For example, in the case of convertible preferred stock issued by a mature company, dividends are paid periodically. This is not the treatment for convertible preferred stock for early-stage funding, where either a dividend payment is made at the time of a liquidation event or dividends are declared by the board of directors to be paid to the common stockholders. The term sheet will set forth how the dividends are to be paid to the convertible preferred stockholders.

Because convertible securities allow investors to convert preferred stock into common stock, the terms of the conversion will be set forth. There are two issues that must be dealt with. The first is the number of common stock shares that each convertible security can convert into. Also described in this section of the term sheet is a provision to protect the investor against the dilution of its equity position as result of future rounds of financing by the founders. This provision, referred to as an *antidilution provision,* will set forth a new conversion price for the convertible security.

The second issue covers the right of conversion itself. The conversion provision grants the investor the right but not the obligation to convert the security into common stock shares. Therefore, the investor has an option to exchange the security for shares (i.e., to convert the convertible security into common stock). A term sheet will specify that the conversion is optional. However, in certain situations the investor has no choice but to convert. That is, the conversion will occur automatically under certain circumstances. For example, automatic conversion occurs when the company does an IPO.

The distribution of proceeds between the investors and founders (including the employees who own the common stock) as a result of liquidation of the company will be described in the second section of the term sheet. The term sheet will define what constitutes a liquidation event. Typically a liquidation event includes an IPO or acquisition of the company.

Investor Protective Provisions   The terms of the offering include provisions that protect the investor's ownership interest in the startup. There are other protective provisions that venture capitalists require of founders that go beyond the terms of the funding. Most of these rights are covered in the *investor rights agreement.* Basically, these are covenants that the founders make with the investor. They include the following:

- *Rights to future stock issuances:* This covenant allows the investor the right of first refusal for the purpose of maintaining a pro rata ownership of the company in the event that the founders elect to have future offerings of common stock or any dilutive security.
- *Information rights:* This right requires that the company furnish the investor with financial information and other reports.
- *Observer rights:* The investor is given the right to be notified of meetings of the board of directors and allowed to attend and participate at those meetings.
- *Inspection rights.* The investor is given the right to inspect the company's financial accounting information and in doing so has the right to discuss the company's financial conditions with the appropriate officers of the company.
- *Redemption rights*: This grants the investor the right to have the company redeem the outstanding shares that it owns at a specified price.
- *Registration rights:* This right grants the investor the right to demand that the company register the security with the SEC at the company's cost so that the investor will be able to sell the shares to the public.
- *Voting rights:* An investor will seek the right to vote based on the number of shares of common stock that would result if the conversion privilege is exercised.
- *Board membership:* An investor has the right to select the number of board members specified in the investor rights agreement.

Another investor protective provision that is included in the company's bylaws rather than the investor rights agreement is the *co-sale right*. This right, also referred to as a *tag-along right*, enables the investor to sell shares owned by the investor on the same terms as the founders. Typically the shares can be sold by the investor on a pro rata basis of the total ownership percentage. The investor wants the co-sale right for the purpose of reducing the incentive of the founders to liquidate a significant portion of their holdings and, as a consequence, reduce the incentive of the founders' motivation in managing the business.

Redemption Rights   Let's take a closer look at the redemption rights granted to an investor. An investor will seek to have included in the agreement the option to have the company repurchase its shares. When such a redemption right is permitted, the right might not be permitted for a specified number of years (usually at least five years) in order to give the company the opportunity to meet its profit or other financial milestones. The more common provision is that the company may redeem the outstanding shares owned by an investor only if there is a majority vote by the board of directors allowing this action. How long the company can take in redeeming the shares will be specified. For example, the shares might be redeemed in three annual installments.

The rationale for the inclusion of this right from the investor's perspective is that it offers downside protection for its investment should the company be successful but has not reached the point where it can be acquired or has not reached a specified price. For a venture capitalist, this right is important because the VC fund that has invested in a startup has a limited life. If the remaining life of a VC fund at the time of the investment is eight years, for example, then the concern is that there will be no exit event for the startup in which the venture capitalist has invested until after that time.

It should be noted that even if there is an option granted to the investor to redeem on request or on a majority board vote for redemption, the company may not legally be permitted to redeem shares if this action would result in the company becoming insolvent and thereby would have an adverse impact on the position of creditors. Consequently, any right of redemption granted to the investor will have a restriction that the right is subject to state law that governs distributions to stockholders.

There is a redemption right that is typically included in an investor's rights agreement that would not require majority board approval even if the investor does not have the right to request redemption. This situation occurs when an "adverse change redemption" right is included. This right gives the investor the option to have shares owned by the investor redeemed immediately if the company experiences a material adverse change. A material adverse change means an event or occurrence that has had or is reasonably expected to have a significant adverse effect on the company's business. This right granted to the investor is called the *material adverse redemption right.*

Despite the granting of liquidation rights, in practice it not common for redemption rights to be exercised by venture capitalists. In negotiating liquidation rights, the founders should seek to have redemption rights removed and, if that is not possible, to make the length of the time period before such rights can be exercised as long as possible (at least five years). With respect to the material adverse redemption right, the founders should make all efforts to have that provision excluded as an investor right.

PRE- AND POST-MONEY VALUATION

The notion of pre- and post-money may seem easy enough to understand. Pre-money valuation means the value assigned to a company by an investor before the investment is made; the post-money valuation is the valuation after the investment is made. So, if a company has a $3 million value before an investor wants to invest $1 million, the pre-money valuation is

$3 million and the post-money valuation is $4 million. That seems easy enough. However, that is not the way it works. Here is why.

An investor knows that as a company grows, the ability to incentivize employees is typically accomplished by granting them the opportunity to purchase the stock at some future date at a price that is set today. If the startup performs well and the stock price increases above the exercise price at which an employee is entitled to buy the stock (i.e., the exercise price), employees who are granted stock options will exercise them and realize a gain. Such plans for employees are called stock option plans and are described in chapter 4. If a company has a stock option plan, then the exercise of the option will increase the number of shares outstanding and therefore reduce the ownership interest of the founders based on the number of new shares issued from the exercise. In fact, it is rare that a high-tech startup fails to have this type of incentive plan.

Option Pools in Financing Rounds and Post-Money Valuation

An important aspect of post-money valuation in financing rounds is the option pool. An option pool during a financing round is the amount of stock reserved for the hiring of new employees as the company grows. What does the option pool, which is just the stock set aside for future employees who would be expected to be granted stock options, have to do with the valuation of a startup seeking to raise funds from an investor? The investor knows two things: (1) eventually the company will have to create more employee stock options and (2) the exercise of the stock options granted to employees will dilute not just the founder's equity and that of current investors but also that of any new investors. Because of this, new investors will take into consideration the potential dilution in determining the pre-money valuation.

Let's illustrate this with an example. We will assume the following:

1. There are one million shares outstanding, and they are all owned by the founders.
2. There are no employee stock options granted.
3. The pre-money valuation, ignoring the dilution by potential stock options, is $3 million.
4. A new investor from whom the company is seeking funds wants a 25% interest in the company and invests $1 million.
5. The new investor wants 15% post-money valuation for the option pool available.
6. The security purchased is a convertible preferred stock that entitles the investor to convert the security into common stock.

There are two questions here. First, what is a 15% option pool? We explain this later. What is important is that it is a negotiable percentage. The second question is, how much of an impact will the percentage have on the pre-money valuation, price, and percentage ownership? As will be shown, it can be significant, and that is why founders need to understand how an investor calculates pre-money valuation.

Returning to the illustration, the founders approach a new investor who is willing to invest $1 million. The pre-money valuation assigned by the investor is $3 million. Since there are one million shares, the pre-money valuation in the view of the founders is $3 per share.

The post-money valuation is $4 million, which is the sum of the pre-money valuation and the $1 million invested. It is clear that after the investment, the founders would own 75% of the company and the investor would own 25%.

Now let's look at the option pool. By assumption, the new investor wants an option pool that is equal to 15% of the post-money valuation. The option pool as well as the founders' shares will be diluted by the 25% investment in the company by the new investor. This means that in determining the pre-money valuation, the option pool must be 15% (i.e., 20% × 75%). Moreover, this means that the new investor is treating the ownership prior to the investment for determining the pre-money valuation as follows: $2.4 million for the founders and $0.6 million for those employees who are assumed to be granted stock options. The $2.4 million is said to be the ***true pre-money valuation*** or the ***effective pre-money valuation***. This valuation is not shown in the term sheet.

When the investor makes the investment, this calculation means that it is the founders that are having their ownership interest diluted, not the new investor, who after the investment still has a 25% ownership of the company (25% of $4 million), and 15% will be treated as being owned by those who will be granted stock options. Thus, the founders will own 60% of the company, not 75%.

A table that shows the ownership interest before and after the investment is called a ***capitalization table***, or simply ***cap table***. The table below shows the cap table for our example:

	Pre-money	Ownership interest	Post-money	Ownership interest
Founders	$2.4 million	80%	$2.4 million	60%
Option pool	0.6 million	20%	0.6 million	15%
New investor	—	—	1.0 million	25%
Total	$3.0 million	100%	$4.0 million	100%

Let's look at the true pre-money price per share. Since the founders' true pre-money valuation is $2.4 million, based on one million shares owned, the per share pre-money price is $2.40. Hence, instead of a valuation of $3 per share pre-money price, the true pre-money share price is $2.40 per share.

A little analysis shows how many shares must be in the option pool. If the total value of the option pool is $600,000 and the per share price is $2.40, then by dividing $600,000 by $2.40 we get 25,000 shares.

To see the impact of the size of the option pool, suppose that instead of a 15% post-money option pool the new investor tries to negotiate for a 30% figure. This means that the ownership interest for the option pool must be 40% so that after it is diluted by 25%, it will have an ownership interest post-money of 30%. Going through the same calculations as above, of the $3 million pre-money valuation, the option pool valuation would be $1.2 million and the founders' valuation would be $1.8 million. The cap table under the above assumptions would be:

	Pre-money	Ownership interest	Post-money	Ownership interest
Founders	$1.8 million	60%	$1.8 million	45%
Option pool	1.2 million	40%	1.2 million	30%
New investor	—	—	1.0 million	25%
Total	$3.0 million	100.0%	$4.0 million	100%

If the founders' value is $1.8 million, this means that the pre-money share price must be $1.80. The number of shares in the option pool is then found by dividing the option pool valuation of $1.2 million by the share price of $1.80 to get 666,667 shares.

KEY POINTS COVERED IN THIS CHAPTER

- The capital structure of a company is the mix of equity and debt that the founders decide to use to finance the company.
- Equity (or equity-type debt) is typically the largest component of the capital structure of a nonfinancial company, particularly in the early stages of financing.
- Equity securities represent an ownership interest in a company and can be classified into two general categories, common stock and preferred stock.
- Holders of the common stock of a company are entitled to receive a pro rata share of the company's earnings and receive dividends when the earnings are paid out.
- Of importance to the founders when common stock shares are issued to obtain financing is the impact on their ownership percentage following a round of financing and on control of the company.
- Preferred stock is a hybrid security that combines the features of common stock and a debt obligation such as a bond. Unlike common stockholders, preferred stockholders typically do not have voting rights except under certain circumstances.
- In the early stages of a startup company, preferred stock that allows investors to convert preferred stock into common stock is the vehicle of choice for investors.
- Preferred stock comes with provisions that convey rights, preferences, and privileges to the investors in this security.

- The par value of preferred stock is important because if there is a liquidating event, where defined in the term sheet, it typically includes the acquisition or merger of the company and the selling off of most of the company's assets.

- Nonparticipating preferred stock does not permit an investor to participate in any proceeds above the amount of the investor's preference when there is a liquidation event.

- Participating preferred stock allows investors to share along with common stockholders in some fashion with respect to any remaining liquidation proceeds.

- Capped participating preferred stock (partially participating preferred stock) is a form of preferred stock in which there is participation but it is capped at a specified amount.

- Convertible preferred stock allows the investor to convert it into common stock.

- A convertible note, typically issued to investors in the early stage of financing prior to a Series A round of financing, is a form of debt.

- Convertible noteholders can either have the option to exchange the note for an equity position or automatically have the position converted into an equity position if there is a Series A round of financing.

- The equity position received by the holder of a convertible note is typically preferred stock.

- Debt with warrants, usually used in the later stages of a company's development, is another form of equity dilutive security whereby the warrants grant the holder the right to acquire a specified number of shares of common stock.

- The terms on which a company raises funds for any type of funding vehicle are set forth in a letter of intent, more popularly referred to as a term sheet.

- Although a term sheet is not a legal document, there are typically two elements of the term sheet that are intended to be legally binding on both parties: the confidentiality provision and the "no-shopping" provision.

- A term sheet for any security or funding instrument is basically divided into three sections: (1) a description of the funding, (2) the terms of the funding, and (3) investor protective provisions.

- Pre-money valuation means the value assigned to a company by an investor before the new investment is made. Post-money valuation is the valuation after the new investment is made.

- An important aspect of post-money valuation in financing rounds is the option pool.

- An option pool during a financing round is the amount of stock reserved for the hiring of new employees as the company grows.

- New investors will take into consideration the potential dilution effect the option pool will have on the pre-money valuation in order to determine the true pre-money valuation or the effective pre-money valuation.

- The capitalization table (cap table) shows the ownership interest before and after a new investment is made.

FURTHER READINGS

Angel Capital Association, *Angel Guide*book, appendix 11, sample 1, http://www.angelcapitalassociation.org/data/Documents/Resources/AngelCapitalEducation/Angel_Guidebook_-_Term_Sheet_1.pdf.

Barnett, Chance, "The Entrepreneur's Guide to Term Sheets and Equity Crowdfunding," *Forbes*, May 30, 2014, http://www.forbes.com/sites/chancebarnett/2014/05/30/the-entrepreneurs-guide-to-term-sheets-and-equity-crowdfunding.

O'Hear, Steve, "A Term Sheet Written in Plain English? Put That in Your Silicon Valley Pipe and Smoke It," *TechCrunch*, June 30, 2013, http://techcrunch.com/2013/06/20/keep-it-simple.

"Sample Term Sheet," *Startup Garage*, September 11, 2014, https://thestartupgarage.com/tsgwiki/sample_term_sheet.

Shontell, Alyson, "What a Straight Forward, Non-Jargony Term Sheet from a VC Looks Like," *Business Insider*, June 20, 2013, http://www.businessinsider.com/a-plain-english-term-sheet-venture-capitalist-2013-6.

Wilmerding, Alex, *Term Sheets & Valuations: A Line by Line Look at the Intricacies of Term Sheets & Valuations (Bigwig Briefs)*, 1st ed. (Aspatore Books, 2006).

8

OBJECTIVES AND PRINCIPLES OF FINANCIAL ACCOUNTING

A company's financial statements provide a summary of the operating, financing, and investing activities of a business. The information contained in financial statements is used by current and potential suppliers of capital, as well as by suppliers of products needed by a firm to generate its offerings of goods and services. The current shareholders of the firm (current suppliers of equity financing) are the firm's owners and will use the information contained in financial statements to assess the performance of management to determine whether to continue to invest in the firm, sell all or part of their interest in the firm, or increase their investment in the firm. Potential new equity investors such as venture capitalists and angels will use the financial statements to assess the investment merits of a startup company. Potential creditors of the firm (i.e., suppliers of capital from whom the firm seeks to borrow funds) will use the financial statements to assess the firm's ability to repay a loan obligation requested. Suppliers of goods and services that agree to provide them in exchange for a promise to pay at some future time will make the decision to extend credit after assessing the firm's ability to repay, much as other creditors do. The bottom line is that financial statements provide the financial information that all of the parties mentioned above will need to assess the future earnings and cash flow of a firm. It is from the financial statements that current and future suppliers of capital and the firm's management are able to determine how efficiently the firm is operating, how efficiently it is using the capital it has available, how its earnings might grow in the future, and where there are currently financial problems or there might be financial problems in the future.

There are four basic financial statements: the balance sheet, the income statement, the statement of cash flows, and the statement of shareholders' equity. Our focus in this chapter is on the objectives and basic principles of financial statements. The balance sheet and the income statement are the subjects of chapters 9 and 10, respectively. Chapter 11 covers the statement of cash flows and the statement of shareholders' equity. In our coverage of financial statements we do not explain how one creates these statements, which begins with the tedious task of recording transactions by means of double-entry bookkeeping. The construction of financial statements for a startup company is typically done by an external accounting firm that specializes in startup companies. Understanding how the financial statements are constructed is not necessary for an entrepreneur. Instead, what is important is how the entrepreneur uses the information in financial statements to make business decisions and to understand how suppliers of capital will be evaluating the firm. With a basic understanding of financial statements, we will see how financial statements are analyzed to provide the information sought about the performance of a startup company. That is, just looking at the raw numbers reported in the financial statements is not sufficient to assess the performance of a startup company; rather, it is the combining of the raw data from the four basic financial statements that is necessary to do so. This task is referred to as financial statement analysis and is the subject of chapter 12.

In seeking to raise capital, ventures provide financial statements to potential investors. In the United States, two financial reporting frameworks can be used, depending on the circumstances: *generally accepted accounting principles* (GAAP) and *special-purpose frameworks* (SPFs). In this chapter, we first describe GAAP accounting and then SPFs. A framework for helping the founders of a company choose between GAAP accounting and SPF accounting is provided.

In explaining financial statements in this chapter and the next, we will use examples from four publicly traded companies: Apple Inc., Bristol-Myers Squibb, iRobot, and MiMedx. The reason is quite simple: financial statements for privately companies are not available. The financial statements for publicly traded companies are distributed to shareholders in the annual report that such companies are required to distribute under U.S. securities law. Moreover, the financial statements become part of the periodic filing with the SEC, Form 10-K, which contains much more information than is contained in the annual report.

THE FOUR FINANCIAL STATEMENTS

In the next three chapters we will describe in detail the four financial statements that must be generated for a publicly traded business. Here we provide an overview of them and then move on to explain the assumptions and principles in constructing financial statements under GAAP.

Balance Sheet

The *balance sheet*, also called the *statement of financial condition*, shows the amount of a company's assets, liabilities, and equity as of the last day of the company's fiscal year, in the case of an annual balance sheet, or the last day of the fiscal quarter, in the case of a quarterly balance sheet. The assets of the company are the resources that management has to operate the firm. How were the assets financed (funded)? That is where the liabilities and equity come into play because they indicate where the funds were obtained. The liabilities represent the amount that the company borrowed. Equity represents the amount of the company assets financed by the owners of the firm (i.e., the stockholders, in the case of a corporation). Since a company can only be financed from debt and equity, there is a well-known accounting identity: assets = liabilities + equity.

Let's look at the 2013 balance sheet of Apple Inc. As of September 28, 2013, Apple's fiscal year end, assets were $207 billion. The liabilities and the equity (shown as shareholders' equity on the balance sheet) were $83.451 billion and $123.549 billion, respectively. As can be seen, the sum of the liabilities and the equity is equal to the assets.

Now for what might seem to be a simple question. If Apple wanted, for whatever reason, to sell off all its assets, approximately how much would it obtain? Let's look at the balance sheet: the assets are shown as having a value of $207 billion. Unfortunately, that is not the right answer. The reason is that the interpretation of the total assets shown on the balance sheet depends on the "rule" used in constructing the financial statements. This means that certain principles are applied in preparing financial statements. We'll discuss the rule later in the chapter and will then be able to understand what $207 billion means.

Here is another question that may seem to have a straightforward answer. By checking the balance sheet, can we determine what the market value of Apple's common stock was on September 28, 2013? The stockholders' equity on the balance sheet shows that value to be $123.549 billion. In fact, around September 30, 2013, Apple's stock was selling for around $480 per share and there were approximately 939.2 million shares outstanding. The approximate market value of the stock outstanding (referred to as its **market capitalization**) on September 28, 2013, was $450.816 billion ($480 per share × 939.2 million shares). Thus, the market value of the stock far exceeded the stockholders' equity as reported on the balance sheet. The reason for this difference lies once again in the rule followed to construct the stockholders' equity.

Income Statement

The **income statement** is a summary of the company's operating performance over a period of time (e.g., a fiscal quarter or a fiscal year). Other terms used for the income statement are the **earnings statement**, the **statement of operations**, and the **profit-and-loss statement**. This financial statement begins with the company's sales or, equivalently, its revenue. That item seems fairly simple to understand. However, that is not always the case for the reasons we explain in chapter 10 when we discuss the rule as to when a company is permitted to recognize revenue so as to include it in the income statement. The last line, the "bottom line," is the company's **net income**, which is also shown in terms of how much was earned per share of common stock, referred to as **earnings per share.**

For 2013 operations, Apple's net income was $37.037 billion. Following the net income on the income statement are two values shown for the company's earnings per share: $40.03 and $39.75. We'll explain why in chapter 10.

Statement of Cash Flows

As we explain in several chapters of this book, the cash flow of a company is critical for a variety of reasons. We provide a formal definition of what cash flow means in the next chapter. The *statement of cash flows* is a summary of a company's cash flows that contains information about where the company received and utilized its cash. More specifically, the statement of cash flows has three components: the cash flow from operations, the cash flow from investment activities, and the cash flow from financing activities.

Statement of Stockholders' Equity

The *statement of stockholders' equity*, also known as the *statement of shareholders' equity*, provides a summary of the changes in the stockholders' equity. In addition, it includes information regarding actions taken that have altered the number of shares outstanding. Such actions include the repurchasing of any stock by the company and the exercise of any stock options granted by the company over the time period,[1] and the sale of treasury stock.[2] The basic structure of this financial statement is to provide a reconciliation of the amount reported in each component of stockholders' equity from the beginning of the fiscal year with that reported at the end of the fiscal year.

GAAP FINANCIAL ACCOUNTING PRINCIPLES

To be useful to users of financial statements, the information contained in financial statements should have three important attributes. It should be relevant, it should be reliable, and it should be presented in a consistent manner so that current and potential suppliers of capital can make an informed decision about the investment merits of a company as an equity investment or its creditworthiness as a borrower of funds.

GAAP are a framework of accounting standards, rules, and practices that have been authoritatively established by recognized accounting bodies in the United States and abroad. In the United States, GAAP for private companies that want to report on a GAAP basis or that must comply under U.S. securities law, as well as GAAP for public companies, are set by the *Financial Accounting Standards Board* (FASB) and the accounting standards promulgated through its *Statement of Financial Accounting Standards* (SFAS). The FASB is an independent organization that the Securities and Exchange Commission (SEC) has designated to develop accounting standards. Here we discuss financial accounting based on U.S. GAAP; later we discuss SPFs and considerations that a company's management should assess and weight if it has the option of using GAAP or SPFs (i.e., non-GAAP financial accounting).

1. We discuss stock options in chapter 4.
2. Treasury stock is explained in chapter 9.

Outside the United States, the ***International Accounting Standards Board*** (IASB) sets GAAP. The IASB's accounting standards are called ***International Financial Reporting Standards*** (IFRS), which we refer to as non-U.S. GAAP. The United States is transitioning to IFRS. Fortunately, generally there are more similarities than differences between U.S. GAAP and non-U.S. GAAP (IFRS) because for most types of transactions, non-U.S. GAAP follow the same basic principles and conceptual framework as U.S. GAAP. In areas where there are differences, the IASB and the FASB have established committees to resolve the differences in accounting treatment. The SEC has encouraged the FASB to resolve any divergences between IFRS and U.S. GAAP because of its goal of requiring companies to report based on a single set of high-quality global accounting standards. Where there are differences between the IFRS and U.S. GAAP, some are just not material. Material differences do occur in important areas that are relevant to high-tech companies, such as the treatment of research-and-development costs. We describe this difference in chapter 9.

GAAP Assumptions

In the recording of financial transactions and in the construction of financial statements, certain assumptions are made and certain principles must be followed. These assumptions and principles are important because they affect the way that users of financial statements interpret the reported numbers. The following three assumptions are made in preparing financial statements in accordance with GAAP:

Assumption 1: monetary unit assumption.

Assumption 2: time period assumption.

Assumption 3: going-concern assumption.

Assumption 1: Monetary Unit Assumption   In the United States, the monetary unit in which financial statements are prepared is the U.S. dollar. The impact of inflation, together with a principle discussed below that assets must be recorded at their historical cost, may cause problems in using and interpreting these values in an inflationary environment.

Assumption 2: Time Period Assumption   Annual financial statements are constructed so as to cover operations over any consecutive twelve-month time period selected by the company, referred to as the ***fiscal year***. The three months covered by the four quarterly financial statements follow from the fiscal year selected. When the annual financial statement covers the period January 1 to December 31, the company is said to have a ***calendar year***.[3]

Many businesses are highly cyclical. Typically a company will select its fiscal year to coincide with the low point of activity in its business cycle. Apple's fiscal year is the

---

3. The Internal Revenue Service appears to use "fiscal year" in a different way for tax reporting. When a taxpayer selects any consecutive twelve-month time period other than a calendar year, the taxpayer is said to be using a fiscal year.

fifty-two- or fifty-three-week period that ends on the last Saturday of September. Its 2013 fiscal year end was September 28, 2013. Because the low point of activity in the business cycle may be selected as the end of the fiscal year, interpretation of the year-end values reported on the annual balance sheet and the statement of shareholders' equity may not be representative of values for the year.

Assumption 3: Going-Concern Assumption   The going-concern assumption is critical in applying the GAAP accounting principles discussed in the next section. To assume that a company will continue its business operations is to say that in the normal course of business (1) the company anticipates realizing what it has paid for its assets at the amount recorded on its balance sheet and (2) the company anticipates satisfying its liabilities to creditors. If the going-concern assumption is unwarranted for a company, then the amount, as well as the classification of assets and liabilities on the balance sheet, as explained in the next chapter, may need to be adjusted. This adjustment will have consequences for the reporting of revenues, expenses, and equity. In the next chapter we will see that on the balance sheet there is a time classification of assets and liabilities referred to as current and noncurrent items. This time classification has to do with a time frame of one year and more than one year. For that time classification to be meaningful, the going-concern assumption must be justified. Similarly, the GAAP principles of historical cost, revenue recognition, and matching are meaningful only within the context of the going-concern assumption.

In preparing financial statements, the auditor is required to evaluate conditions or events that might raise questions about the validity of the going-concern assumption. When an accountant concludes that the going-concern assumption is not warranted, this view is expressed in the accountant's opinion (auditor's opinion), which we discuss later in this chapter.

GAAP Principles

The six GAAP principles are the following:

Principle 1: Full disclosure principle.

Principle 2: Conservatism principle.

Principle 3: Revenue recognition principle.

Principle 4: Cost principle.

Principle 5: Matching principle.

Principle 6: Materiality principle.

Below we briefly explain each of these principles.

Principle 1: Full Disclosure Principle   The full disclosure principle means that for the accounting numbers of such accounting items as revenues, expenses, and assets, there should be narrative and additional numerical disclosures provided in notes accompanying the financial statement. In the absence of this full disclosure, an analysis of financial statements would not be complete.

Principle 2: Conservatism Principle   For certain transactions it is necessary to make an estimate when recording a transaction. Here are two examples of such instances. When a company purchases equipment, an estimate must be made of its economic life. The reason, as explained in the next chapter, is that the economic life is needed to determine how the cost of the equipment will be spread out over time. The periodic cost allocated to future fiscal periods is called *depreciation*. As another example, a company that sells a product that has a one-year warranty must estimate the percentage of items sold that will require repairs or replacement as provided for by the warranty contract. The conservatism principle means that when an accountant prepares financial statements using estimates provided by the company's management of situations equally likely to occur, the least optimistic estimate must be used.

Principle 3: Revenue Recognition Principle   Revenue recognition seems to be something that everyone in a business organization understands and should not be confused about. Yet a number of actions have been brought by the SEC and lawsuits have been brought by investors regarding either fraudulent acts in the recording of revenue from alleged sham transactions or the improper recognition of revenue because the company's reporting failed to truly reflect the economics of a transaction. In fact, a 2010 study of alleged fraudulent financial reporting by 347 companies registered with the SEC for the period 1998–2007 found that in 61% of the cases (including cases involving startup companies), improper revenue recognition was the fraudulent reporting charged.[4] Of the 347 companies in the study, 20% were in computer hardware and software industry and 11% were in the health care and health products industry.

Holding aside fraudulent acts, let's look at why revenue recognition is not as straightforward as one might expect. To do so, let's use an illustration. Suppose that a startup company agrees to provide a client with services for one year for $480,000. Suppose further that:

- the startup company signs an agreement for the delivery of the services with the customer on December 1, 2014;
- on the date of the signing, the company receives a check for the full year of services of $480,000;
- the company provides the service for the full month of December 2014; and

---

4. Committee of Sponsoring Organizations of the Treadway Commission, *Fraudulent Financial Reporting 1998–2007: An Analysis of U.S. Public Companies*, 2010.

- the company's accountant must prepare financial statements for the full year of 2014 (i.e., the time period for the financial statements for its fiscal year beginning on January 1, 2014, and ending on December 31, 2014).

Although the startup company received the amount of $480,000 for one year of services, it performed services for only one month, not for the twelve-month length of the contract. Thus the company earned only $40,000 ($480,000/12) of the $480,000. The financial accounting treatment would then show revenue of $40,000 for the company's 2014 fiscal year. The revenue is shown as part of the company's income statement. What happens to the balance of the payment that is unearned, $440,000? That amount becomes a liability of the company.

Let's change the illustration slightly. Suppose that on the signing of the agreement, the startup company agreed to invoice the customer six months later but still provide the agreed-upon services for December.

Given the above illustrations, we can explain the revenue recognition principle. Under GAAP, revenue is recognized if the following two conditions are satisfied: (1) the revenue is realized or realizable and (2) the revenue is earned. The first condition is satisfied if cash is received (i.e., revenue is realized, in this case). The first condition can still be met if certain criteria, described shortly, are satisfied. Except in fraudulent transactions, it is typically clear whether the service is performed.

Because of the problems that have arisen regarding revenue recognition, the staff of the SEC has intervened by providing guidelines for determining whether the two conditions for revenue recognition are satisfied. The conditions are met when all of the following criteria are established:

- There is persuasive evidence that an arrangement exists.
- Delivery has occurred or services have been performed.
- The price established between the company seeking revenue recognition and the customer is fixed or determinable.
- The collection of any unpaid amounts for the services performed is reasonably assured.

Returning to our illustration, in the case in which the $480,000 was received at the contract signing, the recognition of the $40,000 of revenue for the 2014 fiscal year is the appropriate GAAP treatment: cash was received and the services (by assumption) were performed. The case is not so clear when no cash is received at the signing of the agreement but an amount will be invoiced in the next fiscal year (2015). The first three criteria listed above are satisfied. However, there is insufficient information regarding the customer to determine the collectability of the $40,000. For example, suppose that the customer is another startup company that is strapped for cash and is in a weak financial condition. Then there would be a question as to whether the $40,000 should be recognized. Worse yet, one can imagine a fraudulent act whereby a company enters into sham transactions with an entity that it knows cannot satisfy the payment terms of a service agreement and uses those sham transactions to inflate its revenue.

The revenue recognition principle typically is stated in footnotes to a company's annual report. Here is what is stated in the revenue recognition footnote for the 2012 financial statement of Bristol-Myers Squibb:

Revenue Recognition
Revenue is recognized when persuasive evidence of an arrangement exists, the sales price is fixed and determinable, collectability is reasonably assured and title and substantially all risks and rewards of ownership is transferred, generally at time of shipment.

However, certain sales of non-U.S. businesses are recognized on the date of receipt by the purchaser. See Note 3 "Alliances and Collaborations" for further discussion of revenue recognition related to alliances. Provisions are made at the time of revenue recognition for expected sales returns, discounts, rebates and estimated sales allowances based on historical experience updated for changes in facts and circumstances including the impact of applicable healthcare legislation. Such provisions are recognized as a reduction of revenue.

Revenue is deferred until the right of return no longer exists or sufficient historical experience to estimate sales returns is developed when a new product is not an extension of an existing line of product or there is no historical experience with products in a similar therapeutic category.

We have singled out BMS because, as we note below when we describe the matching principle, there is a practice of manipulating income by what is known as channel stuffing. This practice has been followed by BMS.

Consequently, rules for revenue recognition may seem straightforward under GAAP, but complicated transactions may leave room for interpretation if revenue has been recognized. In particular, historically, revenue recognition for software has been the most difficult area because it involves some thorny issues. Because of questionable or improper treatment of revenue from the sale of software by companies seeking to manipulate earnings, in 1997 the accounting authorities published guidance as how to deal with revenue recognition.[5] Jeffrey Solomon has described the different models that firms may use when they sell software: (1) the software is licensed as a stand-alone canned product; (2) the software is bundled with hardware, other software, or postcontract support; or (3) the software is sold separately as a service.[6] Software can be developed for a customer based on the customer's needs, in which case revenue is generated through the software developer's billable hours, or it may be plug-and-play software. The accounting rules apply to any of these models. Moreover, the accounting rules potentially also apply to firms that sell products where software is one of the components (i.e., products with embedded software). For example, state-of-the art mobile devices include a major software component. Consequently, a telecommunications company that sells such devices may have to follow the accounting rules for software revenue recognition.

---

5. American Institute of Certified Public Accountants, rules, SOP 97–2, "Software Revenue Recognition."
6. Jeffrey D. Solomon, "Accounting Considerations for Start-Up Companies and the Angels Who Invest in Them," http://www.accountab.com/resources/articles/StartUpAccounting.htm.

When a contract for the sale of software involves the bundling of the software with post-contract support or any other services (e.g., helpline support), the fair market value of each component of the bundle must be determined. The financial accounting guidelines, as well as the implementation of those guidelines in practice, for determination of revenue recognition in such cases is complicated, so we won't review it here. What is important is that if management cannot convince its auditors that it is conforming to strict guidelines, some portion of the revenue for bundled software transactions will most likely not be recognized and must be deferred until satisfactory evidence can be presented to the auditor.

To see how complicated this can get, in Apple's 2013 financial statement there is a lengthy footnote (footnotes are common in financial statements and are part of disclosures) that deals with revenue recognition, and more specifically with "revenue recognition for arrangements with multiple deliverables," which is another way of saying bundled sales. The footnote reads:

For multi-element arrangements that include hardware products containing software essential to the hardware product's functionality, undelivered software elements that relate to the hardware product's essential software, and undelivered non-software services, the Company allocates revenue to all deliverables based on their relative selling prices. In such circumstances, the Company uses a hierarchy to determine the selling price to be used for allocating revenue to deliverables: (i) vendor-specific objective evidence of fair value ("VSOE"), (ii) third-party evidence of selling price ("TPE"), and (iii) best estimate of selling price ("ESP"). VSOE generally exists only when the Company sells the deliverable separately and is the price actually charged by the Company for that deliverable. ESPs reflect the Company's best estimates of what the selling prices of elements would be if they were sold regularly on a stand-alone basis. For multi-element arrangements accounted for in accordance with industry-specific software accounting guidance, the Company allocates revenue to all deliverables based on the VSOE of each element, and if VSOE does not exist revenue is recognized when elements lacking VSOE are delivered.

Is this clear? Not likely, but it does suggest that what may seem to be a simple transaction—say, the sale of an iPhone—is not as straightforward as it seems. Moreover, the GAAP accounting rules dealing with revenue recognition are important in developing sales contracts to realize the intended revenue recognition outcome.[7]

As can be seen from this last illustration, it is not just the timing of revenue recognition but its measure under GAAP that is important.

Principle 4: Cost Principle   As we explain in the next chapter when we discuss the balance sheet in more detail, the information in the financial statement identifies assets that have been purchased by a firm. The amount that the firm paid for the assets is initially shown on the balance sheet. The amount on the balance sheet will change over time, but there will not be an upward adjustment as the result of an increase in the fair value of the asset. A downward adjustment may occur for two reasons.

---

7. An excellent discussion as to how sales contracts should be constructed and the involvement of the company's accounting is provided in Solomon, "Accounting Considerations for Start-Up Companies and the Angels Who Invest in Them."

First, a downward adjustment is made for certain types of assets as a result of depreciation or amortization, which will reduce the amount on the balance sheet below the amount paid for an asset. Even the depreciation or amortization figure does not reflect the true amount by which an asset declines, however. Rather, that amount is determined by the accountant using a set of rules, as explained in chapter 10. The second reason for a downward adjustment is evident impairment of an asset recorded on a balance sheet, which requires a reduction in that asset's carrying value on the balance sheet to its fair value. GAAP principles specify how to test for *impairment of an asset*.

Consequently, the amount shown on the balance sheet reflects only historical costs adjusted downward for depreciation, amortization, and any impairments. So a startup company that purchases a patent from another firm for $1 million, even though the patent eventually has an estimated market value of $100 million, will show the amount on the balance sheet as $1 million. (Actually, that amount will be reduced by amortization.)

Principle 5: Matching Principle   For the income statement to be meaningful, the revenues and expenses must be properly matched for the period covered by the statement. That is, revenues are properly recognized (recall the revenue recognition principle) in the period in which they are earned and the expenses associated with the generation of revenues are correctly matched with those revenues.

What is important to understand is that in seeking to create an income statement that reflects a company's operations in generating income, looking at when cash is spent to generate a company's offerings (goods and services) and when it pays cash to purchase the inputs needed to generate revenue will be misleading. That is, the revenues and expenses under GAAP do not necessarily correspond to the inflow and outflow of cash.

In our discussion of the revenue recognition principle, we used the illustration of a company generating $480,000 in cash for consulting services on December 1 of its calendar year for services to be provided for twelve months. It was clear that under GAAP, only $40,000 would be treated as revenue on the company's income statement. Suppose that the company in its previous calendar year purchased equipment costing $3 million and that equipment was used in servicing the $480,000 contract. To fairly represent this company's income for the calendar year, it is necessary to determine how much of that equipment was used in the generation of this calendar year's revenue. This is not done arbitrarily. As we explain in the next two chapters, where we provide more details about the income statement and the balance sheet, there are GAAP rules for determining this amount based on accounting depreciation.

To implement the matching principle requires that the accounting be done on what is called an accrual basis of accounting as opposed to a cash basis of accounting or a modified cash basis of accounting. Under the *cash basis of accounting*, revenue is recognized when cash is received and expenses are recognized when cash is paid out. Obviously, for most businesses this does not satisfy the matching principle. Under the *accrual basis of accounting*, revenue is recognized as we explained earlier, when it is earned and realized (or realizable), and expenses are recognized in the period in which revenue is recognized. The *modified cash basis of accounting*, also referred to as the *modified accrual basis of accounting* or the *hybrid basis of accounting*, blends the cash basis and accrual basis of accounting. Basically, it is the cash basis of accounting that involves modifications that have "substantial support." Although the accounting profession does not clearly define what is meant by substantial support, transactions are recorded recognizing that there is a logical basis that certain transactions should be treated on an accrual basis. The cost of high-priced equipment that has a long useful life would be an example of an asset that should not logically be treated as an expense in the current fiscal period if cash is paid for the equipment under the modified cash basis of accounting.

When an asset is acquired that has expected benefits that extend greater than one year, at the time the asset is acquired, the price paid is recorded on the balance sheet as an appropriately titled asset. For example, it could be "Equipment." When the accountant creates an asset at the time of purchase, the accountant is said to be *capitalizing* the asset, as opposed to expensing the asset. Over time, the asset that has been capitalized will be subject to GAAP rules for the periodic reduction in its value depending on the type of asset, as explained in the next chapter: depreciation, amortization, or impairment.

Because of the matching principle, there are often *timing differences* that result from revenue and expense recognition when the accrual basis of accounting rather than the cash basis of accounting is used. The timing differences that occur lead to "accruals" and "deferred" items on the balance sheet. There are four types of timing differences: accrued revenues, accrued expenses, deferred revenues, and deferred expenses.

Accrued revenue occurs when revenue is recognized before cash is received. This was illustrated earlier when service was performed in the month of December in the amount of $40,000 but the invoicing of this amount occurred in the next calendar year. *Accrued expense* occurs when an expense is recognized before cash is paid. As for deferrals, *deferred revenue* is revenue recognized after cash is received, while a *deferred expense* is an expense that is recognized after cash is paid.

Because the accrual basis of accounting relies on a company's discretion in determining the timing of revenue and expense recognition, there is the potential for manipulation of income. In our discussion of revenue recognition we described how manipulation of when revenue is recognized is one of the major manifestations of accounting fraud. A similar fraudulent outcome can occur if the timing of expenses is manipulated. The manipulation of income is not always to increase income. It could be done by a company to smooth income or revenue in order to meet investor expectations.

The three most common ways in which income smoothing has been used to manipulate income are channel stuffing, the use of pull-in sales schemes, and the use of "cookie jar" reserves.

Channel stuffing **Channel stuffing** is a scheme that accelerates revenues and income in the current fiscal period at the expense of revenues and income in a future fiscal period. The practice involves a company that is in a strong enough position to coerce orders from companies in its distribution channel to order more of its offerings than they expect to sell. The order is shipped at the end of the fiscal quarter, with the coercing company agreeing to accept the return of the shipment and provide full credit to the purchasing company. The result is that the coercing company can report greater revenue and therefore a higher income for the fiscal period.

The SEC has a financial reporting enforcement program. When failure to comply with the GAAP requirements described for revenue recognition is identified, sanctions have been imposed on violating companies. Settlement with the SEC has included payment of substantial financial penalties and incurring of civil injunctions against those executives or senior managers alleged to be involved in the channel-stuffing scheme. The four most notable channeling enforcement actions brought by the SEC were against Bristol-Myers Squibb, Sunbeam, Microtune, and Symbol Technologies.[8]

As noted by two attorneys of the law firm of Sidley Austin LLP, the practice of channel stuffing "is not fraudulent *per se.*"[9] However, when channel stuffing is undertaken to mislead investors, it may constitute fraud.[10] If channel stuffing is followed, the practice should be properly disclosed in the financial statements. For example, the SEC sanctioned Cypress Bioscience, Inc., for (1) failing to disclose the acceleration of a significant amount of sales revenue as a business practice and (2) failing to discuss the financial implications for future fiscal periods.

Pull-in sales Another practice for earnings and revenue management that companies have used is **pull-in sales**. With this practice, there are existing orders that are scheduled to ship to customers in a future fiscal quarter. Instead of shipping the order as scheduled and recognizing the revenue in the future fiscal quarter when it was supposed to be shipped, the order is shipped early and booked in the current fiscal quarter.

Cookie jar reserves Finally, there is the use of what is referred to as "cookie jar" reserves. In a typical cookie jar scheme, a company makes inappropriate assumptions about some expense, overstating the expense in a fiscal period when earnings are good (i.e., in years when earnings are greater than investors might have anticipated). For example, warranty

---

8. For a discussion of each of these enforcement actions, see George B. Parizek and Madeleine V. Findley, "Charting a Course: Revenue Recognition Practices for Today's Business Environment" (Washington, DC: Sidley Austin LLP, 2008), http://www.sidley.com/files/Publication/fc85caf5-4e58-45e6-bc25-cc7ff9f7640c/Presentation/PublicationAttachment/f4ac4695-8da3-4e68-871e-cc9cd27f0a23/ChartingaCourse.pdf.
9. Parizek and Findley, "Charting a Course: Revenue Recognition Practices for Today's Business Environment," 1.
10. Garfield v. NDC Health Corp., 466 F.3d 1255, 1261–62 (11th Cir. 2006).

expenses might be overstated, and the difference between the amount recognized as an expense in the current fiscal period and the lower amount that should have been charged is placed in a "cookie jar." In a future fiscal period when earnings are not as good as investors anticipate, the company dips into the cookie jar and does not charge the true expense for the fiscal period.

The SEC has found such a practice of creating cookie jar reserves when there are expenses for restructuring a company. Restructuring means reorganizing the ownership, legal, operations, or other strategic aspects of a company. Restructuring expenses, which can be substantial, include cash costs, asset write-offs, accrued liabilities, and the cost of severance pay when employees are laid off. For example, the Canadian smartphone maker BlackBerry Ltd. indicated in October 2013 that its restructuring costs would be about U.S. $400 million by the end of May 2014. The restructuring was due to changes in how it manufactured smartphones and in its marketing operations, and to the costs associated with the reduction of its workforce by 4,500 employees. A company that incurs restructuring expenses has considerable discretion in deciding in what future fiscal period to recognize those expenses. A publicly traded company might recognize a substantial portion of restructuring expenses because the company is willing to take a hit to its income in the current fiscal period in order to look more profitable in a future fiscal period. This is referred to as "big bath charges."

Principle 6: Materiality Principle   Accounting as practiced under GAAP recognizes that in the implementation of any of the above accounting principles, there will be transactions or instances in which the financial information contained in the financial statements is of no relevance to users. In such cases, the materiality principle allows the accountant to ignore strict adherence to a principle. For example, suppose that on the first day of the third fiscal quarter Apple Inc. prepays $6,000 for a one-year subscription to several IT magazines for its research staff. The matching principle would require that $500 for the magazines be charged as an expense each month ($6,000/12). That is, for the third and the fourth fiscal quarters there should be an expense charge of $1,500 per quarter. The balance would be charged in the first two fiscal quarters of the next fiscal year. However, charging the entire $6,000 as an expense at the time of purchase for Apple will not in any way materially affect the financial statements of a company whose annual revenue in 2015 was $234 billion.

However, there is no definitive answer to the question of how small a transaction or accounting item has to be in order to be viewed as immaterial. The accounting profession would argue that the accountant must use judgment. One would expect that the size of the transaction relative to the company's size would be an important factor used by an accountant in determining whether the transaction is material.

THE INDEPENDENT AUDITOR AND THE AUDITOR'S REPORT

A company's management is responsible for the preparation and integrity of the financial information presented in the financial statements. More specifically, it is the company's management that has the responsibility of making sure that the financial statements have been prepared and presented fairly and in conformity with GAAP. It is management that is responsible for making sure that certain estimates and judgments mandated by GAAP are made properly. Within the company, this function is performed by the internal auditors.

Users of financial statements are not likely to accept the financial statements as unbiased if no independent analysis was performed to attest that the financial statements were prepared in conformity with GAAP. This independent analysis is performed by an independent accounting firm that has employees who are certified public accountants (CPAs). These firms are retained by the audit committee of the board of directors to audit the financial statements and provide an opinion or a report (the different types of opinions we discuss later). The independent auditor (or external auditor) works together with the internal auditor and the board's audit committee to gather the information needed to form an opinion about the conformity with GAAP of management's financial statement. That is, while an auditor provides an opinion or report about the financial statements, the financial statements are still those of the company's management.

Auditor's Opinion (Report)

One of four possible auditor opinions can be given as a result of an auditor's review of the company's financial statements: an unqualified opinion, a qualified opinion, an adverse opinion, and a disclaimer of opinion.

An ***unqualified opinion*** (also referred to as a "clean opinion") means that it is the belief of the auditor that the financial statements are presented fairly and in conformity with GAAP. For example, the unqualified opinion given to the 2012 financial statements of Bristol-Myers Squibb by its independent auditing firm, Deloitte & Touche LLP, stated:

In our opinion, such consolidated financial statements present fairly, in all material respects, the financial position of Bristol-Myers Squibb Company and subsidiaries as of December 31, 2012 and 2011, and the results of their operations and their cash flows for each of the three years in the period ended December 31, 2012 in conformity with accounting principles generally accepted in the United States of America.

When the auditor believes that the financial statements present the company's financial position, results of operations, and cash flows in conformity with GAAP, except for some matter that remains qualified, a ***qualified opinion*** is issued. The qualification that was the cause of the qualified opinion will be identified and explained in the auditor's opinion. The qualification will result from either a departure from GAAP, or the independent auditor's doubt as to the company continuing as a going concern, or the scope of the audit.

An *adverse opinion* is issued when in the opinion of the independent auditor the financial statements do not present the company's financial position, results of operations, and cash flows in conformity with GAAP. This opinion is issued when there are significant departures from GAAP. When an auditor is unable to formulate an opinion regarding the financial statement, a *disclaimer of opinion* is issued.

If an independent auditor issues an opinion but subsequently discovers a serious error owing to, for example, suspected illegal activities, the auditor will indicate a *withdrawal of opinion*.

Accountant Review of Interim Financial Statements

The annual financial statements must be audited and must carry the independent auditor's opinion. Although interim financial statements (e.g., quarterly financial statements) must be prepared in accordance with GAAP, they are not required to be audited. Instead of an audit, a "review" by an accountant is required. A review does not provide a basis for the accountant to express an opinion about whether the financial statements are presented fairly and in conformity with GAAP. Rather, the purpose of the review is to provide a basis for communicating whether the accountant is aware of any material modifications that should be made to the interim financial statements in order for those statements to conform to GAAP.

When an accountant undertakes a review of interim financial statements, the full set of general accounting auditing standards that guide audits is not used. Auditing requires (1) tests of accounting records through inspection, observation, or confirmation; (2) tests of the company's internal controls for the purpose of evaluating their effectiveness; and (3) obtaining corroborating evidence in response to inquiries. Rather, the scope of the engagement in a review consists primarily of performing analytical procedures and questioning employees responsible for financial and accounting matters. Although it is through these activities that a review may identify for the accountant significant matters affecting the interim financial information; it does not provide assurances that the accountant will be able to identify all significant matters that an audit might disclose.

NON-GAAP ACCOUNTING FOR PRIVATE COMPANIES

The preparation of the financial statements based on GAAP described thus far in this chapter is applicable to companies whose securities are publicly traded, as well as to certain private companies. Small- and medium-sized private companies have a choice of using GAAP accounting as described thus far in this chapter or non-GAAP accounting as provided for by the American Institute of Certified Public Accountants (AICPA). The principles for the preparation of financial statements based on non-GAAP accounting are set forth in what is called a *special-purpose framework*, more popularly referred to as *other comprehensive bases of accounting* (OCBOA). SPFs include, for example, non-GAAP bases of accounting, such as the use of cash basis accounting and modified cash basis accounting, which we discussed earlier in this chapter.

The AICPA's Financial Reporting Framework for Small- and Medium-Sized Entities (referred to hereafter as FRF for SMEs) allows financial reporting on a non-GAAP basis by small and medium-sized companies using a combination of traditional accounting principles (e.g., historical cost principle) and tax-reporting methods of accounting for accruals.[11] When selecting an accounting policy to follow for a transaction, as described in the next chapter, the FRF for SMEs gives management considerable flexibility in making the decision so as to better satisfy the needs of the targeted users of its financial statements. Unlike GAAP accounting, where compliance with the disclosure principle is paramount and requires that considerable information be disclosed by the company, this is not the case for FRF for SMEs. Instead, the framework is intended to provide more intuitive and nontechnical financial information, encouraging the company to employ professional judgment in dealing with transactions. In addition to the ability of the company to provide more customized financial statements for end users, another important factor is the reduced cost of preparing financial statements based on FRF for SMEs compared to preparing financial statements based on GAAP.

According to the AICPA, the FRF for SMEs has the following attributes:

- *Objectivity:* The framework is free from bias.
- *Measurability:* The framework permits reasonably consistent measurements.
- *Completeness:* The framework is sufficiently complete so that those relevant factors that would alter a conclusion about the financial statements are not omitted.
- *Relevance:* The framework is relevant to financial statement users.[12]

HOW TO SELECT AN ACCOUNTING FRAMEWORK

Although all of the frameworks provided for by GAAP and SPFs enable the generation of credible financial reporting, there are factors that a company must consider in selecting an accounting framework. Basically, the decision comes down to weighing the attributes of the different frameworks against the needs of financial statement users. The AICPA has provided a three-part decision tool for selecting the accounting framework decision.[13] We describe the accounting framework decision tool here.

Part 1 of the Decision Tool

Part 1 involves the company's management answering two questions. The first question is: Is there a reporting requirement (e.g., regulatory, legal) that requires GAAP-based financial statements? For example, if a company is required to prepare financial statements that

11. The IASB has also issued international GAAP for small and medium-sized entities.
12. AICPA, "Financial Reporting Framework for Small- and Medium-Sized Entities," 2013, http://www.aicpa.org/ INTERESTAREAS/FRC/ACCOUNTINGFINANCIALREPORTING/PCFR/Pages/Financial-Reporting-Framework.aspx, v.
13. AICPA, "Decision Tool for Adopting an Accounting Framework," 2013.

must be sent to the SEC, then it must use GAAP reporting since that is the accounting framework mandated by that regulator. So if the answer to the first question is yes, then the process stops, and GAAP accounting is used.

If the answer to the above question is no, then the next question to be answered in part 1 of the decision tool is: Does the company operate in an industry where transactions require highly specialized accounting guidance, making the use of a non-GAAP framework insufficient for financial reporting purposes? An affirmative answer means that GAAP should be used and the process ends with GAAP accounting being used. If the answer is negative, the company must consider whether the accounting framework that it currently utilizes satisfies the needs of those who are expected to be its financial statement users or whether another framework might better meet those needs. This is where part 2 of the decision tool is used.

Part 2 of the Decision Tool

In considering GAAP or SPFs, part 2 of the decision framework involves the assessment and weighing by the company's management of the following three groups of considerations:[14]

- overall considerations,
- considerations that are related to GAAP, and
- considerations that are related to the FRF for SMEs accounting framework.

The AICPA document on selecting the accounting framework includes lists of considerations for each of these groups. The list of considerations will not be reproduced here in their entirety. Instead, just a few examples will be given.

Overall Considerations   The following selected overall considerations (taken verbatim) are suggested by the AICPA:

- The nature of the entity and the purpose of the financial statements.
- The users of the financial statements and their financial reporting needs.
- The requirements within existing loan covenants and financing arrangements related to the accounting framework used by the entity and the ability to negotiate such requirements.
- Legal agreements or other arrangements and their implications related to the accounting framework used in the preparation of the financial statements.
- The ability of the accounting framework to result in financial statements that represent the underlying transactions and events in a manner that achieves a fair presentation.
- How the various features among accounting frameworks impact the ability to answer the needs of the financial statement users.
- Short-term and long-term financial reporting needs of the entity and how that factors into the choice of an accounting framework.

---

14. There is actually a fourth group that is not discussed here because it relates to the tax basis of accounting.

Considerations Related to GAAP   The circumstances that may indicate that a company would prefer GAAP-based financial reporting include the following:

- The entity plans to broaden ownership interests in the entity or issue equity in an initial public offering (i.e., go public).
- The entity has significant foreign operations or plans to significantly expand operations globally.
- The entity engages in complex transactions (e.g., complicated financial instruments).
- The entity has significant partnerships with public companies or with other entities that use GAAP-based reporting.
- The entity has the intention of holding itself to public company standards or GAAP.
- The entity competes with public companies for access to credit.
- The entity plans to sell the business to a public company or another entity where GAAP-based reporting is preferred or required.
- The entity plans to access foreign capital or debt markets.
- The entity operates in an industry in which extensive industry-specific accounting rules exist.
- Key users of the entity's financial statements do not have direct access to management.
- Fair-value accounting has significant utility for the financial statement users.
- Topics included in GAAP and omitted in non-GAAP frameworks (e.g., deferred income tax accounting or other comprehensive income) are highly relevant to the entity and its financial statement users.

As can be seen, several of the above circumstances are highly relevant considerations for a startup company.

Considerations Related to the FRF for SMEs Accounting Framework   The AICPA identifies the following characteristics of companies using the FRF for SMEs:

- The owners and management of the entity have no intention of going public.
- The entity may be owner-managed; that is, it is a closely held company where the people who own a controlling ownership interest in the entity are substantially the same set of people who run the company.
- Management and owners of the entity rely on a set of financial statements to confirm their assessments of performance, cash flows, and of what they own and what they owe.
- The entity does not engage in overly complicated transactions.
- The entity does not have significant foreign operations.
- Key users of the entity's financial statements have direct access to the entity's management.

- Users of the entity's financial statements may have greater interest in cash flows, liquidity, statements of financial position strength, and interest coverage.
- The entity's financial statements support applications for bank financing when the banker does not base a lending decision solely on the financial statements but also on available collateral or other evaluation mechanisms not directly related to the financial statements.

Part 3 of the Decision Tool

Given the assessment and weighing of the three considerations discussed above, the company moves on to discuss with the accounting firm it has engaged and with the appropriate stakeholders (such as venture capitalists or angels) before making its final decision. This is part 3 of the decision tool. The decision will then be reviewed periodically based on changes in circumstances and the considerations detailed above.

KEY POINTS COVERED IN THIS CHAPTER

- A summary of the operating, financing, and investing activities of a business used by current and potential suppliers of capital is provided in the company's financial statements.
- The four basic financial statements are the balance sheet, the income statement, the statement of cash flows, and the statement of shareholders' equity.
- The two financial reporting frameworks that can be used, depending on the circumstances, are generally accepted accounting principles (GAAP) and special-purpose frameworks (SPFs).
- A balance sheet (statement of financial condition) shows the amount of a company's assets, liabilities, and equity at a given point in time.
- The assets of the company are the resources that management has to operate the firm.
- The liabilities (i.e., the amount the company has borrowed) and equity (i.e., the amount provided by the owners) indicate how the assets were funded.
- The well-known accounting identity is: assets = liabilities + equity.
- The income statement (also called the earnings statement, the statement of operations, and the profit-and-loss statement) provides a summary of the company's operating performance over a specific period of time (e.g., a fiscal quarter or a fiscal year).
- A company's earnings per share figure is how much was earned per share of common stock.
- The statement of cash flows, a summary of a company's cash flows that contains information about whence the company received and how it utilized its cash, has three components: cash flows from operations, cash flows from investment activities, and cash flows from financing activities.

- The statement of stockholders' equity (statement of shareholders' equity) summarizes changes in the stockholders' equity.

- GAAP is a framework of accounting standards, rules, and practices that have been authoritatively established by recognized accounting bodies in the United States and abroad. Outside the United States, the International Accounting Standards Board (IASB) sets GAAP.

- In recording financial transactions in order to produce financial statements, certain assumptions and principles are made that affect how users of financial statements interpret the reported numbers.

- The three assumptions made in preparing financial statements in accordance with GAAP are (1) the monetary unit assumption, (2) the time period assumption, and (3) the going-concern assumption.

- The six principles are (1) the full disclosure principle, (2) the conservatism principle, (3) the revenue recognition principle, (4) the cost principle, (5) the matching principle, and (6) the materiality principle.

- To implement the matching principle requires that the accounting be done on an accrual basis of accounting as opposed to a cash basis of accounting or a modified cash basis of accounting.

- Under the cash basis of accounting, revenue is recognized when cash is received and expenses are recognized when cash is paid out; for most businesses, this method does not satisfy the matching principle.

- Under the accrual basis of accounting, revenue is recognized when it is earned and realized (or realizable) and expenses are recognized in the period in which revenue is recognized.

- The modified cash basis of accounting (modified accrual basis of accounting or the hybrid basis of accounting) blends the cash and accrual basis of accounting.

- Because of the matching principle, there are often timing differences that result from revenue and expense recognition when the accrual basis of accounting rather than the cash basis of accounting is used, leading to "accruals" and "deferred" items being reported on the balance sheet.

- The responsibility for the preparation and integrity of the information presented in the financial statements falls to the company's management.

- Because users of financial statements are not likely to accept financial statements being unbiased, an independent certified public accountant (CPA) is engaged to judge whether the financial statements were prepared in conformity with GAAP.

- The independent CPA audits the financial statements and provides an opinion, which may be either an unqualified opinion (clean opinion), or a qualified opinion, or an adverse opinion, or a disclaimer of opinion.

- In contrast to annual financial statements, which must be audited and must carry the auditor's opinion, interim financial statements (e.g., quarterly financial statements) involve a review of the financial statements for the purpose of providing a basis for communicating whether the independent auditor is aware of any material modifications that should be made to the interim financial statements in order for those statements to conform with GAAP.

- The preparation of the financial statements based on GAAP is applicable to companies whose securities are publicly traded and to certain private companies, but small- and medium-sized private companies have a choice of using GAAP accounting or non-GAAP accounting as provided for by the American Institute of Certified Public Accountants.

- A special-purpose framework or SPF sets forth the principles for the preparation of financial statements based on non-GAAP accounting.

- All of the frameworks provided for by GAAP and SPFs enable the generation of credible financial reporting; however, there are two factors that management must consider in selecting an accounting framework: (1) whether there is a regulatory or legal requirement mandating the use of GAAP-based financial statements and (2) whether the company operates in an industry where transactions require highly specialized accounting guidance, making the use of a non-GAAP framework insufficient for financial reporting purposes.

FURTHER READINGS

Peterson Drake, Pamela, and Frank J. Fabozzi, *Analysis of Financial Statements,* 3rd ed. (Hoboken, NJ: John Wiley & Sons, 2006), chaps. 1, 2, 3, and 10.

Weil, Roman L., Katherine Schipper, and Jennifer Francis, *Financial Accounting: An Introduction to Concepts, Methods and Uses,* 14th ed. (Mason, OH: South-Western College Publishers, 2013), chap. 1.

Weygandt, Jerry J., Donald E. Kieso, and Paul D. Kimmel, *Financial Accounting,* 9th ed. (Hoboken, NJ: John Wiley & Sons, 2013), chap. 9.

9

BALANCE SHEET

As explained in the previous chapter, there are four basic financial statements: the balance sheet, the income statement, the statement of cash flows, and the statement of shareholders' equity. In this chapter and the two that follow we discuss each of these financial statements. Our focus in this chapter is on the balance sheet.

The **balance sheet**, also referred to as the **statement of financial condition**, is a report of a company's assets, liabilities, and equity, generally at the end of a fiscal quarter or fiscal year. As explained in the previous chapter, the components of the balance sheet are divided into three groups: assets, liabilities, and equity. Assets are what the company owns and liabilities and equity indicate how the company financed those assets.

We will use as our illustration the balance sheet of two actual corporations:

- MiMedx Group Inc. (ticker symbol MDXG): MiMedx is a small regenerative tissue manufacturer whose FDA-approved tissues are designed for the treatment of diabetic foot ulcers. Table 9.1 shows the balance sheet of MiMedx as of December 31, 2012. It had total assets of $35,182,608 as of December 31, 2012.
- iRobot Corporation (ticker symbol IRBT): iRobot designs and builds robots (home care robots) and government and industrial robots that perform tasks such as "battlefield reconnaissance and bomb disposal, multi-purpose tasks for local police and first responders, and long-endurance oceanic missions." Table 9.2 shows the balance sheet of iRobot as of December 29, 2013. iRobot's total assets on December 29, 2013, the end of its fiscal year, were $356.796 million.

ASSETS

The assets of a company are its resources. There are different ways to classify assets. One way is based on how long it would take to convert the asset into cash. When an asset can be converted into cash within one year or one operating cycle, it is said to be a **current asset**. A company's **operating cycle** is the length of time it takes to convert an investment of cash in inventory back into cash through the collections of sales. The operating cycle for most

Table 9.1
Balance Sheet of MiMedx Group Inc. and Subsidiaries as of December 31, 2012

ASSETS	
Current assets:	
Cash and cash equivalents	**$6,754,485**
Accounts receivable, net	7,653,561
Inventory, net	3,022,784
Prepaid expenses and other current assets	657,961
Total current assets	18,088,791
Property and equipment, net of accumulated depreciation of $2,279,840	1,071,625
Goodwill	4,040,443
Intangible assets, net of accumulated amortization of $4,848,756	11,911,749
Deposits and other long term assets	70,000
Total assets	$35,182,608

LIABILITIES AND STOCKHOLDERS' EQUITY	
Current liabilities:	
Accounts payable	$1,251,684
Accrued expenses	3,743,934
Other current liabilities	75,154
Current portion of line of credit with related party	—
Current portion of long term convertible debt related to acquisition	—
Total current liabilities	5,070,772
Earn-out liability payable in MiMedx common stock	5,792,330
Convertible Senior Secured Promissory Notes	4,012,442
Other liabilities	299,762
Total liabilities	15,175,306
Commitments and contingency (Notes 14 and 15)	
Stockholders' equity:	
Preferred stock; $.001 par value; 5,000,000 shares authorized and 0 shares issued and outstanding	—
Common stock; $.001 par value; 130,000,000 shares authorized; 88,423,169 issued and 88,373,169 outstanding for 2012	88,423
Additional paid-in capital	89,627,601
Treasury stock (50,000 shares at cost)	(25,000)
Accumulated deficit	(69,683,722)
Total stockholders' equity	20,007,302
Total liabilities and stockholders' equity	$35,182,608

Table 9.2
iRobot Corporation Consolidated Balance Sheet as of December 29, 2012 (in $ thousands)

ASSETS	
Current assets:	
Cash and cash equivalents	**$126,770**
Short term investments	12,430
Accounts receivable, net of allowance of $111 and $87 at December 29, 2012	29,413
Unbilled revenue	1,196
Inventory	36,965
Deferred tax assets	19,266
Other current assets	11,518
Total current assets	237,558
Property and equipment, net	24,953
Deferred tax assets	8,610
Goodwill	48,951
Intangible assets, net	28,224
Other assets	8,500
Total assets	$356,796

LIABILITIES, REDEEMABLE CONVERTIBLE PREFERRED STOCK AND STOCKHOLDERS' EQUITY	
Current liabilities:	
Accounts payable	$42,515
Accrued expenses	16,527
Accrued compensation	11,864
Deferred revenue and customer advances	6,257
Total current liabilities	77,163
Long term liabilities	3,816
Commitments and contingencies (Note 11):	
Redeemable convertible preferred stock, 5,000,000 shares authorized and no shares issued or outstanding	
Common stock, $0.01 par value, 100,000,000 shares authorized and 27,781,659 shares issued and outstanding	278
Additional paid-in capital	199,903
Retained earnings	75,437
Accumulated other comprehensive income	199
Total stockholders' equity	275,817
Total liabilities, redeemable convertible preferred stock and stockholders' equity	$356,796

companies does not exceed one year. A **noncurrent asset** or a **long-term asset** is an asset that does not satisfy the criterion to be classified as a current asset.

Current Assets

In the presentation of the assets on the balance sheet, current assets appear first and then noncurrent assets. The reason for this is that the order of listing reported on the balance sheet is typically reported in order of liquidity, with the most liquid asset listed first and the least liquid listed last.

There are different types of current assets, as can be seen for MiMedx: cash and cash equivalents, accounts receivable, inventories, and prepaid expenses and other current assets. The footnotes to MiMedx's balance sheet describe the first three current assets as follows:

Cash and Cash Equivalents
Cash and cash equivalents include all highly liquid investments with an original maturity of three months or less.

Accounts Receivable
Accounts receivable represent amounts due from customers for which revenue has been recognized. Generally, the Company does not require collateral or any other security to support its receivables.

The allowance for doubtful accounts is the Company's best estimate of the amount of probable credit losses in the Company's existing receivables. The Company determines the allowance based on factors such as historical collection experience, customer's current creditworthiness, customer concentration, age of accounts receivable balance and general economic conditions that may affect the customer's ability to pay. ...

Inventories
Inventories are valued at the lower of cost or market, using the first-in, first-out (FIFO) method. Inventory is tracked through Raw Material, WIP, and Finished Good stages as the product progresses through various production steps and stocking locations. Within WIP labor and overhead costs are absorbed through the various production processes upon work order closes in our ERP (Enterprise Resource Planning) system. Historical yields and normal capacities are utilized in the calculation of production overhead rates. Reserves for inventory obsolescence are utilized to account for slow-moving inventory as well as inventory no longer needed due to diminished market demand.

Note the following from the excerpt above. First, we see an example of where management must make an estimate: accounts receivable. A company realizes that not all of its customers who have purchased its product on credit will make their payments. Consequently, an estimate must be made for what are referred to as "doubtful accounts." This is the reason why on MiMedex's balance sheet the item is referred to as "Accounts receivable, net." Second, we see another instance in which an estimate must be made by management: reserves for inventory obsolescence. Finally, there are terms used in describing inventories that we have not yet covered: first-in, first-out and WIP (which stands for work in process).

The fourth category of current assets is prepaid expenses. Under GAAP, this category includes prepaid insurance, prepaid rent, prepaid advertising, prepaid royalties, prepaid interest, and prepaid taxes. There is a distinction between a prepaid expense and a deferred expense. The former is a payment that was made less than one year prior to the cost being expensed and is treated as a current asset. A deferred expense is a payment made more than one year prior to the cost being expensed and is treated as a noncurrent asset.

iRobot has a longer list of current assets, so let's look at those categories. The "cash equivalent" component of "Cash and cash equivalents" is defined according to GAAP as "short-term, highly liquid investments that are readily convertible to known amounts of cash and that are so near their maturity that they present insignificant risk of changes in value because of changes in interest rates."[1] A money market fund is given as an example of a cash equivalent. iRobot indicates that the maturity does not exceed three months, which is a common maturity used for cash equivalents. In the case of iRobot, all of the cash equivalents were held in money market funds. Cash equivalents are reported at historical cost based on the historical cost principle described in the previous chapter.

The current asset labeled "Short-term investments" on iRobot's balance sheet differs from the investment classified as "cash equivalents." Debt securities that have a remaining maturity greater than three months but less than one year are classified as short-term investments. The reporting of this current asset is at fair market value, not at historical cost, an exception to the historical cost principle. Robot's short-term investments were corporate bonds, which were purchased for $12.98 million but had a fair market value (based on price quotes in the bond market) of $12.43 million.

The other two items shown on iRobot's balance sheet that were also shown on MiMedx's balance sheet are "Unbilled revenue" and "Deferred tax assets."

Noncurrent Assets

There are two types of noncurrent assets: physical and intangible.

Physical Assets   *Physical assets,* also referred to as *fixed assets,* include property, plant, and equipment and are typically identified on the balance sheet as just *property and equipment.* In the case of iRobot, the cost of property and equipment as shown in footnote 4 of its financial statements was (in $ millions):

Computer and equipment	$16.086
Furniture	2.762
Machinery	3.391
Tooling	10.147
Leasehold improvements	15.758
Software purchased for internal use	8.273
Gross plant and equipment	$56.417

---

1. *Financial Accounting Standards Board Accounting Standards Codification,* paragraph 305–10–20.

When a fixed asset is purchased it is recorded at the cost paid to acquire it and referred to as *gross property and equipment*. For iRobot, the gross property and equipment was $56.417 million. As explained in the previous chapter, this process of creating an asset is referred to as capitalizing the asset. Each year, property and equipment are depreciated according to some permissible accounting policy for depreciation. *Depreciation* is the allocation of the historical cost of a physical asset over its useful life (or economic life). It is required by the matching principle discussed in the previous chapter. The amount of the depreciation for the year is treated as an expense and appears on the income statement, which we discuss in the next chapter.

The company has a choice of the method used to allocate the cost of the fixed asset over the asset's expected life. That allocation is what is referred to as depreciation. The two alternatives are the straight-line method or the accelerated method. With the *straight-line depreciation method*, the cost of the fixed asset (less the amount of its expected salvage value) is charged as an expense in a uniform manner over the asset's expected life. When an a*ccelerated depreciation method* is used, larger annual depreciation charges are taken in the earlier years. If the company elects to use an accelerated depreciation method, then it has a choice between two methods: the declining balance method and the sum-of-the-years' digits method. For our purposes, there is no need to explain these methods in any further detail. What is important is that with straight-line depreciation, the same amount is taken as depreciation each year of the asset's expected life, whereas with an accelerated depreciation method, depreciation is higher in the earlier years of the asset's expected life and less in the later years.

What appears on the balance sheet as "*plant and equipment, net*" is also referred to as the "book value" or "carrying value." It is not the fair market value because of the historical cost principle. The amount of the net property and equipment is the difference between the gross amount and the accumulated depreciation from the initial acquisitions. That is, *accumulated depreciation* for a physical asset is the sum of the depreciation taken each year. As explained in the previous chapter, the amount is reduced further by any impairments that are identified for some of the fixed assets.

In the notes to its financial statement, iRobot stated that there were no impairment charges recorded during any of the periods presented. In contrast, MiMedx did incur impairment charges. MiMedx has biomaterial platform technologies, which include device technologies and tissue technologies. One of the device technologies is HydroFix®, which the company found to be impaired. Specifically, the company stated:

Because the addressable market for our HydroFix® products is somewhat limited and we do not expect significant expansion in the sales of this product line, we recognized an impairment charge in 2012 and reduced the carrying value of the HydroFix® assets.

In the footnotes to the financial statement where significant accounting policies are discussed, the following appears under the subheading "Impairment of Long-lived Assets":

The Company evaluates the recoverability of its long-lived assets (property and equipment) whenever adverse events or changes in business climate indicate that the expected undiscounted future cash flows from the related assets may be less than previously anticipated. If the net book value of the related assets exceeds the expected undiscounted future cash flows of the assets, the carrying amount would be reduced to the present value of their expected future cash flows and an impairment loss would be recognized. (p. 60)

Some companies report just the net plant and equipment figure on the balance sheet, disclosing the details about accumulated depreciation in a footnote in the financial statements. MiMedx shows a property and equipment figure that is net of accumulated depreciation of $1,071,625. The accumulated depreciation is shown, along with the item ($2,279,840). For iRobot, the net plant and equipment as of December 29, 2012, was $24,953.

Intangible Assets   U.S. GAAP principles define *intangible assets* as nonphysical assets that entitle a company to generate rights, privileges, and other economic benefits for the owner. GAAP principles define an intangible asset as "an asset (not including a financial asset) that lacks physical substance." The GAAP definition excludes something that is thought of as an intangible asset called "goodwill," which we discuss shortly. In fact, the footnotes to financial statements refer to "goodwill and intangible assets" or "goodwill and other intangible assets," treating goodwill separately.

Intangible assets can be classified as (1) marketing-related, (2) customer-related, (3) artistic-related, (4) contract-based, and (5) technology-related. Table 9.3 provides examples of each type according to GAAP. Some types of intangible assets appear on the balance sheet while others do not.

Intangible assets are classified under GAAP based on how they were acquired and their economic life. With respect to an acquisition, intangible assets are classified as *internally created* (or *self-created*) *intangible assets* and *purchased intangible assets*. With respect to the latter, this occurs through the direct acquisition of an intangible asset or as a result of some business combination, such as an acquisition of or merger with another company. Under GAAP, when a business combination occurs, a determination is made of identifiable intangible assets. An expert is called in at that time to assess the fair market value of each identifiable intangible asset. So, for example, we now see that an intangible asset can arise by (1) self-creation by the company, (2) purchase of individual intangible assets from other companies, and (3) purchase through a business combination that results in one or more identifiable intangible assets.

Table 9.3

Intangible Asset Categories as per GAAP

---

1. Marketing-related intangible assets

a. Trademarks, trade names

b. Service marks, collective marks, certification marks

c. Trade dress (unique color, shape, or package design)

d. Newspaper mastheads

e. Internet domain names

f. Noncompetition agreements

2. Customer-related intangible assets

a. Customer lists

b. Order or production backlog

c. Customer contracts and related customer relationships

d. Noncontractual customer relationships

3. Artistic-related intangible assets

a. Plays, operas, ballets

b. Books, magazines, newspapers, other literary works

c. Musical works such as compositions, song lyrics, advertising jingles

d. Pictures, photographs

e. Video and audiovisual material, including motion pictures, music videos, television programs

4. Contract-based intangible assets

a. Licensing, royalty, standstill agreements

b. Advertising, construction, management, service or supply contracts

c. Lease agreements

d. Construction permits

e. Franchise agreements

f. Operating and broadcast rights

g. Use rights such as drilling, water, air, mineral, timber cutting,

h. Servicing contracts such as mortgage servicing contracts

i. Employment contracts

5. Technology-based intangible assets

a. Patented technology

b. Computer software and mask works

c. Unpatented technology

d. Databases, including title plants

e. Trade secrets, such as secret formulas, processes, recipes.

Note: The items in the table are examples listed in various places of the document: Statement of Financial Accounting Standards No. 141 (revised 2007), *Business Combinations*, Financial Accounting Standards Board.

Purchased intangible assets   High-tech startup companies typically report large amounts of purchased intangible assets. As Apple noted in its 2013 filing with the SEC, "The Company continues to develop new technologies to enhance existing products and to expand the range of its product offerings through research and development, licensing of intellectual property and acquisition of third-party businesses and technology."

As with physical assets, the matching principle requires that a company allocate the acquisition cost over the expected life (i.e., number of years during which economic benefits are expected) of an asset. In the case of a physical asset, the cost allocated and then shown as an expense on the income statement is called depreciation. For an intangible asset it is called ***amortization***. For purposes of amortization, GAAP distinguishes between an intangible asset that has an indefinite life and one that has a definite life. An intangible asset that has been acquired is classified as having an ***indefinite life*** if there is no foreseeable limit to the period over which it is projected to generate cash benefits for the company. For a purchased intangible asset that has an indefinite life, no amortization is taken. In contrast, a purchased intangible asset with a definite life—which is defined by GAAP as a limited number of periods over which cash benefits are expected by the company—must be amortized.

For the 2013 financial statements of Apple, a footnote with the heading "Goodwill and other intangible assets" states: "The Company's acquired intangible assets with definite useful lives primarily consist of patents and licenses and are amortized over periods typically from three to seven years." In addition, we are told the number of years over which these purchased intangible assets are amortized. The information reported in that footnote (in $ millions) for the period ending September 28, 2013 was as follows:

	Gross Carrying Amount	Accumulated Amortization	Net Carrying Amount
Definite lived and amortizable acquired intangible assets	$6,081	$(2,002)	$4,079
Indefinite lived and non-amortizable trademarks	100	0	100
Total acquired intangible assets	$6,181	$(2,002)	$4,179

Notice that Apple had $100 million in infinite-lived and nonamortizable trademarks, and hence no amortization is shown.

Internally generated intangible assets   Thus far we have discussed the treatment of purchased intangible assets. How are internally created intangible assets treated? This is important because high-tech companies typically create such assets. This often falls under the category of what is referred to as research and development (R&D). The treatment in this case is that, while there are exceptions, U.S. GAAP requires that no intangible asset be reported on the balance sheet. Instead, U.S. GAAP requires that R&D costs be expensed (i.e., taken as an expense on the income statement in the fiscal period when the cost is incurred). For Apple, R&D expenditures for its 2013 fiscal year were $4.475 billion and are not shown on its balance sheet based on GAAP. When we review the income statement, we will see that is where the R&D expenditure appears.

The exceptions deal with elements of costs incurred for internal use software development to support an offering for customers. Prior to 1998, some companies expensed these costs while others capitalized them. Since then, GAAP has provided the following rule, based on the stage of development, to determine whether software development expenses are capitalized or expensed:

- *Preliminary project stage:* Internal and external costs should be expensed as they are incurred. Generally at this stage of development, the costs that are incurred are to determine whether a concept is possible and/or to consider potential applications Completion of this development stage occurs when management approves and subsequently agrees to fund the software project.

- *Application development stage:* Internal and external costs should be capitalized. Completion of this stage occurs when the software project is basically complete and is ready for the use for which it was in development. That is, the testing performed to validate the software has been completed.

- *Postimplementation/operation stage:* At this stage the treatment of costs depends on the purpose of the software. The costs (internal and external) for training must be expensed. Maintenance costs are generally expensed, but not if they are classified as upgrades, in which case such costs are capitalized.

As in the case of a tangible asset, an intangible asset that must be amortized is subject to impairment tests. If there are changes in circumstances or if certain events, referred to as "trigger events," occur, a determination of the impairment must be made and the intangible asset's carrying value reduced or written off totally if it is determined that the impairment is not recoverable. The reduction in the carrying value on the balance sheet owing to impairment results in a corresponding expense amount on the income statement. The economic recession resulting from the 2008–2009 global financial crisis led some companies to reduce their expectations of the future benefits of some of their intangible assets.

As explained in the previous chapter, the transitioning of U.S. GAAP to non-U.S. GAAP (i.e., International Financial Reporting Standards, IFRS) has produced some major differences. The treatment of R&D is one of them. Under IFRS, the costs for research and the costs for development are treated differently. The general rule is that research costs are expensed in the period in which they are incurred, whereas development costs are required to be capitalized when certain criteria set forth in the IFRS are satisfied.[2]

2. It is not important to list the criteria here. The interested reader is referred to International Accounting Standard No. 38, Intangible Assets.

Goodwill   *Goodwill* is an intangible asset that arises when one company acquires another company. Goodwill is measured by the difference between the price paid for the acquired company and the fair value of the net assets acquired. The fair value of the net assets is equal to the following: fair value of all identifiable tangible and intangible assets reduced by the fair value of any liabilities that the acquiring company assumed on behalf of the acquired company. On the acquiring company's balance sheet, the amount of goodwill is shown as an asset. That is, goodwill is capitalized on the balance sheet.

Let's explain how goodwill is created using GAAP, with the June 19, 2013, acquisition of Tumblr, Inc., by Yahoo! as our example. Tumblr is a blog-hosting website that allows users to post their own content as well as follow or reblog posts made by other users. The motivation for Yahoo!'s acquisition of Tumblr was to increase its online presence by introducing it to Tumblr's 300 million unique monthly visitors, to support Yahoo!'s strategy to expand its advertisement business. The cash price paid by Yahoo! was $990.211 million. In addition, Yahoo! assumed the liabilities of Tumblr equal to $113.847 million. Now the question is, what did Yahoo! get when it acquired Tumblr? That is, what assets did it purchase, and what were their fair values? Recall that the financial statements are prepared based on historical costs, adjusted for any impairment. This means that Tumblr's assets had to be revalued by experts hired by Yahoo!'s management to determine the value of the assets acquired. According to the quarterly statement filed by Yahoo!, the company received $353.165 million. The experts determined that the $353,165 million was from the following assets (in $ millions):

Cash and marketable securities acquired	$16.587
Other tangible assets acquired	73.978
Amortizable intangible assets:	
Developed technology	23.700
Customer contracts and related relationships	182.400
Trade name	56.500

The net assets are equal to the $353.165 million of assets received reduced by the liabilities Yahoo! assumed of $113.847 million, or $239.318 million. Since the cash paid was $990.211 million and the net assets were $239.318 million, then goodwill was $750.893 million. Basically, this is how much Yahoo! overpaid for Tumblr. Goodwill was then shown on Yahoo!'s balance sheet as an asset of $750.893 million.

As another example, let's consider the business acquisitions of Apple for its 2013 fiscal year. Apple paid cash of $496 million for these business acquisitions. In addition to cash for those acquisitions, Apple assumed $102 million of liabilities of those companies it acquired. That is, Apple's cost for the business acquisitions was $598 million. It then allocated $179 million to the acquisition of intangible assets and $419 million to goodwill. The $419 million of goodwill from the business acquisitions in fiscal year 2013 was then added to the amount of goodwill at the end of the 2012 fiscal year. The $179 million that was allocated to intangible assets was added to the acquired intangible assets at the end of the 2012 fiscal year.

Goodwill is treated as an intangible asset with an infinite life. Consequently, there is no amortization of goodwill.[3] However, goodwill, like other intangible assets, is subject to impairment tests, which can reduce its value on the balance sheet. As of the end of its 2013 fiscal year, Apple reported $1.6 billion of goodwill and stated that there was no goodwill impairment.

Other Noncurrent Assets

Other noncurrent assets (or simply *other assets*) may include investments, advances to and receivables from subsidiaries, receivables from officers and employees, the cash surrender value of life insurance policies on officers, and the cost of buildings in the process of construction.

For iRobot, "Other assets" of $8.5 million as shown on its balance sheet at December 29, 2012, consisted of (as reported in the notes to the financial statements):

| Investment in Advanced Scientific Concepts, Inc. | $2.500 million |
| Investment in InTouch Technologies, Inc. | 6.000 million |

LIABILITIES

The liabilities of a company represent the amount of funds it has borrowed to finance the purchase of the assets that appear on the balance sheet. The terms "liabilities" and "debt" are used interchangeably.

On the balance sheet, the liabilities are listed in the order of their due date. Typically they appear in two categories: current liabilities and long-term liabilities. Liabilities that are due within one year or one operating cycle (whichever is longer) are classified as *current liabilities*. *Long-term liabilities* are obligations that are due beyond one year.

Current Liabilities

At the end of its 2012 fiscal year, MiMedx reported for its total current liabilities $5,070,772, consisting of the following:

---

3. At one time, the acquiring company had to amortize goodwill over a period of time no less than forty years.

Accounts payable	$1,251,684
Accrued expenses	3,743,934
Other current liabilities	75,154
Current portion of line of credit with related party	—
Current portion of long-term convertible debt related to acquisition	—

Accounts payable represents the amount owed to suppliers for purchases on credit. *Accrued expenses* are expenses that have been realized but not paid out. Footnote 8 of the financial statements provided more information on accrued expenses:

Accrued Personnel Related Costs	$1,761,760
Accrued Commissions	1,469,925
Other Accrued Expenses	512,249

Other current liabilities cover a range of liabilities that fit the definition of a current liability.

Notice that there is nothing shown for the last two items in MiMedx's current assets. For the 2011calendar year end the following was reported:

Current portion of line of credit with related party	$1,295,980
Current portion of long-term convertible debt related to acquisition	1,128,806

What do these current liabilities represent? To understand these two items we need to know the liabilities with which each is associated. The first was a "Convertible Line of Credit with Related Party with 5% interest; principal and interest payable in full December 31, 2012." Since the financial statement was for calendar year 2011, this means that the liability was due in the following year, making it a current liability. The second liability we will discuss when we describe the company's long-term liabilities. What is important to understand here is that if there is any long-term liability incurred by a company, then the portion of that liability that is due within one year is treated as a current liability.

Let's look at iRobot's 2012 balance sheet. The total current liabilities are $77.163 million, broken down as follows (in millions):

Accounts payable	$42.515
Accrued expenses	16.527
Accrued compensation	11.864
Deferred revenue and customer advances	6.257

We discussed the first two items earlier. Footnote 6 in the financial statements reported the accrued expenses of $16.527 million as of year-end 2012 as follows (in $ millions):

Accrued warranty	$6.057
Accrued direct fulfillment costs	0.999
Accrued rent	0.696
Accrued sales commissions	0.475
Accrued accounting fees	0.155
Uncertain tax positions—short-term	2.884
Accrued other	5.261

"Accrued compensation" is the amount owed to employees that have not been paid yet and are due within one year. Some companies title this account "Wages and salaries payable." The second account, "Deferred revenue and customer advances," represents payments made by customers for whom services have yet to be performed or a product is yet to be delivered. However, the services and the products are due within one year.

Long-Term Liabilities

Examples of typical long-term liabilities are borrowings from notes and bonds issued, capital leases, and deferred taxes. "Capital leases" are lease obligations that represent long-term commitments of lease payments.

"Deferred taxes" are taxes that may have to be paid in the future but that are currently not due. Although for financial reporting purposes they are expensed (in accordance with the matching principle), they are due or may not be due in the future. *Deferred income taxes* are the net tax effects of temporary differences between the carrying amounts of assets and liabilities as computed for financial reporting purposes (GAAP) and the amounts computed for income tax purposes.

Now let's look at MiMedx's total liabilities of $15,185,306 at the end of its 2012 fiscal year. The following is reported on the balance sheet:

Earn-out liability payable in MiMedx common stock	$5,792,330
Convertible Senior Secured Promissory Notes	4,012,442
Other liabilities	299,762

The first liability above is an estimate of what the company had to pay to Surgical Biologics for the acquisition of its intellectual property in order to extend it biomaterials product lines. The payment to Surgical Biologics is to be made in MiMedx common stock.

The liability is a contingent liability, and for that reason we discuss the topic of contingent liability further below and continue the MiMedx example there.

The second liability for MiMedx is for $5 million of Convertible Senior Secured Promissory Notes used for the acquisition of Surgical Biologics' intellectual property. The estimated current portion for calendar year 2011 is the amount shown in the current liabilities section: $1,128,806. In footnote 9 of the financial statements the amount shown for the current portion of the long-term liabilities for year-end 2011 is $2,480,400, which includes the $1,128,806 plus the amount on the convertible line of credit.

For iRobot, there is just one entry for long-term liabilities. The amount shown for the 2012 fiscal year is $3.186 million. The reader is then referred to "Commitments and contingencies (Note 11)."

Contingent Liabilities   A *contingent liability* is a potential cost that a company might incur. Under GAAP, a contingency liability is accounted for based on the probability of that cost occurring. There are three categories of contingent liabilities and for each category there is a mandated accounting treatment under GAAP. The three categories are based on the likelihood of the contingent liability occurring: probable, reasonably possible, and remote. The accounting treatment also depends on the ability to estimate (measure) the amount of the liability that would be incurred. Of course, over time, the classification of a contingent liability may change.

The GAAP rules are as follow:

- If a contingent liability is both probable and the company can reasonably estimate the amount of the loss that would occur, then the amount must be shown on the (1) balance sheet as part of long-term liabilities and (2) income statement as an expense.
- If the company cannot reasonably estimate the amount of the loss that would occur, then there is a disclosure about the contingency, but no amount is shown on the balance sheet. (For example, litigation for patent infringement is typically shown as a contingent liability.)
- If the amount is reasonably possible, the treatment is the same as if the contingent liability cannot be estimated: by note disclosure only.
- If a contingent liability is viewed to be remote, it does not appear on the balance sheet and need not be disclosed in notes to the financial statements.

Let's look at three note disclosures ("11. Commitments and Contingencies") of iRobot. The first two are simply note disclosures and the third is a contingency liability.

For "Legal," the following appears:

From time to time and in the ordinary course of business, the Company is subject to various claims, charges and litigation. The outcome of litigation cannot be predicted with certainty and some lawsuits, claims or proceedings may be disposed of unfavorably to us, which could materially affect the Company's financial condition or results of operations.

For "Sales tax," the following appears:

The Company collects and remits sales tax in jurisdictions in which it has a physical presence or it believes nexus exists, which therefore obligates the Company to collect and remit sales tax. The Company continually evaluates whether it has established a nexus in new jurisdictions with respect to sales tax. The Company has recorded a liability for potential exposure in several states where there is uncertainty about the point in time at which the Company established a sufficient business connection to create nexus. The Company continues to analyze possible sales tax exposure, but does not currently believe that any individual claim or aggregate claims that might arise will ultimately have a material effect on its consolidated results of operations, financial position or cash flows.

For "Warranties," the following appears:

The Company provides warranties on most products and has established a reserve for warranty based on identified warranty costs. The reserve is included as part of accrued expenses (Note 6) in the accompanying consolidated balance sheets.

In our listing for accrued warranties for iRobot in our discussion of current liabilities, the $6.057 million is shown.

Commitments   Under GAAP, a company must disclose

- commitments under unconditional purchase obligations that are associated with suppliers' financing arrangements,
- obligations under lease agreements, and
- future payments on long-term borrowings and redeemable stock.

The commitments under unconditional purchase obligations are associated with suppliers' financing arrangements. One such arrangement is a take-or-pay contract, which is a long-term contract to make periodic payments over the life of the contract in certain minimum amounts as payments for a service or a product. The obligation to make minimum payments is unconditional and must be met whether or not the service or product is actually furnished or delivered by the supplier.

Obligations under lease agreements are long-term payments that are unconditional. For example, in the 2012 iRobot financial statement, the following was disclosed:

The Company leases its facilities. Rental expense under operating leases for fiscal 2012, 2011 and 2010 amounted to $4.4 million, $4.1 million, and $3.7 million, respectively. Future minimum rental payments under operating leases were as follows as of December 29, 2012 (in thousands):

2013	$3,158
2014	2,837
2015	2,820
2016	2,747
2017	2,505
Thereafter	5,682
Total minimum lease payments	$ 19,749

In the case of long-term borrowings and of redeemable stock, the disclosures include maturities and the required redemption for each of the next five years, respectively.

STOCKHOLDERS' EQUITY

The ownership interest of a company is represented by equity. *Stockholders' equity*, also referred to as *shareholders' equity*, is the book value (carrying value) of equity. It is the book value because, as we have explained, the valuation of the assets and the liabilities follows GAAP rules does not reflect market values (with some exceptions). We'll explain how stockholders' equity is computed later in this section.

Preferred Stock versus Common Stock

As explained in chapter 7, a corporation may issue two types of stock, common and preferred. Preferred stockholders have priority over common stockholders with respect to the distribution of dividends and in the case of the liquidation of the company. That is, common stockholders cannot receive dividends until the preferred stockholders receive their specified dividends. For preferred stockholders the dividends may be a fixed dollar amount or an amount that varies based on some formula. In the liquidation of a company, preferred stockholders have priority over common stockholders with respect to the distribution of assets. In exchange for this preference with respect to dividends and asset distribution in the case of liquidation, preferred stockholders give up the appreciation potential for the price of their shares, unlike common stockholders. Under special circumstances, preferred stockholders are permitted special voting rights.

As explained in chapter 7, typically for startup companies preferred stock has a feature that is added to make it more appealing to investors who do want upside potential. This feature is the conversion privilege, which allows the preferred stockholder to convert shares of preferred stock into a designated number of shares of common stock. The treatment of convertible preferred stock when calculating an important measure of profitability, earnings per share, will be explained in the next chapter.

The common stockholders, in contrast, are the residual owners of the company. Dividends are paid to common stockholders after all debtholders have had their obligations fulfilled by the company and after preferred stockholders have received their dividends.

Classification of Common Stock

In chapter 7 we provided a classification of common stock based on voting rights. Here we describe how, for balance sheet reporting purposes, common stock is classified in terms of authorized shares, issued shares, unissued shares, outstanding shares, and treasury stock.

When a corporation is formed, its charter states the total number of shares that may be sold. This is referred to as the *authorized shares*. Authorized shares are then classified as *issued shares* (the number of authorized shares sold to investors) and *unissued shares* (the number of authorized shares that have not been sold to investors).

Outstanding shares are the number of shares sold to investors. It would seem that the number of outstanding shares should be the same as the number of issued shares. This need not be the case because a company may repurchase shares from investors. Shares that are repurchased are referred to as *treasury stock*. Therefore, the number of outstanding shares plus the number of treasury shares is equal to the number of issued shares.

Par Value of Common Stock

All financial instruments have a par value. In the case of debt obligations, par value is a meaningful concept because (1) it indicates how much the issuer must repay the bondholder prior to the maturity date and (2) coupled with the coupon rate, it indicates the amount of interest that will be paid annually. So a bond with a par value of $1,000 and a 5% coupon rate will pay the bondholder $50 annually in interest.

For preferred stock, the par value has a similar meaning. First, if the preferred stock is to be redeemed, then the company must repay the par value unless there is some participation as explained in chapter 7. If there is a liquidation, the maximum amount to which the preferred stockholders is entitled is fixed. Preferred stock has a dividend rate, and the dollar amount is the product of the par value and the dividend rate.

When we get to common stock, the par value is often a meaningless value in terms of its relationship to the market value of the stock. The state in which a firm incorporates will require either a par value or a stated value. As with par value, the stated value too has no relationship to the market value. The par value or stated value is important only for legal reasons. Specifically, the number of issued shares multiplied by the par or stated value establishes the company's minimum legal capital. This minimum legal capital imposes a constraint on the company with respect to the payment of dividends and the repurchasing of stock. Neither action can be taken if it would result in the company's capital falling below the minimum legal capital. The company's board of directors sets the par value or stated value, typically $1 or less to avoid the problem of falling below the minimum legal capital while providing flexibility for dividend and stock repurchase decisions.

Book Value of Stockholders' Equity

The book value (or carrying value) of stockholders' equity is determined as follows:

Common stock issued based on par value or stated value	
+	Additional paid-in-capital
+	Retained earnings
+	Accumulated other comprehensive income (or minus for loss)
−	Treasury stock
=	Stockholders' equity

Let's describe each of these components of stockholders' equity.

The first component is just the legal capital based on the par value or stated value for issued shares. The second component is the result of selling the common stock at an amount in excess of its par value or stated value and is referred to as ***additional paid-in-capital***.

The third component is the amount in the current fiscal period that was not distributed to shareholders since the inception of the company. "Accumulated other comprehensive income" is explained in the next chapter. Basically, it includes unrealized gains and losses on certain investments, and the amount reported in the stockholders' equity is the accumulated amount since the company's inception. The stockholders' equity is then reduced by the issued shares that were repurchased by the company, which we stated earlier is called treasury stock. The reduction is equal to the amount paid for the treasury stock.

For example, the stockholders' equity for iRobot reported on its 2012 fiscal year-end balance sheet was (in $ millions):

Common stock, $0.01 par value (100,000,000 shares authorized; 27,781,659 shares issued and 27,216,555 shares outstanding)	$0.278
+Additional paid-in capital	199.903
+Retained earnings	75.437
+Accumulated other comprehensive income	0.199
Total stockholders' equity	$275.817

Let's see the link between the income statement (discussed in the next chapter) and the balance sheet with respect to retained earnings. The amount of iRobot's 2011 retained earnings as reported on its balance sheet was $58.140 million. For 2012, the amount of retained earnings was $75.437 million, as shown in the tabulation above. The difference is $17.297 million. Where did that positive difference come from? In the next chapter when we describe the income statement we will see that iRobot in 2012 had net income of $17.297 and that no dividend payments were made to shareholders in 2012. So the increase in retained earnings from 2011 to 2012 was net income. Basically, iRobot had earnings of $58.140 million that it had accumulated and not paid out to shareholders from its inception to the end of its 2011 fiscal year. In 2012, it earned $17.297 million and retained all of it, increasing retained earnings to $75.437 million.

For MiMedx, stockholders' equity as reported on its year-end 2012 balance sheet was:

Preferred stock, $0.001 par value (5,000,000 shares authorized; 0 shares issued and outstanding)	—
Common stock, $0.001 par value (130,000,000 shares authorized; 88,423,169 shares issued and 88,373,169 shares outstanding)	$88,423
+Additional paid-in capital	89,627,601
−Treasury stock (50,000 shares at cost)	(25,000)
−Accumulated deficit	(69,683,722)
Total stockholders' equity	$20,007,302

Notice that MiMedx was authorized to issue preferred stock but did not issue any. We see that treasury stock was repurchased at cost, and this reduced stockholders' equity. Where are retained earnings? Up to this point in its corporate life, MiMedx had not in fact accumulated any earnings (i.e., there were no retained earnings). Instead, the company accumulated losses of about $69.7 million.

LIMITATIONS OF THE BALANCE SHEET

In the end, the information on the balance sheet will be used with the information provided in the income statement to assess a company's performance. Consequently, it is necessary to be aware of the limitations of the balance sheet when using the information it contains. There are three limitations:

- Information provided on the balance sheet is based on historical costs and therefore reflects only the book value of assets.
- There are intangible assets that add value to a company that are not reflected on the balance sheet, such as brand loyalty, trademarks, and employee loyalty.
- The recording of some assets involves estimates.

KEY POINTS COVERED IN THIS CHAPTER

- The balance sheet (statement of financial condition) contains information about a company's assets, liabilities, and equity, generally at the end of a fiscal quarter or fiscal year.

- An asset can be classified based on how long it would take to convert the asset into cash.
- A current asset can be converted into cash within one year or one operating cycle (i.e., the length of time it takes to convert an investment of cash in inventory back into cash through the collections of sales).
- The operating cycle for most companies does not exceed one year.
- A noncurrent asset or a long-term asset is an asset that does not satisfy the criterion to be classified as a current asset.
- Typically current assets include cash and cash equivalents, accounts receivable, inventories, and prepaid expenses and other current assets.
- Noncurrent assets include physical assets and intangible assets.
- Physical assets, also referred to as fixed assets, include property, plant, and equipment.
- At the time of purchase, a fixed asset is recorded at the cost paid to acquire it and referred to as gross property and equipment.
- Each year property and equipment are depreciated based on some permissible accounting policy for depreciation.
- Depreciation is the allocation of the historical cost of a physical asset over its useful life (or economic life) and is required by the matching principle under GAAP.
- The amount of depreciation is treated as an expense on the income statement.
- The company can select from one of two methods to compute depreciation over a fixed asset's expected life: the straight-line method or the accelerated method (declining balance method and sum-of-the-years' digits method).
- Accumulated depreciation for a physical asset (i.e., the sum of the depreciation taken each year) is used to reduce the gross plant and equipment value to obtain the net plant and equipment value (referred to as the book value or carrying value).
- The amount of gross plant and equipment value must be reduced by any impairments identified.
- Intangible assets are nonphysical assets that entitle a company to generate rights, privileges, and other economic benefits and can be classified as (1) marketing-related, (2) customer-related, (3) artistic-related, (4) contract-based, and (5) technology-related.
- Intangible assets are classified under GAAP based on how they were acquired and on their economic life.
- With respect to acquisitions, intangible assets are classified as internally created (or self-created) intangible assets and purchased intangible assets.
- Large amounts of purchased intangible assets are typically reported by high-tech startup companies.

- The matching principle requires that a company allocate the acquisition cost over the expected life of a purchased intangible asset, and that the allocated cost be shown in the income statement as amortization.

- Amortization differs for an intangible asset that has an indefinite life and one that has a definite life.

- For a purchased intangible asset that has an indefinite life, no amortization is taken. A purchased intangible asset with a definite life must be amortized.

- Goodwill, an intangible asset that arises when one company acquires another company, is classified as having an infinite life, and therefore there is no amortization of goodwill.

- The accounting treatment for internally generated intangible assets typically falls under the category of research and development (R&D), and while there are exceptions for certain software development, no intangible asset is reported; instead, the costs are taken as an expense when they are incurred.

- Other noncurrent assets (or simply other assets) may include investments, advances to and receivables from subsidiaries, receivables from officers and employees, the cash surrender value of life insurance policies on officers, and the cost of buildings in the process of construction.

- A company's liabilities represent the amount of funds that it has borrowed to finance the purchase of the assets and are listed on the balance sheet in the order of their due date.

- Liabilities are classified as current liabilities (due within one year or one operating cycle, whichever is longer) and long-term liabilities (due beyond one year).

- Current liabilities include accounts payable, accrued expenses, other current liabilities, the current portion of a line of credit with a related party, and the current portion of a long-term convertible debt related to acquisition.

- Typical long-term liabilities are borrowings from notes and bonds issued, capital leases, and deferred taxes.

- A contingent liability is a potential cost that a company might incur and is accounted for based on the probability of that cost occurring.

- The ownership interest of a company is represented by stockholders' equity.

- On the balance sheet, common stock is classified in terms of authorized shares, issued shares, unissued shares, outstanding shares, and treasury stock.

- The limitations of balance sheet information are (1) reported values are based on historical costs and therefore reflect only the book value of assets; (2) there may be intangible assets that add value to a company but are not reflected on the balance sheet; and (3) the recording of some assets involves estimates.

FURTHER READINGS

Berman, Karen, Joe Night, and John Case, *Financial Intelligence for Entrepreneurs: What You Really Need to Know about the Numbers* (Boston: Harvard Business School Press, 2008), chaps. 8–11.

Weil, Roman L., Katherine Schipper, and Jennifer Francis, *Financial Accounting: An Introduction to Concepts, Methods and Uses,* 14th ed. (Mason, OH: South-Western College Publishers, 2013), chaps. 2, 4, 10, 11, and 12.

Weygandt, Jerry J., Donald E. Kieso, and Paul D. Kimmel, *Financial Accounting,* 9th ed. (Hoboken, NJ: John Wiley & Sons, 2013), chaps. 9–12.

10

INCOME STATEMENT

The statement that summarizes the operating performance of a company over a period of time (a fiscal quarter or a fiscal year) is the statement of income (or simply income statement). In this chapter, we explain the income statement and its components.

STRUCTURE AND COMPONENTS OF THE INCOME STATEMENT

Although the presentation of the income statement varies from company to company, the basic structure and components are as follows, *assuming that there is no preferred stock outstanding*:

	Sales or revenue
−	Cost of goods sold
=	Gross margin (or gross profit)
−	Selling, general and administrative expenses
−	Research-and-development expenses
=	Operating income (or earnings before interest and taxes)
−	Interest expense
=	Net income before taxes
−	Income taxes
=	Net income
−	Net income attributable to noncontrolling interests
=	Net income attributable to the company
+	Other comprehensive income (minus if loss)
=	Comprehensive income
−	Comprehensive income attributable to noncontrolling interests
=	Comprehensive income attributable to the company

When a company has preferred stock outstanding, then:

	Net income
–	Preferred stock dividends
=	Earnings available to common stockholders

We'll detail all of the components of the income statement in this chapter. For now, here is the fundamental idea behind the presentation of the income statement. It begins by providing information about the company's operating results (labeled "gross margin") by taking into account only the cost of producing the company's offerings. The cost of producing the offerings is called the cost of goods sold (COGS) (or the cost of sales). The gross margin ignores the nonoperating expenses associated with producing the offerings. Once these are accounted for, the operating income of the company is determined and summarizes the company's performance with respect to business operations.

One of the nonoperating costs not included in this category is the financial cost. This is the cost of borrowing funds; that is, it is the interest expense. Note that neither preferred stock nor common stock dividends that a company might pay are a financial cost to the company. What is important to highlight here is that interest paid is a tax-deductible expense for both financial accounting purposes and tax purposes.

Then there are other adjustments that must be made. These adjustments are for any other income or cost that is not a part of the company's core business.

Notice the distinction between "net income" and "earnings available to common stockholders." Net income is the amount earned for all stockholders—preferred stockholders and common stockholders. The focus of common stockholders is what has been earned for them. We will see another measure later that gives us that information: earning per share.

As noted above, the presentation in the income statement can vary. Tables 10.1 and 10.2 show the 2012 income statements for MiMedx and iRobot, respectively. We will use them in this chapter to illustrate the classifications in the income statement, along with the note disclosures from their financial statements.

SALES/REVENUE

The proceeds received or to be received from the sale of a company's offerings is referred to as sales or revenue. Here we will simply use the term revenue. In chapter 8, we explained the revenue recognition principle and the matching principle.

We'll begin by considering the revenue of iRobot. The company derives revenue from product sales (which include sales of various home-cleaning robots and defense and security robots and related accessories) and from execution of research-and-development contracts with the U.S. federal government and commercial entities. In its income statement,

Table 10.1
Mimedx Group, Inc. and Subsidiaries 2012 Consolidated Statements of Operations

Net sales:	$ 27,053,773
Operating costs and expenses	
Cost of products sold	5,188,378
Research and development expenses	2,884,546
Selling, general and administrative expenses	20,970,687
Impairment of intangible assets	1,798,495
Fair value adjustment of earn-out liability	1,567,050 5,803
Loss from operations	(5,355,383)
Other income (expense)	net
Amortization of debt discount	(1,714,101)
Interest expense, net	(592,892)
Loss before income taxes	(7,662,376)
Income taxes	—
Net loss	$ (7,662,376)
Net loss per common share	
Basic and diluted	$ (0.09)
Shares used in computing net loss per common share	
Basic and diluted	81,646,295

shown in table 10.2, the company breaks out the revenue from each accordingly: "Product revenue" and "Contract revenue."

In the notes to the financial statements, the revenue recognition policy is described. For "product revenue" generated from sales directly to customers and indirectly through resellers and distributors, the following is stated:

The Company recognizes revenue from sales of home robots under the terms of the customer agreement upon transfer of title and risk of loss to the customer, net of estimated returns, provided that collection is determined to be reasonably assured and no significant obligations remain. Sales to domestic resellers are typically subject to agreements allowing for limited rights of return, rebates and price protection. Accordingly, the Company reduces revenue for its estimates of liabilities for these rights of return at the time the related sale is recorded. The Company makes an estimate of sales returns for products sold by domestic resellers directly based on historical returns experience and other relevant data. The Company's international distributor agreements do not currently allow for product returns and, as a result, no reserve for returns is established for this group of customers.

Table 10.2
iRobot Corporation 2012 Consolidated Statements of Income (in $ thousands)

Revenue:	
Product revenue	$418,550
Contract revenue	17,694
Total revenue	436,244
Cost of revenue:	
Cost of product revenue(1)	239,745
Cost of contract revenue(1)	16,783
Total cost of revenue	256,528
Gross margin	179,716
Operating expenses:	
Research and development[a]	37,215
Selling and marketing[a]	71,631
General and administrative[a]	45,698
Total operating expenses	154,544
Operating income	25,172
Other income (expense), net	435
Income before income taxes	25,607
Income tax expense	8,310
Net income	$17,297
Net income per share	
Basic	$0.63
Diluted	$0.61
Number of shares used in per share calculations	
Basic	27,577
Diluted	28,301

Author's note: Footnote a to this statement shows how stock-based compensation breaks down by expense classification.

The note then continues on to explain in general terms the method iRobot employed to obtain the estimates.

The same note also explained how revenue is recognized for the different types of "contract revenue":

Under cost-plus-fixed-fee ("CPFF") type contracts, the Company recognizes revenue based on costs incurred plus a pro rata portion of the total fixed fee. Costs incurred include labor and material that are directly associated with individual CPFF contracts plus indirect overhead and general and administrative type costs based upon billing rates submitted by the Company to the Defense Contract Management Agency ("DCMA").

Revenue on firm fixed price ("FFP") contracts is recognized using the percentage-of-completion method. For government product FFP contracts, revenue is recognized as the product is shipped or in accordance with the contract terms. Costs and estimated gross margins on contracts are recorded as revenue as work is performed based on the percentage that incurred costs compare to estimated total costs utilizing the most recent estimates of costs and funding.

Finally, the same note explains: "Revenue earned in excess of billings, if any, is recorded as unbilled revenue. Billings in excess of revenue earned, if any, are recorded as deferred revenue."

Revenue Recognition for Long-Term Contracts

Because it is common for high-tech companies to generate revenue and gross profit (gross margin) from contracts that span more than one accounting year, we briefly describe the method for revenue recognition in such cases. The GAAP methods for accounting for long-term contracts are (1) percentage-of-completion method and (2) completed-contract method.

The *percentage-of-completion method* requires that revenues for the contract be recognized each period based on the progress of the construction (i.e., the percentage of completion). iRobot's note cited above uses this method for its contract work. The major problem in implementing this method is that reasonably accurate estimates of completion may not be that simple to measure. Accounting under GAAP requires the use of this method when estimates of progress toward completion, revenues, and costs are reasonably dependable and all of the following conditions are met: (1) the contract clearly specifies the enforceable rights regarding goods or services to be provided and received by the parties, the consideration to be exchanged, and the manner and terms of settlement; (2) the buyer can be expected to satisfy all obligations under the contract; and (3) the company performing the contracted service can be expected to perform the contractual obligations.

In contrast to the percentage-of-completion method, the *completed-contract method* specifies that revenue and gross profit are recognized only at the point of sale (i.e., when the contracted work is completed). The costs associated with the long-term contracts in process are accumulated, but there are no interim expenses charged to the income statement. This method should be used only (1) when a company has primarily short-term contract, or (2) when the conditions for using the percentage-of-completion method discussed above cannot be satisfied, or (3) when there are inherent hazards in the contract beyond the normal, recurring business risks. That is, the guiding principle is that the percentage-of-completion method is the more suitable method for accounting for long-term contracts and that the completed-contract method should be used only when the percentage-of-completion method is inappropriate.

OPERATING COSTS

In the basic income statement shown above, two types of costs are shown: (1) COGS and (2) selling, general, and administrative expenses. In practice, these costs can be represented in different ways in the income statement. For example, MiMedx reports "Operating Costs and Expenses" and lists the following:

- Cost of products sold
- Research and development expenses
- Selling, general and administrative expenses
- Impairment of intangible assets
- Fair value adjustment of earn-out liability

The "cost of products sold" on the MiMedx income statement is what we referred to in the basic income statement structure as "cost of goods sold." The calculation of COGS involves the valuation of inventory for determining the cost of each item sold and the depreciation of the fixed assets used, and the amortization of amortized intangible assets. We'll explain how the COGS is computed shortly.

As explained in the previous chapter, R&D expenses in general are expenses in the period in which they are incurred. iRobot states that its R&D expenses consist primarily of

- salaries and related costs for our engineers;
- costs for high technology components used in product and prototype development; and
- costs of test equipment used during product development.

GAAP has a special provision for dealing with internally developed software, as explained in the previous chapter. Here is what iRobot stated in a note to its financial statements about "Internal Use Software":

The Company capitalizes costs associated with the development and implementation of software for internal use. At December 29, 2012 and December 31, 2011, the Company had $8.3 million and $8.3 million, respectively, of costs related to enterprise-wide software included in fixed assets. Capitalized costs are being amortized over the assets' estimated useful lives. The Company has recorded $1.0 million, $0.9 million and $0.9 million of amortization expense for the years ended December 29, 2012, December 31, 2011 and January 1, 2011, respectively.

Recall that "capitalizing costs" means the creation of an asset on the balance sheet equal to the acquisition price. So on iRobot's balance sheet the costs associated with the software for internal use is part of the amount shown as fixed assets. The portion of fixed assets representing the software development cost is then amortized. The amortization appears as part of the COGS, as will be explained.

Selling, general, and administrative expenses are expenses not directly related to the production or creation of the products sold. These expenses, as listed by iRobot in a note to its financial statements, consist primarily of

- "salaries and related costs for sales and marketing personnel;
- salaries and related costs for executives and administrative personnel;
- advertising, marketing and other brand-building costs;
- fulfillment costs associated with direct-to-consumer sales through our on-line store;
- customer service costs;
- professional services costs;
- information systems and infrastructure costs;
- travel and related costs; and
- occupancy and other overhead costs."

Let's look at the last two of the five operating expenses for MiMedx; they were not listed in the basic income statement structure earlier. The first, "Impairment of intangible assets," is an expense we described in the previous chapter. This expense results from the estimated reduction in value of an intangible asset. On the balance sheet, the intangible asset's value is reduced; the deduction hits the income statement as an expense. The expense for "Fair value adjustment of earn-out liability" is the amount that was earned by another entity as a part of an acquisition and is therefore an expense.

The depreciation expense is not just part of the COGS but also applies to the other categories of expenses. For example, MiMedx reported the following allocation of its total $465.367 million in depreciation in one of its notes to the financial statements for the 2012 fiscal year (in $ millions):

Depreciation expense included in:

Cost of products sold	$155.987
Research and development	120.260
Selling, general and administrative	189.120

When we look at iRobot's income statement, we see the presentation items listed as follows:

Cost of revenue:
Cost of product revenue
Cost of contract revenue
Total cost of revenue

Operating expenses:
Research and development
Selling and marketing
General and administrative

What is labeled the "cost of revenue" is the equivalent of the COGS. In the note to the financial statement, the "cost of product revenue" is explained as follows:

Cost of product revenue includes the cost of raw materials and labor that go into the development and manufacture of our products as well as manufacturing overhead costs such as manufacturing engineering, quality assurance, logistics and warranty costs.

The "cost of contract revenue" is explained as follows:

Cost of contract revenue includes the direct labor costs of engineering resources committed to funded research and development contracts, as well as third-party consulting, travel and associated direct material costs. Additionally, we include overhead expenses such as indirect engineering labor, occupancy costs associated with the project resources, engineering tools and supplies and program management expenses.

Cost of Goods Sold

The calculation of COGS (or its equivalents, as explained earlier) is as follows:

+	Cost of inventory purchased/manufacturing during the accounting period
−	Cost of inventory at the end of the accounting period
=	Cost of goods sold

Or, equivalently,

	Cost of inventory available for sale during the accounting period
−	Cost of inventory at the end of the accounting period
=	Cost of goods sold

Inventory includes raw materials inventory, work-in-process inventory, and finished goods inventory. As of the 2012 fiscal year for MiMedx, the following was reported in a note to its financial statements:

Raw materials	$ 233,747
Work in process	1,598,537
Finished goods	1,349,121

As can be seen, calculating the COGS depends on the costs of inventory at the beginning and the end of the accounting period and the cost of creating or purchasing inventory during the period. Determining the cost of inventory is referred to as *inventory valuation* or *inventory costing*. Fundamentally, the process involves the allocation of the costs of inventory available for sale between the ending inventory and the COGS.

Inventory Valuation/Costing Under GAAP a company has considerable discretion in selecting the accounting method for determining the cost of inventory. We will keep the discussion brief when describing the alternative methods, what is included in the cost of inventory, and how the method adopted affects a company's net income. It should be noted that there are hi-tech companies that may not have any inventory.

Accounting under GAAP requires that the following costs go into the costing of inventory:

- *Parts and raw materials cost.*
- *Direct labor costs:* Direct labor costs are work-related wages and fringe benefits that can be attributed to the direct production of a product or a service.
- *Manufacturing overhead costs:* Also referred to as factory overhead, factory burden, and manufacturing support costs, manufacturing overhead costs are the indirect manufacturing-related costs associated with manufacturing a product. Three examples of manufacturing overhead costs are depreciation of the fixed assets used in the production process, labor other than direct labor (referred to as indirect labor) involved in the production process (e.g., material handlers, maintenance personnel, equipment maintenance personnel, and product inspectors), and utilities used to operate the manufacturing plant and the equipment.

Using one of the following four inventory costing methods, the company determines how costs are allocated to COGS and ending inventory:[1] (1) specific identification, (2) first in, first out (FIFO), (3) last in, first out (LIFO), and (4) average cost. Once a company

---

1. There are other methods, but they are less frequently used.

selects a method, it cannot simply change methods because this would make financial statements between two accounting periods difficult to fairly compare with one another.

When the specific identification method is used for inventory costing, the cost of each item sold is individually identified and recorded under COGS. The method tends to be impractical to use when a company sells large quantities of similar items. However, the method is suitable if a company sells items that are unique from one another and each item has a high cost.

The other three methods of inventory—FIFO, LIFO, and average cost—determine inventory cost based on an inventory cost flow assumption. More specifically, the inventory cost flow assumptions are as follows:

- FIFO: assumes that the first units in are the first units sold.
- LIFO: assumes that the last units in are the first units sold.
- Average cost: uses the average cost per unit to value the cost of those items sold.

The most commonly used method is FIFO.

In chapter 12, we will explain how to analyze the financial statements of a company in order to assess its performance and appeal to different investor groups. The selection of the inventory costing method will have an impact on net income. During an inflationary period or a period in which prices are rising within the sector, FIFO will produce a higher net income than LIFO or average cost.

There is one more aspect of inventory valuation that is important. The historical cost principle explained in chapter 8 states that an asset should be reported at historical cost. Consequently, fixed assets whose market value exceeds their historical cost are not restated at the higher market value. In the case of inventory, there is a revaluation of inventory when the market value declines because the inventory may become obsolete or is simply not saleable. The rule for inventory valuation is that inventory is reported at the *lower of cost or market* (LCM). Inventory revaluation is not uncommon in high-tech industries where there are different generations of a product.

The inventory valuation method described in a note to MiMedx's 2012 financial statements is:

Inventories are valued at the lower of cost or market, using the first–in, first-out (FIFO) method. Inventory is tracked through Raw Material, WIP, and Finished Good stages as the product progresses through various production steps and stocking locations. Within WIP labor and overhead costs are absorbed through the various production processes upon work order closes in our ERP (Enterprise Resource Planning) system. Historical yields and normal capacities are utilized in the calculation of production overhead rates. Reserves for inventory obsolescence are utilized to account for slow-moving inventory as well as inventory no longer needed due to diminished market demand.

For iRobot, the note to its 2012 financial statement says the following regarding inventory valuation:

We value our inventory at the lower of the actual cost of our inventory or its current estimated market value. We write down inventory for obsolescence or unmarketable inventories based upon assumptions about future demand and market conditions. Actual demand and market conditions may be lower than those that we project and this difference could have a material adverse effect on our gross margin if inventory write-downs beyond those initially recorded become necessary. Alternatively, if actual demand and market conditions are more favorable than those we estimated at the time of such a writedown, our gross margin could be favorably impacted in future periods.

INCOME TAXES

U.S.-based companies pay taxes in the United States, various states, and foreign jurisdictions. There are differences between currently due taxes and future potential taxes owing to differences in financial accounting and tax reporting, as well as other timing issues. In iRobot's 2012 note to its financial statement, the following is stated about deferred taxes:

Deferred taxes are determined based on the difference between the financial statement and tax basis of assets and liabilities using enacted tax rates in effect in the years in which the differences are expected to reverse. Valuation allowances are provided if based upon the weight of available evidence, it is more likely than not that some or all of the deferred tax assets will not be realized.
 The Company monitors the realization of its deferred tax assets based on changes in circumstances, for example recurring periods of income for tax purposes following historical periods of cumulative losses or changes in tax laws or regulations. The Company's income tax provisions and its assessment of the ability to realize its deferred tax assets involve significant judgments and estimates."

In another note to the 2012 financial statements, iRobot reports the components of income tax expense of $8.31 million (reported on the income statement shown in table 10.2) as follows ($ millions):

Current	
Federal	$12.540
State	0.473
Foreign	(0.008)
Total current tax provision	$13.005
Deferred	
Federal	(4.003)
State	(0.692)
Total deferred tax provision	(4.695)
Total income tax provision	$8.310

Table 10.3a

2012 Consolidated Statement of Earnings and Comprehensive Income: Bristol-Myers Squibb (Year Ended December 31, 2012): Consolidated Statement of Earnings ($ and Shares in Millions, Except Per Share Data)

Earnings:	
Net sales	$17,621
Cost of products sold	4,610
Marketing, selling and administrative	4,220
Advertising and product promotion	797
Research and development	3,904
Impairment charge for BMS-986094 intangible asset	1,830
Other (income)/expense	(80)
Total expenses	15,281
Earnings before income taxes	2,340
Provision for/(Benefit from) Income Taxes	(161)
Net Earnings	2,501
Net Earnings Attributable to Noncontrolling Interest	541
Net Earnings Attributable to BMS	$ 1,960
Earnings per Common Share	
Basic	$1.17
Diluted	$1.16
Cash dividends declared per common share	$1.37

NET INCOME

When people talk about the "bottom line," what they mean is some form of net income. Net income is the amount earned for all stockholders (common and preferred) after deducting all expenses (including taxes). There are other names used to describe net income such as net income after taxes and net earnings. For example, iRobot's 2012 net income reported in table 10.2 was $17.297 million. Bristol-Myers Squibb (BMS), whose income statement for 2012 is shown in panel a of table 10.3, had a net income of $2.501 billion; however, BMS refers to net income as "net earnings."[2] When there is a loss in the fiscal period being reported, the term used is "net loss." A net loss is not uncommon for many startup companies. MiMedx reported a net loss for its 2012 fiscal year.

Net Income Attributable to Noncontrolling Interests

Let's look at BMS's income statement (which is referred to as an earnings statement). Notice that there is a net earnings amount shown and two other types of net earnings

---

2. The reasons for including BMS in our discussion will be apparent shortly.

Table 10.3b

2012 Consolidated Statement of Earnings and Comprehensive Income: Bristol-Myers Squibb (Year Ended December 31, 2012 (Concluded)): Consolidated State of Comprehensive Income ($ in Millions)

Comprehensive income	
Net Earnings	$2,501
Other Comprehensive Income/(Loss), net of taxes:	
Derivatives qualifying as cash flow hedges:	
Unrealized gains	9
Realized gains	(36)
Pension and postretirement benefits:	
Actuarial losses	(311)
Amortization	90
Settlements and curtailments	103
Available for sale securities:	
Unrealized gains	12
Realized gains	(9)
Foreign currency translation	(7)
Foreign currency translation on net investment hedges	(8)
Total Other Comprehensive Income/(Loss), net of taxes	(157)
Comprehensive Income	2,344
Comprehensive Income Attributable to Noncontrolling Interest	535
Comprehensive Income Attributable to BMS	$1,809

reported: "Net Earnings Attributable to Noncontrolling Interest" and "Net Earnings Attributable to BMS." What does the former mean?

A *noncontrolling interest* is the portion of stockholders' equity in a subsidiary that is not attributable directly or indirectly to a parent company. On financial statements this may be referred to as a *minority interest*. It is common for a company, even a startup, to have an ownership interest in another company or a partnership with another company in which it does not have a controlling interest. Consequently, a portion of the earnings of a company may be attributable to other companies in which it has a noncontrolling or minority interest.

So the question is, how does one handle noncontrolling interest on the financial statements? GAAP requires that the following be clearly identified and presented in the financial statements: (1) the ownership interests in subsidiaries, (2) the net income attributable to both the parent and the subsidiaries, (3) changes in the parent's ownership interests, (4) gain or loss on deconsolidation, and (5) disclosures that distinguish the interests of the parent and the subsidiary.

GAAP requires that the noncontrolling interest be reported on the consolidated balance sheet in the stockholders' equity section, but shown separately from the parent's equity. That amount is to be clearly identified and labeled as a noncontrolling interest in subsidiaries. Should a company have a noncontrolling interest in more than one subsidiary, the amount can be aggregated. In the income statement, that portion of net income (and comprehensive income, which we discuss later) is shown as net income attributable to noncontrolling interest.

For example, let's consider BMS. The company has agreements with Sanofi for the codevelopment and cocommercialization of Avapro/Avalide (an angiotensin II receptor antagonist indicated for the treatment of hypertension and diabetic nephropathy) and Plavix (a platelet-aggregation inhibitor). BMS acts as the operating partner and owns a 50.1% majority controlling interest in certain regions of the world. For certain of these partnerships throughout the world, BMS consolidates the revenues generated with Sanofi's 49.9% share. The operating results are reflected as a noncontrolling interest by BMS. In other territories, BMS recognizes net sales in territories and in comarketing countries outside such territories. In the COGS, as shown on BMS's income statement, royalties owed to Sanofi are included (other than development royalties). In other territories, Sanofi acts as the operating partner and owns a 50.1% majority controlling interest in the territories and BMS has a 49.9% ownership interest in those territories, which is included in equity in net income of affiliates. Distributions of profits relating to the partnerships are included in operating activities. In addition, there is a separate partnership agreement between BMS and Sanofi for the copromotion in the United States of irbesartan, for which Sanofi paid BMS $350 million to acquire an interest in the irbesartan license.

As a result of these agreements, BSM states that it has a noncontrolling interest primarily related to the Plavix and Avapro/Avalide partnerships with Sanofi. Its net earnings in 2012 were $2.501 billion. Of that amount, net earnings attributable to noncontrolling interest was $541 million. The portion of the net earnings that is not attributed to noncontrolling interest, $1.96 billion, is the net earnings attributable to BMS.

NET INCOME AVAILABLE TO COMMON STOCKHOLDERS

The net income reported is the amount earned for all stockholders: preferred stockholders (if any) and common stockholders. Common stockholders, however, are interested in the amount earned and available to them. To obtain *net income available to common stockholders*, preferred stock dividends paid must be deducted from net income.

COMPREHENSIVE INCOME AND OTHER COMPREHENSIVE INCOME

We have seen net income that is not distributed to stockholders as dividends are retained by the company and increase stockholders' equity. So one would expect that if a company's net income was $10 million for the fiscal year and its stockholders' equity was $80 million at the beginning of the fiscal year, then stockholders' equity at the end of the fiscal year would be $90 million, assuming that no dividends were distributed to stockholders. However, at one time, there were transactions that had an adverse impact on stockholders' equity but were not shown in the income statement. In our example, suppose that the stockholders' equity at the end of the fiscal year was $75 million instead of $90 million. What happened to the missing $15 million in stockholders' equity? Companies would basically bury a transaction or series of transactions that had an adverse impact on stockholders' equity in the statement of stockholders' equity. That is, it might be expected that anything that affected stockholders' equity would be identified in the income statement, but such was not the case. As a result of this abuse, GAAP dealt with this issue by requiring a company report what it refers to as "comprehensive income" and "other comprehensive income."

Under GAAP, *comprehensive income* is defined as

the change in equity [net assets] of a business enterprise during a period from transactions and other events and circumstances from nonowner sources. It includes all changes in equity during a period except those resulting from investments by owners and distributions to owners.[3]

Thus comprehensive income includes net income. The part of comprehensive income that is added to net income to obtain comprehensive income is called *other comprehensive income* (OCI) and is defined as revenue, expenses, gains, and losses that under GAAP are recorded as part of shareholders' equity on the balance sheet but are excluded from net income. Therefore,

Comprehensive income = Net income + OCI.

Three examples of OCI are (1) adjustments made in foreign currency from foreign subsidiaries that do not use as their functional foreign currency the U.S. dollar, (2) a loss realized on the derivative instruments as a company attempts to hedge its position using certain financial derivatives (swaps, futures, forward), and (3) a gain or loss on the sale of marketable securities.

For example, Apple in its 2013 financial statement reported a total loss on OCI after taxes of $970 million, consisting of the following three components:

- A net loss after tax effects of $112 million owing to a change in foreign currency translation, net of tax effects of $35 million.
- A net gain after tax effects of $64 million owing to a change in unrecognized gains/losses on derivative instruments, consisting of two parts: (1) a $522 million gain net of taxes of the fair value of derivatives and (2) a $458 million net loss after taxes as the result of an adjustment for losses realized and included in net income.

---

3. Paragraph 70 in *Statement of Financial Accounting Concepts 6* (Financial Accounting Standards Board, 1985).

- A net loss of $922 million after tax effects owing to change in unrealized gains/losses on marketable securities, attributable to the following: (1) a $791 million net loss after taxes owing to a change in the fair value of marketable securities and (2) a $131 million net loss after taxes owing to an adjustment for losses realized and included in net income.

Since Apple's 2013 net income was $37.037 billion and OCI was a loss of $0.970 billion, the comprehensive income was $36.067 billion.

Panel b of table 10.3 shows the components of OCI for BMS's 2012 fiscal year. Because BMS has noncontrolling interest, as explained earlier, the comprehensive income is reported as "Comprehensive Income Attributable to Noncontrolling Interest" and "Comprehensive Income Attributable to BMS."

In the presentation in the income statements, the two components of comprehensive income must be shown: net income and OCI. The information provided for OCI is classified according to the nature of the income. Examples include foreign currency items and unrealized gains and losses on investments in financial instruments.

The presentation for comprehensive income must be made either in a single-statement format or in a two-consecutive-statements format. A company that elects the single-statement approach must present the following:

- net income, together with the components that make up net income;
- OCI, together with the components that make up OCI; and
- comprehensive income (i.e., the sum of net income and OCI).

In the basic structure of the income statement listed earlier in this chapter, the single-statement format is shown (without the detailed components).

A company choosing the two-consecutive-statements format must present two financial statements: the net income statement followed immediately by a *statement of comprehensive income*. An example from the 2012 BSM financial statements is shown in table 10.3. Panel a of the table is the income statement; panel b of the table is the statement of comprehensive income. Apple used the same two-statement format.

On the balance sheet, the *accumulated OSI* (AOSI) must be reported in the stockholders' equity section. It is a line item that is usually titled: "Accumulated other comprehensive income/(loss)." Just like retained earnings, it is an accumulated amount up to and including the operations since the inception of the company.

In Apple's 2013 financial statements, the AOCI reported on its 2012 balance sheet was $499 million and on its 2013 balance sheet a loss of $471 million. This means that there was a swing of $970 million from +$499 million to −$471 million. As explained earlier, Apple's 2013 OSI was a net loss of $970 million.

As another example, we can consider BMS. The AOCI reported on its 2011 balance sheet was a loss of $3.045 billion and on its 2012 balance sheet a loss of $3.202 billion. This means that there was an increase in the AOCI loss of $157 million. Looking at part b of table 10.3, the 2012 comprehensive income statement, one can see where that $157 million loss came from.

EARNINGS PER SHARE

In their financial statements, companies report the **earnings per share** (EPS). This measure shows how much was earned for each share of common stock. It is calculated as follows:

$$\text{EPS} = \frac{\text{Net income available to common stockholders}}{\text{Number of shares outstanding}}.$$

The numerator uses only the amount earned for common stockholders by removing the dividend payments made to preferred stockholders.

The number of common shares to use in the denominator must be calculated. The reason is that EPS is for an accounting period but the number of common shares may change over that period. That is, it is not necessarily the case that the same number of common shares is outstanding for the entire accounting period. For this reason, the accountant calculates the weighted average number of shares outstanding.

In addition, GAAP requires that companies report two EPS measures: basic EPS and diluted EPS.[4] **Basic earnings per share** is precisely what is in the equation above for the calculation of EPS.

Diluted EPS

Diluted earnings per share takes into account the potential for the conversion of securities into common stock, such as securities that allow the holder to exchange them for a specified number of common stock shares, and options issued by the company that grant certain parties the right to exercise an option to obtain a specified number of shares. A convertible security such as convertible preferred stock or convertible debt, discussed in chapter 7, is an example. Collectively, all of the financial arrangements made by the company that allow a third party to potentially acquire the company's common stock shares are referred to as **dilutive securities**. Diluted EPS figures allow the user of the financial statements to see the potential impact on basic EPS if holders of dilutive securities actually exercise their right to obtain shares.

The formula for calculating diluted EPS is

$$\text{Diluted EPS} = \frac{\text{Net income available to common stockholders adjusted for exercise of dilutive securities}}{\text{Number of common shares if dilutive securities are exercised}}.$$

4. Prior to 1998, companies reported three EPS measures: simple, primary, and fully diluted EPS.

The reason for the adjustment in the numerator is that the net income must be adjusted for what would happen to this measure if a dilutive security were exercised. We may take as an example a convertible debt. Interest is paid on that debt. If the debtholders converted those securities to common stock, the interest expense would be reduced by the amount paid to the convertible debtholders. The same would true with convertible preferred stock, but in that case it would be the amount of dividends paid to that class of stockholders.

There is a restriction as to what dilutive securities can be included in the calculation. Any dilutive security that can potentially make diluted EPS exceed basic EPS is excluded from the calculation of diluted EPS. Such dilutive securities are referred to as antidilutive securities.

Let's use Apple's 2013 financial statements to illustrate diluted EPS. In a note to its financial statements, Apple described its dilutive securities as "potentially dilutive securities include outstanding stock options, shares to be purchased under the Company's employee stock purchase plan and unvested RSUs." (RSUs are restricted stock units discussed in chapter 4.) The following table shows the computation of Apple's basic and diluted EPS for 2013 (in $ thousands, except net income in $ millions and per share amounts):

Numerator:	
Net income	$37,037
Denominator:	
Weighted-average shares outstanding	925,331
Effect of dilutive securities	6,331
Weighted-average diluted shares	931,662
Basic earnings per share	$40.03
Diluted earnings per share	$39.75

Apple also disclosed that potentially dilutive securities representing 4.2 million shares of common stock for 2013 were excluded from the computation of diluted EPS because their effect would have been antidilutive.

KEY POINTS COVERED IN THIS CHAPTER

- The statement of income (income statement) is a financial statement that summarizes a company's operating performance over a period of time (a fiscal quarter or a fiscal year).
- The presentation of the income statement begins with information about the company's operating results (labeled gross margin) that takes into account only the cost of producing the company's offerings (the cost of goods sold or the cost of sales).

- Because gross margin ignores nonoperating expenses, the operating income of the company is determined, and this figure summarizes the company's performance with respect to business operations.
- Sales/revenue are the proceeds received or to be received from the sales of a company's offerings; the amount and recognition depend on the principle of revenue recognition and the matching principle.
- Because some companies generate revenue from contracts that span more than one accounting year, there are two GAAP methods for accounting for long-term contracts: the percentage-of-completion method and the completed-contract method.
- The percentage-of-completion method requires that a contract's revenues be recognized each period based on the progress of the construction.
- GAAP requires the use of the percentage-of-completion method when estimates of progress toward completion, revenues, and costs are reasonably dependable and certain conditions are met.
- The completed-contract method specifies that revenue and gross profit are recognized only at the point of sale (i.e., when the contracted work is completed), with the costs associated with the long-term contracts in process accumulated, but there are no interim expenses charged to the income statement.
- The completed-contract method should be used only (1) when a company has primarily short-term contracts, or (2) when the conditions for using the percentage-of-completion method cannot be satisfied, or (3) when there are inherent hazards in the contract beyond the normal, recurring business risks.
- Two general categories of operating costs are shown in the income statement: (1) the cost of goods sold (COGS) and (2) selling, general, and administrative expenses.
- Selling, general, and administrative expenses are expenses not directly related to the production or creation of the products sold.
- The COGS is computed as follows: the cost of inventory at the beginning of the accounting period plus the cost of inventory purchased or manufactured during the accounting period reduced by the cost of inventory at the end of the accounting period.
- Inventory valuation (inventory costing) is important because calculation of the COGS depends on the cost of inventory at the beginning and end of the accounting period and the cost of creating or purchasing inventory during the period.
- Fundamentally, inventory valuation involves allocation of the costs of inventory available for sale between the ending inventory and the COGS.
- Under GAAP, a company has considerable discretion in selecting the accounting method for determining the cost of inventory.

- Accounting under GAAP requires that the costs that must be included for computing the costs of inventory are parts and raw materials costs, direct labor costs, and manufacturing overhead costs.

- The four inventory costing methods that a company can use to determine how costs are allocated to COGS and ending inventory are (1) specific identification, (2) first in, first out (FIFO), (3) last in, first out (LIFO), and (4) average cost.

- Once a company selects an inventory costing method, it cannot simply change methods.

- There are differences between currently due taxes and future potential taxes owing to differences in financial accounting and tax reporting methods, as well as other timing issues; these differences result in deferred taxes.

- A noncontrolling interest is the portion of stockholders' equity in a subsidiary that is not attributable directly or indirectly to a parent company; in financial statements it may be referred to as a minority interest.

- GAAP requires that the noncontrolling interest be reported on the consolidated balance sheet in the stockholders' equity section but be shown separately from the parent company's equity; in the income statement, that portion of net income (and comprehensive income) is shown as net income attributable to noncontrolling interest.

- The earnings available to common stockholders are equal to net income reduced by any preferred stock dividends.

- According to GAAP, comprehensive income is the change in equity during a period resulting from transactions and other events and circumstances from nonowner sources except transactions resulting from investments by owners and distributions to owners.

- Comprehensive income includes net income.

- Other comprehensive income is that part of comprehensive income added to net income to obtain comprehensive income; it is defined as revenue, expenses, gains, and losses that under GAAP are recorded as part of shareholders' equity on the balance sheet but are excluded from net income.

- In an income statement, two components of comprehensive income must be shown: net income and other comprehensive income.

- A company's earnings per share (EPS) is computed by dividing net income available to common stockholders by the number of common shares outstanding.

- GAAP requires that companies report two EPS measures: basic EPS and diluted EPS.

- Dilutive securities are all financial arrangements made by the company that allow a third party to potentially acquire the company's common stock shares.

- Diluted EPS takes into account the potential for the conversion of securities into common stock, such as securities that allow the holder to exchange them for a specified number of common stock shares, and options issued by the company that grant certain parties the right to exercise an option to obtain a specified number of shares.

- Diluted EPS is computed by net income available to common stockholders adjusted for the exercise of dilutive securities divided by the number of common shares if dilutive securities are exercised.
- Any dilutive security that can potentially make diluted EPS exceed basic EPS (referred to as antidilutive securities) is excluded from the calculative of diluted EPS.

FURTHER READINGS

Berman, Karen, Joe Night, and John Case, *Financial Intelligence for Entrepreneurs: What You Really Need to Know about the Numbers* (Boston: Harvard Business School Press, 2008), chaps. 3, 4, 5, and 12.

Peterson Drake, Pamela, and Frank J. Fabozzi, *Analysis of Financial Statements,* 3rd ed. (Hoboken, NJ: John Wiley & Sons, 2006), chap. 5.

Weil, Roman L., Katherine Schipper, and Jennifer Francis, *Financial Accounting: An Introduction to Concepts, Methods and Uses,* 14th ed. (Mason, OH: South-Western College Publishers, 2013), chaps. 3, 5, and 8.

11

STATEMENT OF CASH FLOWS AND STATEMENT OF STOCKHOLDERS' EQUITY

In this chapter we describe our last two financial statements: the statement of cash flows and the statement of stockholders' equity.

STATEMENT OF CASH FLOWS

The *statement of cash flows* provides a summary of a company's cash flows. The summary presentation is in terms of

- cash flow from operations,
- cash flow from investment activities, and
- cash flow from financing activities.

From these three components of the statement of cash flows, the following will be obtained:

- net cash flows from operating activities,
- net cash flows from investing activities, and
- net cash flows from financing activities.

The sum of the above is called the *net change in cash*. By adding the cash (including cash equivalents) on the balance sheet at the beginning of the fiscal year (i.e., the end of the previous fiscal year) to the net change in cash, the result is the cash (including cash equivalents) on the balance sheet at the end of the fiscal year. That is,

Net change in cash + Cash at beginning of year = Cash at end of year.

Basically, the statement of cash flows reconciles the beginning-of-the-year cash with the end-of-year cash, detailing the different sources and uses of cash that caused the change.

We will use iRobot's 2012 statement of cash flows, reproduced in table 11.1, and MiMedx's 2012 statement of cash flows, reproduced in table 11.2, to explain this statement and its three components.

Table 11.1
iRobot Corporation 2012 Consolidated Statements of Cash Flows (December 29, 2012) (in $ thousands)

Cash flows from operating activities:	
Net income	$ 17,297

Adjustments to reconcile net income to net cash provided by operating activities:	
Depreciation and amortization	11,672
Loss on disposal of property and equipment	1,332
Stock based compensation	10,983
Deferred income taxes, net	(3,763)
Tax benefit of excess stock based compensation deductions	(1,445)
Non-cash director deferred compensation	87
Changes in operating assets and liabilities—(use) source	
Accounts receivable	15,560
Unbilled revenue	1,166
Inventory	(807)
Other assets	(2,892)
Accounts payable	(8,684)
Accrued expenses	(656)
Accrued compensation	(6,106)
Deferred revenue	4,730
Long term liabilities	(613)
Net cash provided by operating activities	37,861

Cash flows from investing activities:

Additions of property and equipment	(6,770)
Change in other assets	(6,000)
Purchase of Evolution Robotics, Inc., net of cash received	(74,530)
Purchase of investments	(5,086)
Sales of investments	10,000
Net cash used in investing activities	(82,386)

Cash flows from financing activities:

Income tax withholding payment associated with restricted stock vesting	(784)
Proceeds from stock option exercises	4,326
Tax benefit of excess stock based compensation deductions	1,445
Net cash provided by financing activities	4,987
Net increase (decrease) in cash and cash equivalents	(39,538)
Cash and cash equivalents, at beginning of period	166,308
Cash and cash equivalents, at end of period	$ 126,770

A great deal can be learned about a company's economic prospects by examining the sources of the company's cash flows. For example, a company that is financially strong tends to consistently generate positive cash flows from operations and invests such that it has negative cash flows from investing. To remain competitive and attractive to investors, a company must be able to generate cash flows from its operations, and to grow the company it must continually make capital investments. We'll look at this more closely in the next chapter when we discuss the analysis of financial statements.

Cash Flow from Operating Activities

Cash flow from operating activities is the cash flow from day-to-day operating activities and is basically net income adjusted for (1) noncash expenditures and income and (2) changes in current assets and current liabilities. This section of the statement of cash flows begins with net income, which is divided into the two types just described.

Noncash Expenditures and Income   For iRobot and MiMedx, in the section "Cash flows from operating activities" is the net income, followed by a line that provides the first adjustment mentioned above, noncash expenditures and income, referred to by iRobot as "Adjustments to reconcile net income to net cash provided by operating activities" and by MiMedx as "Adjustments to reconcile net loss to net cash flows from operating activities." From that section, one can see the various types of adjustments: depreciation for fixed assets, amortization for intangibles, impairment of intangibles, and share-based compensation (i.e., compensating employees with stock rather than with cash).

Changes in Current Assets and Current Liabilities   In the case of changes in current assets and current liabilities, the "change" is from the prior accounting period to the current accounting period. The reason why it is necessary to adjust net income for changes in current assets and current liabilities is because of the use of the accrual basis of accounting under GAAP.[1] The procedure is as follows:

Adjustment to net income		
to obtain cash flow	**Current assets**	**Current liabilities**
Add to net income	Increase	Decrease
Subtract from net income	Decrease	Increase

In the section on cash flows from operating activities shown in tables 11.1 and 11.2, the change for each current asset and current liability is shown in a separate section: for iRobot it is labeled "Changes in operating assets and liabilities — (use) source" and for

---

1. Accrual accounting is explained in chapter 8.

Table 11.2
MiMedx Group, Inc. and Subsidiaries 2012 Consolidated Statements of Cash Flows (December 31, 2012)

Cash flows from operating activities:	
Net loss	$ (7,662,376)
Adjustments to reconcile net loss to net cash flows from operating activities:	
Depreciation	465,367
Amortization of intangible assets	1,380,241
Impairment of intangible assets	1,798,495
Amortization of debt discount and deferred financing costs	1,714,101
Employee share-based compensation expense	2,075,680
Other share-based compensation expense	463,041
Change in fair value of earn-out liability	1,567,050
Increase (decrease) in cash resulting from changes in (net of effects of acquisition):	
Accounts receivable	(5,761,642)
Inventory	(2,310,182)
Prepaid expenses and other current assets	(466,060)
Other assets	96,657
Accounts payable	(81,112)
Accrued expenses	2,960,744
Accrued interest	387,896
Other liabilities	(12,731)
Net cash flows from operating activities	(3,384,831)

Cash flows from investing activities:	
Purchases of equipment	(582,931)
Proceeds from grant	—
Cash paid for acquisition, net of cash acquired	—
Net cash flows from investing activities	(582,931)

Cash flows from financing activities:	
Proceeds from exercise of warrants	6,001,063
Proceeds from exercise of stock options	1,052,668
Repayment of convertible debt related to acquisition	(427,126)
Repayment of equipment lease	(16,116)
Repurchase of warrants	(568)

Table 11.2 (continued)

Cash flows from operating activities:	
Net loss	$ (7,662,376)
Proceeds from Senior Secured Promissory Notes	—
Proceeds from Line of Credit with related party	—
Repayment of Line of Credit	—
Repayment of Note Payable	—
Proceeds from sale of common stock and warrants and common stock with registration rights, net	—
Net cash flows from financing activities	6,609,921
Net change in cash	2,642,159
Cash, beginning of period	4,112,326
Cash, end of period	$6,754,485

Author note: Items where a dash is shown are reported in the 2012 financial statement. However, they were not applicable for the 2012 statement but had values for the 2011 financial statement. Since two years' worth of accounting information is provided on financial statements for the 2012 year end, these items are shown.

MiMedx it is labeled "Increase (decrease) in cash resulting from changes in (net of effects of acquisition)."

Cash Flow from Investing Activities

The *cash flow from investing activities* consists of the cash flow related to the acquisition of fixed assets (property, plant, and equipment), intangible assets, and companies; offsetting this amount are the proceeds from the disposal of such assets.

The largest component of cash flow from investing activities by iRobot was for the purchase of Evolution Robotics, Inc., representing $74.53 million of the total $82.386 million net cash outflow from investing activities. Notice that the amount shown for this purchase is "net of cash received." This is because in the purchase, one of the assets iRobot received was cash or cash equivalents. For MiMedx, the only use of cash was for purchasing equipment.

Cash Flow from Financing Activities

Cash flow from financing activities is the cash flow from activities related to the sources of capital funds. Examples of how cash flow is used include repurchasing common stock, paying off maturing debt, and paying dividends to stockholders. Note that interest paid for debt is part of net income, so it is not included here. Examples of how cash flow from financing activities is obtained include selling common stock, selling bonds, and exercising options to purchase common stock.

For iRobot, cash flow from financing activities had to do with restricted stock and the exercise of options. For MiMedx, it was for a wider range of financing activities.

Net Change in Cash

The net change in cash is the sum of the net cash flows from the three activities:

- net cash flows from operating activities,
- net cash flows from investing activities, and
- net cash flows from financing activities.

Table 11.1 summarizes for iRobot and table 11.2 summarizes for MiMedx the net change in cash, as well as how the end-of-period cash is determined:

STATEMENT OF STOCKHOLDERS' EQUITY

The changes in stockholders' equity between two years is shown in the ***statement of stockholders' equity***, also referred to as the ***statement of shareholders' equity***. Basically, this statement reconciles the balance of each component of stockholders' equity (common stock, paid-in capital, retained earnings, accumulated comprehensive income) from the beginning of the fiscal year (i.e., end of the prior fiscal year) to the end of the fiscal year. For each component of stockholders' equity, the statement begins with the balance at the beginning of the fiscal year. From there, the adjustments that are made to obtain the balance at the end of the fiscal year are shown.

Table 11.3 shows the statement of stockholders' equity for 2012 for iRobot for each component of stockholders' equity. It provides a description of what resulted in a change in stockholders' equity from January 2, 2012 (equivalently, December 31, 2011) to the end of the calendar year for which iRobot reports, December 29, 2012. Notice that the first line is the beginning period balance and the last line is the ending balance. A comparison of the stockholders' equity components on iRobot's balance sheet shown in table 9.2 of chapter 9 with the last line in table 11.3 shows that they agree.

KEY POINTS COVERED IN THIS CHAPTER

- The statement of cash flows provides a summary of a company's cash flows in terms of (1) cash flow from operations, (2) cash flow from investment activities, and (3) cash flow from financing activities.
- The net change in cash is the sum of (1) net cash flows from operating activities, (2) net cash flows from investing activities, and (3) net cash flows from financing activities.
- The cash (including cash equivalents) on the balance sheet at the end of the fiscal year is found by adding the cash (including cash equivalents) on the balance sheet at the

Table 11.3
iRobot 2012 Consolidated Statements of Stockholders' Equity (in $ thousands)

	Common Stock		Additional Paid-In Capital	Deferred Compensation	Retained Earnings (Accumulated Deficit)	Accumulated Other Comprehensive Income (Loss)	Stockholders' Equity
	Shares	Value					
Balance at December 31, 2011	27,216,555	$272	$184,395		$58,140	$151	$242,958
Issuance of common stock for exercise of stock options	390,956	4	4,322				4,326
Conversion of deferred compensation	823						
Vesting of restricted stock units	204,053	2	(2)				
Tax benefit of excess stock-based compensation deduction			902				
Amortization of deferred compensation relating to stock options			10,983				902
Stock withheld to cover tax withholdings requirements upon vesting of restricted stock units	(30,728)		(784)				(784)
Unrealized gain on short-term investment						48	48
Directors' deferred compensation	87	87					
Net income							
Balance at December 29, 2012	$27,781,659	$278	$199,903		$75,437	$199	$275,817

beginning of the fiscal year (i.e., end of the previous fiscal year) to the net change in cash, the result is the cash (including cash equivalents) on the balance sheet at the end of the fiscal year.

- Basically, the statement of cash flows reconciles the beginning-of-the-year cash with the end-of-year cash, detailing the different sources and uses of cash that caused the change.

- A great deal can be learned about a company's economic prospects by examining the sources of a company's cash flows.

- Cash flow from operating activities is the cash flow from day-to-day operating activities and is basically net income adjusted for (1) noncash expenditures and income and (2) changes in current assets and current liabilities.

- The cash flow from investing activities consists of the cash flows related to the acquisition of fixed assets (property, plant, and equipment), intangible assets, and companies, reduced by the proceeds from the disposal of such assets.

- Cash flow from financing activities is the cash flow from activities related to the sources of capital funds.

- The net change in cash is the sum of the net cash flows from three activities: (1) net cash flows from operating activities, (2) net cash flows from investing activities, and (3) net cash flows from financing activities

- The statement of stockholders' equity (the statement of shareholders' equity) shows the changes in stockholders' equity between two years, reconciling the balance of each component of stockholders' equity from the beginning of the fiscal year to the end of the fiscal year.

- Each component of stockholders' equity begins with the balance at the beginning of the fiscal year and from there adjustments are made to obtain the balance at the end of the fiscal year.

FURTHER READINGS

Berman, Karen, Joe Night, and John Case, *Financial Intelligence for Entrepreneurs: What You Really Need to Know about the Numbers* (Boston: Harvard Business School Press, 2008), chaps. 15 and 16.

Peterson Drake, Pamela, and Frank J. Fabozzi, *Analysis of Financial Statements,* 3rd ed. (Hoboken, NJ: John Wiley & Sons, 2006), chap. 6.

Weil, Roman L., Katherine Schipper, and Jennifer Francis, *Financial Accounting: An Introduction to Concepts, Methods and Uses,* 14th ed. (Mason, OH: South-Western College Publishers, 2013), chaps. 6 and 15.

Weygandt, Jerry J., Donald E. Kieso, and Paul D. Kimmel, *Financial Accounting,* 9th ed. (Hoboken, NJ: John Wiley & Sons, 2013), chap. 13.

12

FINANCIAL RATIOS

The previous four chapters provided the financial accounting information needed to understand how to assess the performance of a company and how to assess its ability to satisfy its debt obligations. In this chapter we explain various financial ratios, computed from the financial statements, that are useful in assessing the performance of management. Our purpose here is not to provide an in-depth explanation of how to use this financial information to value a startup. We discuss the valuation of a private company in chapter 16 and appendix B.

Here the purpose is to show how financial ratios created from the financial statements can be used to learn something about a firm's profitability, how efficiently it utilizes its resources, and its reliance on debt and its ability to satisfy that debt. A complete analysis involves an analysis of the industry in which a firm operates and the competition the firm faces in the marketplace. Several Internet sources provide these financial measures and performance measures.

KEY FINANCIAL RATIOS

Financial ratios are classified into five categories, based on information about the activities of the firm:

- profitability margin ratios,
- return on investment ratios,
- asset efficiency ratios,
- financial leverage ratios, and
- liquidity ratios.

We describe each below.

A summary of the calculation for each ratio is provided in table 12.1. To illustrate these ratios, we will apply them to iRobot Corporation for the 2013 and 2012 fiscal years. The income statements for the 2013 and 2012 fiscal years are shown in table 12.2. The balance

Table 12.1
Summary of Key Financial Ratios

Profitability margin ratios	
Gross profit margin	$\dfrac{\text{Gross profit}}{\text{Revenues}}$
Operating profit margin	$\dfrac{\text{Operating income}}{\text{Revenues}} = \dfrac{\text{EBIT}}{\text{Revenues}}$
Net profit margin	$\dfrac{\text{Net income}}{\text{Revenues}}$

Return on investment ratios	
Return on assets	$\dfrac{\text{Net income}}{\text{Average total assets}}$
Return on any asset	$\dfrac{\text{Net income}}{\text{Any asset}}$

Asset efficiency ratios	
Total asset turnover ratio	$\dfrac{\text{Revenues}}{\text{Average total assets}}$
Inventory turnover ratio	$\dfrac{\text{Cost of goods sold}}{\text{Average inventory}}$
Accounts receivable turnover ratio	$\dfrac{\text{Credit sales to customers}}{\text{Average accounts receivable}}$

Financial leverage ratios	
Percentage of financial leverage ratios	
Debt-to-assets ratio	$\dfrac{\text{Debt}}{\text{Total assets}}$
Long-term debt-to-assets ratio	$\dfrac{\text{Long-term debt}}{\text{Total assets}}$
Debt-to-stockholders' equity ratio (debt ratio)	$\dfrac{\text{Debt}}{\text{Common stockholders' equity}}$
Equity multiplier	$\dfrac{\text{Common stockholders' equity}}{\text{Debt}}$
Coverage ratios	
Times-interest-earned ratio (interest coverage ratio)	$\dfrac{\text{EBIT}}{\text{Interest}}$
Fixed charge coverage ratio	$\dfrac{\text{EBIT} + \text{Annual lease payments}}{\text{Interest} + \text{Annual lease payments}}$

Liquidity ratios	
Current ratio	$\dfrac{\text{Current assets}}{\text{Current liabilities}}$
Quick ratio	$\dfrac{\text{Current assets} - \text{Inventory}}{\text{Current liabilities}}$

Table 12.2
Income Statement for iRobot Corporation for 2013 and 2012 ($ thousands)

	12/29/2013	12/29/2012
Sales or revenue	$487,401	$436,244
Cost of goods sold (cost of revenue)	266,247	241,896
Gross margin (or gross profit)	221,154	194,348
Total operating expenses	188,536	169,176
Operating income (or earnings before interest and taxes, EBIT)	32,618	25,172
Interest expense	0	0
Net income before taxes	32,415	25,607
Income tax expense	4,774	8,310
Net income	$27,641	$17,297

sheets for three fiscal years—2013, 2012, and 2011—are shown in table 12.3. The reason for including three fiscal years is because the average of the beginning and ending fiscal year account values on the balance sheet are used when a balance sheet item is used in the calculation of a financial ratio. In table 12.3 the average balance is shown. The financial ratios are shown in table 12.4.

Profitability Margin Ratios
Profitability margin ratios measure a company's profit relative to its revenues. The denominator for profitability margin ratios is revenues. The numerator for these ratios is some measure of income. Let's recap the income statement structure as provided in chapter 10, ignoring other comprehensive income and assuming no preferred stock, to help us understand the different profitability margin ratios:

	Sales or revenues
−	Cost of goods sold
=	Gross margin (or gross profit)
−	Selling, general and administrative expenses
−	Research-and-development expenses
=	Operating income (or earnings before interest and taxes, EBIT)
−	Interest expense
=	Net income before taxes
−	Income taxes
=	Net income

Table 12.3
Balance Sheet for iRobot Corporation for 2013, 2012, and 2011 ($ thousands)

	Balance Sheet Item by Year ($ thousands)				
	12/29/2013	12/29/2012	Avg. 2013	12/29/2011	2012 Avg.
Assets					
Current assets:					
Cash and cash equivalents	$165,404	$126,770	$146,087	$166,308	$146,539
Short-term investments	21,954	12,430	17,192	17,811	15,121
Accounts receivable, net	39,348	29,413	34,381	43,338	36,376
Unbilled inventory	856	1,196	1,026	2,362	1,779
Inventory	46,107	36,965	41,536	31,089	34,027
Deferred tax assets	20,144	19,266	19,705	15,344	17,305
Other current assets	6,848	8,853	7,851	7,928	8,391
Total current assets	$300,661	$234,893	$267,777	$284,180	$259,537
Property, plant, and equipment, net	23,661	24,952	24,307	29,029	26,991
Deferred tax assets	10,095	8,792	9,444	6,127	7,460
Goodwill	48,751	48,951	48,851	7,910	28,431
Intangible assets, net	22,668	28,224	25,446	2,467	15,346
Other assets	10,501	8,500	9,501	2,500	5,500
Total assets	$416,337	$354,313	$385,325	$332,213	$343,263
Liabilities					
Current liabilities:	$80,915	$77,163	$79,039	$85,000	$81,082
Long-term liabilities	4,733	3,816	4,275	4,255	4,036
Total liabilities (debt)	85,648	80,979	83,314	89,255	85,117
Preferred stock	0	0	0	0	0
Common stock	330,689	275,817	303,253	242,958	259,388
Total liabilities and stockholders' equity	$416,337	$356,796	$386,567	$332,213	$344,505

Table 12.4
Financial Ratios for iRobot for 2013 and 2012

Financial ratio	2013	2012
Profitability margin ratios		
Gross profit margin	0.454	0.446
Operating profit margin	0.067	0.058
Net profit margin	0.057	0.040
Return on investment ratios		
Return on assets ratio	0.07	0.05
Asset efficiency ratios	2013	2012
Total asset turnover	1.26	1.27
Inventory turnover ratio	6.41	7.11
Accounts receivable turnover ratio	14.18	11.99
Financial leverage ratios		
Percentage of financial leverage ratios		
Debt-to-assets ratio	0.22	0.25
Long-term debt-to-assets ratio	0.01	0.01
Debt-to-equity ratio (debt ratio):	0.01	0.02
Equity multiplier	70.94	64.28
Coverage ratios		
Times-interest-earned ratio (interest coverage ratio)	No interest	No interest
Fixed charge coverage ratio		
Liquidity ratios		
Current ratio	3.39	3.20
Quick ratio	2.86	2.78

The first measure of profitability above is the gross margin (gross profit). When this measure is used, the profitability margin measure is called the **gross profit margin**:

$$\text{Gross profit margin} = \frac{\text{Gross margin}}{\text{Revenues}}.$$

The gross profit margin indicates the profit per dollar of revenues based solely on the cost of goods sold.

The second measure of profitability that we see in the income statement is operating income (also called earnings before interest and taxes, EBIT) and the ratio is called the **operating profit margin**:

$$\text{Operating profit margin} = \frac{\text{Operating income}}{\text{Revenues}} = \frac{\text{EBIT}}{\text{Revenues}}.$$

The operating profit margin indicates the profit per dollar of revenues generated from operations, ignoring the interest expense and taxes.

Our last measure of profitability listed above is net income, which takes into account interest expense and taxes. When that measure is used in the numerator, the profitability margin ratio is called the **net profit margin**:

$$\text{Net profit margin} = \frac{\text{Net income}}{\text{Revenues}}.$$

Return on Investment Ratios

Financial ratios that measure the return on the amount that the company invests in an asset or in stockholders' equity are referred to as **return on investment ratios** or ROI ratios. The numerator in these ratios is some measure of profitability and the denominator is either total assets or any specific asset. In addition, a return on stockholders' equity can be computed to determine what return was earned for the company's common stockholders.

The return that was earned on the company's total assets uses as its profit measure net income. The resulting measure, called the **return on assets**, is then

$$\text{Return on assets} = \frac{\text{Net income}}{\text{Average total assets}}.$$

The general formula for the calculation of the return on any asset is

$$\text{Return on any assets} = \frac{\text{Net income}}{\text{Any asset}}.$$

For example, if the assets whose return we seek are fixed assets, then

$$\text{Return on fixed assets} = \frac{\text{Net income}}{\text{Average fixed assets}}.$$

The return on common stockholders' equity shows the net income generated for the common stockholders as a percentage of the common stockholders' equity:

$$\text{Return on common stockholders' equity} = \frac{\text{Net income}}{\text{Average common stockholders' equity}}.$$

Asset Efficiency Ratios

Asset efficiency ratios seek to quantify how well specific asset types (i.e., inventory, accounts receivable, fixed assets) are being used by a company's management. For each of these ratios, the higher the value, the greater the amount generated per dollar invested in the specific asset. What is a good turnover ratio? That depends on the industry in which the company being evaluated falls.

Let's begin with the ***total asset turnover***, which is the ratio of revenues to average total assets:

$$\text{Total asset turnover} = \frac{\text{Revenues}}{\text{Average total assets}}.$$

This ratio indicates how much revenue each dollar that the company invests in total assets is able to generate.

If we are looking at management's efficiency in investing in inventory, the question is how much did inventory generate in the cost of goods sold. So the ***inventory turnover ratio*** is

$$\text{Inventory turnover ratio} = \frac{\text{Cost of goods sold}}{\text{Average inventory}}.$$

The inventory turnover can be viewed as an estimate of how many times during the accounting period that inventory was either created or purchased and sold. Although the inventory turnover is for all of the company's products, it can be calculated by product line.

The efficiency of funds tied up in accounts receivable, the ***accounts receivable turnover ratio***, looks at the average amount of accounts receivable relative to the approximate amount of sales the company makes on credit to its customers:

$$\text{Accounts receivable turnover} = \frac{\text{Credit sales to customers}}{\text{Average accounts receivable}}.$$

Recall from our review of financial statement that amount of credit sales to customers was not shown anywhere. What must be done by someone trying to evaluate the efficiency of accounts receivable management to obtain an estimate of annual credit sales to customers? Often what is done is to assume that all sales are on credit. This assumption was made in calculating the accounts receivable turnover ratio for iRobot in table 12.4.

Financial Leverage Ratios

The capital structure of a company shows how the founders have decided to finance the company. The balance sheet shows how this was done by reporting the amount of liabilities and equity. The liabilities are the debt used to finance the firm.

Briefly, the disadvantage of debt is that unlike with equity, there is an obligation to pay interest and repay the principal borrowed. Failure to do so will result in the bankruptcy of a company unless terms for extending or reducing a loan can be reached with all creditors. Moreover, lenders often impose restrictions on certain activities of a company; these restrictions are called covenants. Violating any of the covenants results in a technical default and requires the immediate repayment of the loan unless terms can be worked out with creditors.

The advantage of debt is that it is a cheaper form of financing than equity. Effectively, the cost of debt, which is the interest that must be paid to borrow funds, has the advantage that it is tax deductible. This also makes debt unlike equity, for with equity, any dividends paid represent a distribution of profit and are not tax deductible. The true benefits are realized based on operating performance. Since the cost of borrowing funds is fixed, if the company can use the borrowed funds to generate a return greater than the cost of borrowing, earnings will benefit, as the greater return increases earnings. The higher the return that can be earned on the borrowed funds, the greater is the benefit. Of course, this works in the opposite direction: earnings less than the cost of borrowing will result in poor performance compared to raising funds by issuing equity.

The ratio of the amount of funds borrowed relative to the amount of equity indicates the amount of financial leverage used by the company. The higher the financial leverage ratio, the greater is the company's financial risk. Financial leverage ratios seek to identify the amount of financial risk by using debt rather than equities. Two types of leverage can be used in the calculation. The first is simply a measure of the proportion of debt to the amount of the company financed by equity. Ratios of this sort are referred to as ***percentage of financial leverage ratios.*** The missing aspect when just the percentage of financial leverage is used is that it does not indicate the company's ability to meet its financial obligations from the sources it has available to pay off its creditors. For example, two companies in the same industry may have the same amount of percentage of debt in their capital structure but one company may have a better ability to pay off its debtholders through its operations. Financial leverage ratios that measure a company's ability to pay off debt are called ***coverage ratios.***

We discuss percentage of financial leverage ratios and coverage ratios below. The real-world company that we use for our illustration, iRobot, has very little debt.

Percentage of Financial Leverage Ratios   In computing percentage of financial leverage ratios, four questions must be dealt with.

The first question is whether to use the book value (carrying value) as shown on the balance sheet or the market value. Financial analysts use book values. However, the book value reported on a balance sheet is the ending book value. In calculating financial ratios using values on the balance sheet, the practice is to use the average book value of the accounting period. So if a financial ratio is being calculated for a fiscal year, the average of the beginning-of-the-year book value and the end-of-the-year book value is used. The beginning-of-the-year book value is equal to the end-of-the-prior-year's book value.

The second question is the measure that should be used for debt. Debt is classified as two types on the balance sheet, as explained in chapter 9: current liabilities and long-term (noncurrent) liabilities. Analysts have used as a measure of debt either all debt (current liabilities plus long-term liabilities) or just long-term liabilities. However, there are reasons to include debt not shown on the balance sheet as part of debt. For example, there are obligations, such as capital leases, that analysts view as a form of debt. Capital leases are effectively an alternative to borrowing funds to purchase a plant or equipment. In turn, an analyst would treat the capital lease as an asset.

The third is the treatment of preferred stock. Stockholders' equity includes preferred stock and common stock. Some analysts treat preferred stock as a form of debt because it has a fixed dividend rate even though failure to pay a preferred stock dividend does not have the same legal implications as defaulting on a debt payment.

Finally, should the book value of equity be used to measure common stockholders' equity or should market value be used? Either measure can be used as long as the ratio is clearly identified as the market value of stockholders' equity. Most services that report percentage of financial leverage ratios use book value. If the market value of equity is used, it is important to determine the market capitalization as of some date using the fiscal year or by using some average of different points in time. The market capitalization is the market price per share times the number of shares outstanding. The calculation may be done for the beginning of the fiscal year and the end of the fiscal year, which requires determining the market price and the number of shares outstanding on those two dates.

Now let's look at the four commonly used percentage of financial leverage ratios.

The ***debt-to-assets ratio*** indicates the percentage of the company's total assets that is financed by all debt (current liabilities and long-term debt):

$$\text{Debt-to-assets ratio} = \frac{\text{Debt}}{\text{Total assets}}.$$

If the focus is on just the use of long-term debt as a funding source for all of the company's total assets, the ***long-term debt-to-assets ratio*** is used:

$$\text{Long-term debt-to-assets ratio} = \frac{\text{Long-term debt}}{\text{Total assets}}.$$

For these two percentage of financial leverage ratios, the larger the ratio, the greater the reliance on debt, and accordingly the greater the financial risk to equity investors.

The two ratios above show debt as a percentage of total assets. The next ratio calculates a percentage of financial leverage ratio in terms of the amount of debt relative to stockholders' equity. The ratio is the ***debt-to-equity ratio*** (also known as the ***debt ratio***):

$$\text{Debt-to-stockholders' equity} = \frac{\text{Debt}}{\text{Common stockholders' equity}}.$$

The greater this ratio, the greater is the financial risk. The reciprocal of this ratio is called the ***equity multiplier***. That is,

$$\text{Equity multiplier} = \frac{\text{Common stockholders' equity}}{\text{Debt}}.$$

Coverage Ratios   As explained earlier, the percentage of financial leverage ratios look just at the portion of the company's capital structure financed by debt. Coverage ratios provide information about the company's ability to satisfy its debt obligations. Covenants for debt agreement typically specify a minimum level for coverage ratios. This means that if a coverage ratio falls below the required minimum, the company has breached its agreement and the amount owed is immediately payable, along with accrued interest.

The two most common coverage ratios are (1) the times-interest-earned ratio and (2) the fixed charge coverage ratio. The ***times-interest-earned ratio*** (also called the ***interest coverage ratio***) measures the amount available to pay only one fixed financing obligation, interest, from the funds available from the company's operating income. Since operating income is earnings before interest and taxes (EBIT), the ratio is expressed as

$$\text{Times-interest-earned ratio} = \frac{\text{EBIT}}{\text{Interest}}.$$

Interest is not the only fixed financing financial obligation. For example, since leasing is effectively a financing vehicle that is a substitute for borrowing to buy, lease payments represent a fixed financial charge.[1] When the coverage ratio takes into account all fixed

---

1. Although preferred stock is a form of equity and the dividends are not a fixed financing charge in the sense that failure to pay will result in adverse legal consequences, the required dividend payment (properly adjusted) can be considered in a coverage ratio. The procedure for handling an obligation in the denominator that is paid out of after-tax earnings, such as preferred stock dividends, is to gross up these obligations to place them on a pre-tax basis by dividing the obligation by a factor equal to one minus the tax rate.

financial obligations, the ratio is called the *fixed charge coverage ratio*, and is computed as follows:

$$\text{Fixed charge coverage ratio} = \frac{\text{EBIT} + \text{Annual lease payments}}{\text{Interest} + \text{Annual lease payments}}.$$

Liquidity Ratios

Ratios that are used to measure the ability of a company to satisfy its short-term obligations (liabilities due within one year) are referred to as *liquidity ratios* or *short-term solvency ratios*. The assets that are assumed to provide the needed liquidity for the company to meet its short-term obligations (i.e., its current liabilities) are the company's current assets. The company's current assets are also referred to as its *working capital*, and the excess of working capital over current liabilities is referred to as *net working capital*.

The two common liquidity ratios are the current ratio and the quick ratio, shown below:

$$\text{Current ratio} = \frac{\text{Current assets}}{\text{Current liabilities}}.$$

$$\text{Quick ratio} = \frac{\text{Current assets} - \text{Inventory}}{\text{Current liabilities}}.$$

The *current ratio* shows the amount of current assets relative to current liabilities. In most industries, this ratio exceeds one. There is no rule of thumb here about what a good current ratio is because in some industries the ratio could be slightly greater than one. The *quick ratio* differs from the current ratio in that it removes the least liquid of the current assets, inventory.

PUTTING IT ALL TOGETHER: DETERMINANTS OF EARNINGS PER SHARE

The presentation thus far explains the key financial ratios and their meaning. It is fair to say that at this point, we merely have a listing of these ratios. Our purpose in this section is to put together the first five key financial ratios to show how they affect the earnings per share (EPS) of a company. In this presentation, we will ignore the difference between basic EPS and diluted EPS described in chapter 10.

We start with basic EPS, and for convenience we assume no preferred stock:

$$\text{EPS} = \frac{\text{Net income}}{\text{Number of common shares outstanding}}.$$

We will now use a simple mathematical manipulation to break up a financial ratio into two parts. If we multiple EPS by "common stockholders' equity," we can rewrite EPS as

$$\text{EPS} = \frac{\text{Net income}}{\text{Common stockholders' equity}} \times \frac{\text{Common stockholders' equity}}{\text{Number of common shares outstanding}}.$$

Here we have two ratios. The first ratio, one we have already seen, is the return on common stockholders' equity. The second ratio is one we have not seen thus far. It is the ratio of the book value of the common stockholders' equity divided by the number of shares of common stock outstanding. This ratio is referred to as the ***book value per share of common stock***; that is,

$$\text{Book value per share of common stock} = \frac{\text{Common stockholders' equity}}{\text{Number of common shares outstanding}}.$$

Thus, EPS can be written as

EPS = Return on common stockholders' equity × Book value per share of common stock.

Increasing either of the two ratios without reducing the other will increase EPS. Suppose that a founder is considering another round of common equity financing. The impact on EPS is twofold. The book value per share of common stock will increase. However, for the EPS to increase, the change in the return on common stockholders' equity must be such that this ratio cannot decline by more than the increase in book value per share of common stock. Thus, if a founder is contemplating another round of common equity financing, the opportunities for investment within the company must be such that the return on common stockholders' equity will not decline.

A Closer Look at Return on Common Stockholders' Equity
Let's take a closer at the return on common stockholders' equity to determine what has an impact on EPS. We rewrite that ratio as

$$\text{Return on common stockholders' equity} = \frac{\text{Net income}}{\text{Total assets}} \times \frac{\text{Total assets}}{\text{Common stockholders' equity}}.$$

We have seen both of these ratios: an ROI ratio and a financial leverage ratio. The first ratio is the return on assets. To see how the second ratio is linked to a financial leverage ratio, recall that

Total assets = Common stockholders' equity + Total liabilities,

or equivalently,

Total assets = Common stockholders' equity + Debt.

Substituting into the second ratio for the return on common stockholders' equity, we get:

$$\frac{\text{Total assets}}{\text{Common stockholders' equity}} = \frac{\text{Common stockholders' equity} + \text{Debt}}{\text{Common stockholders' equity}}.$$

$$\frac{\text{Common stockholders' equity}}{\text{Common stockholders' equity}} + \frac{\text{Debt}}{\text{Common stockholders' equity}}$$

$$= 1 + \frac{\text{Debt}}{\text{Common stockholders' equity}}.$$

Now we see why we said the second ratio for the return on common stockholders' equity is a leverage ratio: the ratio above is the debt-to-equity ratio. Thus, the return on common stockholders' equity can be written as

Return on common stockholders' equity = Return on assets × (1 + Debt-to-equity ratio).

This means that to improve EPS by increasing the return on common stockholders' equity, one can increase one or both of return on assets and greater financial leverage (i.e., take on more debt). So a firm seeking debt financing (which will increase the debt-to-equity ratio) must be confident that the proceeds received will be used by the firm in such a way as not to reduce return on total assets. The reduction in the return on total assets will occur if the return earned on the proceeds from the borrowed funds is less than the cost of funds. Furthermore, notice that there a magnifying impact that the second factor has (1 + Debt-to-equity ratio).

Analysis of Return on Assets   For the return on assets, the analysis can be carried further to see the factors that have an impact on that ROI measure. To see how, the return on assets can be rewritten as

$$\text{Return on assets} = \frac{\text{Net income}}{\text{Revenues}} \times \frac{\text{Revenues}}{\text{Average total assets}}.$$

The first ratio is a profit margin ratio: net profit margin. The second ratio is an asset efficiency ratio: total asset turnover. Thus, the return on assets can be expressed as

Return on assets = Net profit margin × Total asset turnover.

So to improve the return on assets, which in turn improves the return on common stockholders' equity, and then EPS, founders can improve the profit margin and asset turnover. The asset efficiency ratio for each type of asset can be analyzed to improve total asset turnover.

How does one improve the net profit margin? Let's first concentrate on profit margin based on operations, without taking into account interest and taxes, which gives us the net profit margin. As explained in chapter 10, operating income or earnings before interest and taxes reflects earnings from operations ignoring interest and taxes. The ratio of EBIT to total assets is called **basic earning power**; that is,

$$\text{Basic earning power} = \frac{\text{EBIT}}{\text{Total assets}}.$$

Multiplying the numerator and denominator by revenues, we get:

$$\text{Basic earning power} = \frac{\text{EBIT}}{\text{Revenues}} \times \frac{\text{Revenues}}{\text{Total assets}}.$$

The second ratio is the total asset turnover. The first ratio is a profitability margin ratio, the operating profit margin, and reflects the profit margin, ignoring the capital structure (i.e., the amount paid in interest to borrow funds) and the tax rate that the company must make to tax authorities.

Consequently, basic earning power can be expressed as

Basic earning power = Operating profit margin × Total asset turnover.

Let's take into account taxes. We know that

Net income = Earnings before taxes − Taxes.

Abbreviating earnings before taxes as EBT, we can write:

$$
\begin{aligned}
\text{Net income} &= \text{EBT} - (\text{EBT} \times \text{Effective tax rate}) \\
&= \text{EBT} \times (1 - \text{Effective tax rate}) \\
&= \text{EBIT} \times \left[\frac{\text{EBT}}{\text{EBIT}} \right] \times (1 - \text{Effective tax rate}).
\end{aligned}
$$

The ratio of EBT/EBIT reflects the **tax burden** of the company based on its capital structure and the interest cost it must pay for debt and therefore equity's share of earnings. The measure (1 − Effective tax rate) is the **tax retention rate** (i.e., the amount that is retained by equity after payment of taxes).

With some manipulation, the return on total assets can be written as

$$\text{Return on total assets} = \left[\frac{\text{EBIT}}{\text{Revenues}} \right] \times \left[\frac{\text{Revenues}}{\text{Total assets}} \right] \times \left[\frac{\text{EBT}}{\text{EBIT}} \right] \times (1 - \text{Effective tax rate}).$$

The first ratio above is the operating profit margin. The second ratio is the total asset turnover (an asset efficiency ratio). The third ratio is equity's share of earnings after taxes are paid. The last factor is the tax retention rate. Consequently, we can write:

Return on assets = Operating profit margin × Total asset turnover

× Equity's share of earnings × Tax retention rate .

Now we can see the factors that influence the return on assets and in turn EPS.

COMMON SIZE ANALYSIS

Another useful tool in the analysis of financial statements over different time periods is *common size analysis*. In this analysis, sometimes referred to as *vertical analysis*, each item in the income statement and on the balance sheet is compared to some benchmark item. The resulting ratio is referred to as a *common size ratio*. That is,

$$\text{Common size ratio} = \frac{\text{Item of interest on a financial statement}}{\text{Benchmark item}}.$$

For the income statement, the benchmark item is revenues; for the balance sheet it is total assets. Tables 12.5 and 12.6 show common size ratio analysis for iRobot's income statement and balance sheet for 2012 and 2013.

Common size analysis is useful for two reasons. First, when applied to a given company, it helps identify trends and changes in a company's expenses as a percentage of revenues in the case of an income statement and investing/financing activities in the case of the balance sheet. Second, it is a useful tool in comparing the performance of different companies of different sizes.

Common size analysis does have its limitations. For example, as explained in chapters 4, 5, and 6, companies have a choice of accounting policies with respect to certain accounting items in the income statement and on the balance sheet. This may make intercompany

Table 12.5
Common Size Analysis for iRobot for 2013 and 2012: Income Statement (Percent of Revenues)

	2013	2012
Sales or revenue	100.00	100.00
Cost of goods sold (cost of revenue)	54.63	55.45
Gross margin (or gross profit)	45.37	44.55
Total operating expenses	38.68	38.78
Operating income (or earnings before interest and taxes, EBIT)	6.69	5.77
Interest expense	0.00	0.00
Net income before taxes	6.65	5.87
Income tax expense	0.98	1.90
Net income	5.67	3.96

Table 12.6
Common Size Analysis for iRobot (2013 and 2012): Balance Sheet (Percent of Total Assets)

	2013	2012
Assets		
Current assets:		
Cash and cash equivalents	39.73	35.78
Short-term investments	5.27	3.51
Accounts receivable, net	9.45	8.30
Unbilled inventory	0.21	0.34
Inventory	11.07	10.43
Deferred tax assets	4.84	5.44
Other current assets	1.64	2.50
Total current assets	72.22	66.30
Property, plant, and equipment, net	5.68	7.04
Deferred tax assets	2.42	2.48
Goodwill	11.71	13.82
Intangible assets, net	5.44	7.97
Other assets	2.52	2.40
Total assets	100.00	100.00
Liabilities		
Current liabilities:	19.43	21.78
Long-term liabilities	1.14	1.08
Total liabilities (debt)	20.57	22.86
Preferred stock	0.00	0.00
Common stock	79.43	77.85
Total liabilities and stockholders' equity	100.00	100.70

comparisons difficult to interpret. In such situations, an in-depth analysis would require adjustment of the financial statements. Second, the companies being compared may have different fiscal years, which could affect the interpretation of the analysis.

KEY POINTS COVERED IN THIS CHAPTER

- Financial ratios computed from the financial statements are useful in evaluating a firm's profitability, how efficiently it utilizes its resources, its reliance on debt, and its ability to satisfy debt obligations.

- A complete analysis involves an analysis of the industry in which a firm operates and the competitors the firm faces in the marketplace.
- Financial ratios are classified based on the information about the activities of the firm and include: profitability margin ratios, return on investment ratios, asset efficiency ratios, financial leverage ratios, and liquidity ratios.
- Profitability margin ratios measure a company's profit relative to its revenues and includes gross profit margin and operating profit margin.
- Return-on-investment ratios measure the return on the amount that the company invests in an asset or on stockholders' equity.
- Asset efficient ratios seek to quantify how well specific asset types are being used by a company's management and include total asset turnover, inventory ratio, and accounts receivable ratio.
- Financial leverage ratios indicate the amount of financing of the firm obtained by borrowing, as well as the ability of the firm to repay its debt obligations, referred to as coverage ratios. The debt-to-assets ratio, long-term debt-to-assets ratio, and debt-to-equity ratio are percentage financial leverage ratios. Coverage ratios include times-interest-earned ratio (also called the interest coverage ratio) and fixed charge coverage ratio.
- Liquidity ratios or short-term solvency ratios are used for measuring the ability of a company to satisfy it short-term obligations (liabilities due within one year) and include the current ratio and the quick ratio.
- The earnings per share of a company can be decomposed in various financial ratios to explain performance.
- Common size analysis is a useful tool in the analysis of financial statements over different periods of time. In this analysis, each item on the income statement and the balance sheet is compared to some benchmark item with the resulting ratio referred to as the common size ratio.

FURTHER READINGS

Drake, Pamela Peterson, and Frank J. Fabozzi, *Analysis of Financial Statements,* 3rd ed. (Hoboken, NJ: John Wiley & Sons, 2006), chaps. 1, 4, and 10.

Weil, Roman L., Katherine Schipper, and Jennifer Francis, *Financial Accounting: An Introduction to Concepts, Methods and Uses,* 14th ed. (Mason, OH: South-Western College Publishers, 2013), chap. 7.

Weygandt, Jerry J., Donald E. Kieso, and Paul D. Kimmel, *Financial Accounting,* 9th ed. (Hoboken, NJ: John Wiley & Sons, 2013), chap. 14.

13

FINANCIAL PLANNING

In our discussion of the business plan in chapter 2, we described the financial plan component. A financial plan sets forth the company's projected financial position, cash flows, net income, and external financing needs. The starting point is the projected revenues and sales of the company. The financial plan provides the entrepreneur with information about when and how much funds need to be raised and whether those are permanent needs or seasonal needs resulting from the company's operating cycle.

Fundamentally, the financial plan involves the use of budgets to make quantitative statements about the funding needs of a company. Typically the budgeting process that is part of a financial plan will include a short budget covering a time period of less than one year, referred to as an *operating budget*, and a long-term budget covering a time period of three to five years, referred to as a *long-term planning budget*. These two budgets are not constructed independently from one another. Rather, the two budgets are dependent on each other because the long-term planning budget depends on what the entrepreneur plans to do in the short run.

Financial planning requires forecasting. There is no way around it. In entrepreneurs' pitches to investors, one is often struck by the high level of confidence many entrepreneurs seem to have in their forecasts of sales and sales growth, as well as in the cost elements affecting profitability, such as production costs, distribution costs, and marketing costs. But forecasting is more of an art than a science. Although there are different methods of forecasting, typically the forecasts are wrong except by fluke. So starting with the assumption that forecasts are wrong is a prudent practice in financial planning. That does not mean forecasts should not be used. Rather, it means that relying on one number to develop the critical component of a business plan could lead to lower profitability and potentially the failure of a business. Consequently, testing using alternative assumptions is warranted. Moreover, monitoring actual versus forecasted sales and costs is imperative for revising the financial plan. The difficulties of forecasting sales and costs are compounded for entrepreneurs in high-tech industries when the offerings to be sold are still in the research-and-development stage. Uncertainty as to when the offerings (products or services) can be brought to market and the cost of producing the offering make sales forecasts highly questionable because sales depend on costs, but the costs can only be estimated.

The end point of a financial plan is the projected or forecasted income statement and balance sheet for a company based on budgets. This allows the entrepreneur to assess where the company will be, given assumptions about sales and other activities to be undertaken. Deviations from the projected values can help the entrepreneur identify early what actions might have to be taken. They also help the entrepreneur identify when certain milestones are likely to be achieved.

In this chapter we describe the basics of financial planning. We begin with the importance of financial planning and an explanation of two key budgets, sales and cash budgets, and then show how to project the income statement and balance sheet given these two budgets. The difficulties of formulating a sales budget are explained. We conclude the chapter with the topic of strategic acquisitions.

WHY FINANCIAL PLANNING IS IMPORTANT

The financial plan is important for two reasons. First, the insights offered by a properly formulated financial plan provide an entrepreneur with a tool with which to assess and then react to changing market conditions, such as sales that are less than forecasted, increases in the cost of raw materials, or increases in funding costs. This is because the tools available in financial planning allow entrepreneurs to test the sensitivity of their financial plan to unanticipated adverse market conditions before they occur.

Second, there are trade-offs that entrepreneurs will face in making business decisions. These trade-offs have to be evaluated by applying financial planning tools to the financial plan. For example, a financial plan provides an entrepreneur with information to better evaluate the trade-off between having sufficient inventory to satisfy customer demands and the need to obtain financing to invest in inventory. It also allows an entrepreneur to assess the trade-off associated with other decisions, such as the introduction of a new product, a change in product pricing, and production using alternative systems (high fixed cost/low variable cost versus low fixed cost/high variable cost).

BUDGETS AND FORECASTED FINANCIAL STATEMENTS

The tool that founders use to quantitatively express their objective of achieving financial milestones is the budget. The budget also functions as a device that allows founders and investors to monitor the progress of the venture to see whether it is on track to accomplish its financial milestone and, if not, allows the founders to take the necessary corrective action to get the venture back on track.

The period of time that a budget encompasses depends on the type of budget. Operating budgets cover a period of one year or less and are broken down into either weeks, months, or quarters, with updates at the of each period. Budgets for capital expenditures cover periods greater than one year and up to ten years and are referred to as long-term budgets.

Many budgets could be prepared for every activity of a firm's operations. Here our focus is on the sales budget and the cash budget. From these two budgets we can construct pro forma financial statements, which is the end point of the budgeting process.

Sales Budget

The starting point in the construction of the sales budget in a financial plan is projected sales. Forecasts that are inaccurate can have adverse financial consequences. Forecasts that understate sales will result in lost revenues from sales that could not be fulfilled by the company because of a shortage of inventory, insufficient personnel, or lack of short-term funding. Overly optimistic sales forecasts result in excessive inventory, which ties up funds; overstaffing, which increases labor costs; and unnecessary borrowing costs to accommodate the greater than actual sales.

The classic example of the devastating impact that can arise from missing the market in sales forecasting is that of Coleco Industries. In 1983 this company introduced a new toy, the Cabbage Patch doll; to say it became very popular would be an understatement. The runaway demand for this toy can be seen from the depletion of inventory by retailers, which resulted just before Christmas in the alleged bribing of store managers by customers to obtain the scarce doll, physical confrontations among customers for any dolls available on the shelves at a store, and the smuggling in of fake dolls manufactured outside the United States. Despite the opportunity to enhance sales had more dolls been manufactured, this substantial underestimation encouraged other toy manufacturers to produce dolls with similar features, thereby creating competitors in the market for toy dolls. Moreover, Coleco's reputation in the eyes of consumers was severely damaged. Not being able to introduce a second toy that enjoyed the success of the Cabbage Patch doll, Coleco filed for bankruptcy in 1988, with most of the assets, including its doll line, sold to a rival toy company, Hasbro, Inc. The Cabbage Patch doll, which was included in the assets purchased by Hasbro, was then acquired by Mattel, Inc., when it acquired Hasbro. With the marketing power of Mattel, there was a resurgence of interest in the Cabbage Patch doll.

The difficulties that arise in sales forecasting and in relying on one number even when the forecaster is an experienced and well-respected firm specializing in global analysis can be seen in the following example of ultrabook shipment forecasts for 2012. The forecaster, IHS iSupply (hereafter IHS), is a global information service with 8,000 employees in more than thirty-one countries that provides industry forecasting. The illustration here is not a criticism of IHS but rather supports our main thesis that sales forecasting even by professionals is difficult. IHS originally forecasted worldwide ultrabook sales for 2012 of 22 million units, but then in 2012 revised the prediction to 10.2 million units, a more than 50% reduction. Furthermore, the original prediction based on statements by IHS was for growth to 72 million in 2013 and 181 million by 2016.[1] The forecast was revised before the end of the fourth quarter, when sales were expected to pick up, but not enough to hit the original forecast. The two main reasons for the below-forecast worldwide ultrabook sales given by one of IHS's senior principal analysts were (1) prohibitively high pricing of ultrabooks and (2) little consumer interest because of poor advertising campaigns. Those computer manufacturers who relied on the forecast in formulating their revenues from this sector of the computer market now had to revise their financial plan, as did suppliers to those manufacturers, such as companies in the hard disk drive industry.

Even well-established companies that have access to market sector historical data and are industry leaders can miss the mark when forecasting sales. We need only consider the case of Nikon Corporation. In November 2013, this Japanese company reduced its unit sales forecast for the year for its high-end cameras (i.e., its single-lens reflex [SLR] model) from 6.55 million units to 6.20 million units.[2] Nikon had anticipated that the demand among overseas photography enthusiasts would decline in 2013; however, the decline occurred faster than anticipated. The depressed market for SRL cameras was the result of consumers switching to the use of smartphones to take digital photographs. As a result, Nikon's operating profit dropped by 41%.

Types of Sales Forecasting   Several factors must be considered in forecasting sales. A statistical model for forecasting requires historical data. In some markets there is ample historical information about sales. For products in the mature phase of their product life cycle, there is typically a wealth of sales data available for all states of the economy (i.e., growth periods and recessionary periods). In contrast, new technological products that are still on the drawing board lack any sales information. Instead, a sales history for closely related products or for products that the new product is anticipated to replace is used.

In certain industries, there are trade associations that compile information about sales and sometimes project sales growth. There are marketing research reports that are available for purchase that provide forecasted sales estimates. However, the task of an entrepreneur is not just to forecast the market size but also to estimate the potential market share given the competition in the industry, alternative pricing schemes, and different expenditure levels for alternative marketing campaigns.

The purpose for which the sales forecast is being used is important. The sales forecast becomes part of some budget. As noted earlier, there is an operational budget and a long-term planning budget. The operational budget calls for forecasts of near-term sales. The accuracy of this forecast may leave little room for error since a major forecasting error can cut the life of a venture short. For a long-term budget, or to identify the viability of the

1. See Joel Hruska, "Ultrabook Sales Forecasts Plummet, Short-Sighted Analysts Call for Price Cuts," ExtremeTech.com, October 2, 2013, http://www.extremetech.com/computing/137248-ultrabook-sales-forecasts-plummet-short-sighted-analysts-call-for-price-cuts. A further discussion as to why the forecasts were off is provided.
2. "Nikon Drops Sales Forecast as High-End Camera Market Stalls," Reuters, November 7, 2013, http://www.reuters.com/article/2013/11/07/nikon-earnings-idUSL3N0IR39F20131107.

economic prospects of a new venture, the forecast does not have to be precise. An entrepreneur can work with a reasonable range for this purpose.

The sales forecast for a product can be calculated individually for defined customer segments and defined geographic regions and then aggregated.

Sales forecasts can be based on the following types of customer-generated information:

- the stated intentions of customers about continuing to buy products in the industry,
- the actual behavior of customers in the current market regarding purchases, and
- an analysis of historical behavior by customers in purchasing the product.

To obtain customer intentions, typically a survey is conducted by a market research firm engaged by the entrepreneur or, as noted above, one may purchase a report of survey results from a marketing research firm that undertakes surveys of different industries. Alternatively, to acquire supplementary data, an industry expert can be used.

Cash Budget

A detailed analysis of cash that is expected to come into the company (i.e., cash inflows) and going out of the company (i.e., cash outflows) over the planning period is provided by the *cash budget*. Because of the importance of liquidity for any company, but particularly for a startup, the cash budget is a critical component of the budgeting process. The cash budget provides a warning about potential cash positions that may disrupt production and marketing plans such that it would be difficult for the firm to achieve a key milestone to obtain a round of financing or embark on a liquidation strategy. Moreover, chronic cash deficits identified by the cash budget might suggest that more permanent financing is needed rather than short-term borrowing.

The cash inflows used in a cash budget primarily come from three activities: operations, financing, and investing. More specifically, cash inflows are generated from

- operations, from cash sales and collections on accounts receivables;
- financing, from raising funds through either debt (i.e., bank borrowing or the sale of bonds), the sale of preferred stock, and the sale of common stock; and
- investing, from income received from financial assets or the sale of tangible and intangible assets.

Cash outflows arising from the same three activities include:

- operations, from payments of materials and wages, payments on accounts payable, and payment of taxes;
- financing, from the payment on debt obligations (interest and any portion of the amount borrowed due currently), the redemption of preferred stock, and the repurchase of common stock; and
- investing, such as the purchase of plant and equipment, the purchase of another company, or the purchase of intangibles.

Estimates must be made of the timing of a credit sale and the length of time it will take to collect cash. Moreover, an estimate of the percentage of credit sales that will not be paid (i.e., customer defaults) must be made. For a startup with no historical experience with customers, the credit quality of customers must be analyzed. A startup trying to break into an existing market by offering attractive credit terms must be concerned about a higher percentage of uncollectible sales if it elects to sell to credit-impaired customers.

As with sales, a company will not necessarily make cash payments when it receives an invoice for a purchase. There will be a relationship between an expense and cash disbursement. As examples, wages may be paid weekly, bimonthly, or monthly; vendors may offer term credit (which is accounts payable) that allows a payment to be made without any interest for one month or more; or federal and state taxes may be paid with a quarterly lag.

Illustration

To illustrate the sales budget and cash budget, we will use a hypothetical company, Surgical Robot Device Corporation. The company wants to project its cash flow based on its sales budget for the first six months of Year 1. Table 13.1 shows the sales budget for the time period for each month.

We will assume that Surgical Robot Device Corporation's projected sales for the six-month period of January through June of Year 1 is reproduced in table 13.2 as the projected sales. Also shown in table 13.2 are (assumed) actual sales from November and December of the prior year (which we refer to as Year 0). The cash flow from operations will be from these projected sales and the two months of actual sales. As we noted earlier, to move from sales to cash receipts, assumptions must be made about the collection of sales. We will assume the following:

- 10% of the sales in a month will generate a cash inflow in the month of the sale.
- 60% of the sales in a month will generate a cash inflow in the first month following the month of the sale.

Table 13.1
Monthly Sales Budget for Surgical Robot Device Corporation: January–June of Year 1

Month	Budget
January	$1,200,000
February	2,400,000
March	3,600,000
April	2,400,000
May	1,200,000
June	1,200,000

- 30% of the sales in a month will generate a cash inflow in the second month following the month of the sale.

Now let's look at the cash flows related to Surgical Robot Device Corporation's cash out-flows from operations arising from its costs of production. We will assume the following:

- Excluding labor costs, the cost of goods is 55% of projected sales.
- The company purchases the goods for producing its products two months in advance of sales, with the amount purchased based on projected sales.
- The company pays 20% of its accounts payable in the month it purchases the goods.
- The company pays 80% of its accounts payable in the month after it purchases the goods.
- Wages are 5% of the projected current month's sales and are paid in that month.
- Selling and administrative expenses are 10% of the projected current month's sales and are paid in that month.

These assumptions are then used to determine the cash outflows in each month resulting from operations. This is shown in table 13.2. Based on these assumptions, the operating net cash flow indicates that there will be a positive cash flow from operations in all months except for February, when there will be a cash shortfall of $720,000. Thus, although cumu-latively there is a positive cash flow for the entire six-month period, the founder must be prepared to obtain financing for February.

However, cash flow from operations does not tell the entire story because it fails to take into consideration nonoperating (financing and investing) cash flows. Assume with respect to nonoperating decisions that the following financing activities are planned:

- In February a five-year bank loan for $3.6 million will be received.
- Long-term debt of $1.2 million will be retired in April.
- Interest payments on long-term debt will cost $12,000 per month.
- Dividend payments of $120,000 will be made for the months of March and June.

Also assume that the following investing activities are planned:

- Equipment owned by the company will be sold in March for $600,000, with the cash to be received in April.
- Acquisitions of plant and equipment will cost $1.2 million in January, $3.6 million in February, and $4.2 million in May.

Finally, assume that the estimated taxes to be paid in each month are as shown in table 13.2. Based on these assumptions, the nonoperating cash flows are shown in the next-to-last row of table 13.2.

In the last row of table 13.2 is the net cash flow for each month, which is found by adding the net cash flow from operations and the net cash flow from nonoperations (financing

Table 13.2
Monthly Cash Budget for Surgical Robot Device Corporation: January–June of Year 1

	November	December	January	February	March	April	May	June
Sales (actual for November and December; projected otherwise)	$2,400,000	$1,200,000	$1,200,000	$2,400,000	$3,600,000	$2,400,000	$1,200,000	$1,200,000
Operating cash flows								
Cash inflows from accounts receivable								
Cash from current month's sales (10%)			120,000	240,000	360,000	240,000	120,000	120,000
Cash from prior month's sales (60%)			720,000	720,000	1,440,000	2,160,000	1,440,000	720,000
Cash from two months' prior sales (30%)			720,000	360,000	360,000	720,000	1,080,000	720,000
Operating cash inflows			1,560,000	1,320,000	2,160,000	3,120,000	2,640,000	1,560,000
Cash outflows								
Purchases based on sales in two months		1,200,000	1,800,000	1,200,000	600,000	600,000	600,000	600,000
Cash payment for purchases in month (20%)		240,000	360,000	240,000	120,000	120,000	120,000	120,000
Cash payment for previous month's purchase (80%)			960,000	1,440,000	960,000	480,000	480,000	480,000
Cash payment for wages (5%)			60,000	120,000	180,000	120,000	60,000	60,000
Cash payment for selling and administrative expenses (10%)			120,000	240,000	360,000	240,000	120,000	120,000
Operating cash outflows			1,500,000	2,040,000	1,620,000	960,000	780,000	780,000
Net cash flows from operations			60,000	(720,000)	540,000	2,160,000	1,860,000	780,000
Nonoperating cash flows								

Table 13.2 (continued)

	November	December	January	February	March	April	May	June
Cash inflows from financing and investing decisions								
Cash inflow from issuance of long-term liabilities in February				3,600,000	—	—	—	—
Cash inflow from sale of equipment in April				—	—	600,000	—	—
Cash inflows from non-operations activities				3,600,000	—	600,000	—	—
Cash outflows from financing and investing activities (+ taxes)								
Cash purchase of plant and equipment			1,200,000	3,600,000	—	—	4,200,000	—
Cash payment for Interest on debt			12,000	12,000	12,000	12,000	12,000	12,000
Cash payment for common stockholders' dividends			—	—	120,000	—	—	120,000
Estimated taxes			82,800	198,000	325,000	201,600	63,600	63,600
Cash outflows from financing and investing activities			1,294,800	3,810,000	457,200	213,600	4,275,600	1,395,600
Net cash flows from financing and investing activities			(1,294,800)	(210,000)	(457,200)	386,400	(4,275,600)	(1,395,600)
Net cash flow for month			($1,234,800)	($930,000)	$82,800	$2,546,400	($2,415,600)	($615,600)

and investing activities). This is the cash flow in each month assuming no actions by the founders.

Now let's see how to use the net cash flow each month in table 13.2. We will make the following assumptions about Surgical Robot Device Corporation's decision as to how much cash to hold:

- The minimum monthly cash that the company wants is $1.2 million.
- If the cash flow exceeds $2.4 million in a given month, the excess above that amount can be used to pay off any financing debt.
- The cash balance at the beginning of January of Year 1 is $1.8 million.

With these assumptions, let's look at table 13.3. The cash at the beginning of January is assumed to be $1.8 million. The next line in the January column shows the net cash flow for the month of January, as given in table 13.2 (a negative $1,234,800). Without any financing, the cash at the end of January would be $565,200, which is found by subtracting the beginning balance of $1.8 million from the net cash flow for January. This is shown on the line labeled "Balance without any financing." So at this point, without any financing, Surgical Robot Device Corporation will have a projected cash balance of $565,200, which is less than the required minimum cash balance of $1.2 million. This means there will be a shortfall of $634,800, found by subtracting $565,200 from the $1.2 minimum cash required. Thus the company must arrange for financing of $634,800. We will assume that this financing will come from a bank loan.

In February, the beginning balance if the financing is obtained is the minimum $1.2 million. Since the net cash flow for February is negative $930,000, the cash balance for that month would be $270,000 without any financing. An amount of $930,000 is needed in financing to bring the cash up to the minimum level. Moving on to March, the net cash flow for that month is $82,800, and therefore no financing is needed that month. The cash for April is then $1,282,800. The net cash flow for April is $2,546,500. Adding that amount to the beginning balance in April gives a projected cash of $3,829,200. Since by assumption any amount in excess of $2.4 million can be used to pay off any financing that has been obtained to maintain the cash balance in prior months, in April $1,429,200 is available to pay off any financing. The May and June figures in table 13.3 are self-explanatory.

As can be seen from table 13.3, financing is needed in all months except March and April. Hence the founders may seek to obtain financing on a short-term basis through bank loans. An alternative interpretation the founders may reach is that additional capital is needed, not short-term financing.

FORECASTING THE BALANCE SHEET AND INCOME STATEMENT

Assuming that the sales and cash budgets described above are realized, then the founders can use them to create a forecasted or pro forma balance sheet and income statement. As

Table 13.3
Cash Flow Analysis of Cash Budget for Surgical Robot Device Corporation: January–June of Year 1

	January	February	March	April	May	June
Beginning-of-month balance	$1,800,000	$1,200,000	$1,200,000	$1,282,800	$2,400,000	$1,200,000
Net cash flow for month	(1,234,800)	(930,000)	82,800	2,546,400	(2,415,600)	(615,600)
Balance without any financing	565,200	270,000	1,282,800	3,829,200	(15,600)	584,400
Financing needed to maintain minimum balance	634,800	930,000	—	—	1,215,600	615,600
Available to pay off financing	—	—	—	1,429,200	—	—
Balance at end of month	$1,200,000	$1,200,000	$1,282,800	$2,400,000	$1,200,000	$1,200,000

long as the budget amounts are realized, the founders and investors should not be surprised by the results. If the forecasted income statement does not result in the achievement of financial milestones, then the founders should reconsider the various budgets and assess how they can reasonably be revised to achieve the targeted milestone.

Making unreasonable assumptions to get to the targeted milestone is simply foolish. If under the most reasonable assumptions used in the budgets the target cannot be achieved, then alternative marketing strategies, distribution channels, or possibly production processes might be considered. In the design of a cost structure at the outset of production, the budgeting process can be helpful in assessing the effect of different cost structures on the financial statements, particularly income and cash flow.

Periodic updating of the budgets as new information is obtained or as actual amounts deviate from budgeted amounts will yield a new forecasted financial statement that the founders can assess in terms of the milestones they seek to achieve.

Illustration

Let's continue with our illustration of Surgical Robot Device Corporation to show how a pro forma balance sheet and income statement can be constructed.

We begin with the balance sheet for the company at the end of December Year 0. These amounts for the balance sheet accounts are known. In our illustration, they are shown in table 13.4. Since the end-of-December Year 0 balance sheet is the beginning-of-January Year 1 balance sheet, we have our starting amounts. The total assets are $19.2 million. Notice that the amount shown as cash of $1.8 million is the amount shown for the cash budget in table 13.3.

Table 13.4
Balance Sheet of Surgical Robot Device Corporation as of December of Year 0

Assets	
Cash	$1,800,000
Account receivable	2,400,000
Inventory	3,000,000
Plant and equipment	12,000,000
Total	$19,200,000

Liabilities and stockholders' equity	
Accounts payable	$2,400,000
Bank loans	1,200,000
Long-term liabilities	6,000,000
Common equity	9,600,000
Total	$19,200,000

Let's walk through how we can get the balance sheet account for each month using the information from the cash budget shown in table 13.2 and the analysis of the cash flow shown in table 13.3. We begin with accounts receivable and show the analysis in table 13.5.

The first line shows the opening balance of $2.4 million from the balance sheet. To that amount is added the credit sales during the month. In table 13.2 we can see that sales for January are $1.2 million. Recall that an assumption in constructing the cash budget is that the amount of sales on credit is 90% of sales. Therefore, the credit sales during the month are 90% of $1.2 million, or $1,080,000, and this amount is added to the opening accounts receivable balance. Accounts receivable will be reduced by the amount collected. In table 13.2, the amount that will be paid off is shown. For January it is December Year 0 sales on credit of $720,000 and the same amount for November Year 0 sales. The total is $1,440,000. Adding to the beginning balance the net credit sales and subtracting the collections gives an ending balance for January of $2,040,000. This January ending balance is then the beginning-of-February balance. The rest of table 13.5 is computed in the same manner. For our pro forma balance sheet for each month, which we present later, we will have the balances shown in the last line of the table.

For inventory, the beginning balance as per table 13.6 is $3 million. By assumption, purchases are 50% of projected sales two months forward and wages are 5% of sales. Both of these are added to beginning inventory. Inventory is then reduced by the cost of goods sold, which is assumed to be 55% of sales. The analysis is shown in table 13.6. The analysis of the final asset, plant and equipment, is shown in table 13.7. The assumption in the calculation of depreciation is that it is 1% per month of gross plant and equipment (i.e., the beginning balance plus the acquisitions for the month).

Table 13.5

Analysis of Accounts Receivable for Surgical Robot Device Corporation: January–June of Year 1

	January	February	March	April	May	June
Beginning balance	$2,400,000	$2,040,000	$3,120,000	$4,560,000	$3,840,000	$2,400,000
+ Credit sales during month	1,080,000	2,160,000	3,240,000	2,160,000	1,080,000	1,080,000
– Collections of receivables	1,440,000	1,080,000	1,800,000	2,880,000	2,520,000	1,440,000
Monthly ending balance	$2,040,000	$3,120,000	$4,560,000	$3,840,000	$2,400,000	$2,040,000

Table 13.6

Analysis of Inventory for Surgical Robot Device Corporation: January–June of Year 1

	January	February	March	April	May	June
Beginning balance	$3,000,000	$4,200,000	$4,200,000	$3,000,000	$2,400,000	$2,400,000
+ Purchases	1,800,000	1,200,000	600,000	600,000	600,000	
+ Wages	60,000	120,000	180,000	120,000	60,000	60,000
– Cost of goods sold (55% of sales)	660,000	1,320,000	1,980,000	1,320,000	660,000	660,000
Monthly ending balance	$4,200,000	$4,200,000	$3,000,000	$2,400,000	$2,400,000	$2,400,000

Table 13.7

Analysis of Plant and Equipment ($) for Surgical Robot Device Corporation: January–June of Year 1

	January	February	March	April	May	June
Beginning balance	$12,000,000	$13,068,000	$16,501,320	$16,336,306	$15,572.944	$19,575,214
+ Acquisitions	1,200,000	3,600,000	—	—	4,200,000	—
– Sales of equipment	—	—	—	600,000	—	—
– Depreciation	132,000	166,680	165,013	163,363	197,729	195,752
Monthly ending balance	$13,068,000	$16,501,320	$16,336,307	$15,572,944	$19,575,214	$19,379,462

Table 13.8
Analysis of Accounts Payable for Surgical Robot Device Corporation: January–June of Year 1

	January	February	March	April	May	June
Beginning balance	$2,400,000	$2,880,000	$2,400,000	$1,920,000	$1,920,000	$1,920,000
+ Purchases on account	1,440,000	960,000	480,000	480,000	480,000	480,000
− Payments on account	960,000	1,440,000	960,000	480,000	480,000	480,000
Monthly ending balance	$2,880,000	$2,400,000	$1,920,000	$1,920,000	$1,920,000	$1,920,000

Table 13.9
Analysis of Bank Debt for Surgical Robot Device Corporation: January–June of Year 1

	January	February	March	April	May	June
Beginning balance	$1,200,000	$1,834,800	$2,764,800	$2,764,800	$1,335,600	$2,551,200
+ Financing to meet minimum cash requirements	634,000	930,000	—	—	1,215,600	615,600
− Loan repayment	—	—	—	1,429,200	—	—
Monthly ending balance	$1,834,800	$2,764,800	$2,764,800	$1,335,600	$2,551,200	$3,166,800

We now turn to liabilities, beginning with accounts payable. In table 13.8 the beginning accounts payable each month is added to the purchases on credit (which increases the accounts payable balance). The amount purchased is shown in table 13.2, which is based on 50% of projected sales two months from now. However, recall that it is assumed that only 80% of the purchases are on credit. The amount of accounts payable is reduced by the amount of accounts payable paid down in the month. That amount is shown in table 13.8 for each month. Adding the beginning accounts payable balance to the new purchases on credit and reducing that sum by the amount of the accounts payable balance paid off during the month gives the end-of-month accounts payable balance.

For bank debt, the beginning balance in January is $1.2 million. Now here is where we use the information in table 13.3 to determine how much must be financed. We will assume that the financing is done with a short-term bank loan. Table 13.9 shows the financing that must be obtained as calculated in table 13.3 and the amount that can be repaid.

Long-term liabilities analysis is straightforward, as shown in table 13.10. It begins with the balance at the beginning of January of $6 million and adds to that issuance of long-term

Table 13.10

Analysis of Long-Term Liabilities for Surgical Robot Device Corporation: January–June of Year 1

	January	February	March	April	May	June
Beginning balance	$6,000,000	$6,000,000	$9,600,000	$9,600,000	$9,600,000	$9,600,000
+ Insurance of long-term liabilities	—	3,600,000	—	—	—	—
− Retirement of long-term liabilities	—	—	—	—	—	1,200,000
Monthly ending balance	$6,000,000	$9,600,000	$9,600,000	$9,600,000	$9,600,000	$8,400,000

liabilities in each month as shown in table 13.2, where cash flows from investing and financing activities are shown.

Finally, we get to common stockholders' equity. Note that there is no preferred stock class for Surgical Robot Device Corporation. The calculation for each month would be as follows:

Beginning balance for the month	
+	Earnings for the month
−	Dividends paid in the month
+	Common stock issued
−	Common stock repurchased
=	Balance for the month

For Surgical Robot Device Corporation, there was no repurchase or sale of common stock in any month. To get the net earnings, however, we must determine that amount from the pro forma income statement. Thus, we will look at the construction of this statement and then return to the analysis of the common stockholders' equity account for the balance sheet.

The pro forma income statement for each month can be computed as shown in table 13.11. It begins with monthly sales and then deducts the various expenses, including the estimated taxes. Net income is shown as the last line in the table.

Now we can return to the analysis of the common stockholders' equity. The beginning balance in January is $8 million. To that amount is added the net income, and the sum is then reduced by the dividends, as shown in table 13.12.

We now have all the components to construct the pro forma balance sheet for each month, as shown in table 13.13. The first asset is cash. Notice that cash can be held as

Table 13.11
Pro forma Income Statement for Surgical Robot Device Corporation: January–June of Year 1

	January	February	March	April	May	June
Sales	$1,200,000	$2,400,000	$3,600,000	$2,400,000	$1,200,000	$1,200,000
– Cost of goods sold	660,000	1,320,000	1,980,000	1,320,000	660,000	660,000
– Depreciation	132,000	166,680	165,013	163,363	197,729	195,752
Gross profit	408,000	913,320	1,454,987	916,637	342,271	344,248
– Selling and administrative expenses	120,000	240,000	360,000	240,000	120,000	120,000
Operating income	288,000	673,320	1,094,987	676,637	222,271	224,248
– Interest	12,000	12,000	12,000	12,000	12,000	12,000
Net income before taxes	276,000	661,320	1,082,987	664,637	210,271	212,248
– Taxes (around 30%)	82,800	198,000	325,200	201,600	63,600	63,600
Net income	$193,200	$463,320	$757,787	$463,037	$146,671	$148,648

Table 13.12
Analysis of Common Stockholders' Equity for Surgical Robot Device Corporation: January–June of Year 1

	January	February	March	April	May	June
Beginning balance	$9,600,000	$9,793,200	$10,256,520	$10,894,307	$11,357,344	$11,504,014
+ Net income	193,200	463,320	757,787	463,037	146,671	148,648
– Dividends	—	—	120,000	—	—	120,000
+ Common stock issued	—	—	—	—	—	—
– Common stock repurchased	—	—	—	—	—	—
Monthly ending balance	$9,793,200	$10,256,520	$10,894,307	$11,357,344	$11,504,014	$11,532,662

Table 13.13
Pro Forma Balance Sheet ($) for Surgical Robot Device Corporation: January–June Year 1

	January	February	March	April	May	June
Assets						
Cash (marketable securities)	$1,200,000	$1,200,000	$1,282,800	$2,400,000	$1,200,000	$1,200,000
Accounts receivable	2,040,000	3,120,000	4,560,000	3,840,000	2,400,000	2,040,000
Inventories	4,200,000	4,200,000	3,000,000	2,400,000	2,400,000	2,400,000
Plant and equipment	13,068,000	16,501,320	16,336,307	15,572,944	19,575,214	19,379,462
Total assets	20,508,000	25,021,320	25,179,107	24,212,944	25,575,214	25,019,462
Liabilities and common stockholders' equity						
Accounts payable	2,880,000	2,400,000	1,920,000	1,920,000	1,920,000	1,920,000
Bank loans	1,834,800	2,764,800	2,764,800	1,335,600	2,551,200	3,166,800
Long-term liabilities	6,000,000	9,600,000	9,600,000	9,600,000	9,600,000	8,400,000
Common stockholders' equity	9,793,200	10,256,520	10,894,307	11,357,344	11,504,014	11,532,662
Total liabilities and stockholders' equity	$20,508,000	$25,021,320	$25,179,107	$24,212,944	$25,575,214	$25,019,462

a short-term marketable security. The values for that account are obtained from the cash budget shown in table 13.2. The other values are obtained as follows:

Accounts receivable	Table 13.5
Inventories	Table 13.6
Plant and equipment	Table 13.7
Accounts payable	Table 13.8
Bank loans	Table 13.9
Long-term liabilities	Table 13.10
Common stockholders' equity	Table 13.12

ACQUISITIONS AS A STRATEGIC GROWTH PLAN

Investors expect new high-tech firms to grow their earnings and enhance other performance metrics to justify their valuation. A company can do so using its own resources (current tangible and intangible assets and management team/research groups), referred to as ***organic growth***, and by acquisitions. Here we will look at the factors that the founders should consider in performing their due diligence to determine whether an acquisition should be made. The discussion here is purely qualitative. The analytical tools that can be utilized for projecting the impact of a potential acquisition on the acquiring firm's performance were described earlier in this chapter. The estimation of the value of the candidate acquisition firm is not simple, as noted in chapter 16, where the various valuation methods are explained.

It is not easy for founders who are attempting to assess how acquisitions in their industry have worked out because often the stated reason given for an acquisition is not the true reason for the acquisition. Empirical studies of acquisitions, although providing some insight into what makes for a successful acquisition, are also hampered by the same problem of differentiating between the stated and actual reasons for an acquisition.

The staff of the consulting firm McKinsey & Company, based on its work in the acquisitions area, has offered strategic reasons as to why an acquisition creates value.[3] The authors of the McKinsey study report that acquisitions that create value usually fit at least one of the following five archetypes:

- they improve the performance of the company acquired;
- they create market access for products;
- they acquire skills or technologies faster than or at a lower cost compared to what can be built in-house;
- they remove excess capacity from an industry; and
- they are winning companies that are identified early in their life and developed further by the acquiring company.

Announcements in the press by the acquiring company's representative may state reasons for the acquisition other than the five given above. However, according to the authors of the McKinsey study, an acquisition that fails to conform to one or more of the above archetypal reasons for an acquisition is "unlikely to create value." The other reasons mentioned by corporate representatives, according to the McKinsey study, may create value but seldom do so.

Let's consider Google's acquisitions from the inception of the company to the beginning of 2015. During this period Google made more than 170 acquisitions. Seven examples of recent acquisitions (from 2013 and 2014) by Google and the strategic motivation for each acquisition are shown in table 13.14.

The reason for the acquisition should be used to assess the projected impact on the financial performance on the acquiring company that would result from the acquisition, using

3. Marc Goedhart, Tim Koller, and David Wessels, "The Five Types of Successful Acquisitions," McKinsey & Company, July 2010, http://www.mckinsey.com/business-functions/strategy-and-corporate-finance/our-insights/the-five-types-of-successful-acquisitions.

Table 13.14
Examples of Recent Google Acquisitions (2013 and 2014)

Acquisition	Year	Cost	Strategic reason given
Nest Labs	2014	$3.2 billion	Nest Labs manufactured high-tech thermostats and smoke detectors and the acquisition strengthened Google's presence in the urban household market by gaining access to web-connected household appliances. (In addition to the products, the sales to homeowners generated a good deal of data about the habits exhibited by a homeowner that could be leveraged to sell other Google products or services.)
SkyBox Imaging	2014	$500 million	The acquisition of SkyBox Imaging's satellite technology gave Google the ability to enhance its real-time imagery for its Google Maps.
Titan Aerospace	2014	$60 million	Titan Aerospace manufactures high-flying solar-powered drones, allowing Google to obtain photos that can be contributed to Google Maps and Google Earth. (It was also expected to play an important role in Google's Project Loon, a project that seeks to bring Internet connectivity to regions without such service by sending balloons into the atmosphere that can allow Internet connectivity.)
DeepMind Technologies	2014	$650 million	The acquisition of DeepMind Technologies gave Google the ability to organize the world's data multimedia by giving machines perception capabilities. Using the company's technology, Google is teaching computers to perform such tasks as annotate videos and images and describe visual objects.
Makani Power	2014	$30 million	Makani Power's acquisition allowed Google to enter into the clean energy business. The acquired company was a green energy startup.
Waze	2013	$966 million	The acquisition of Waze, a GPS and navigation company, allowed Google to greatly enhance its real-time mapping data with respect to road status (e.g., showing closures and accident sites in real time) and to obtain data about information submitted by the 44 million users of Waze.
DNNresearch Inc.	2013	$5 million	DNNresearch Inc. at the time of acquisition was a three-person Toronto-based startup company doing experimental research in the neural network field. Using a computer to simulate and mimic processes of the human brain, neural networks seek to make the processes followed by the brain more efficient. Google believes that the research on neural networks can optimize operations in its global data centers.

the tools described earlier in this chapter. The outcome of the due diligence process is also used in determining the price that the acquiring company should pay for the acquisition.

Moreover, if an acquisition does occur, actual performance can be compared to the projected performance used to determine whether the acquisition should be made as a way of assessing the success or failure of the acquisition and management's method for evaluating performance. For example, in projecting synergies that arise because of cost cutting, although the first few years of cost savings may materialize, in the long run they may not, for a variety of reasons. Consequently, in evaluating future acquisitions, those responsible for that decision should avoid repeating that forecasting error. In the case of expanding product lines, an acquisition may not perform as expected because of too optimistic forecasts of future sales, which the acquisition team must be sure to avoid in considering future acquisition candidates.

Instead of value creation, some acquisitions end up destroying value for the acquiring company. Some of the reasons why strategic acquisitions fail to meet expectations and result in value destruction are the following:

- a clash of corporate cultures, making integration of the acquired company into the acquiring company unsuccessful;
- the departure of key personnel or research teams that were expected to remain in place after the acquisition;
- an overstatement of the projected benefits to be derived from the acquisition;
- failure of the technology acquired to perform up to expectations, or legal issues associated with the ownership or use of the technology;
- changes in the acquiring company's management's view of the strategic importance of the acquired company or a complete change in the direction of management that results in the acquired company no longer fitting the acquirer's business plan or business model.

In a study seeking to identify why some high-tech companies succeed and others do not, Saikat Chaudhuri and Benham Tabrizi investigated the practices of twenty-four global leaders in the IT, communications, and engineering industries in their execution of fifty-three acquisitions.[4] The size of the acquired companies ranged from startup companies to companies with sales of several billion dollars. In their investigation, Chaudhuri and Tabrizi conducted interviews with employees from both the acquiring and the acquired companies, and reviewed confidential internal information made available to them. This information included corporate strategies, technology decision-making processes, due

---

4. Saikat Chaudhuri and Benham Tabrizi, "Capturing the Real Value in High-Tech Acquisitions," *Harvard Business Review,* September–October 1999, 123–130.

diligence reports, integration procedures, and post-acquisition analysis. A major conclusion of their study was the following:

High-tech industries are fundamentally different from other industries, so it's not surprising that high-tech companies need to approach acquisitions differently. Although product life cycles for all industries have shortened, high-tech products can become obsolete in a matter of months. A successful new product may boost market share and profits, but the relentless pace of innovation means that any one gain is likely to be brief. Long-term success depends on the sustained ability to build on excellent products—to develop or recognize rising technologies and incorporate them into new versions that satisfy changing markets.[5]

This suggests that arguments for acquisitions based on expanding market share or new products may not be the right way to approach acquisitions in a rapidly changing technology. As Chaudhuri and Tabrizi point out, the position even of companies "first to market" with a product is no assurance that they will maintain their leadership in future generations of that product. To do so, the company must develop technical capabilities. Developing technical capabilities is also important for a company to recover from missing an important shift in technology or the development of a new product within an industry.

Acquisitions provide a means for acquiring capabilities in dealing with rapidly changing technologies and markets. Chaudhuri and Tabrizi argue that in seeking acquisitions, companies should strive to obtain real capacities rather than focusing on acquisitions that might allow the creation of specific products or enhance market share.

Consequently, to obtain a successful acquisition, Chaudhuri and Tabrizi suggest that the first step for a board is to systematically identify what capabilities are needed. Once those basic competencies are identified, founders can determine whether the company has the ability to develop those capabilities in-house or whether to acquire them. To identify those capabilities, founders must formulate plans for what businesses that they want to be in over the next few years. Once their future offerings are determined by line of business, an analysis is performed to determine whether the company will have the necessary technological capabilities to effectively create the products, and to do so in a way that will generate a profit.

Once the needs assessment is completed and needs are determined, the choice of whether to develop in-house or purchase by means of an acquisition will be influenced by several factors. One of the key factors is the speed at which the needed capability can be obtained to achieve the objectives sought by the founders. Chaudhuri and Tabrizi, for example, report that several of the companies they studied were able to reduce the time to market by one half by means of an acquisition.

5. Chaudhuri and Tabrizi, "Capturing the Real Value in High-Tech Acquisitions," 123.

Due Diligence Screening Process

The typical due diligence process involves strategic, financial, and legal screening. Although a good performance record of the candidate company is important and may favorably impact the short-term performance of the acquiring company if the acquisition is at a fair price, there should be a focus on long-term capabilities as mentioned above. Founders should look carefully to investigate the real capabilities of the candidate company in terms of matching the identified needs of the founders from its needs assessment.

Once the founders identify how the candidate company can fill any gaps in the expected future technological capability needs, founders must assess whether those employees of the candidate company with those skills will be likely to remain after an acquisition. One indicator of the ability of the acquiring company's ability to retain key employees whose technical capabilities are sought is the incentive package that the candidate company provides them prior to an acquisition. If key employees have the right to cash in on the proceeds received from their company being acquired, they are less likely to remain with the acquiring company following the acquisition, and therefore the likelihood of the acquisition being successful in acquiring special talents will be reduced.

Consequently, a key part of the acquisition process is creating the necessary incentive package for retaining key employees, as well as devising a well-structured plan for integrating those employees into the team of the acquiring company where they will be placed, to make it clear to those employees what the new company expects of them. These steps should be done before the transaction is completed. Chaudhuri and Tabrizi report that for the companies that they studied, many key employees did not remain with the company because of the absence of such direction from the acquiring company's management.

Integrating an acquired company into an acquiring company's organization is challenging. When a company seeks to acquire another company to acquire to fill gaps in capabilities, the degree of integration will depend on the type of capability that the acquiring company seeks. Chaudhuri and Tabrizi describe three cases. When the acquiring company is seeking innovation from the employees of the company being acquired, less integration might be more appropriate to avoid stifling the creativity of those employees who had the opportunity to exercise creative freedom at the acquired company prior to the acquisition. In the rare case in which a company makes an acquisition just to extend its current business lines in-house and seeks to do so through an acquisition rather than through the in-house development of capability, the acquiring company should fully integrate into its organizational structure the acquired company. In the most common case, the purpose of the acquisition is to develop new platforms. For such acquisitions, the personnel of the company being acquired should be integrated over time into the central equivalents of the acquiring company. With respect to the engineering teams whose special capabilities motivated the acquisition, it is recommended that for the acquisition to satisfy its objective, they should be retained as a team within the same business unit as existed before the acquisition rather than being individually assigned to other business units of the acquiring firm.

Negotiating the Terms of an Acquisition

Both parties to an acquisition will have their own assessment of the value of the company to be acquired. The methods for valuing a company are the subject of chapter 16 and appendix B. Overpaying for an acquisition because of overestimates of the potential benefits will result in a disappointing outcome.

It is common in a negotiation that the board of the candidate company believes that the offer made by the potential acquirer is low and does not properly account for the candidate company's potential future performance. This is often the view of early startup high-tech companies that become the targets of acquirers. If the company to be acquired cannot get the board of the acquiring company to raise its offer, it can seek to negotiate a higher purchase price whereby some portion of the purchase price is paid out if earned (i.e., based on post-acquisition performance). The amount above the cash purchase price paid is called an "earnout."

The board of the acquiring company will seek to structure the transaction so as to achieve the maximum tax benefits and (if applicable) favorable financial reporting treatment. In addition to structuring the transaction for these benefits, the board of the acquiring company will seek to negotiate long-term employment contracts with the right economic incentives for the key personnel of the candidate firm it seeks to retain and will strive to obtain a reasonable noncompete agreement or restrictive covenant for an appropriate period of time for certain personnel.

Acquisition As an Exit or Harvesting Strategy

Thus far, we have looked at strategic acquisitions as a means to grow a business. In some cases, however, the founders of a company may want the company to be acquired. It is the board that must decide on the reasons why the company might want to be acquired. High-tech companies are often willing to be acquired if an acquisition provides for one or more of the following:

- It improves the distribution capability, which reduces costs and/or allows sales to expand in order to realize economies of scale.
- The acquisition means obtaining access to technology that would take too much time to develop or be too costly to produce with current resources.
- The acquisition provides founders and investors with a better way to realize a liquidity event compared to an initial public offering (IPO).
- The target company will gain access to a broader market customer base than can be achieved in the absence of the acquisition.
- The acquisition may facilitate future financing in the capital market as the target company becomes part of the acquiring company.
- The target company can avoid utilizing resources (cash and management time) to build an infrastructure when the acquiring company can provide them.

Of particular interest to founders and investors is whether an acquisition provides a better liquidity event than an IPO, which we discussed in chapter 6. There are several advantages of being acquired versus undergoing an IPO.

First, the cost of an IPO offering can be more expensive than the cost of an acquisition. In an IPO, all fees associated with going public must be borne by the company. In contrast, the target company's board can negotiate with the acquiring company to pay the costs (fees) associated with the acquisition.

Second, key information in an IPO must be disclosed to the public so that investors have sufficient information to evaluate whether the stock should be purchased. Some of the information the company may want to remain confidential because of its strategic importance must be disclosed under federal securities law. In an acquisition, that information need only be shared with the acquiring company.

Third, there are ongoing financial reporting costs associated with an IPO. By contrast, there are no ongoing financial reporting requirements and therefore no such costs associated with an acquisition. Security analysts closely watch the performance of a publicly traded company, causing management decisions to be based on the impact on short-term performance rather than based on the long-run benefit to investors. The advantage of an acquisition is that this problem is reduced, though it is not entirely eliminated. Management of the acquiring company may impose similar pressures, but the risk of such unwise behavior falls on the acquiring company's investors.

Finally, to go public, a company must have built the necessary infrastructure to operate efficiently. With an acquisition, that infrastructure need not be developed if it is available from the acquiring company or at the expense of the acquiring company.

An argument in favor of an IPO is that it provides founders and other investors in the company with market liquidity. Support for this view comes from the many well-known high-tech companies that have gone public. However, that is not necessarily the case for smaller IPOs. The stocks of such companies may not be traded frequently, and interest in the company may be limited by the lack of coverage by security analysts. When an acquisition results in the receipt of shares of a large, publicly traded company, those shares typically offer better liquidity than an IPO for a small company.

KEY POINTS COVERED IN THIS CHAPTER

- The financial plan provides an entrepreneur with information about when and how much funds need to be raised and whether those are permanent needs or seasonal needs resulting from the company's operating cycle.
- The financial plan involves the use of budgets to make quantitative statements about the funding needs of a company.

- Financial planning requires forecasting, with the end point of a financial plan being the projected or forecasted income statement and balance sheet for a company based on budgets.

- Deviations from the projected values can identify early what actions might have to be taken by the entrepreneur and identify when certain milestones are likely to be achieved.

- A financial plan is important because it is a tool a founding team can use to assess and then react to changing market conditions and allows an assessment of trade-offs that the founding team will face in making business decisions.

- Operating budgets cover a period of one year or less.

- Long-term budgets are for capital expenditures covering periods greater than one and up to ten years.

- Forecasting future sales is the starting point in the construction of a financial plan's sales budget.

- Sales forecasts that are too conservative will result in lost revenues from sales that could not be fulfilled by the company because of a shortage of inventory, insufficient personnel, or lack of short-term funding.

- Sales forecasts that are overly optimistic will result in excessive inventory; overstaffing, which increases labor costs; and unnecessary borrowing costs to accommodate the greater than actual sales.

- A statistical model for forecasting sales requires historical data. Although in some markets there is ample historical information about sales, in the development of new technological products there may not be any sales information.

- The operational budget calls for forecasts of near-term sales, and its accuracy is important. For a long-term budget, the sales forecast does not have to be precise; entrepreneurs can work with a reasonable range for this purpose.

- The sales forecast for a product can be calculated separately for customer segments and geographic regions, and these figures then aggregated.

- A cash budget provides a detailed analysis of cash that is expected to come into the company and go out of the company over the planning period.

- Because of the importance of liquidity, the cash budget is a critical component of the budgeting process: it provides a warning about potential cash positions that may disrupt production and marketing plans and make it difficult to achieve key milestones.

- A cash budget plays an important role in planning financing since any chronic cash deficits identified would suggest that more permanent financing is needed rather than short-term borrowing.

- In the preparation of a cash budget, the cash inflows primarily come from (1) operations, from cash sales and collections on accounts receivable; (2) financing, from raising funds through either debt, the sale of preferred stock, and the sale of common stock; and (3) investing, from income received from financial assets or the sale of tangible and intangible assets

- In the preparation of a cash budget, the cash outflows primarily arise from (1) operations, from payments of materials and wages, payments on accounts payable, and payment of taxes; (2) financing, from the payment on debt obligations, the redemption of preferred stock, and the repurchase of common stock; and (3) investing, such as from the purchase of plant and equipment, the purchase of another company, and the purchase of intangibles

- From the sales and cash budgets the founders can construct a forecasted or pro forma balance sheet and income statement.

- If the forecasted income statement does not result in the achievement of financial milestones, then the founders should reconsider the various budgets and assess how they can reasonably be revised to achieve the targeted milestone.

- If under the most reasonable assumptions used in the budgets a specified target cannot be achieved, then alternative marketing strategies, distribution channels, or possibly production processes might be considered.

- Investors expect new high-tech firms to grow their earnings and enhance other performance metrics in order to justify their valuation.

- A company's growth can occur through organic growth (i.e., growth using the company's own resources) and strategic acquisitions.

- It is not easy for founders to assess how acquisitions in their industry have worked out because often the reason given for an acquisition is not the true reason for the acquisition.

- It has been observed that acquisitions that create value usually fit at least one of the following archetypes: (1) they improve the performance of the company acquired, (2) they create market access for products, (3) they acquire skills or technologies faster than or at a lower cost compared to what can be built in-house, (4) they remove excess capacity from an industry, and (5) they are winning companies that are identified early in the life and developed further by the acquiring company

- The outcome of the due diligence process during the acquisition decision process is used in determining the price that the acquiring company should pay for the acquisition.

- After an acquisition occurs, actual performance should be compared to projected performance to assess the success or failure of the acquisition and to assess management's methodology for evaluating performance.

- Some strategic acquisitions destroy value rather than create value for the acquiring company for one or more of the following reasons: (1) a clash of corporate cultures, (2) the departure of key personnel or research teams, (3) overstated projected benefits,

- (4) the technology acquired underperformed or legal issues emerge associated with the ownership or use of the technology, and (5) changes in the acquiring company's assessment of the strategic importance of the acquired company.
- The typical due diligence process involves strategic, financial, and legal screening.
- A critical aspect of the acquisition process is creating the necessary incentive package to retain key employees, as well as devising a well-structured plan for integrating those employees into the team of the acquiring company to make it clear what the new company expects of them.
- Both parties to an acquisition will have their own assessment of the value of the company to be acquired.
- If the company to be acquired cannot get the board of the acquiring company to raise its offer, it can seek to negotiate a higher purchase price whereby some portion of the purchase price is based on an earnout.
- High-tech companies are willing to be acquired for one or more of the following reasons: (1) to improve distribution capability, (2) to obtain access to technology, (3) to provide founders and investors with a better way to realize a liquidity event compared to an IPO, (4) to gain access to a broader market base, (5) to facilitate future financing, and (6) to avoid utilizing resources to build an infrastructure.
- The advantages of being acquired versus an IPO are the following: (1) the cost of an IPO can be more expensive than being acquired; (2) key information that a company wishes to hold close must be publicly disclosed in an IPO, but in an acquisition that information need only be shared with the acquiring company; (3) there are ongoing financial reporting costs associated with an IPO but not with an acquisition; and (4) a company need not build the necessary infrastructure to go public.

FURTHER READINGS

Benninga, Simon, *Financial Modeling,* 4th ed. (Cambridge, MA: MIT Press, 2014).

Fabozzi, Frank J., Pamela Peterson Drake, and Ralph S. Polimeni, *The Complete CFO Handbook: From Accounting to Accountability* (Hoboken, NJ: John Wiley & Sons, 2008), chap. 6.

Samonas, Michael, *Financial Forecasting, Analysis and Modelling: A Framework for Long-Term Forecasting* (Chichester: John Wiley & Sons, 2015).

14

PROFIT PLANNING

Profit planning requires the founding team to make operating decisions involving the introduction of new products, the volume of production, the pricing of products, and the selection of alternative production processes. To increase the likelihood that the best decision will be made, the founding team must understand the relationship among costs, revenues, and profits. Break-even analysis and cost-volume-profit analysis take this interrelationship into account and can provide an entrepreneur with useful guidelines for decision making.

The key to profit planning is understanding the cost structure of a firm. Therefore, this chapter begins with a discussion of the nature of production costs.

THE NATURE OF PRODUCTION COSTS

The costs of a company can be classified into four functional areas: production costs (or manufacturing costs), marketing costs, administrative costs, and financing costs. Production costs, the costs related to the creation of a product or products, is discussed in this section.

As explained in chapter 2, the cost structure is influenced by the value proposition, with the two cost structures at the extreme ends being cost-driven, when the value proposition is low price, and value-driven, when the value proposition is premium value. Once a cost structure is selected, it is essential for the founders to understand the various types of costs and the behavior that they exhibit as the company grows.

Production Cost Components

The starting point for projecting the income statement and for pricing a new product is understanding the components of the cost of producing a product (i.e., the production costs). When a new venture produces multiple products, being able to identify the costs associated with each product requires the ability to trace costs to each product. The three components of product cost are direct material costs, direct labor costs, and factory overhead costs. The task is easier in the situation in which a venture has only one product; however, as a venture grows and is expected to introduce new products, the task becomes

Table 14.1

Function	Includes Manufacturer of Parts or Parts	Cost
Memory	Toshiba Semiconductor, Samsung Semiconductor	$14.40
Display/touchscreen module		11.50
Application processor with supporting DRAM	Toshiba Semiconductor	4.95
User interface	Cyprus Logic, ST Microelectronics, Cyprus Semiconductor, Silicon Laboratories, Intersil; also includes Analog Ics, switches, connectors, and other circuitry supporting nondisplay user interface	3.49
Box contents	Headset, USB cable, packaging, and literature	2.42
Other	Passive components	2.05
Mechanical	Enclosure metal components, plastic components, insulators, shields	2.00
Power management	Dialog; also includes minor power components	1.33
Electromechanical	PCBs, connectors	0.89
Battery	Battery Li-Ion Polymer	0.70

Source: The web page http://appleinsider.com/articles/10/09/28/materials_cost_for_sixth_gen_ipod_nano_estimated_at_43. It should be noted that this information is provided only for illustration purposes. iSupplier is a third-party company, and estimates by any such party are subject to considerable estimation error.

more challenging and, if not done properly, can lead to the production of new products that are mispriced.

The costs of acquiring the materials for the production for a product are called ***material costs***. In turn, material costs can be divided into direct material costs (typically the largest component of material costs) and indirect material costs. Material costs that can be easily traced to the direct production of a product are classified as ***direct material costs***. For example, iSupplier, a company well known for its cost analysis of electronic products, provided a component analysis of the direct materials (i.e., parts) for Apple's sixth generation of iPod, released in September 2010, along with the estimated costs, as shown in table 14.1.

As another example, estimates of the direct material costs of the main cost drivers of the Apple Mac Mini (A1347) computer (constituting 80% of the estimated total material costs) by Electronics 360 are shown in table 14.2.

Material costs that cannot be easily traced back to the production of the product are referred to as ***indirect material costs***. Indirect material costs are included as part of factory overhead costs, which we describe below.

As with material costs, labor costs are divided into direct and indirect components. All labor costs that are directly involved in the production of a product are classified as direct labor costs and all remaining labor costs associated with production are classified as indirect labor costs. Typically the major component of labor costs is direct labor costs. The

Table 14.2

Supplier/Manufacturer	Parts	Cost
Intel	AV80577SH0563M—CPU—Intel Core 2 Duo P8600 Processor, 2.40GHz, 3MB L2 Cache, 1066MHz FSB, 45nm	$69.38
Nvidia	MCP89MZ-A2—Chipset—GeForce 320M, 40nm	44.27
Toshiba Storage Device	MK3255GSXF—Hard Drive—320 GB, 2.5", SATA 3 Gb/s, 5400RPM, 8 MB Buffer	43.00
Hitachi-LG Data Storage	GA32N—CD/DVD RW Drive—Slim Internal Type, Slot Load, SATA	40.00
Hynix	HMT112S6TFR8C-G7—SODIMM DDR3–1066–1GB, 128Mx64, 1.5V (Qty:2)	38.00
Compeq	10-Layer—FR4, Lead-Free, Halogen Free	16.28
Enclosure, Outer Case	Machined Aluminum, Printed, Anodized	13.5
Broadcom	BCM943224PCIEBT—WLAN/Bluetooth Module Value Line Item—IEEE802.11a/b/g/n, 2 × 2, Bluetooth V2.1+EDR	9.90
Delta Electronics	ADP-85AF—Power Supply Module Value Line Item— 12V, 7.1A, 85W, w/ Plastic Housing	8.17
Texas Instruments	XIO2211ZAY—PCI-E to IEEE1394b Controller	3.65
Cooler Assembly	Die-Cast Aluminum Alloy Mounting Bracket, 2 copper blocks, 2 copper tubes, aluminum fins, painted, w/ thermal transfer material	3.15
Delta Electronics	BUB0712HC-HM01—Blower—DC Brushless, 12VDC, 0.66A, w/ Integral 4-Wire Harness and 4-Postion Pin Socket Connector	2.40
Broadcom	BCM57765A0KMLG—Ethernet Transceiver/Memory Card Reader Controller—10/100/1000Base-T, 65nm	1.75
Renesas	R4F2117LP—MCU—16-Bit, H8S/2600 CPU Core, 160KB ROM, 8KB RAM, 20MHz, 3.0–3.6V, 112 I/Os	1.57
International Rectifier	IR3841WMTRPbF—Regulator—DC-DC Converter, Synchronous Buck, 8A, 1.5MHz (Qty: 2)	1.22

Note: The costs shown in the table constituted 80% of the estimated total material cost.
Source: Web page http://electronics360.globalspec.com/article/2192/apple-mac-mini-a1347-computer-teardown.

salary of a plant supervisor would be an example of an indirect labor cost. Indirect labor costs are included as part of factory overhead costs, along with indirect material costs.

Factory overhead costs include indirect costs that cannot be assigned to a product. We have already described two such components: indirect material costs and indirect labor costs. Other indirect manufacturing costs that are part of factory overhead costs are utilities to operate a plant, rental payments for a production plant if the plant is leased or depreciation of the production plant if it is owned, and depreciation of equipment used in production. Factory overhead costs are categorized as fixed costs, variable costs, and mixed costs.

Production Cost-Volume Relationship

The behavior exhibited by costs as volume changes is information needed to assess the volume of sales needed to break even and the scalability of a product from a production perspective. Although scalability of a product can be achieved from economies arising from marketing and distribution, it is more likely to come from the production process. The concepts of fixed, variable, and mixed costs are needed to understand the relationship of production costs to volume.

Variable costs are those costs where the total cost changes in direct proportion to changes in volume while the unit cost remains unchanged over some relevant range of production. The implication for entrepreneurs in terms of achieving a milestone such as break-even operating profit or a positive operating profit is that, holding the selling price per unit and the total fixed costs constant, for each unit increase in sales there will be an incremental change in total variable costs equal to a constant amount per unit. Assuming the product is properly priced so that the selling price per unit exceeds the variable cost per unit, an increase in sales will be beneficial.

It should be borne in mind that variable costs, as well as fixed costs, change at different levels of production. For example, we gave illustrations of components of variables costs earlier in this chapter when listing the raw material costs for the sixth generation of iPod nano and the main cost drivers of the Apple Mac Mini (A137) computer. In estimating the costs for the latter, Electronics360 stated that the estimates applied to a lifetime production of about two million units. How much could the cost estimates change for different levels of output? As stated by Electronics360: "Unless assumed volumes are different by an order of magnitude, minor changes in volume (say 1 million vs. 2) rarely have a large net effect on our final analysis because of this."

Fixed costs are those costs that remain constant within a relevant range of output. This means that fixed costs per unit (i.e., unitized fixed costs) decline as output increases.

Mixed costs have attributes of both variable and fixed production costs. One type of fixed cost is *semivariable fixed costs*, which may arise for the use of a service. There would be a minimum fee for the service (the fixed cost component) plus a per use charge for the service (the variable cost component). A second type of mixed cost occurs when there is a fixed cost of a specified amount up to some level of activity and then beyond that level the fixed cost jumps to a higher amount. This type of mixed cost is called a *step cost* and arises because some production costs can be obtained only in indivisible portions. For example, suppose in the assembling of a product there is one floor supervisor for every twenty assembly workers. Suppose further that thirty-three assembly workers are needed. That means that two floor supervisors are needed. So the addition of thirteen workers above the twenty will increase production cost by an amount equal to the salary of one supervisor.

Nonaccounting Other Costs and Profit Planning

For purposes of planning and decision making regarding business operations, there are ways to think about costs that go beyond the definitions given above. More specifically, in decision making it is important to understand relevant versus irrelevant costs and opportunity costs. These concepts do not appear on financial statements but their application in conducting business has an impact on the financial statements.

A cost is said to be a ***relevant cost*** if the projected future cost differs among alternative courses of action and may be eliminated if activity is changed or no longer exists. If a cost is unaffected by the actions of a founder, then such a cost is referred to as an ***irrelevant cost***. An example of an irrelevant cost is a sunk cost, which is a cost incurred in a prior period and is now irrevocable.

To see why it is important to distinguish between a relevant and irrelevant cost, let's consider the case of a founder thinking about introducing another product into an existing product line. Suppose that the new product is to be manufactured at a plant where the company's other products are manufactured. In making a decision whether or not to launch the new product, the founder attempts to estimate its cost. In performing this task, the founder may allocate a portion of the factory overhead costs to estimate the cost of the new product. That allocation would be correct from an accounting perspective (i.e., in terms of computing the cost of goods sold), but for addressing the question of whether or not to launch the new product, that allocation might not be correct. The reason is that part of the factory overhead costs such as depreciation of the plant[1] or the rental payments for the plant if it is not owned will not change if the new product is introduced. Hence the depreciation or the rental payment would be an irrelevant cost for pricing the new product. So for decision-making purposes, it important for a founder to think carefully about whether costs are relevant.

When a decision is made to pursue one alternative, the benefits of other options are forgone. Benefits lost from rejecting the next best alternative are called the ***opportunity costs*** of the chosen action. Although they are not recorded in the financial statements, they are relevant costs for decision-making purposes and must be considered in evaluating a proposed alternative. The Coleco Inc. case described in chapter 13 is a good example. By failing to produce sufficient Cabbage Patch dolls to meet customer demand, the company realized a loss in potential revenue and profit, which was its opportunity cost.

Estimating the Cost of a New Product

There are standard product costing techniques for established products that are used by a company's internal accounting staff. However, for the introduction of a product that is in the early stage of product development, cost estimates using such techniques may not be very helpful to founders. What is needed is an approach that can provide a fairly accurate

---

1. Remember that the depreciation is an accounting number and is not based on the actual physical deterioration of the plant.

cost estimate so that given a suitable markup over cost, the venture can provide price quotations to potential customers. Misestimating the price because the cost estimate for a new product is off the market can result in either a loss of current and future business from a customer requesting a quote (i.e., an opportunity cost) or the sale of a product at less than its true cost to manufacture. Insofar as the product life cycle for many high-tech products is brief, cost estimates are critical for entrepreneurs in deciding whether to launch a new product.

Although building a prototype may provide some estimate about production costs, the information is flawed for two reasons. First, in the building of the prototype, customized parts may have to be used, adding to the production costs. However, normal production may eventually involve the use of the same parts, which can then be purchased at a lower unit cost. Moreover, the cost of those parts will decline as production volume increases. Consequently, it is imperative in estimating costs for determining the potential profitability of a new product to distinguish between customized component costs for the building of a prototype and component costs that are estimated assuming normal production. The second reason is that labor costs may decline as employees' productivity in producing the new product increases. That is, there is a learning curve associated with a new production process, and as more units are produced, labor time per unit declines. Eventually there are no further productivity gains, but the labor costs associated with producing a unit at that point are far less than the labor costs associated with building a prototype.

Two techniques for estimating production costs of a new technology have been suggested by Adnan Niazi, Jian S. Dai, Stavroula Balabani, and Lakmal Seneviratne: qualitative and quantitative.[2] Qualitative techniques try to estimate the cost of a new product based on a comparison with the cost of manufacturing a similar product. The technique involves identifying products with a similar design feature and similar components as the new product and using those costs as a rough estimate for the cost of producing a new product. Quantitative techniques entail a more detailed decomposition of the component parts of a similar design product using the statistical technique of regression analysis.

BREAK-EVEN ANALYSIS

A simple example will introduce break-even analysis and cost-volume-profit (CVP) analysis. Suppose that Dr. Gregory Xu develops a personal medical device that improves testing for diabetes and obtains a patent on the device. Dr. Xu's research leads him to believe that the cost of renting a facility sufficient to satisfy his expected needs would be about $12,000 per month, or $144,000 per year. The rent would include all utilities except telephone expenses and office furniture. He estimates telephone expenses to be about $18,000 per year; this cost would not vary with the level of sales as long as sales did not exceed

2. Adnan Niazi, Jian S. Dai, Stavroula Balabani, and Lakmal Seneviratne, "Product Cost Estimation: Technique Classification and Methodology Review," *Journal of Manufacturing Science and Engineering,* May 2006, 563–575.

$1 million per year. Dr. Xu also estimates that it would cost $138,000 per year to hire an administrative staff. A freelance manufacturer agrees to manufacture and sell to him the device for $10 per unit. Dr. Xu is confident that he can sell each unit for $90.

Dr. Xu must now make a decision as to whether or not to start the business. The decision is based on the expected number of units of the device that he can sell in a year. He understands that he will incur the annual fixed cost of the facility—rent, telephone expense, and the cost of the administrative staff—regardless of the number of units sold. This total annual fixed cost is estimated to be $300,000 (= $144,000 rent + $18,000 telephone expense + $138,000 administrative staff). Since $90 in revenue is expected to be received for each device sold, and since it costs $10 to purchase a unit, this means that a "profit" of $80 per unit will be realized for each unit sold. Just to break even, 3,750 ($300,000/$80) units must be sold to cover the total annual fixed costs expense of $300,000.

Although Dr. Xu, based on his market analysis, feels he could sell every year at least 3,750 devices, that is not sufficient to generate a profit. Dr. Xu has targeted a profit before taxes of at least $400,000 a year or it would not be worth his time to start this business. To generate a pre-tax profit of $400,000 with each unit sale increasing his profit by $80, he would need to sell 5,000 additional units. Adding the 3,750 units necessary to break even to the 5,000 units means that annual unit sales must be at least 8,750 to earn a pre-tax profit of $400,000. The decision then comes down to the likelihood that Dr. Xu assigns to selling 8,750 units.

In determining the break-even point in our illustration, Dr. Xu divided the total annual fixed cost by the "profit" on each unit sold. This profit is the difference between the selling price per unit and the cost of purchasing each unit, which is the variable cost per unit. In this example, the only component of the variable cost per unit is the price of acquiring a unit. In practice, the variable cost per unit will include all the costs that vary with the level of sales.

The difference between the selling price per unit and the variable cost per unit is called the ***contribution margin per unit*** or ***unit contribution***. Therefore, to obtain the number of units necessary to break even, we divide the total fixed cost by the contribution margin per unit. That is,

$$\text{Break-even point (in units)} = \frac{\text{Total fixed costs}}{\text{Selling price per unit} - \text{Variable cost per unit}},$$

or equivalently,

$$\text{Break-even point (in units)} = \frac{\text{Total fixed costs}}{\text{Contribution margin per unit}}.$$

Dollar Break-Even Point
The formula for the break-even point given above indicates the number of units necessary to break even. In some applications, it is useful to know the break-even point in terms

of sales dollars. For example, the selling price may vary slightly from one customer to another; therefore, dollar sales may be more informative than units. In the case of a single product line and a single price per unit, the break-even point in dollars can be obtained by multiplying the break-even point in units by the selling price per unit. When the selling price per unit varies by customer, a different formula can be used to determine the break-even point in dollars.

The break-even point in dollars can be found using the following formula:

$$\text{Break-even point (in \$)} = \frac{\text{Total fixed costs}}{1 - \text{Variable costs as a \% of dollar sales}}.$$

The denominator of the above formula is the contribution margin per unit divided by the selling price and is called the **contribution margin ratio**. Thus the previous formula can be rewritten as

$$\text{Break-even point (in \$)} = \frac{\text{Total fixed costs}}{1 - \text{Contribution margin ratio}}.$$

To illustrate the above formula, suppose that, instead of formulating the earlier example for determining the break-even point for the medical device that Dr. Xu must sell in terms of units, the following information is given. The total annual fixed cost is $300,000. Since the variable cost per unit is equal to $10 and the selling price is $90, the variable cost is 11.1111% of sales ($10/$90). The contribution margin ratio is then $1 - 0.111111 = 0.888889$. Substituting these two values into the formula for the break-even point in dollars gives

$$\text{Break-even point (in \$)} = \frac{\$300,000}{0.888889} = \$337,500.$$

Therefore, if sales are $337,500, Dr. Xu's startup company will break even. Since each unit sells for $90, this means that the number of units required to break even if all customers pay that price is 3,750 ($337,500/$90). This result, of course, agrees with the number of units needed to break even when the formula for the break-even point in units is used.

COST-VOLUME-PROFIT ANALYSIS

Break-even analysis indicates the level of sales at which profits will be zero. Entrepreneurs want to know the level of sales necessary to achieve a pre-tax target profit. The analysis to determine the level of sales to answer this question is referred to as **cost-volume-profit analysis** and the solution is given by the following formula:

Sales to realize a given pre-tax target profit (in units)

$$= \frac{\text{Pre-tax target profit} + \text{Total fixed costs}}{\text{Contribution margin per unit}}.$$

For example, if Dr. Xu wants to know the number of units necessary to generate a pre-tax profit of $400,000, using the above formula gives the following:

$$\text{Sales to realize a }\$400,000\text{ pre-tax target profit (in units)} = \frac{\$400,000 + \$300,000}{\$80}$$

$$= 8,750 \text{ units.}$$

Using the following formula gives the dollar sales level necessary to realize a given pre-tax target profit:

Sales to realize a given pre-tax target profit (in dollars)

$$= \frac{\text{Pre-tax target profit} + \text{Total fixed costs}}{1 - \text{Contribution margin ratio}}.$$

Risk and Profit Analysis

A useful measure for an entrepreneur in profit planning is the maximum percentage by which expected sales can decline and the entrepreneur will still realize a profit. This is referred to as the *margin of safety* and is computed as follows (for both units and dollar sales):

$$\text{Margin of safety} = \frac{\text{Expected sales} - \text{Break-even sales}}{\text{Expected sales}}.$$

For example, if Dr. Xu expects sales of 7,000 units and the break-even point is 3,750 units, the margin of safety is computed as follows:

$$\text{Margin of safety} = \frac{7,000 - 3,750}{7,000} = 0.46 = 46\%.$$

Therefore, as long as actual sales are not less than 46% of what Dr. Xu expects, then the target profit will be realized.

Comparing Different Production Processes

A problem faced by an entrepreneur is selecting from among alternative production processes that have different fixed and variable costs. For example, an entrepreneur may be considering two alternative production processes. The first has a high fixed cost but low variable cost per unit; the other has a low fixed cost but a high variable cost per unit. Which is the best production process that should be adopted by the entrepreneur?

The following formula for determining the break-even number of units where two production processes, say 1 and 2, will provide the same profit can be used to help evaluate which production process should be adopted:

Sales at which two production processes produce the same profit (in units) =

$$\frac{\text{Total fixed costs for 1} - \text{Total fixed costs for 2}}{\text{Variable cost per unit for 2} - \text{Variable cost per unit for 1}}.$$

To illustrate how, assume that the two production processes that the entrepreneur is considering have the following cost structure:

	Process 1	Process 2
Total fixed costs	$500,000	$2,500,000
Variable cost per unit	$20	$10

Assume that regardless of the production process selected, the entrepreneur is confident that each unit can be sold for $30.

The break-even point for the two production processes can be shown to be 50,000 units for process 1 and 125,000 units for process 2. So, as expected, production process 2 has a higher break-even point because of its higher total fixed costs.

Using the previous formula we find the number of units where the same profit will be generated by both production processes:

Sales at which two production processes produce the same profit (in units) =

$$\frac{\$500,000 - \$2,500,000}{\$10 - \$20} = 200,000 \text{ units}.$$

At 200,000 units, the profit will be $1,500,000 for both production processes, as shown below:

	Process 1	Process 2
Sales ($30 per unit)	$6,000,000	$6,000,000
– Variable costs	4,000,000	2,000,000
– Total fixed costs	500,000	2,500,000
= Profit	$1,500,000	$1,500,000

Given the break-even number of units for both production processes and the number of units needed to generate the same profit for both production processes, table 14.3 provides the entrepreneur with key information in considering which of the two production processes to select.

Although there is a greater profit with process 2 if expected sales are in fact 250,000 units, there is also greater risk. The margin of safety is 80% for process 1 and 50% for process 2, as shown below:

$$\text{Margin of safety for process 1} = \frac{\text{Expected sales} - \text{Break-even sales for process 1}}{\text{Expected sales}}$$

$$= \frac{250,000 - 50,000}{250,000} = 0.80 = 80\%$$

Table 14.3
Information for Selecting Between Two Production Processes

Expected Level of Sales (in units)	Best Process	Comment
Fewer than 50,000	1	Both production processes will sustain a loss; the loss is less for process 1.
50,000	1	Process 1 will break even; process 2 will sustain a loss.
50,001–124,999	1	Process 1 will realize a profit; process 2 will sustain a loss.
125,000	1	Process 1 will realize a profit; process 2 will break even.
125,001–199,999	1	Both production processes will realize a profit, but it will be greater for process 1.
200,000	Same	Both production processes will realize the same profit ($1,500,000).
More than 200,000	2	Both production processes will realize a profit, but it will be greater for process 2.

$$\text{Margin of safety for process 2} = \frac{\text{Expected sales} - \text{Break-even sales for process 2}}{\text{Expected sales}}$$

$$= \frac{250,000 - 125,000}{250,000} = 0.50 = 50\%$$

Consequently, unit sales can decline by as much as 80% and the company will still break even under process 1; however, unit sales can fall by only 50% under process 2 before a loss will be realized. The best process will depend not only on the expected level of sales but also on the probability that different levels of sales may be realized.

LIMITATIONS OF BREAK-EVEN AND COST-VOLUME-PROFIT ANALYSIS

Break-even and CVP analyses as they have been described in this chapter are useful tools for an entrepreneur. One of the most often cited virtues of these tools is their simplicity. It is this simplicity, however, that limits their usefulness in practice. In some circumstances, limitations can be overcome by using more sophisticated techniques in conjunction with the basic break-even and CVP analyses. The limitations associated with these two tools are described below.

Difficulties of Cost Classification
The classification of costs as either fixed or variable is not as simple in practice. Some costs are mixed. That is, they can be fixed costs up to a certain level of output but will vary within certain ranges of output. Although mixed costs complicate the analysis, if they can be identified and measured, then the basic models presented in this chapter can be modified to reflect their impact.

Difficulties in Estimating the Cost-Volume Relationship

Assuming that costs can be properly classified as either fixed or variable, it is necessary to estimate the relationship between cost and volume. This relationship can be estimated using a statistical technique known as regression analysis. For now, it is sufficient to point out that the data generally used in regression analysis are historical data. The relationship estimated is therefore representative of past relationships and based on production technology prevailing at that time. Clearly, the estimated relationship between cost and volume may not be indicative of future cost relationships if production technology has changed.

The Linearity Assumption of Cost and Revenue

The break-even and CVP models described in this chapter assume that the selling price and the variable cost are independent of the level of output. A more plausible assumption is that to increase sales, the selling price must be lowered. Moreover, as production approaches capacity, the variable cost per unit will probably increase because workers will be required to work overtime or the plant may be operating at a less efficient level.

The implication of all this is that the relationship between total cost and output and between total revenue and output will be nonlinear. Figure 14.1 graphically depicts these two relationships. Total cost will increase with output, but at an increasing rate. Total revenue will also increase with output; however, it will do so at a decreasing rate. When the relationships are nonlinear, as shown in figure 14.1, there will be two break-even points. With linear relationships there is only one break-even point. Also, with linear relationships, the company can maximize its profit by selling as many units as possible given the relevant range. In contrast, with nonlinear relationships, there is a level of sales that will produce a maximum profit.

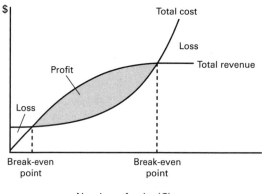

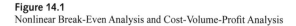

Figure 14.1
Nonlinear Break-Even Analysis and Cost-Volume-Profit Analysis

Difficulties in Multiproduct Applications

The illustrations have demonstrated how break-even and CVP analyses can be used when there is a single product. In many applications an entrepreneur is concerned with profit planning when the company produces more than one product line.

The problem that arises is that the contribution margin per unit can be determined only for a particular product mix. If the actual product mix sold differs from the product mix used in the analysis, there will be a divergence between the expected profit based on the CVP model and the realized profit. Also, the break-even point will not be the same if the product mix actually sold differs from the product mix used in the analysis.

To see this, let's consider a startup company that produces three products, X, Y, and Z. Suppose that the entrepreneur has determined that the optimal product mix for these three products is 5:4:1. That is, for every ten units sold, five will be product X, four will be product Y, and one will be product Z. The assumed selling price and variable cost per unit for each product line are given below:

Product	Selling price per unit	Variable cost per unit	Contribution margin per unit
X	$10	$2	$8
Y	20	6	14
Z	30	28	2

The fixed cost associated with all three products is $4.9 million.

The contribution margin per unit for the optimal product mix is the weighted average of the contribution margin per unit for each product. The weight for each product is determined by the product mix determined by the entrepreneur. In this illustration, the weights are 50% for product X, 40% for product Y, and 10% for product Z. The contribution margin per unit for the product mix is therefore $9.80, as shown below:

Weighted average contribution margin for a product mix = $8 (0.5) + $14 (0.4) + $2 (0.10) = $9.80.

The break-even point in units would be 500,000, as shown below:

$$\text{Break-even point (in units)} = \frac{\text{Total fixed costs}}{\text{Weighted average contribution margin for a product mix}}.$$

$$= \frac{\$4,900,000}{\$9.80} = 500,000 \text{ units}$$

If 700,000 units are sold, the break-even analysis just performed indicates that there will be a profit. The profit can be determined by multiplying the weighted average contribution margin per unit by the number of units and subtracting fixed costs. In this illustration, therefore, the profit if 700,000 units are sold should be $1,960,000 (700,000 ($9.80) − $4,900,000).

Suppose that 700,000 units are sold, but that the product mix actually sold was not the same as the product mix assumed in the analysis by the entrepreneur. Suppose instead that sales were as follows: 200,000 units of product X, 100,000 units of product Y, and 400,000 units of product Z. It can easily be shown that this product mix results in a loss of $1.1 million, even though the number of units sold exceeded the number that was computed to break even.

To overcome this problem, an entrepreneur could, of course, perform break-even analysis and CVP analysis separately for each product line. The problem that arises with that approach is allocating the common fixed expenses shared by all product lines to each product line.

Short-Term Nature of the Model

Break-even analysis and CVP analysis are used for short-term profit planning. One of the weaknesses of this approach is that it does not take into account the time value of money, a concept presented in chapter 16. That is, the tools discussed in this chapter, which are commonly employed in industry, do not take into account the timing of the revenues and costs. When a break-even point of X units is computed, for example, it is assumed that those units will be sold within a short period of time, not over an extended period.

To see how failure to recognize the timing of revenue can lead to catastrophic results, consider the case of Lockheed's TriStar program. In 1971, Lockheed sought congressional approval for a federal guarantee of $250 million in loans to help the company complete the program. Lockheed's management argued that the TriStar program was economically sound. The reason why the program was in trouble, Lockheed's management argued, was that the company faced a severe liquidity crisis. Lockheed estimated that the break-even point for the program was between 195 and 205 aircraft. Unfortunately, in its break-even analysis, Lockheed failed to take into consideration the timing of revenue. In fact, an independent analysis estimated that had the timing of revenues been considered, the break-even point would have been almost double that estimated by Lockheed.[3]

CASH FLOW VERSUS PROFIT

As will be explained in chapter 16, the key concept in analyzing the economic merit of an investment is its expected cash flow. Cash flow is simply the cash inflow minus the cash outflow expected to result from an investment. In the break-even analysis model described in this chapter, the focus was on all costs, both current costs and those costs for which a

---

3. See Uwe E. Reinhardt, "Break-Even Analysis for Lockheed's TriStar: An Application of Financial Theory," *Journal of Finance*, September 1973, 821–838.

noncash outlay in the current period is not required. Depreciation is an example of a non-cash outlay that is included in the fixed cost component of total cost.

To overcome the criticism that break-even analysis does not recognize cash flow, an entrepreneur can determine the *cash break-even point*. This information is useful to an entrepreneur because it indicates that during a period of temporary decline in sales, the company's cash obligations can still be satisfied from the cash flow generated from operations, even though a loss may result, as long as the firm operates at or above the cash break-even point.

The cash break-even point is usually approximated by subtracting noncash outlays from total fixed costs in the break-even formulas presented earlier in this chapter. The cash break-even formulas are given below:

$$\text{Cash break-even point (in units)} = \frac{\text{Total fixed costs} - \text{Noncash outlays}}{\text{Contribution margin per unit}}.$$

$$\text{Cash break-even point (in \$)} = \frac{\text{Total fixed costs} - \text{Noncash outlays}}{1 - \text{Contribution margin ratio}}.$$

The cash break-even point is only an approximation.

KEY POINTS COVERED IN THIS CHAPTER

- New product introduction, production volume, product pricing, and production process selection are part of the profit planning and operating decisions that entrepreneurs must make.
- The key to profit planning is understanding the firm's cost structure.
- A firm's costs can be classified into four functional areas: production costs (or manufacturing costs), marketing costs, administrative costs, and financing costs.
- The cost structure is influenced by the value proposition, and once a cost structure is selected, it is essential for the founders to understand the various types of costs and the behavior that they exhibit as the firm grows.
- There are two extreme cost structures: a cost-driven structure, in which the value proposition is low price, and a value-driven structure, in which the value proposition is premium value.
- The projection of future income and new product pricing begin with understanding the components of production costs.
- When a firm sells multiple products, management must be able to identify the costs associated with each product.
- There are three components of product cost: (1) direct material costs, (2) direct labor costs, and (3) factory overhead costs.

- As a firm grows and introduces new products, the task of tracing costs to each product becomes increasingly challenging and, if not done properly, can lead to the production of new products that are mispriced.

- Material costs are the costs of acquiring the materials for the production of a product and consist of direct material costs (typically the largest component of material costs) and indirect material costs.

- Direct material costs are material costs that can be easily traced to the direct production of a product.

- Indirect material costs are material costs that cannot be easily traced back to the production of the product and are included as part of factory overhead costs.

- Labor costs are divided into direct and indirect components, with the former being the major component of labor costs.

- Factory overhead costs include indirect costs that cannot be identified to a product, indirect material costs, and indirect labor costs.

- Other indirect manufacturing costs that are part of factory overhead costs are utilities to operate a plant, rental payments for a production plant if it is leased or depreciation of the production plant if it owned, and depreciation of production equipment.

- Factory overhead costs are categorized as fixed costs, variable costs, and mixed costs.

- The behavior exhibited by costs as volume changes is needed to assess the volume of sales required for the firm to break even (zero profit) and the scalability of a product from a production perspective.

- Variable costs are those costs where the total cost changes in direct proportion to changes in volume, with the unit cost remaining unchanged over some relevant range of production.

- Fixed costs are those costs that remain constant within a relevant range of output; as a result, fixed costs per unit decline as volume increases.

- Variable costs, as well as fixed costs, do in fact change at different levels of production.

- Mixed costs have attributes of both variable and fixed production costs and include semivariable fixed costs and step costs.

- Although not so classified in financial statements, for purposes of planning and decision making, costs can also be classified as relevant versus irrelevant costs and opportunity costs.

- A cost is said to be a relevant cost if the projected future cost differs among alternative courses of action and may be eliminated if activity is changed or no longer exists.

- An irrelevant cost is a cost that is unaffected by management decision, with sunk costs being one example.

- Opportunity costs are the benefits lost from rejecting the next best alternative course of action.

- For the introduction of a new product that is in the early stage of product development, accurate cost estimates may be difficult to obtain.

- Product price misestimating resulting from inaccurate cost estimates for a new product can result in either a loss in current and future business from a customer requesting a quote or the sale of a product at less than its true cost to manufacture.

- Although building a prototype may provide some estimate of production costs, the information is flawed for the following reasons: (1) in building the prototype, customized parts may have been used, adding to the production costs compared to the cost of a normal production process, which may eventually involve the use of the same parts which can be purchased at a lower unit cost; and (2) labor costs may decline as employees' productivity in producing the new product increases.

- Two techniques for estimating the production costs of a new technology are (1) qualitative techniques, which seek to estimate the cost of a new product based on a comparison with the cost of manufacturing a similar product already on the market, and (2) quantitative techniques, which use a more detailed decomposition of the component parts of a similar design product based on statistical methods.

- Contribution margin per unit or unit contribution is the difference between the selling price per unit and the variable cost per unit.

- The contribution margin ratio is the contribution margin per unit divided by the selling price.

- The break-even point is the point at which zero profit is generated. It can be expressed either in units of production or sales dollars.

- Cost-volume-profit (CVP) analysis allows estimation of the sales needed to achieve a pre-tax target profit.

- A useful measure in profit planning is the margin of safety, which is the maximum percentage by which expected sales can decline and the firm will still realize a profit.

- Profit planning analysis can be used in selecting from among alternative production processes that have different fixed and variable costs.

- One of the most often cited virtues of break-even and CVP analyses is their simplicity; however, this simplicity limits their usefulness in practice.

- One difficulty in the application of break-even and CVP analyses is the need to classify costs as either fixed, variable, or mixed costs.

- Break-even and CVP analyses assume that the selling price and the variable cost are independent of the level of output, though in fact the relationship between total cost and output and between total revenue and output is more likely to be nonlinear.

- A problem that arises in many applications of profit planning when a company produces more than one product line is that the contribution margin per unit can be determined only for a particular product mix.

- A potentially important weakness of break-even and CVP analyses is that they fail to recognize the time value of money.

- To overcome the criticism that break-even analysis does not recognize cash flow, the analysis can be based on the cash break-even point.

- The cash break-even point is important because it provides information that indicates that during a period of temporary decline in sales, the company's cash obligations can still be satisfied from the cash flow generated from operations, even though a loss may result as long as the firm operates at or above the cash break-even point.

FURTHER READINGS

Bouter, Ernst-Jan, *Pricing: The Third Business Skill: Principles of Price Management* (The Netherlands: First-Price BV, 2013).

Gopalkrishnan, Vivekenand, Kim Thi Nhu Quynh, and Wee-Keong Ng, "Regression Models for Estimating Product Life Cycle Cost," *Journal of Intelligent Manufacturing* 20, no. 4 (2009): 401–408.

Gregson, Andrew, *Pricing Strategies for Small Business* (Self-Counsel Press, 2008).

"JD Edwards EnterpriseOne Applications Product Costing and Manufacturing Accounting Implementation Guide," http://docs.oracle.com/cd/E16582_01/doc.91/e15130/intro_to_jde_e1_pcma.htm#EOAPM00370.

"JD Edwards World Product Costing and Manufacturing Accounting Guide," http://docs.oracle.com/cd/E26228_01/doc.93/e21775/ch_ov_prod_cost_mfg_acc.htm#WEAMA108

Meehan, Julie, Mike Simonetto, Larry Montan, and Chris Goodin, *Pricing and Profitability Management: A Practical Guide for Business Leaders* (Singapore: John Wiley & Sons, 2011).

15

FINANCIAL OPTIONS

As explained in chapter 4, stock options and other option-type awards granted to founders and employees must be valued for tax purposes. These options are referred to as "financial options" and are one of several types of a more general category of financial instruments referred to as "financial derivatives." Moreover, the principles of financial options have been used in valuing a startup company and in making capital project decisions (i.e., valuing a capital project), as explained in chapter 18. The approach to valuation of a company or a proposed capital project using the principles of financial options by looking at the managerial flexibility provided by real assets in place or real assets to be acquired is referred to as the *real options approach*.

Because of the applications of the principles of financial options in valuing stock option plans and in the real options approach, in this chapter we describe their basic principles.

BASIC FEATURES OF FINANCIAL OPTIONS

A *financial option* is a contract in which the writer of the option grants the buyer of the option the right, but not the obligation, to purchase from or sell to the writer a financial asset at a specified price within a specified period of time (or at a specified date). The *writer*, also referred to as the *seller*, grants this right to the buyer in exchange for a certain sum of money, which is called the *option price* or *option premium*. The price at which the financial asset may be bought or sold is referred to as the *exercise price* or *strike price*. The date after which an option is void is called the *expiration date*.

When an option grants the buyer the right to purchase the financial asset from the writer (seller), it is referred to as a *call option*, or simply a *call*. When the option buyer has the right to sell the financial asset to the writer, the option is referred to as a *put option*, or *put*.

An option is also categorized according to when the option buyer may exercise the option. This is referred to as the option's *exercise style*. The two most common exercise styles are American and European. An *American option* may be exercised at any time up to and including the expiration date. A *European option* may be exercised only at the expiration date. Note that labeling the exercise style as American or European is arbitrary. It has nothing to do with the geographic location of the option involved.[1]

For example, suppose that an investor buys a call option for $3 (the option price) with the following terms: (1) the underlying instrument is one share of the common stock of Company XYZ, (2) the exercise price is $100, (3) the expiration date is three months from now, and (4) the option can be exercised any time up to and including the expiration date (i.e., it is an American option).

At any time up to and including the expiration date, the investor can decide to buy from the writer of this option one share of XYZ stock, for which the investor will pay a price of $100. If it is not beneficial for the investor to exercise the option, the investor will not exercise it, and we explain shortly how the investor decides when it will be beneficial. Whether the investor exercises the option or not, the $3 paid for the option by the investor will be kept by the option writer. If the investor buys a put option rather than a call option, then the investor will be able to sell one share of XYZ to the option writer for a price of $100.

The maximum amount that an option buyer can lose is the option price. The maximum profit that the option writer can realize is the option price. The option buyer has substantial upside return potential, while the option writer has substantial downside risk. The risk/reward relationship for option positions is discussed later in this chapter. What is critical to understand is that the buyer of an option has the right but not the obligation to perform.

RISK AND RETURN CHARACTERISTICS OF OPTIONS

Here we illustrate the risk and return characteristics of the two basic option purchase positions: buying a call option and buying a put option. The illustrations assume that *each option position is held to the expiration date and not exercised early.*

Buying Call Options

To illustrate the financial position of the buyer of a call option, assume that a call option on XYZ stock expires in one month and has an exercise price of $100.The option price is $3. Suppose that the current price of XYZ stock is $100. The profit and loss from the strategy will depend on the price of the stock at the expiration date. A number of outcomes are possible.

1. If the stock price at the expiration date is less than $100, then the investor will not exercise the option. It would be foolish to pay the option writer $100 when the stock can be purchased in the market at a lower price. In this case, the option buyer loses the entire option price of $3. Notice, however, that it is the maximum loss that the option buyer will realize regardless of how low the stock's price declines.

---

1. There are variants of these two exercise styles. An option can be created with an exercise style in which the option can be exercised at several specified dates, as well as at the expiration date of the option. Such options are referred to as **limited exercise options**, **Bermuda options**, and **Atlantic options**.

2. If the stock price is equal to $100 at the expiration date, the option buyer would again find no economic value in exercising the option. As in the case where the price is less than $100, the buyer of the call option loses the entire option price, $3.

3. If the stock price is more than $100 but less than $103 at the expiration date, the option buyer exercises the option. By exercising, the option buyer can purchase the stock for $100 (the exercise price) and sell it in the market for the higher market price. Suppose, for example, that the stock price is $102 at the expiration date. The buyer of the call option will realize a $2 gain by exercising the option. Of course, the cost of purchasing the call option was $3, so $1 is lost on this position. By failing to exercise the option, the option buyer would lose $3 instead of only $1.

4. If the stock price at the expiration date is equal to $103, the investor exercises the option. In this case the option buyer breaks even, realizing a gain of $3, which offsets the cost of the option, $3.

5. If the stock price at the expiration date is more than $103, the investor exercises the option and realizes a profit. For example, if the price is $113, exercising the option generates a profit of $13. Reducing this gain by the cost of the option ($3), the option buyer realizes a net profit from this position of $10.

Figure 15.1 graphically portrays the result. Even though the break-even point and the loss depend on the option price and the exercise price, the profile shown in figure 15.1 holds for all buyers of call options. The shape indicates that the maximum loss is the option price and that there is substantial upside potential.

Buying Put Options

To illustrate the financial position of the buyer of a put option, assume that a put option on XYZ stock expires in one month and has an exercise price of $100. Assume the put option is selling for $2.The current stock price is $100.The profit or loss for this position at the expiration date depends on the market price of XYZ stock. The following outcomes are possible:

1. If the stock price is greater than $100, the buyer of the put option chooses not to exercise it because exercising would mean selling XYZ stock to the writer for a price that is less than the market price. A loss of $2 (the option price) would result in this case from buying the put option. Once again, the option price represents the maximum loss to which the buyer of the put option is exposed.

2. If the stock price at expiration is equal to $100, the put is not exercised, leaving the put buyer with a loss equal to the option price of $2.

3. Any stock price that is less than $100 but greater than $98 results in a loss. However, exercising the put option limits the loss to less than the option price of $2. For example, suppose that the price is $99 at the expiration date. By exercising the option, the option

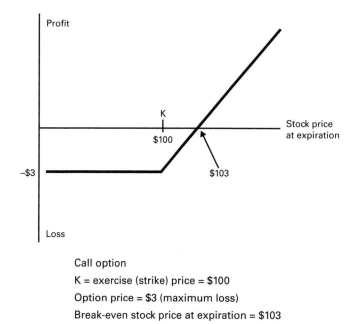

Call option
K = exercise (strike) price = $100
Option price = $3 (maximum loss)
Break-even stock price at expiration = $103

Figure 15.1
Profit/Loss for a Long Call Option at Expiration Date

buyer realizes a loss of $1 because the buyer of the put option can sell the stock that can be purchased in the market for $99 to the writer for $100, realizing a gain of $1. After deducting the $2 cost of the option, a loss of $1 is realized.

4. At a $98 price at the expiration date, the put buyer breaks even, realizing a gain of $2 by selling the stock to the option writer for $100, offsetting the cost of the option ($2).

5. If the stock price is below $98 at the expiration date, the put buyer realizes a profit by exercising the option. For example, suppose the price falls at expiration to $80. The put buyer realizes a profit of $18: a gain of $20 for exercising the put option less the $2 option price.

The profit-and-loss profile for the long put position is shown in graphical form in figure 15.2. As with all long positions, the loss is limited to the option price. The profit potential, however, is substantial: the theoretical maximum profit is generated if XYZ's price falls to zero.

BASIC COMPONENTS OF THE OPTION PRICE

The option price reflects the option's intrinsic value and any additional amount over its intrinsic value. The premium over intrinsic value is often referred to as the *time value* or

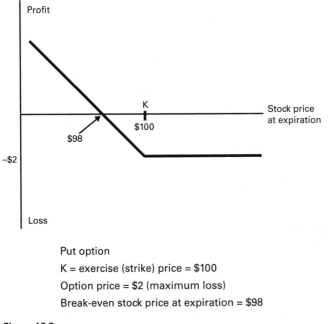

Put option
K = exercise (strike) price = $100
Option price = $2 (maximum loss)
Break-even stock price at expiration = $98

Figure 15.2
Profit-and-Loss Profile for a Long Put Position

time premium. The former term is more common; however, we use the term *time premium* to avoid confusion between the time value of money and the time value of the option.

Intrinsic Value

The *intrinsic value* of an option is the economic value of the option if it is exercised immediately. If no positive economic value will result from exercising immediately, the intrinsic value is zero.

The intrinsic value of a call option is the difference between the current price of the underlying asset and the exercise price if positive; it is otherwise zero. For example, if the exercise price for a call option is $100 and the current asset price is $105, the intrinsic value is $5. That is, an option buyer exercising the option and simultaneously selling the underlying asset would realize $105 from the sale of the asset, an amount that would be covered by acquiring the asset from the option writer for $100, thereby netting a $5 gain.

An option that has intrinsic value is said to be "in the money." When the exercise price of a call option exceeds the current asset price, the call option is said to be "out of the money"; it has no intrinsic value. An option for which the exercise price is equal to the current asset price is said to be "at the money." The intrinsic value of both at-the-money and out-of-the-money options is zero because it is not profitable to exercise the option. Our call option with an exercise price of $100 would be (1) in the money when the current asset price is greater than $100, (2) out of the money when the current asset price is less than $100, or (3) at the money when the current asset price is equal to $100.

For a put option, the intrinsic value equals the amount by which the current asset price is below the exercise price. For example, if the exercise price of a put option is $100 and the current asset price is $92, the intrinsic value is $8.That is, the buyer of the put option who exercises the put option and simultaneously sells the underlying asset nets $8 by exercising. The asset is sold to the writer for $100 and purchased in the market for $92. For our put option with an exercise price of $100, the option would be (1) in the money when the asset price is less than $100, (2) out of the money when the current asset price exceeds the exercise price, or (3) at the money when the exercise price is equal to the asset's price.

Time Premium

The *time premium* of an option is the amount by which the option price exceeds its intrinsic value. The option buyer hopes that at some time prior to expiration, changes in the market price of the underlying asset will increase the value of the rights conveyed by the option. For this prospect, the option buyer is willing to pay a premium above the intrinsic value. For example, if the price of a call option with an exercise price of $100 is $9 when the current asset price is $105, the time premium of this option is $4 ($9 minus its intrinsic value of $5). A current asset price of $90 instead of $105 means that the time premium of this option would be the entire $9 because the option has no intrinsic value. Clearly, other things being equal, the time premium of an option increases with the amount of time remaining to expiration.

FACTORS THAT INFLUENCE THE PRICE OF A FINANCIAL OPTION

Six factors influence the price of an option: (1) the current price of the underlying asset, (2) the exercise price, (3) the time to expiration of the option, (4) the expected price volatility of the underlying financial asset over the life of the option, (5) the short-term risk-free interest rate over the life of the option, and (6) anticipated cash payments on the underlying asset over the life of the option

The impact of each of these factors may depend on whether the option is a call or a put, and whether the option is an American option or a European option. Table 15.1 presents a summary of the effect of each factor on put and call option prices.

Current Price of the Underlying Financial Asset

The option price changes as the price of the underlying financial asset changes. For a call option, as the price of the underlying financial asset increases (all other factors being constant, the exercise price in particular), the option price increases. The opposite holds for a

Table 15.1
Summary of Factors That Affect the Price of an Option

	Effect of an Increase in Factor on:	
Factor	Call Price	Put Price
Current price of underlying financial asset	Increase	Decrease
Exercise price	Decrease	Increase
Time to expiration of option	Increase	Increase
Expected price volatility	Increase	Increase
Short-term interest rate	Increase	Decrease
Anticipated cash payments	Decrease	Increase

put option. As the price of the underlying financial asset increases, the price of a put option decreases.

Exercise (Strike) Price
The exercise price is fixed for the life of the option. All other factors being equal, the lower the exercise price, the higher the price of a call option. For put options, the higher the exercise price, the higher the price of a put option.

Time to Expiration of the Option
An option is a "wasting asset." That is, after the expiration date the option has no value. All other factors being equal, the longer the time to expiration of the option, the greater the option price, because as the time to expiration decreases, less time remains for the price of the underlying financial asset to rise (for a call buyer) or fall (for a put buyer)—that is, to compensate the option buyer for any time premium paid—and therefore the probability of a favorable price movement decreases. Consequently, for American options, as the time remaining until expiration decreases, the option price approaches its intrinsic value.

Expected Price Volatility of the Underlying Financial Asset over the Life of the Option
All other factors being equal, the greater the expected price volatility of the underlying financial asset, the more an investor would be willing to pay for the option, and the more an option writer would demand for it. The greater the volatility, the greater is the probability that the price of the underlying financial asset will move in favor of the option buyer at some time before expiration. To measure volatility, the standard deviation (or variance) of the underlying financial asset's price is used.

Short-Term Risk-Free Interest Rate over the Option's Life
By buying the underlying financial asset, an investor ties up funds. Buying an option on the same quantity of the underlying financial asset makes the difference between the financial

asset's price and the option price available for investment at (at least) the risk-free rate. Consequently, all other factors being constant, the higher the short-term risk-free interest rate, the greater the cost of buying the underlying financial asset and carrying it to the expiration date of the call option. Hence, the higher the short-term risk-free interest rate, the more attractive the call option will be relative to the direct purchase of the underlying financial asset. As a result, the higher the short-term risk-free interest rate, the greater is the price of a call option.

Anticipated Cash Payments on the Underlying Financial Asset over the Option's Life

Cash payments on the underlying financial asset tend to decrease the price of a call option because the cash payments make it more attractive to hold the underlying financial asset than to hold the option. For put options, cash payments on the underlying financial asset tend to increase their price.

DETERMINING THE VALUE OF A FINANCIAL OPTION: PRICING MODELS

Given the factors that have an impact on the value of an option, the next step is to determine the option's theoretical value. Theoretical boundary conditions for the price of an option can be derived using arbitrage arguments. That is, there must be a relationship between the price of an option and the price of the underlying asset and the exercise price. For example, using arbitrage arguments it can be shown that the minimum price for an American call option is its intrinsic value. That is,

Call option price $\geq$ Max (0, Price of asset − Exercise price).

This expression says that the call option price will be greater than or equal to the difference between the price of the underlying asset and the exercise price (intrinsic value) or zero, whichever is higher.

The boundary conditions can be "tightened" by using arbitrage arguments coupled with certain assumptions about the cash distribution of the asset. The extreme case is an option pricing model that uses a set of assumptions to derive a single theoretical price rather than a range. As we shall see, deriving a theoretical option price is complicated because it depends on the expected price volatility of the underlying asset over the option's life.

The major breakthrough in the development of an option pricing model was the model developed by Fischer Black and Myron Scholes, appropriately referred to as the Black-Scholes *option pricing model*.[2] There are two other methods of valuing a financial option that can be used, the lattice model (a special case being the binomial model) and the Monte Carlo simulation method. These two methods are more easily applied to the valuation of real options, the subject of chapter 18, than is the Black-Scholes model.

---

2. Fischer Black and Myron Scholes, "The Pricing of Corporate Liabilities," *Journal of Political Economy,* May/June 1973, 637–659.

Black-Scholes Option Pricing Model

The Black-Scholes option pricing model was first developed for pricing call options on common stock. The inputs in the model are those described earlier that affect the value of an option. The assumptions of the model are as follow:

- *Assumption 1:* The call option is a European call option for a non-dividend-paying common stock.
- *Assumption 2:* The return distribution for the underlying common stock follows a lognormal distribution.
- *Assumption 3:* The stock price is generated by a diffusion process, meaning that the stock price can take on any positive value, but when it moves from one price to another, it must take on all values in between. That is, the stock price does not jump from one stock price to another, skipping over interim prices.
- *Assumption 4:* The variance of the stock's return is the appropriate measure of volatility. It meets two criteria: (a) it is constant over the life of the option and (b) it is known with certainty.
- *Assumption 5:* The short-term interest rate for borrowing and lending are the same, and the short-term interest rate is constant over the life of the option.
- *Assumption 6:* There are no transaction costs or taxes that must be considered.

It is critical to understand these assumptions because the model is often applied to other types of financial assets or real assets where the assumptions are unwarranted, and as a result, the resulting option price is unreliable. Extensions of the Black-Scholes option pricing model that have been proposed over the years have sought to modify the model by relaxing one or more of the above assumptions.

Based on these assumptions, the fair value of a European call option on a non-dividend-paying common stock is

$$C = SN(d_1) - Xe^{-rt}N(d_2),$$

where

$$d_1 = \frac{ln(S/X) + (r + 0.5s^2)t}{s\sqrt{t}},$$

$$d_2 = d_1 - s\sqrt{t},$$

C = European call option price,

S = current stock price,

X = strike price,

r = short-term risk-free interest rate over the life of the option,

t = time remaining to the expiration date (measured as a fraction of one year),

s = standard deviation of the stock's return,

Table 15.2
Price of a European Call Option Using the Black-Scholes Option Pricing Model

Assumed Standard Deviation of Stock's Return, s	Time Remaining to the Expiration Date (Measured as a Fraction of One Year), t			
	0.25 (3 mos)	0.50 (6 mos)	1.00 (1 yr)	1.5 (18 mos)
20%	$1.31	$2.51	$4.42	$6.03
25%	1.92	3.42	5.74	7.63
30%	2.55	4.34	7.06	9.23

Notes: Inputs: S = current stock price = $66.00; X = exercise price = $70.00; r = short-term risk-free interest rate over the life of the option = 3.00%. Figures in the table were calculated using the Money-Zine Black-Scholes Calculator (http://www.money-zine.com/calculators/investment-calculators/black-scholes-calculator).

e = base of the natural logarithm,

ln = natural logarithm, and

$N(.)$ = the cumulative probability density (the value for $N(.)$ is obtained from a normal distribution function, which is tabulated in most statistics textbooks).

Note that all of the inputs needed to apply the formula are known except for the standard deviation of the stock's return, s.

The formula can be interpreted as follows.[3] (In chapter 16 we will explain the concept of the time value of money and the meaning of the present value of a future value.) The formula indicates that the option price is the difference in two terms that represent the expectations of two present values. The term $SN(d_1)$ is the expected present value of owning the stock at the option's expiration date contingent on the option being exercised. The expected value is obtained using the probability given by $N(d_1)$. The term $Xe^{-rt}N(d_2)$ is the expected present value of paying the exercise price at the expiration date, where $N(d_2)$ is the probability that the option will be exercised. Therefore, the formula says that the value of a call option is the benefit that the buyer is expected to receive by receiving the stock at the option's expiration date contingent on the option being exercised, reduced by the cost of paying the exercise price at the option's expiration date.

Since software is available to calculate the option price, we will not walk through an application of the model. Instead, we will just show the option price for a European call option with a current price of $66, an exercise price of $70, and a short-term interest rate of 3%. The option prices are shown in table 15.2 for four different maturities (three months, six months, one year, and eighteen months) and three different standard deviations (20%, 25%, and 30%).[4]

It is important to emphasize that the Black-Scholes option pricing model holds only in the special case in which the underlying is a European call option on a non-dividend-paying

---

3. Lars Tyge Nielsen, "Understanding $N(d_1)$ and $N(d_2)$: Risk-Adjusted Probabilities in the Black-Scholes Model," *Finance* 14 (1993): 95–106.

4. See the web page http://www.money-zine.com/calculators/investment-calculators/black-scholes-calculator.

Table 15.3
Price of a European Put Option Using the Put-Call Relationship

Assumed Standard Deviation of Stock's Return, s	Time Remaining to Expiration Date (measured as a fraction of one year), t			
	0.25 (3 mos)	0.50 (6 mos)	1.00 (1 yr)	1.5 (18 mos)
20%	$4.79	$5.46	$6.63	$6.95
25%	5.39	6.38	7.67	8.55
30%	6.02	7.03	8.99	10.15

Notes: Inputs: S = current stock price = $66.00; X = exercise price = $70.00; r = short-term risk-free interest rate over the life of the option = 3.00%. Figures in table were calculated using the Money-Zine Black-Scholes Calculator at http://www.money-zine.com/calculators/investment-calculators/black-scholes-calculator.

stock. The model has been extended, but there are still assumptions that may not apply if the model is used to value real options, as described in chapter 18.

Once the the option price for a call option is known, the price of a put option with the same exercise price and same expiration can be calculated. This can be done because of the relationship between the price of a call option and the price of the corresponding put option. This relationship for European options for a non-dividend-paying common stock is as follows:

Put option price – Call option price = Present value of exercise price – Price of underlying stock.

This relationship is referred to as the put-call parity relationship. Table 15.3 shows the put option prices for the call options whose call prices are shown in table 15.2.

BEYOND THE SIMPLE FINANCIAL OPTION

We have just described a basic or simple financial option. There is a wide array of more complex or what are more popularly referred to as exotic options available in the financial markets. Our principal interest here is the more complex options that are routinely found when applying the real options approach. Here we will confine our discussion to the three types of options that are encountered in real options—a compound option, a rainbow option, and a barrier option.

Compound Option
A *compound option* gives the option buyer the option to buy another option. As an example, we'll consider the buyer of a compound call option who has the right to purchase a put option at some future date.[5] This compound option gives the buyer of the option the right

---

5. An option that allows the option buyer to purchase a put option is called a callonput. A calloncall grants the option buyer the right to purchase a call option.

but not the obligation to require the writer of the compound option to sell the buyer a put option at some future date. The compound option would specify the following terms:

1. The day on which the buyer of the compound option has the choice of either requiring the writer of the option to sell the buyer a put option or allowing the option to expire, which is called the **extension date**.

2. The exercise price and the expiration date of the put option that the buyer acquires from the writer, which is called the **notification date**.

The payment that the option buyer makes to acquire the compound option is called the **front fee**. If the buyer exercises the call option in order to acquire the put option, a second payment is made to the writer of the option. That payment is called the **back fee**.

When a compound option involves resolving uncertainty about the market for a product or resolving private uncertainty, such as the cost of producing new technology or the feasibility of new technology, it is called a **learning option**.

Rainbow Option

In a simple option, there is one source of uncertainty. For example, in the simple financial options described earlier, the source of uncertainty is the future price of the underlying asset. With a **rainbow option**, there is more than one source of uncertainty. For example, in the case of a real option, the uncertainty can be about both the price at which a product can be sold and the timing as to when the option may be exercised. In the case of real options, some options are actually compound rainbow options.[6]

Barrier Option

In some cases the option's value depends on whether or not the underlying asset has breached a predetermined barrier level (exercise price) sometime during the option's life. An option with this feature is referred to as a **barrier option**. There are two types of barrier options: a knock-out option and a knock-in option. With a **knock-out option**, the option expires worthless if the price of the underlying asset at any time during the option's life does not breach a barrier level (exercise price); with a **knock-in option**, the option has no value until the underlying asset price breaches a barrier level (the exercise price).

When we say that the underlying asset breaches a barrier level, this could mean that the underlying asset price exceeds or falls below the barrier level. The term "up" means that the underlying asset price must exceed the barrier level while the term "down" means that the underlying asset price must be below the barrier level. An option that is said to be an "up and in" option is a knock-in option where the underlying asset price must exceed the barrier level, while a "down and in" option is a knock-in option where the underlying asset price must be below the barrier level. Similarly, an "up and out" and a "down and out"

---

6. Thomas E. Copeland and Vladimir Antikarov, *Real Options: A Practitioner's Guide* (New York: Texere Publishing, 2001).

option are knock-out options where the underlying asset price must be above or below the exercise price, respectively.

KEY POINTS COVERED IN THIS CHAPTER

- Stock options and other option-type awards granted to founders and employees are financial options and must be valued for tax purposes (Section 409a of the U.S. tax code).

- The principles of valuing financial options are used in valuing a startup company and in valuing a capital project being considered by management.

- The real options approach to valuation of a company or a proposed capital project uses the principles of valuing financial options by looking at the managerial flexibility provided by real assets in place or real assets to be acquired.

- A financial option is a contract whereby the writer (seller) of the option grants the buyer of the option the right, but not the obligation, to purchase from or sell to the writer a financial asset at a specified price within a specified period of time (or at a specified date).

- The option writer grants the option buyer the right to buy or sell a financial asset in exchange for the option price or option premium.

- The exercise or strike price is the price at which the financial asset may be bought or sold, and the expiration date is the date after which an option is void.

- A call option grants the buyer the right to purchase the financial asset; a put option buyer has the right to sell the financial asset to the writer.

- An option's exercise style specifies when the option buyer may exercise the option: an American option may be exercised at any time up to and including the expiration date and a European option may be exercised only at the expiration date.

- The maximum amount that an option buyer can lose is the option price, while there is substantial upside return potential.

- The option price reflects the option's intrinsic value and any additional amount over its intrinsic value.

- An option's time value or time premium is the amount of the option price that exceeds the intrinsic value.

- The intrinsic value of an option is the economic value of the option if it is exercised immediately; if no positive economic value will result from exercising immediately, then the intrinsic value is zero.

- The intrinsic value of a call option is the difference between the current price of the underlying asset and the exercise price if positive; it is otherwise zero.

- An at-the-money option has no intrinsic value; an out-of-the money option has no intrinsic value.

- The six factors that influence an option's price are (1) the current price of the underlying asset, (2) the exercise price, (3) the time to expiration of the option, (4) the expected price volatility of the underlying financial asset over the life of the option, (5) the short-term risk-free interest rate over the life of the option, and (6) anticipated cash payments on the underlying asset over the life of the option

- All other factors being equal, the greater the expected price volatility of the underlying financial asset, the more an investor would be willing to pay for the option and the more an option writer would demand for it.

- If the factors that have an impact on an option's value are known, its theoretical boundary conditions can be derived using arbitrage arguments.

- An option pricing model that uses a set of assumptions to derive a single theoretical price rather than a range.

- Several different option pricing models are used in practice, with the most popular one for valuing common stock being the Black-Scholes model.

- There is a wide array of more complex or exotic options available in the financial markets.

- Three types of options that are encountered in real options are a compound option, a rainbow option, and a barrier option.

- A compound option gives the option buyer the option to buy another option.

- With a rainbow option, there is more than one source of uncertainty.

- With barrier options, the option's value depends on whether or not the underlying asset has breached a predetermined barrier level (exercise price) sometime during the option's life.

- There are two types of barrier options: a knock-out option and knock-in option.

FURTHER READINGS

Clarke, Roger G., Harindra de Silva, and Steven Thorley, *Fundamentals of Futures and Options* (Charlottesville, VA: Research Foundation of the CFA Institute, 2013), chaps. 1 and 6.

Hull, John C., *Options, Futures, and Other Derivatives*, 9th ed. (Upper Saddle River, NJ: Prentice Hall, 2014), chaps. 1, 10, and 15.

Whaley, Robert E., *Derivatives: Markets, Valuation, and Risk Management* (Hoboken, NJ: John Wiley & Sons, 2006), chaps. 6–8.

16

METHODS FOR VALUING PRIVATE COMPANIES

In the valuation of a publicly traded company, an investor will employ well-known models to assess whether the stock price fairly reflects the economic value of the business. The investor will decide whether the price is fair, low, or high relative to the market price. In contrast, the valuation task confronting an investor such as an angel investor or a venture capital firm contemplating investing in a private company or an investment banker working with a private company to take it public is far more complex and challenging. The challenges faced are the selection of the standard of value, how to adjust reported financial information for valuation purposes, and how to select an appropriate valuation model and to estimate the inputs needed to implement the valuation model. Additional complexities are encountered when an investor must adjust these estimated values for the lack of liquidity of a private company. There is considerable debate regarding the magnitude of these liquidity discounts.

Valuation of a private company is needed for more than just acquiring funding from potential equity investors and determining the sale price for an initial public offering (IPO) or being acquired. In chapter 4, we explained how under Section 409a of the tax code it is necessary to determine the value of stock awards or options provided to founders and employees so as to mitigate the risk of adverse tax consequences (i.e., deferring taxes). Founders need a valuation for determining the buyout price to be paid to any member of the founding team who has decided to leave the company. In a divorce resolution involving a founding partner, a valuation is needed for determining the value of marital assets. For estate tax purposes, the death of a member of the founding team will prompt a valuation to determine the value of the founder's estate.

In this chapter we describe the methods for the valuation of a private company and the issues that arise in doing so. We begin with a discussion of the differences between public and private companies and their implications, and then discuss the different valuation methods that can be used and when they should be used based on the stage of a company's business development. Typically the most difficult valuations are those for early-stage,

This chapter is co-authored with Dr. Stanley Jay Feldman, chairman of Axiom Valuation Solutions.

pre-revenue companies. The various methods suggested by practitioners (angel investors and venture capitalists) for valuing pre-revenue companies are also described in this
chapter.

VALUATION OF PRIVATE VERSUS PUBLIC COMPANIES

There are two major differences between private and public firms. First, private companies are predominantly distinguished from public companies in that their securities do not
trade on national exchanges. Because a private company's underlying securities—common
stock, for example—are not routinely transacted, owners have little or no idea of the value
of their ownership at any point in time. Second, typically there is no or only very little separation between management and ownership of a private company (i.e., a private company
is a closely held company). Consequently, owners in their management of the company do
not have to answer to a board of directors in any meaningful sense, and as a result, they can
make decisions as they deem appropriate. Nor, as a general matter, do the owners have to
confer with minority (i.e., noncontrolling) shareholders about these decisions.

There are three ways in which these two major differences between private and public
companies influence the valuation of private companies. First, in the valuation of a private
company it is assumed that there is a hypothetical transaction in which the hypothetical
buyers and sellers are assumed to be fully informed about the nature of the risks and opportunities that characterize the hypothetical transaction.

Second, because this hypothetical transaction is not occurring in an organized-exchange
market, by definition, the number of buyers and sellers is limited, which results in a lack of
liquidity. Consequently, in estimating the value of a private company's securities, an investor must consider what suitable discount should be applied for the lack of marketability or
liquidity.

Finally, while the lack of marketability or liquidity reduces the value of a private
company, from an owner's perspective, the ownership value in a private company may
warrant a premium. This is because ownership typically is not widely dispersed, resulting
in the value of this ownership position always being worth more than the shares held by
minority owners. Generally speaking, a minority position in a company means less than
50% ownership. Since control confers further benefits on a company's owners, the value
of this position commands a value premium in relation to the shares owned by minority
owners. The difference in value is often referred to as the ***control premium***—control value
divided by minority value—or the minority discount (1 − Minority value/Control value).

THE STANDARD OF VALUE

Although there are exceptions, the standard of value applied in the valuation of private
companies is the ***fair market value*** (FMV). The U.S. Internal Revenue Service (IRS)
defines FMV the following way:

FMV is the price at which the property would change hands between a willing buyer and a willing seller when the former is not under any compulsion to buy and the latter is not under any compulsion to sell, both parties having reasonable knowledge of the relevant facts. Court decisions frequently state in addition that the hypothetical buyer and seller are assumed to be able, as well as willing to trade and to be well informed about the property and concerning the market for such property.[1]

The terms "fair value" and "fair market value" are often used interchangeably. Whereas the IRS uses FMV, financial accounting authorities such as the Financial Accounting Standards Board (FASB) use the term "fair value." The reason the FASB prefers this term is that FMV is associated with a large body of case law developed in the context of tax regulation. In addition, the FASB has developed a criterion that specifically defines the fair value standard, in contradistinction to FMV, and thus in most practical applications the differences between the standards are not material. Because our focus in this chapter is on the valuation of companies, we will use the FASB convention of using "fair value" to mean fair market value.

The concept of fair value is based on the price paid for an item by one party (the buyer) to another party (the seller) in a transaction between two unrelated parties. That is, it is an exchange-based concept whereby there is an orderly exchange between the two parties. (When the transaction is not characterized by an orderly exchange, another standard of value, described later, is used.) A transaction involving the financial securities of a private company is conceptually a hypothetical exchange at a given point in time, the *valuation date*. The price is the result of this hypothetical exchange and is therefore itself a hypothetical price, referred to as the *exit price*—the price that the buyer is willing to pay and the seller is willing to accept. The exit price is based on information that the two informed parties to the exchange would utilize to price the transacted instrument whose valuation is sought. This information would include the current and expected state of the economy and the industry segment in which the company operates, as well as a host of risk factors that would be used to evaluate the company's risk profile. One of these risk factors, which we describe later in this chapter, is the appropriate cost of capital that the company must pay to attract investors. It is the cost of capital that reflects both the business and the financial risks of the company.

This view of the pricing of a company's specific risk flies in the face of the well-developed (but unproven) theory in finance known as capital market theory. According to this theory, investors hold well-diversified portfolios such that the process of diversification in constructing their optimal portfolios will eliminate a company's specific risk. However, this is not the case if the marginal investor in a private firm is not well diversified, and so these investors require an incremental risk premium that reflects a company's unique risks.

1. IRS Revenue Ruling 59–60 (1959, p. CB237).

Other Standards of Value

There are standards of value other than fair value. They are

- orderly liquidation value,
- intrinsic value, and
- investment or strategic value.

Liquidation value is the probable price that would be obtained by the seller when the seller is forced to dispose of an item within a reasonable period of time and the market condition is orderly. By "orderly" we mean the seller retains the right to withdraw the item from the market for some defined period of time for the purpose of determining whether a higher price could be obtained from other market participants.

Intrinsic value embodies two components: the monetary value and personal preference value. An example is the stock certificate of a company that went bankrupt ten years ago and no longer has a legal existence. The stock certificate may have virtually no monetary value. However, it might be valuable to the heir of a family member who started the company or to a bankruptcy lawyer who worked on the proceedings early in his or her legal career. In this case, the stock certificate has no monetary value but has intrinsic value to an interested party.

Investment value, also referred to as *strategic value*, is a standard of value that represents the value placed on a company in excess of fair value on a stand-alone basis. This excess value arises in the acquisition of a company because the buyer (i.e., acquiring company) believes that when its own operations are combined with those of the company it is seeking to acquire, the buyer will be able to realize synergies as a result of the acquisition that would not be possible otherwise. For this reason, investment value is also referred to as strategic value. The potential synergies resulting from an acquisition are those in excess of the market-based synergies that would be included as part of fair value, such as buyers initiating improvements in productivity or negotiating cost reductions with key suppliers. An example of a non-market-based synergy that results in generating an excess value above an acquiring company's stand-alone fair value is when the acquirer has a unique distribution network through which the purchased firm's products and services can be sold. This then would result in a reduction in the marginal cost of sales, thereby giving the acquirer the potential to garner greater unit profit than a typical market buyer who does not have the distribution the acquirer's network could generate. Strategic value is typically used by the management of companies such as Google, Yahoo!, and Facebook to justify paying more than fair value for a company they acquire.

VALUATION METHODS

Two valuations are of interest: (1) the company's value, which is referred to as its *enterprise value*, and (2) the value of the company from the perspective of just its common shareholders (for illustration purpose, this chapter simplifies the equity structure and assumes there are only common shareholders), which is referred to as its *equity value*. Several methods have been proposed for valuing a private company. Basically, these methods fit one of the following four valuation models:

- asset-based method (cost method),
- income method (discounted cash flow method),
- market method (or method of comparables), or
- option-based method.

We describe each of these methods in the sections that follow.

ASSET-BASED METHOD

The *asset-based method* requires determining the fair value of every tangible and intangible asset (excluding goodwill) on the balance sheet. Aggregation of the fair values of identified assets less the fair value of current liabilities (excluding any short-term debt) gives the company's enterprise fair value. As explained in chapter 9, goodwill is an intangible asset. When the asset-based method is applied, goodwill is excluded because by construction, the asset-based method assumes that all value is allocated to the identifiable assets. Because of the difficulties of estimating intangible assets, the asset-based approach, when used, is used when the firm primarily consists of tangible assets and specific identifiable intangible assets such as patents and trademarks.

The underlying principle of the asset-based method is that each identified asset has a stand-alone value. For example, a truck with 40,000 miles on it will have a price that is far lower than the price of the same truck purchased new. There are active second-hand markets for a variety of tangible assets. This is also the case for patents and to a lesser extent for trademarks. In cases where there is no second-hand price information, value is often determined by calculating the cost of reproducing the asset in its current state. In these cases, one obtains the price of the asset when new and reduces it by an estimate of depreciation reflecting years in service and other factors such as technological obsolescence.

According to the American Institute of Certified Public Accountants (AICPA), the asset-based approach (using the replacement cost of the assets) has been applied primarily to value companies classified as being in stage 1 in table 1.1 in chapter 1 and some enterprises in stage 2.[2] The justification for using the asset-based approach is that the information needed to apply the income and market methods is limited because the company has virtually no financial history and so it is difficult to make any forecasts, or the company at the time of valuation may have a patent application pending despite not yet having developed a product. The asset-based method is typically not used once a company passes stage 2. The

2. American Institute of Certified Public Accountants, *Valuation of Privately-Held-Company Equity Securities Issued as Compensation: Accounting and Valuation Guide* (New York: AICPA, 2013).

reason is that the asset-based method assumes that the business is a collection of assets and the company has not generated any organic goodwill. Because most companies should be ongoing and established once they are beyond stage 2, it is assumed that they have sustainability, and that occurs in part because organic goodwill has been created. In contrast, the asset-based method may be appropriate when the company is in an early stage and has seed capital but little else.

INCOME METHOD

The *income method* involves the application of three important financial concepts: (1) the discounted value of future value, (2) free cash flow, and (3) the cost of capital. The income method then requires the following three steps:

Step 1: Project for each year the company's free cash flow.

Step 2: Determine the discounted value of the projected free cash flow for each year.

Step 3: Aggregate the discounted value of the projected free cash flow for each year to obtain the company's valuation as of the valuation date.

Note that although this valuation method is referred to as the "income" method, it is free cash flow that is used in the process, not net income after taxes. Although some methods that fall under the umbrella of the income method use different forms of adjusted income to project cash flows, the method described here is the most common method and is referred to as the *discounted cash flow method* or *DCF method.*

According to the AICPA, the income method typically is used to value later-stage companies (i.e., companies in stages 3 through 6) rather than early-stage companies. The reason is there is a greater probability that companies in later stages will have some financial history on which to base a forecast of future results. Although companies in stage 3 have little or no revenue, they typically have demonstrated proof of concept. Companies beyond stage 3 have revenue and a customer base, and are in a position to expand their presence in the market. Companies in stage 6 have established financial histories.

Free Cash Flow

The principle underlying the DCF method is that the valuation, whether it be for the entire company (enterprise value), the equity owners (equity valuation), or even for a project being considered by a company (as in the case of capital budgeting, described in the next chapter), should be based on the cash flow that is expected to be received from any investment. Valuation using the DCF method entails determining the sum of those expected cash flows adjusted to reflect the fact that they will be received in future periods. Consequently, equity valuation requires the projection of the cash flows that are expected to be received by common stockholders, whereas enterprise valuation requires the projection of the cash flows that are expected to be received by the company and therefore includes not only what would be received by common stockholders but also what would be received by creditors.

Several measures have been proposed in the valuation literature for measuring a company's cash flow. We have already discussed in previous chapters the concept of cash flow. For the purpose of valuation, using cash flow without any adjustment may be misleading because financial measures based on historical data fail to reflect the cash outflows that are necessary for the future existence of a company. An alternative measure of cash flow, known as free cash flow, was developed by Michael Jensen of Harvard University.[3] Broadly stated, *free cash flow* is the cash flow of the firm less the capital expenditures necessary to stay in business (i.e., replacing facilities as necessary) and grow at the expected rate (which requires an increase in working capital).

The perspective taken in this definition of free cash flow to equity is that of the shareholders because it is what remains for shareholders after the company makes necessary capital expenditures. Thus this definition of free cash flow is referred to as *free cash flow to equity* (FCFE). From the shareholders' perspective, any net borrowings that a company makes are available for shareholders, so net borrowings are often added to FCFE. The *net borrowings* item refers to the difference between any new debt issuance and any debt repayment. The projected FCFE for a given period is calculated as follows:

	Projected net operating profit after taxes
−	Projected change in capital expenditures
−	Projected after-tax interest
+	Projected change in net borrowings
=	Projected free cash flow to equity

The projected change in capital expenditures above includes two components. The first component is the change in net fixed capital, where net fixed capital is the difference between fixed capital and accumulated depreciation. The amount used in the expression above is the projected change in net fixed capital from one year to the next. This component measures how much the company must provide to maintain its operations over time. The second component is the change in working capital. Working capital is defined as the difference between current assets and current liabilities less short-term debt and the current portion of long-term debt. The projected change in the working capital is the change in working capital from one year to the next and measures how much working capital the company will need over time. Thus,

	Projected change in net fixed capital
+	Projected change in working capital
=	Projected change in capital expenditures

3. Michael Jensen, "Agency Costs of Free Cash Flow, Corporate Finance, and Takeovers," *American Economic Review* 76, no. 2 (1986): 323–329.

A broader perspective would consider the *free cash flow to the firm* (FCFF), which is FCFE with after-tax interest added and net borrowings subtracted. The after-tax interest is found by multiplying the interest expense by one minus the marginal tax rate. That is,

After-tax interest expense = Interest expense $\times$ (1 – Tax rate).

For example, if a firm that has a 40% tax rate is projected to have an interest expense in some year of $300,000, then the after-tax interest is computed as follows:

After-tax interest = $300,000 $\times$ (1 – 0.40) = $180,000.

The reason for adding after-tax interest to FCFE is that it produces a cash flow that indicates how much cash flow was available before paying suppliers of debt funding. FCFF therefore provides a measure of how much cash flow is available to all suppliers of capital, both common stockholders and creditors. The calculation of FCFF is as follows:

	Projected free cash flow to equity
–	Projected change in net borrowings
+	Projected after-tax interest
=	Free cash flow to the firm

When FCFF is used, the resulting valuation is the firm's enterprise value. When FCFE is used in a valuation, it yields the firm's *equity value*. Subtracting the market value of debt from the enterprise value gives the firm's equity value.

Valuation using cash flow FCFE and FCFF produces equivalent results if the inputs to each valuation are consistent. If the firm's capital structure (i.e., the relative amounts of equity and debt) is expected to change substantively over the projection period, both measures will yield results that are inconsistent with fair value.[4] The reason is that both values produced using these measures assume that the capital structure remains constant or, if it changes, that the changes will not materially affect the fair value estimate. In most cases, the assumption of a fixed capital structure is consistent with market participants' expectations. However, if the capital structure is expected to change radically over the projection period, as in the case of a highly leveraged firm whose debt percentage is expected to significantly decline, FCFE is the preferred free cash flow measure to use. In this approach, the firm is first valued as an all-equity firm; that is, the firm is valued as if it had no debt on its balance sheet. To this value is added the value of the firm's cost of debt (also known as the interest tax shield), which then yields the firm's enterprise value.

---

4. As explained earlier in this chapter, fair value is a financial reporting standard. Fair market value (FMV) and fair value, while technically different, are used interchangeably here.

Time Value of Money

In describing the valuation process, we stated that it is necessary to determine the "discounted" value of the future cash flow. What does that mean? The valuation of any of asset, whether it is a company, a financial instrument (stock or bond), an intangible asset (such as a patent), or a capital project, involves translating a future cash flow that is expected to be received to the present. Translating the value of a future cash flow to the present is referred to as *discounting the cash flow* or simply *discounting*.

Basically, discounting involves determining how much must be invested today to make that amount grow to a specific future value. That amount is referred to as the *discounted value*, or more commonly the *present value*. The future value itself is said to be an undiscounted value. The equation for the present value of any future value is a simple formula. We begin by asking how much an amount today if invested at some interest rate will grow to in the future.

If we let I denote the amount invested today, FV the future value, n the number of years when the future value is to be received, and i the interest rate that can be earned on the amount invested, then, allowing for annual compounding of interest, the following equation obtains:

$$FV = I (1 + i)^n. \tag{16.1}$$

For example, suppose that $185,116 is invested today for four years and assume that a 15% annual interest rate can be earned on the investment. Then we know that

$I = \$185,116$, $n = 4$, and $i = 0.15$.

Substituting these values into equation (16.1), we get

$FV = \$185,116 (1 + 0.15)^4 = \$323,769$.

That is, if $185,116 is invested today for four years earning an annual interest rate of 15%, then at the end of four years, that amount will grow to $323,769.

Notice two properties about the future value:

- For a given number of years for which the investment compounds, the higher the interest rate earned, the greater the future value is.

- For a given interest rate at which the amount can be invested, the greater the number of years the amount can be invested, the higher the future value is.

Present Value of a Future Value   The *present value of a future value,* or simply the *present value,* is the amount that has to be invested today at some interest rate that will make that amount grow to the future value. Looking at equation (16.1), we can see that the amount that must be invested today (i.e., the present value) to grow to the future value is just I in the equation. Therefore, solving for I in equation (16.1), we get

$I = FV/(1 + i)^n$.

And since I is the present value, we get the equation for the present value (PV):

$$PV = FV/(1 + i)^n. \tag{16.2}$$

The interest rate in the above formula is commonly referred to as the ***discount rate***. Saying that the present value is obtained by "discounting at some interest rate" is the same thing as saying "discounting at some discount rate."

For example, suppose $323,769 is expected to be received four years from now and the annual interest rate that can be earned on any amount invested today is 15%. Then we know that

FV = $323,769, $n = 4$, and $i = 0.15$.

Substituting these values into equation (16.2), we get

$PV = \$323,769/(1 + 0.15)^4 = \$185,116$.

Of course, this agrees with our earlier calculation, namely, that if $185,116 is invested today for four years at an annual interest rate of 15%, it will generate a future value of $323,769.

In equation (16.2), the value of $1/(1 + i)^n$ is referred to as the ***present value of $1***.

Note two properties of the present value:

- For a given number of years, the higher the discount rate earned, the lower the present value is.
- For a given discount rate, the further into the future that the future value will be received, the lower the present value is.

Present Value of a Series of Future Values What we have just explained is how to calculate the present value of a single future value to be received in the future. In practice, the valuation process involves more than one future value (i.e., a series of future values) that are expected to be received in the future. The process for determining the present value is straightforward. The present value for each future value must be calculated and then summed.

For example, suppose that the future value expected to be received from an asset for each of the next six years is as shown in the second column in table 16.1, with two future values shown in Year 6 for a reason explained later in this chapter. Notice that the sum of the future values is $7,714,182. This sum, which reflects the future values ignoring the time

Table 16.1
Calculation of Present Value of a Series of Future Values

Year	Future Value	Present Value of $1 at 15%	Present Value	Present Value of $1 at 25.25%	Present Value
1	$466,237	$0.8696	$405,423	$0.7984	$372,245
2	516,963	0.7561	390,898	0.6374	329,537
3	606,211	0.6575	398,594	0.5089	308,525
4	671,528	0.5718	383,948	0.4063	272,868
5	710,145	0.4972	353,068	0.3244	230,387
6	724,280	0.4323	313,126	0.2590	187,603
6	4,018,818	0.4323	1,737,446	0.2590	1,040,955
Total	$7,714,182		3,982,503		$2,742,121

value of money (i.e., not discounting), is the undiscounted value. The third column shows the future value of $1 assuming a discount rate of 15%. The fourth column is the present value of each year's future value using a discount rate of 15% and found by multiplying the present value of $1 at 15% by the corresponding future value. The sum of the present values, $3,982,503, is the present value of all the future values.

The last three columns of table 16.1 shows the same calculation but assuming a discount rate of 25.25%. The present value of the future values in this case is $2,742,121. This agrees with the property for the present value noted above: the higher the discount rate, the lower the present value is.

Present Value of an Amount in Perpetuity Before leaving the present value concept, there are two more very simple formulas to discuss because, as will be seen later, they are typically used in valuation when applying the DCF method. Suppose that an asset is expected to provide the same after-tax cash flow forever (i.e., in perpetuity). How does one obtain the present value of such an asset? It turns out that the formula is simply the amount to be received in perpetuity divided by the discount rate. The present value of such a cash flow stream is given by

$$PV \text{ (in perpetuity, constant amount)} = \text{After-tax cash flow}/i. \tag{16.3}$$

Suppose, for example, that $100,000 is expected to be received in perpetuity and the discount rate is 15%. Then the present value is given by

$$PV \text{ (in perpetuity, constant amount)} = \$100,000/0.15 = \$666,667.$$

Rather than assume that the same amount will be received in perpetuity, suppose that the amount is expected to grow by a certain percentage per year. The formula for the present value of an amount that is assumed to grow at a rate of g per year (where the growth rate is assumed to be less than the discount rate) is

$$PV = \text{After-tax cash flow} \times (1 + g)/(i - g). \tag{16.4}$$

Considering our $100,000 perpetuity and a 15% discount rate, if the growth rate of the amount to be received per year is expected to be 5%, then the present value is

$$PV = (\$100,000(1 + 0.05))/(0.15 - 0.05) = \$1,050,000.$$

In practice, the reason for needing to understand the present value of future payments in perpetuity in valuation is that often future cash flow payments are projected for a specified number of years and then at the end of that time period the asset is assumed to have some value, which is referred to as its **terminal value**. What is assumed in modeling is that the terminal value is a perpetuity where the expected after-tax cash flow in that future year is the starting cash flow for the perpetuity calculation. For example, look again at table 16.1, where two future values for Year 6 are shown. The second of the two future values is there because it reflects an assumed terminal value, which we will explain later in this chapter. Suppose the future values in column 2 assume that the terminal value at the end of Year 6 is $4,018,818. That amount must then be discounted to determine the present value as of Year 0.

While it may seem that the assumption of expected cash flows to be received far into the future may be subject to considerable forecasting error, particularly when the expected cash flows are highly uncertain, as in the case of a firm with little history to go on, this uncertainty is typically adjusted for by applying a high discount rate to the uncertain cash flows to calculate their present values and thereby mitigating the inherent risk associated with this process. For example, $100,000 that may be projected for a cash flow fifteen years from now will have a present value of only $12,289 if the discount rate is 15% and $4,237 if the discount rate is 23.46%.

Midyear Convention in Computing Present Value   There is one more nuance that is important in discounting future values. In the calculations in table 16.1, it is assumed that the future cash flows will be received at the end of the year. That is, in equation (16.2), n is an integer. In reality, future cash flows from an asset are distributed over the year, not necessarily at year end. To adjust the discounting process to reflect the future cash flows being received throughout the year, we apply the **midyear convention.** This convention assumes that instead of a future cash flow being received at year end, it is received in the middle of year. The adjustment to equation (16.2) for the present value is found by reducing the number of years from n to $(n - 0.5)$, as shown below:

$$PV = FV/(1 + i)^{(n - 0.5)}. \tag{16.5}$$

Table 16.2
Calculation of Present Value of a Series of Future Values Using the Midyear Convention

Year	Future Value	Present Value of $1 at 15%	Present Value	Present Value of $1 at 25.25%	Present Value
1	$466,237	$0.9325	$434,768	$0.8935	$416,599
2	516,963	0.8109	419,191	0.7134	368,801
3	606,211	0.7051	427,444	0.5696	345,286
4	671,528	0.0.6131	411,739	0.4548	305,381
5	710,145	0.5332	378,623	0.3631	257,838
6	724,280	0.4636	335,791	0.2899	209,956
6	4,018,818	0.4636	1,863,203	0.2899	1,164,986
Total	$7,714,182		$4,270,759		$3,068,848

Table 16.2 shows the calculation of the present value of the same series of future values shown in table 16.1 but using the midyear convention. The present value of the future value series using the midyear convention is $4,270,759 if the discount rate is 15% and $3,068,848 if the discount rate is 25.25%.

Cost of Capital

So far we know the following regarding valuation: (1) what the appropriate measure that should be used in valuation (i.e., free cash flow) is and (2) how to discount future cash flows (i.e., how to calculate the present value of the projected free cash flow). The last concept to understand in the DCF method is determining the appropriate discount rate for discounting the projected free cash flow.

The appropriate discount rate to use in valuing a company's expected free cash flow is the company's *cost of capital*. The reason is that this is the rate of return that is required by the suppliers of long-term capital to the company—creditors and stockholders. Therefore, for a company that finances its operations or investments using both debt and equity, the cost of capital includes not only the explicit interest on the debt (i.e., borrowings) but also the implicit minimum return that stockholders would require. This minimum return to stockholders is necessary so that stockholders maintain their investment in the company.

The cost of each source of capital must reflect the risk of the assets in which the company invests. A company that invests in assets that investors perceive as having little risk will be able to obtain capital at a lower cost than a company that investors believe invests in high-risk assets. Another way of saying this is that a company's whose assets are expected to generate cash flows that are risky will have to pay a higher cost to raise capital than a company whose assets are expected to generate cash flows that have less risk. Hence the link between the cost of capital and the riskiness associated with what we want to value, free cash flow. Recall that the discounted value and the value of expected future cash flows have an inverse relationship: the higher the discount rate, the lower is the discounted value. Consequently, the higher the cost of capital (which reflects greater risk associated with a company's expected future cash flows), the lower is the valuation. For this reason, one would expect the cost of capital to be related to the stage of business development of a company. The more milestones a company has reached (i.e., the later the stage of its business development), the lower is the cost of capital.

Moreover, the cost of each source of capital reflects the hierarchy of the risk associated with its seniority over the other sources in the capital structure. For a given company, the cost associated with funding that is obtained by incurring debt is less than the cost from preferred stock, which in turn is less than the cost from common stock. This is because creditors have seniority over preferred stockholders, who have seniority over common stockholders. If the company has difficulties meeting its obligations, the creditors receive their promised interest and principal before the preferred stockholders, who in turn receive their contractual dividends and principal before the common stockholders receive anything. Common shareholders are residual claimants on the firm's cash flow. The preference in the case of a Chapter 7 bankruptcy (i.e., the liquidation of a company) is the same as just described for meeting interest and dividend payments. For a startup company that has Series A financing in the form of convertible preferred stock, the cost of preferred stock will reflect the extent of participation in liquidation proceeds, as explained in chapter 7 of this book. Consequently, for a given firm, debt is less risky than preferred stock, which is less risky than common stock. Therefore, preferred shareholders require a greater return than creditors and common stockholders require a greater return than preferred stockholders.

The estimation of a company's cost of capital involves first determining the cost of each source of capital that it is expected the owners will use to finance the business, along with the relative amounts of each source of capital it is expected the company will raise. Basically, this means that the estimated cost of capital is based on an assumed capital structure (i.e., the proportion of debt, preferred stock, and common stock). Estimation of a company's cost of capital entails three steps:

Step 1: Determine the proportions of each source from which capital is to be raised (i.e., determine the capital structure).

Step 2: For each source of financing, determine its cost (i.e., determine how much that supplier of capital will want for providing funds to the company).

Step 3: Calculate the weighted average of these costs by multiplying the costs obtained in step 2 for each source of capital by the proportion of the source obtained in step 1 and then summing the values.

The resulting rate is called the ***weighted average cost of capital*** (WACC).[5]

---

5. WACC is based on the after-tax costs of financing. Since the interest rate on debt is quoted on a before-tax cost basis, it must be placed on an after-tax cost basis when calculating the WACC. No adjustment needs to be made to the costs of common and preferred equity since these are based on after-tax return measures.

To make sure we understand what is meant by a company's capital structure, let's use an illustration. Suppose that the founders have used a capital structure that consists of 20% debt, 25% preferred stock, and 55% common stock. That means that in the future, if the capital structure is kept constant, every $100 of additional funding will consist of $20 of debt, $25 of preferred stock, and $55 of common stock.

It is important to note here the difference between preferred stock as used for a mature company and the preferred stock we described in chapter 7 as used by venture capitalists and some angel investors for early seed financing. The preferred stock used in early seed financing is convertible preferred stock. As a startup matures, the preferred stockholders will convert their shares to common stock. Consequently, in our discussion of the capital structure, we will ignore preferred stock in computing the cost of capital for a startup since the type of preferred stock used will eventually be converted to common stock. Moreover, preferred stock is not commonly used by mature nonfinancial firms, so we will ignore it to simplify our discussion.

The decision regarding a company's capital structure is a critical one that the founders must make. Financial theory offers a good deal of guidance for how a founder might want to think about obtaining an "optimal" capital structure. In practice, determining an optimal capital structure is difficult. In the estimation of a company's cost of capital, the assumption is that the current capital structure (or something close to it) will be similar to its historical capital structure, so long as the founders have access to debt funding.

When the WACC of a publicly traded company is sought, information about the company's capital structure reported on the balance sheet does not reflect the market values of the company's debt or equity. The market value of common stock can be obtained from public trades and the number of shares of common stock outstanding.

The cost of debt can be approximated by looking at how the prices of different bonds issued by the company trade in the market. The problem becomes much more complicated for a private company, particularly for common stock. Certain methods, described later, can be used to get a good feel for the market value of debt. However, if we want to figure out what the percentage of common stock is in the capital structure, we need to know the market value of the common stock. Therein lies the problem: it is common stock whose value we seek to determine.

So in practice, in the valuation of private companies, no attempt is made to measure the market value of debt and common stock. Instead, relative weights that would be appropriate for the startup in the future are assumed.

Given an assumed capital structure, the next step is to compute the cost of what we are assuming the two components of the capital structure will be: debt and common stock.

Estimating the Cost of Debt Like public firms, most private firms have debt on their balance sheet. Yet the cost of debt that was raised during different time periods reflects credit market conditions at those times and is not necessarily what the cost of new debt financing

Table 16.3
U.S. Federal Corporate Tax Rates: 2014

Taxable Income Over	Taxable Income Not Over	Tax Rate
$0	$50,000	15%
50,000	75,000	25%
75,000	100,000	34%
100,000	335,000	39%
335,000	10,000,000	34%
10,000,000	15,000,000	35%
15,000,000	18,333,333	38%
18,333,333		35%

with different maturities would be. This cost can be approximated by undertaking a credit analysis of the firm using traditional credit analysis or using some statistical method.

Traditional credit analysis involves assessing the risk that the issuer will default by undertaking an economic analysis of the issuer's ability to meet its obligations, the protections afforded creditors provided by covenants (i.e., restrictions) imposed on the firm's management, and the collateral available to creditors to satisfy the debt obligation should the issuer fail to meet its contractual payments.[6] The product of traditional credit analysis is an internal rating that can then be used to assign a credit rating to the firm. Based on the credit rating and the term to maturity, a cost of debt can be estimated.

Instead of traditional credit analysis, statistical models can be used to estimate the credit rating or its equivalent, which in turn can be used to estimate the cost of debt. These credit scoring models include discriminant analysis, contingent claims analysis, and artificial intelligence systems such as expert systems and neural networks. In appendix B, we describe a popular statistical model for estimating the cost of equity, the linear discriminant model, and apply it to determine the cost of debt in our case study.

There is an adjustment that must be made in estimating the cost of debt owing to the tax treatment of interest. The U.S. tax code allows a company to deduct from taxable income the interest it pays on debt. Thus, how much a company pays its lenders is not reflected in a company's cost of borrowing. The cost has to be adjusted for the marginal tax rate that the company pays. The marginal tax rate is the tax rate on the next dollar of a company's taxable income. In the United States the corporate tax structure in 2014 was as shown in table 16.3. So, for example, the marginal tax rate for an early-stage firm that had $5 million in taxable income in 2014 was 34%.

---

6. For a further discussion of corporate credit analysis, see Frank J. Fabozzi, *Bond Markets, Analysis and Strategies*, 9th ed. (Upper Saddle River, NJ: Pearson, 2015), chap. 22.

The reason for the focus on the marginal tax rate is that in calculating the cost of debt, we are interested in determining how the interest deduction changes the amount of taxes paid. For example, suppose that before considering interest expense an early-stage corporation has taxable income of $5 million and faces a marginal tax rate of 34%. Its taxes would be $1.7 million (34% × $5 million). Suppose the startup corporation's interest expense on debt is $1 million. Then the taxable income is reduced from $5 million to $4 million and the taxes would then be $1.36 million (34% × $4 million). Thus, taxes are reduced as a result of the interest expense of $1 million from $1.7 million to $1.36 million, or by $0.34 million. The amount of taxes by which the interest expense is reduced is referred to as the *tax shield*.

In general, the after-tax cost of debt can be calculated as follows, given the pre-tax cost of debt and the marginal tax rate:

After-tax cost of debt = Pre-tax cost of debt × (1 − Marginal tax rate).

For example, if the pre-tax cost of debt is estimated to be 8% and the company is in the 34% marginal tax rate, then

After-tax cost of debt = 8% × (1 − 0.34) = 5.28%.

Estimating the Cost of Common Stock   Estimating the cost of common stock is more difficult than estimating the cost of debt and entails the following steps:

Step 1: Identifying the risk factors for which investors want to be compensated when investing in a company's common stock

Step 2: For each risk factor identified in step 1, providing a financial metric to quantify that risk factor.

Step 3: For the financial metric for each risk factor formulated in step 2, estimating the risk for the company.

These steps are not simple to do. Moreover, some of the financial metrics that are used as proxies for risk require market information to compute that might not be available for the startup companies whose cost of common stock we wish to estimate.

Financial theory does provide suggestions for the risks that investors want to be compensated for when taking a position in common stock. The models that are used are called *asset pricing models*. In general, asset pricing models have the following form:

Expected equity return =

Risk-free rate + β_1 (market risk premium for risk factor 1) + … + β_K (market risk premium for risk factor K).

In words, the return on equity that an investor should expect is the sum of the risk-free rate (i.e., the interest rate that can be earned on a risk-free security such as a short-term U.S. Treasury security) plus compensation for each of the K risk factors. There are two elements of the risk factor. The first is the betas (β_i's), which represent the estimated quantity of risk factor i that the stock exposes the investor, and the second is the estimated compensation for risk factor i that the market requires for accepting the risk (i.e., the market risk premium for the risk factor i).

The link between the expected equity return and the cost of equity that we seek for estimating the cost of capital is that the former is the appropriate measure for the latter. But look at how difficult it is to estimate the expected equity return! The unknowns are the risk factors, the number of risk factors, and the market risk premium for each risk factor. Financial theory provides various asset pricing models, which we describe in the case study in appendix B.

Determining the Value of a Private Company

We now have an understanding of the concepts of free cash flow (i.e., FCFE and FCFF), the time value of money (i.e., the discounting process), and the cost of capital (i.e., the weighted average cost of capital, WACC). We also know the issues associated with their calculation. Now we can estimate the enterprise value and the equity value of a private company using the DCF method.

This is done by completing the following steps to compute the enterprise value:

Step 1: Project for each year the company's projected free cash flow.

Step 2: Determine the discounted value of the projected free cash flow to the firm for each year using as the discount rate the WACC.

Step 3: Aggregate the discounted value of the projected free cash flow for each year to obtain the enterprise value.

Once these three steps are completed, the result is what we term the firm's operating enterprise value. This value is the value of the firm prior to adjustments for liquidity, or its preliquidity enterprise value, and any cash on the balance sheet that is in excess of the firm's cash operating needs. Adding excess cash to the operating enterprise value yields the firm's preliquidity enterprise value.[7] We describe the issue of excess cash below and the discount for liquidity later in this chapter. By following the next two steps, we obtain the *enterprise value including excess cash*:

Step 4: Determine any excess cash flow that is on the current balance sheet.

Step 5: Add any excess cash found in step 4 to the amount in step 3 to obtain the enterprise value including excess cash.

---

7. Not to belabor this point, but it should be kept in mind that enterprise value can be calculated as the sum of operating working capital (e.g., inventory plus receivables less payables), tangible and intangible assets, and goodwill, which is equal to equity plus debt. Hence any liquidity adjustment to equity and debt implies that the asset side of the balance sheet is also adjusted accordingly. Thus enterprise value after liquidity adjustment is equal to liquidity-adjusted equity plus liquidity-adjusted debt.

To obtain the equity value, it is necessary to reduce the enterprise value including cash, found in step 5 by the value of debt, since that portion of the enterprise value does not belong to the common stockholders. Thus, to compute the equity value, we start with step 5 and do the following:

Step 6: Estimate the value of debt.

Step 7: Subtract the amount in step 6 from the amount in step 5 to obtain the equity value.

We explain how to estimate the market value of debt below. The problem with the equity value as found in step 7 is that it does not consider the discount for liquidity. Given an estimated discount for liquidity, the *liquidity-adjusted equity value* can be determined. Therefore,

Step 8: Estimate the discount for liquidity for (8a) equity and (8b) debt.

Step 9: Subtract the amount in step 8a from the equity value computed in step 7 to obtain the liquidity-adjusted equity value and then subtract the amount in step 8b from the value in step 6.

Finally, to obtain a *liquidity-adjusted enterprise value with excess cash*, the following step must be performed:

Step 10: Subtract from step 5 the amount in step 8, which adjusts the enterprise value, with excess cash for the liquidity discounts.

Determining Any Excess Cash on the Balance Sheet   A company needs cash as part of its working capital in order to operate. However, it is not unusual for private companies to have excess cash buildup on the balance sheet. This is particularly the case for C corporations, whose excess cash is taxed at the stockholder level when it is distributed. If the firm has a pass-through tax status—S corporations, partnerships, and limited liability corporations, for example—there is no additional tax burden, and so there is often less excess cash on the balance sheet of these firms than on the balance sheet of their C corporation counterparts.[8]

In general, any excess cash on the current balance sheet belongs to the common stockholders and should be included in both the equity value and the enterprise value. Thus, for proper valuation, it is necessary to determine whether there is any excess cash. In practice, it is common to estimate the amount of cash needed by determining the cash needs based on the firm's revenue. For example, suppose that the cash needs of a firm are estimated to be 5% of its revenue and that the current year's revenue is $4,526,341. Thus the amount of cash needed for operations is $226,317 ($4,526,341 × 0.05). Any amount on the current balance sheet cash and cash equivalent item(s) in excess of that amount is excess cash.

---

8. The tax treatment of corporations is explained in chapter 3.

Estimating the Preliquidity Value of Debt A firm's preliquidity equity value is its estimated enterprise value reduced by the value of debt. Therefore, to obtain a firm's equity value, the market value of debt must be estimated. This is done using the following four steps:

Step 1: Estimate the credit rating of the debt.

Step 2: Estimate the maturity of the current debt on the firm's balance sheet.

Step 3: Based on the maturity of the debt and the credit spreads in place at the valuation date, estimate the pre-tax cost of debt as the sum of the risk-free rate for the given maturity plus the credit spread for that maturity.

Step 4: Based on step 3, discount the interest expense and principal repayments over the maturity of the debt.

Keep in mind that this value is not liquidity adjusted. We will see in appendix B how to estimate the credit risk rating of the debt using a statistical model and how to calculate the cost of debt.

Limitations of the Discounted Cash Flow Method

The DCF method is based on reasonable economic principles. The problem lies in the implementation. We explained all of the estimates needed to obtain the enterprise value and the equity value. If the estimated inputs are misestimated, the valuations will not reflect a reasonable fair value.

The major criticism has to do with estimating the future benefits that arise from the managerial flexibility that may be embedded in the firm's existing assets to allow management to take advantage of various opportunities that may arise in the future. It is argued that under certain circumstances, the estimated free cash flow as computed under the DCF method underestimates future benefits and therefore underestimates enterprise value and equity value. An approach that addresses this drawback is the real options approach, briefly mentioned later but described in more detail in chapter 18.

MARKET METHOD

The market method entails identifying ***comparable companies*** to the company whose valuation is being sought, and so this method is also referred to as the ***method of comparables***. The companies used in the analysis, also referred to as ***peer companies***, can be publicly traded companies or, for purposes of valuation, private firms that have transacted at or near the valuation date. As with the income method, the market method is appropriate for companies in stages 3 through 6 of business development. According to the AICPA, the identification of comparable companies with readily determinable fair values is unlikely for companies in earlier stages.

The method of comparables falls into two general categories: guideline public company analysis and guideline transactions analysis.

Guideline Public Company Analysis

Comparability is a matter of degree. Companies included in the group of comparable companies fall into two categories: clone companies and guideline companies. ***Clone companies***, the most desirable of the two types for obvious reasons, generally are companies that are very close in asset size and revenue, have close to the same cost structure, operate in the same industry segment, produce equivalent products and services, have equivalent capital structures (i.e., use the same percentage of debt), and have virtually identical expected revenue and profit growth opportunities.

Guideline companies are those that have several but not all of the characteristics of the company whose valuation is sought. In practice, clone companies are typically not readily available, and therefore in performing a valuation one is forced to use data from guideline companies. Given the guideline companies in the group of comparable companies, as we explain later in this chapter, a multiple is a financial metric to obtain a company's valuation using the market method. Since the multiple is based on the trades in the common stock of guideline companies, the multiple is referred to as the "trading multiple." However, because one is dealing with guideline companies, not clone companies, guideline valuation using a trading multiple of some financial metric requires an estimated valuation multiple based on both guideline information and the unique characteristics of the private firm being valued.

The application of the guideline market method is based on multiples of some suitable financial ratio. Once a suitable financial ratio is identified and, based on findings for comparable companies, a reasonable value for that ratio is determined, a valuation can be determined as follows. Suppose that a suitable ratio, that is, the multiple (M), is determined as the ratio of equity value to free cash flow. Then, given the free cash flow of the private company whose valuation is sought, the equity value is the product of free cash flow and M. Keep in mind that this simple multiplication is not a valuation model but a valuation metric. Put differently, M is really telling us what the relationship of free cash flow in this case is to equity value. It is a way to "normalize" equity values of different firms so that they can be compared. Generally the M for each firm will be different, and these differences are generally related to multiple factors. For example, if the M of firm 1 is larger than the M of firm 2 in the same industry, this may mean that expected growth in free cash flow is greater in firm 1 or that firm 1 is less risky; in either case it is assigned a lower cost of capital by investors.

Financial Ratios Used for Multiples   Various financial ratios have been proposed as suitable multiples. When the goal is to estimate the equity value, for the three most common ratios the numerator is the equity value and the denominator is a measure that serves as a proxy for values that apply to equity investors. These values include free cash flow and two measures described in considerable detail in chapter 12, net income and the book value of equity. That is,

$$\frac{\text{Equity value}}{\text{Net income}}$$

and

$$\frac{\text{Equity value}}{\text{Book value of equity}} .$$

Once an M is accepted, the equity value is found by multiplying the measured used to obtain M (either free cash flow, net income, or book value of equity) by the accounting measure used. For example, if the ratio of equity value to net income is estimated to be 5 (i.e., $M = 5$) and the company whose equity value is sought has a net income of $2 million, the equity value is $10 million (= 5 × $2 million).

One of the complications in estimating equity value using one of the above financial ratios is that comparable firms are likely have substantial differences in their amount of financial leverage and growth rates, requiring an adjustment of the ratios. We discuss this later.

When the valuation being sought is the enterprise value, the numerator is the enterprise value. The denominator is some measure of value to all investors (common stockholders and creditors), with the three most popular measures being revenue, earnings before interest and taxes (EBIT), and earnings before interest, taxes, depreciation, and amortization (EBITDA). (The latter two measures are explained in chapter 10.) Thus the following financial ratios have been suggested:

$$\frac{\text{Enterprise value}}{\text{Revenue}} ,$$

$$\frac{\text{Enterprise value}}{\text{EBIT}} ,$$

and

$$\frac{\text{Enterprise value}}{\text{EBITDA}} .$$

Adjusting for Growth   It is important to remember in any business valuation that wide variation in firm size and in the values of relevant financial variables across firms within the same industry is not uncommon. Firms in the same business segment are often at different stages of their business life cycle, and thus one can expect that reported financial performance and the various financial ratios that we described in chapter 12 will show sizable variation from firm to firm. These variations aside, what is important when applying the market approach is that the target firm and comparable firms face similar systematic risks. If this is the case, as it is in the valuation of startup companies, then we can combine multiple data from comparable firms and the target firm's unique characteristics to calculate a "shadow" multiple for the target firm, a multiple that an informed investor would use to value the target.

To see how the required adjustment is done, we proceed by applying a valuation model commonly used in finance called the **Gordon-Shapiro constant growth model**.[9] The formula for this model turns out to be an application of the future value of an annuity as given by equation (16.4). Applying equation (16.4) to obtain the Gordon-Shapiro constant growth rate model, the inputs would be as follows:

g = assumed growth in net operating profit after taxes (NOPAT);

i = discount rate, which in this model is the WACC;

CF = amount to be received each year, which in this model is NOPAT; and

PV = enterprise value.

Substituting the values into equation (16.4), we get

$$\text{Enterprise value} = \frac{\text{NOPAT}\ (1+g)}{(\text{WACC}-g)}. \tag{16.6}$$

By dividing both sides of equation (16.6) by revenue, we can get the following for the financial metric that relates the enterprise value to the revenue:

$$\frac{\text{Enterprise value}}{\text{Revenue}} = \frac{\text{NOPAT}}{\text{Revenue}\ (\text{WACC}-g)} \times (1+g). \tag{16.7}$$

As can we can see from equation (16.7), the multiple for the financial metric of enterprise value to revenue is adjusted based on the current NOPAT margin, expected growth of NOPAT, and the company's WACC.

Also, note that once a set of comparable companies is available, equation (16.7) can be used to obtain an implied growth rate, g. This is done by solving the equation for g to obtain the following:

$$\text{Implied } g = \frac{\left(\dfrac{\text{Enterprise value}}{\text{Revenue}} \times \text{WACC}\right) - \dfrac{\text{NOPAT}}{\text{Revenue}}}{\dfrac{\text{Enterprise value}}{\text{Revenue}} + \dfrac{\text{NOPAT}}{\text{Revenue}}}. \tag{16.8}$$

9. Myron J. Gordon and Eli Shapiro, "Capital Equipment Analysis: The Required Rate of Profit," *Management Science* 3, no. 1 (October 1956): 102–110, and Myron J. Gordon, *The Investment, Financing, and the Valuation of the Corporation* (Homewood, IL: Richard D. Irwin, 1962).

For example, suppose that for some comparable company, the inputs for equation (16.8) are as follows:

$$\frac{\text{Enterprise value}}{\text{Revenue}} = 11.51;$$

$$\text{WACC } 19.12\% = 0.1912;$$

$$\frac{\text{NOPAT}}{\text{Revenue}} = 5.81\% = 0.0581.$$

Substituting these values into equation (16.8), we get

$$\text{Implied } g = \frac{(11.51 \times 0.1912) - = 0.0581}{11.51 + 0.0581} = 0.1852 = 18.52\%.$$

That is, for this comparable, the implied growth rate is 18.52%.

What does this actually mean? The way to think about this is that the growth reflected is the geometric average growth over an extended period of time. So in a startup case one might expect the growth in NOPAT to be over 100% a year for the next two years and then begin leveling off over the next eight years such that the geometric average of these annual growth rates over a ten-year period is 18.52%. When one backs out long-term growth rates for publicly traded firms, it is not unusual to find that even for firms in the same industry or the same segment within an industry, implied firm growth rates are materially different. What this indicates is that industry and segment classification is a necessary but not a sufficient condition to explain firm valuation. Unique firm characteristics will in most cases make a difference.

Financial Accounting Adjustments   In addition to the complication of identifying comparable companies and adjusting for differences in growth, it is necessary to adjust the financial metrics used in the analysis for differences in accounting treatments that we describe in chapters 9, 10, and 11.

Guideline Transactions Analysis

In addition to public firm comparables, valuation multiples indicated by transactions involving the sale of comparable companies can often provide meaningful input into a fair value analysis of a closely held company. Rather than using market trading data, this method, referred to as guideline transactions analysis or the precedent transactions method, uses transactions that have occurred in the recent past for similar firms. That is, when a company is sold to another company, the price paid by the acquiring company can be used as a benchmark for determining the enterprise value of the private company whose valuation is sought.

The concern with this method is that the transaction price may reflect a value that might not be the fair value but the strategic value to the acquiring firm, as explained in chapter 13. However, guideline transactions analysis provides two key pieces of information that can be used in estimating the value of a private company. It provides information not just about the multiples paid in the startup company's industry but also about the premium that investors are willing to pay in order to obtain control of a company (referred to as the "control premium"). Thus, analyzing recent acquisitions using guideline transactions analysis provides a perspective on the premium paid to gain control. The control premium found will result in a multiple that is typically greater than the trading multiples found using the comparable company method.

OPTION-BASED METHOD

One drawback to valuing early-stage technology companies using the income method is that it fails to take into account the flexibility offered to management of technology platforms that have not been brought to market yet (i.e., have not been commercialized). Even for startups with technology platforms that have realized a few applications, the income method is inadequate because it does not consider the venture's opportunity to expand into different areas. Basically, certain technology platforms offer management the flexibility or "option" to expand into other applications. How does one quantify in a company's valuation this flexibility or option available to management? This can be done by using an approach developed in finance and known as *real options valuation*, which applies the option pricing method. This approach to company valuation, referred to as the option-based method, is discussed in chapter 18.

VALUATION OF PRE-REVENUE AND POSITIVE EARNINGS STARTUP FIRMS

The most difficult valuations are early-stage companies in stages 1 and 2. Such startup firms are referred to as pre-revenue startup companies or pre-earnings startup companies. As noted earlier, although the appropriate valuation method might be asset-based valuation, this typically is not done. Some academics believe that the other methods described earlier can be used if an investor is willing to put in the necessary time to analyze the company. However, investors such as angels and venture capitalists have proposed methods to estimate the pre-money value of pre-revenue-startup companies seeking funding in the absence of financial data on which to apply the other valuation methods. Pre-money valuation means a company's value prior to a round of financing. These proposed valuation methods are creative ways to compensate for the lack of financial data and inputs needed in the other valuation methods described above.

Pre-revenue startup company valuation methods have been put forth by academics specializing in the valuation of pre-revenue startup companies, with subsequent refinements by investors to the original proposal; as well, some methods have been proposed by well-known angel investors and venture capitalists. The more popular methods for valuing pre-revenue startup companies are the venture capital method, the scorecard method, the Berkus method, and the risk factor summation method. We briefly describe each of these methods below. The last three methods are based purely on an analysis in which dollar values are assigned according to the various risks associated with a startup company that the investor views as having been eliminated or mitigated by the founders as of the valuation date.[10] All four methods have been used as starting points for negotiations between founders and suppliers of capital to pre-revenue startup companies, such as angel groups and venture capitalists.

Venture Capital Method

One of the more popular methods for the valuation of pre-revenue startup companies is the venture capital (VC) method. The approach was first suggested in a Harvard Business School case study by William Sahlman.[11] An important assumption in applying the VC method is that no additional equity financing will occur in the future. Although modifications of the method have been proposed to attempt to deal with this unrealistic assumption, here we describe only the basic model.

The application of this method begins with forecasting the future revenue at the exit date. The exit date can be as short as four years and as long as eight years. This is not a simple forecasting task insofar as what is being sought is the valuation of a pre-revenue company. With a figure assigned to the forecasted revenue at the exit date, the next step is to estimate what the after-tax earnings rate will be. This estimate can be obtained using data from the industry of the target company. Then the forecasted earnings at the exit date can be formalized as follows:

Forecasted earnings at the exit date = Forecasted revenue at exit date × After-tax profit margin.

Now that we have the forecasted earnings at the exit date, we can apply the market method to get the forecasted terminal value at the exit date by identifying comparable companies or comparable transactions. The market method provides the multiple at which the comparable companies trade over earnings. The metric used in this case is the price/earnings (PE) ratio. So, for example, if a comparable publicly traded company with earnings after taxes of $100 million sells in the market for $1.5 billion, the PE ratio (or multiple) is 15. If a target company has forecasted earnings at the exit date, then the target company's forecasted terminal value at the exit date is simply found by multiplying that value by the PE ratio. That is,

---

10. In appendix B where we explain a critical input needed to apply the income method, a company's cost of capital, we use a similar approach of identifying firm-specific risk and assign weights based on the investor's assessment of those risks.

11. William A. Sahlman, "The Venture Capital Method," *Harvard Business School Case #9–288–006,* 1987, and William A. Sahlman, "The Basic Venture Capital Formula," *Harvard Business School note* 9–804–042, revised May 13, 2009.

Forecasted terminal value at the exit date = Forecasted earnings at the exit date ×
Assumed PE ratio.

Bear in mind that the forecasted terminal value is as of the exit date, not today (the day of valuation). Earlier we said that values to be received in the future must be discounted. This is where the time value of money, discussed earlier, needs to be introduced. The basic principle of the time value of money is that the value of an amount in the future has a present value that must take into consideration how much can be earned on that sum of money if invested today. In terms of our analysis, the terminal value today depends on the target return on an investment required by an investor.

For example, suppose that an investor wants a 20% return on an investment in order to invest in a startup company where the planned exit is six years from now. Computing the future value, it can be shown that this means that for every $1 the investor agrees to invest in the startup company, that amount will grow to $2.986. This can be scaled for any investment amount. Another way of putting it that is more helpful for our discussion is that an investor who expects to receive $2.986 six years from now per $1 invested now has realized a return on investment of 20% per annum.

With the terminal value at the exit date set, the terminal value today is computed as follows:

$$\text{Terminal value today} = \frac{\text{Forecasted terminal value at the exit date}}{\text{Target return on investment factor for \$1}}. \tag{16.9}$$

The target return on investment factor is based on the target return on the investment that the investor seeks and is nothing more than the future value of $1. That is, the target rate of return factor is simply the dollar amount by which $1 will increase from the time of valuation to the exit date based on the target return on investment. For example, the table below gives the target return on investment factor of $1 for various exit dates and target returns on investment:[12]

| No. of years to exit | Target return on investment factor: | | | |
| | Target rate of return sought | | | |
	20%	25%	28%	30%
4	$2.074	$2.441	$2.684	$2.856
5	2.488	3.052	3.436	3.713
6	2.986	3.815	4.398	4.827
7	3.583	4.768	5.629	6.275
8	4.300	5.960	7.206	8.157

12. The target return on investment factors in the table are obtained by using equation (16.9).

The terminal value today is the company's post-money valuation. Therefore,

$$\text{Post-money valuation} = \frac{\text{Forecasted terminal value at the exit date}}{\text{Target return on investment factor for \$1}}.$$

For example, if the forecasted terminal value at an exit date is assumed to be six years from now is $5.972 million and the investor seeks a 20% return on investment (a target return on investment factor of 2.986 from the table above), then the post-money valuation is

$$\text{Post-money valuation} = \frac{\$5,972,000}{2.986} = \$2 \text{ million}.$$

Given the post-money valuation, the pre-money valuation is

Pre-money valuation = Post-money valuation − Amount of new funding.

In our example, the post-money valuation is $2 million. Suppose that the amount of new funding sought is $1.5 million. Then the pre-money valuation is $0.5 million (= $2 million − $1.5 million).

Note that the VC method utilizes principles from both the income method and market method. The income method requires that any future amounts be converted to a current amount based on a target return. In the VC method, the only conversion from a future value to a present value is for the one cash flow that is assumed: the terminal value at the exit date. The VC method uses the market method to obtain the PE multiple that can be used to estimate the terminal value at the exit date based on forecasted earnings.

In our illustration, the terminal value at the exit date is based on a forecast of revenue and an assumed after-tax earnings rate. In practice, investors have used only a forecasted revenue to obtain the terminal value at the exit date. When doing so, the investor would look for comparable companies or comparable transactions, but instead of forecasting the terminal value at the exit date using future earnings obtained using a PE multiple, the investor can forecast a terminal value at the exit date using a price/revenue multiple.

A variation of the venture capital approach is to use different scenarios to estimate the pre-money valuation, assigning a probability to each scenario. The pre-money valuation is then a weighted average of the different scenarios. For example, what is referred to as the *First Chicago method*[13] uses three scenarios, success, survival, and chance, with corresponding probabilities of 30%. 50%, and 20%.

Scorecard Method

Also referred to as the benchmark method, the scorecard method was introduced by Bill Payne in his 2006 book on obtaining funding through angel investing.[14] This method was then modified by the Ohio TechAngels in 2008 and subsequently expanded by its originator,

13. This method was developed by First Chicago Corporation Venture Capital, a subsidiary of First Chicago Bank.
14. William H. Payne, *The Definitive Guide to Raising Money from Angels* (Bedford, MA: Aspatore Books, 2006).

Bill Payne, in 2010.[15] The method begins by identifying the typical startup ventures in the target company's geographic region and in the same stage of development that were recently funded by angels. In this case, the stage of development is pre-revenue startups. For the identified comparable startups, the average pre-money valuation is determined.

Next, the investor using the scorecard method compares factors that are expected to affect the valuation of the target pre-revenue company with the same factors associated with the similar angel-funded deals in the same region that the investor identified. The seven factors and their weights suggested by Bill Payne are:

Factor	Maximum factor weight
Strength of the management team	30%
Size of the opportunity	25%
Product/Technology	15%
Competitive environment	10%
Marketing/Sales channels/Partnerships	10%
Need for additional investment	5%
Other	5%

For the target company, a value as assessed by the investor is assigned to each factor and the sum of the factor values is then computed. For example, suppose that the factor values assigned by the investor to the target company based on an assessment of the identified startup ventures in the region that are angel-funded are as follows:

Factor	Maximum factor weight	Investor value assigned	Factor value
Strength of the management team	30%	80%	24%
Size of the opportunity	25%	100%	25%
Product/Technology	15%	100%	15%
Competitive environment	10%	50%	5%
Marketing/Sales channels/Partnerships	10%	40%	4%
Need for additional investment	5%	100%	5%
Other	5%	80%	4%
Sum			12%

The total factor value is found by summing up the last column, giving 82%. This value is then multiplied by the average pre-money valuation of the company identified. For

15. A recent discussion of the scorecard method is provided by Bill Payne, "Valuations 101: Scorecard Valuation Methodology," blog post, October 20, 2011, http://blog.gust.com/2011/10/20/valuations-101-scorecard-valuation-methodology.

example, suppose that the average pre-money valuation of the company is $1.8 million. Then the pre-money valuation for the target company is found by multiplying the average pre-money valuation of $1.8 million by 82%, giving a pre-money valuation of $1.476 million according to the scorecard method.

Berkus Method

Proposed by David Berkus, an active angel investor and lifelong entrepreneur, the Berkus method identifies five risk-reduction components that angel investors are exposed to when investing in a startup company. A value is assigned to each risk-reduction component based on the degree to which the angel investor believes the corresponding risk has been reduced.

With the Berkus method, there are five components that add value to an early-stage startup company seeking angel funding. The five components all involve the reduction of risk that angel investors face in investing in an early-stage company. The risk reduction components are

1. a sound idea: basic value, reducing product risk;
2. a prototype: reducing technology risk;
3. a quality management team: reducing execution risk;
4. strategic relationships: reducing market risk and competitive risk; and
5. product rollout or sales: reducing financial or production risk.

Berkus proposes that each risk-reduction component be assigned a value up to $500,000. Precisely what value should be assigned between zero and $500,000 is subjectively determined by an angel investor. Of course, for a pre-revenue company, the last risk-reduction component would not be satisfied and a zero value would be assigned.

Risk Factor Summation Method

Similar to the scorecard and Berkus methods, wherein an early-stage startup company accrues value to the degree to which the investor subjectively believes a risk component is reduced, the risk factor summation method provides for twelve risk-reduction components. This method, described by the Ohio TechAngels, considers twelve risk components: (1) management, (2) stage of the business, (3) legislation or political risk, (4) manufacturing risk, (5) sales and marketing risk, (6) funding or capital raising risk, (7) competition risk, (8) technology risk, (9) litigation risk, (10) international risk, (11) reputation risk, and (12) potential lucrative exit risk.

For each of these risk components one of the following grades, along with the corresponding dollar values attributed to each risk component, is assigned:

Grade	Dollar value to be added or subtracted
+ +	Add $500,000
+	Add $250,000
0	0
−	Subtract $250,000
− −	Subtract $500,000

DISCOUNT FOR LACK OF LIQUIDITY

Since the equity of a private company does not freely trade in a market, its value must be discounted because it is illiquid. This discount is referred to as the *liquidity discount*. The terms "marketability discount" and "liquidity discount" are often used synonymously, but this is technically incorrect. The marketability discount occurs because there are unique security characteristics that limit the exchange of the security, while lack of liquidity refers to a market where the number of buyers and sellers is limited. Unlike in a liquid market, where the next transaction price is very close to the previous transaction price, in an illiquid market the sequential transaction price differences can be very large, and generally this is the case for securities issued by private firms. When a market is liquid, it means that there are many buyers and sellers, and therefore securities can be bought and sold quickly and cost-effectively. This means that the spread between the bid price and the ask price in a liquid market is narrow. When a market is highly illiquid, the bid-ask spread is large, indicating that when securities are purchased, the costs of finding the next buyer are likely to be high, so the acquirer factors these costs into the purchase price. This cost is the opportunity cost of the time associated with searching for and identifying a buyer and concluding a transaction. In public markets, the liquidity discount for the most liquid stocks is a tiny fraction of the value being transacted. In private market, these transaction costs are far larger.

Unfortunately, the size of the liquidity discount is difficult to measure, and the literature on the subject—both academic and practitioner—is voluminous. Values for the discount range from a low of 6.5% to more than 40%. There are also discounts for the sale of large blocks of stock, and this sort of discount is separate from the liquidity discount associated with sales of smaller lots. To the extent these larger block sales confer control rights on the buyer, their value reflects both a discount for liquidity and a premium for control. Our focus here is on the pure liquidity discount: the discount applied to the sale of an individual security or a small group of securities where the sale does not in effect trigger a change in control.[16]

---

16. For a review of this literature, see Stanley J. Feldman, *Principles of Private Firm Valuation* (Hoboken, NJ: John Wiley & Sons, 2005).

Table 16.4
Average Discount or Discount Range

Study by	Average Discount or Discount Range
Emory-Dengell-Emory (pre-IPO) study[a]	46%
Silber study[b]	14%–40%
Hertzel-Smith study[c]	13.50%
Bajaj-Denis-Ferri-Sarin study[d]	7.2%
Koeplin-Sarin-Shapiro study for control transactions[e]	20.39%–28.26%
Feldman study[f]	17%
Overall average with Emory study	23.36%
Average for minority shares without Emory study	18.34%
Average for controlling shares	4.38%

Notes: a. John D. Emory, Sr., F. R. Dengell, and John D. Emory, Jr., "Discounts for Lack of Marketability," *Business Valuation Review* 21 (2002): 190–193. b. William Silber, "Discounts on Restricted Stock: The Impact of Illiquidity on Stock Prices," *Financial Analysts Journal* 47, no. 4 (1991): 60–64. c. Michael Herzel and Richard L. Smith, "Market Discounts and Shareholder Gains for Placing Equity Privately," *Journal of Finance* 48, no. 2 (1993): 459–485. d. Mukesh Bajaj, Dylan C. Shapiro, "The Private Company Discount," *Journal of Applied Corporate Finance* 12, no. 4 (2000): 94–101. f. Stanley J. Feldman, *Principles of Private Firm Valuation* (Hoboken, NJ: John Wiley & Sons, 2005).

Table 16.4 summarizes several of the major studies that estimate the size of the liquidity discount. As can be seen from the table, there is wide variation in the estimated size of the discounts. The Koeplin-Sarin-Shapiro study estimates discounts for control transactions in contrast to the other studies that focus on minority interests. The discount for control transactions is generally greater than for minority transactions. The pre-IPO study by Emory, Dengell, and Emory is based on IPO data that generally do not represent change-in-control transactions. Nevertheless, the reported average discount is far greater than those reported by other investigators. The Emory-Dengell-Emory results are likely to overstate the size of the discount since the reported results compare a private transaction price some time before the IPO to a price immediately after the event. Since expectations about the future are likely to be more optimistic at the IPO date than at the last valuation date prior to the IPO, the difference in price in part reflects this difference in expectations. Hence the implied liquidity discount calculated using the raw results reported by Emory, Dengell, and Emory would necessarily overstate the size of the discount. While this conclusion is speculative, it does suggest that the Emory-Dengell-Emory results need to be further vetted before one can conclude they measure a liquidity discount. The overall results indicate that control transactions have a greater discount than minority transactions, but the difference does not appear to be substantial. In our case study presented in appendix B, we assume that the discount for lack of liquidity is 20%, which is consistent with the liquidity discount literature.

KEY POINTS COVERED IN THIS CHAPTER

- Although there are well-known models for valuing a publicly traded company, the valuation of a private company is far more complex and challenging.

- The challenges in private company valuation are selecting the standard of value, determining how to adjust reported financial information for valuation purposes, and selecting an appropriate valuation model and estimating the inputs needed to implement the valuation model, with additional complexities arising in adjusting estimated values for the lack of liquidity of a private company.

- Valuation is required not only in fundraising but also under Section 409a of the tax code for determining the value of stock awards or options to founders and employees so as to mitigate the risk of adverse tax consequences.

- Two major differences that arise in valuing private and public firms are (1) the stock of private companies is not traded on national exchanges, and therefore little or no idea of the value is available, and (2) typically there is no or very little separation between management and ownership of private companies.

- The major differences that influence the valuation of private companies compared to public companies are the following: (1) it is assumed that there is a hypothetical transaction in which the hypothetical buyers and sellers are assumed to be fully informed about the nature of the risks and the opportunities that characterize the hypothetical transaction; (2) because this hypothetical transaction is not occurring in an organized-exchange market, by definition, the number of buyers and sellers is limited, which results in a scarcity of liquidity; and (3) while the lack of marketability or liquidity reduces the value of a private company, from an owner's perspective the ownership value in a private company may warrant a premium.

- Although there are exceptions, the fair market value (FMV) is the standard of value applied to the valuation of private companies. According to the IRS, the FMV is "the price at which the property would change hands between a willing buyer and a willing seller when the former is not under any compulsion to buy and the latter is not under any compulsion to sell, both parties having reasonable knowledge of the relevant facts."

- Typically, the terms "fair value" and "fair market value" are used interchangeably, but financial accounting authorities use the former term and the IRS uses the latter term.

- The concept of fair value is based on the price paid for an item by one party (the buyer) to the other party (the seller) in a transaction between two unrelated parties.

- A transaction involving the financial instruments issued by a private company is conceptually a hypothetical exchange at a given point in time, the valuation date, and the resulting price of this hypothetical exchange is called the exit price.

- The exit price is based on information that the two informed parties to the exchange would utilize to price the transacted instrument whose valuation is sought, and the information used to obtain this price should take into account the current and expected state of the economy and the industry segment in which the company operates, as well as a host of risk factors that would be used to evaluate the company's risk profile.

- A key risk factor in valuation is the appropriate cost of capital that the company must pay to attract investors. The cost of capital in turn reflects both the company's business risks and its financial risks.

- Standards of value other than fair value are orderly liquidation value, intrinsic value, and investment value (or strategic value).

- Liquidation value is the probable price that would be obtained by the seller if the seller were forced to dispose of an item within a reasonable period of time and the market condition were orderly.

- Intrinsic value takes into account monetary value and personal preference value.

- Investment value, or strategic value, is a standard of value that represents the value placed on a company in excess of fair value on a stand-alone basis.

- The two valuations of interest are the company's enterprise value and its equity value.

- A company's enterprise value is the value of the company; a company's equity value is the value from the perspective of just its common shareholders.

- The methods for valuing a private company fall into four categories: asset-based method (cost method), income method (discounted cash flow method), market method (or method of comparables), and the option-based method.

- Value according to the asset-based method is computed as the aggregation of the fair value of every tangible and intangible asset (excluding goodwill) on the balance sheet.

- The aggregated fair values of identified assets less the fair value of current liabilities (excluding any short-term debt) gives the company's fair value.

- The underlying principle of the asset-based approach is that each identified asset has a stand-alone value. According to the AICPA, the asset-based approach (using the replacement cost of the assets) has been applied primarily to value companies classified as being in stage 1 and some enterprises in stage 2, but is typically not used once a company is beyond stage 2.

- The asset-based approach is used when the information needed to apply the income method or market method of valuing an enterprise is limited because the company has virtually no financial history and it is difficult to make any forecasts, or when the company at the time of valuation may have a patent application pending despite not yet having developed a product.

- The income method involves the application of (1) the discounted value of future value, (2) free cash flow, and (3) the cost of capital.

- Despite being referred to as the income method, this method uses a company's free cash flow, not any income measure, in the valuation process, and the income method is therefore more commonly referred to as the discounted cash flow (DCF) method.

- According to the AICPA, the income method typically is used to value later-stage companies (those in stages 3 through 6) rather than early-stage companies.

- Broadly stated, free cash flow is the cash flow of the firm less the capital expenditures necessary to stay in business (i.e., replacing facilities as necessary) and grow at the expected rate (which requires an increase in working capital).

- The perspective taken in defining free cash flow to equity (FCFE) is that of the shareholders because it is what remains for shareholders after the company makes necessary capital expenditures.

- A broader perspective of free cash flow is the free cash flow to the firm (FCFF), which is the after-tax interest added and net borrowings subtracted.

- When the FCFF is used, the resulting valuation is the firm's enterprise value; when the FCFE is used in the valuation, it results in the firm's equity value.

- Valuation using FCFF or FCFE generates equivalent results if the inputs to each valuation are consistent.

- The process of discounting the cash flow (or discounting) involves converting the value of a future cash flow to its present value.

- The present value of a future value (or simply present value) is the amount that has to be invested today at some interest rate to make that amount grow to the future value; the interest rate used to compute this value is called the discount rate.

- Two properties of the present value are (1) for a given number of years, the higher the discount rate, the lower the present value is, and (2) for a given discount rate, the further into the future the future value will be received, the lower the present value is.

- The midyear convention is used to adjust the discounting process to reflect future cash flows being received throughout the year rather than at the end of the year.

- The cost of capital is the appropriate discount rate to value a company's expected free cash flow because it is the rate of return required by suppliers of long-term capital to the company—creditors and stockholders.

- The cost of capital includes the explicit interest on the debt (i.e., borrowings) and the implicit minimum return that stockholders would require.

- The cost of each component of the cost of capital must reflect the risk of the assets in which the company invests.

- The higher the cost of capital, the lower is the value of the company.

- The estimated cost of capital is based on an assumed capital structure (i.e., the proportion of debt, preferred stock, and common stock) and is called the weighted average cost of capital (WACC).

- In estimating a company's WACC, an adjustment must be made in estimating the cost of debt because of the tax treatment of interest.

- Estimating the cost of common stock is more difficult than estimating the cost of debt and involves (1) identifying the risk factors for which investors want to be compensated when investing in a company's common stock, (2) for each risk factor identified, providing a financial metric to quantify that risk factor, and (3) for the financial metric for each risk factor formulated, estimating the risk for the company.

- In the valuation of startup companies, when computing the cost of equity, some of the financial metrics that proxy for risk require market information that is typically unavailable.

- There are asset pricing models proposed by financial theory that suggest the risks that common stock investors want to be compensated for; the expected return on equity that an investor wants is the sum of the risk-free rate plus compensation for each risk factor.

- Estimating the value of the enterprise value of a private company using the discounted cash flow method involves three steps: (1) projecting for each year the projected free cash flow, (2) computing the discounted value of the projected FCFF for each year using the WACC as the discount rate, and (3) aggregating the discounted value of the projected free cash flow for each year.

- Adding excess cash to the operating enterprise value gives the firm's preliquidity enterprise value.

- The enterprise value's excess cash is found by determining any excess cash flow that is on the current balance sheet.

- To obtain the equity value, it is necessary to reduce the enterprise value including cash by the value of debt since that portion of the enterprise value does not belong to the common stockholders.

- With an estimated discount for liquidity determined, the liquidity-adjusted equity value can be determined.

- In general, any excess cash on the current balance sheet belongs to the common stockholders and should be included in both the equity value and the enterprise value.

- A firm's preliquidity equity value is its estimated enterprise value reduced by the value of debt.

- Although the DCF method is based on reasonable economic principles, the major criticism is in estimating the future benefits that arise from the managerial flexibility that may be embedded in the firm's existing assets to allow management to take advantage of various opportunities that may arise in the future.

- It is argued that under certain circumstances, the estimated free cash flow as computed under the DCF method underestimates future benefits and therefore underestimates enterprise value and equity value.
- To value a company using the market method (or method of comparables) it is necessary to identify companies comparable to the company (i.e., peer companies) whose valuation is being sought. These companies may be publicly traded companies or, for purposes of valuation, private firms that have transacted at or near the valuation date.
- The method of comparables falls into two general categories: guideline public company analysis and guideline transactions analysis.
- Companies included in the group of comparable companies fall into two categories, clone companies (the most desirable) and guideline companies.
- Clone companies are companies that are very close in asset size and revenue, have close to the same cost structure, operate in the same industry segment, produce equivalent products and services, have equivalent capital structures (i.e., use the same percentage of debt), and have virtually identical expected revenue and profit growth opportunities.
- Guideline companies are those that have several but not all of the characteristics of the company whose valuation is sought.
- With information obtained from the guideline companies or a group of comparable companies, a multiple of some suitable financial metric is used to obtain a company's valuation using the market method
- Various financial ratios have been proposed as suitable multiples for estimating equity value. In the three most common ratios the numerator is the equity value and the denominator is a measure that is a proxy for values that apply to equity investors (free cash flow, net income, and book value of equity).
- In estimating equity value using financial ratios, it should be kept in mind that the comparable firms are likely to have substantial differences in the amount of financial leverage and growth rates, requiring an adjustment of the ratios.
- In addition to the complication of identifying comparable companies and adjusting for differences in growth, it is necessary to adjust the financial metrics used in the analysis for differences in accounting treatment.
- Rather than using market trading data for valuation, guideline transactions analysis (also known as the precedent transactions method) uses transactions that have occurred in the recent past for similar firms.
- The concern with using the guideline transactions method is that the transaction price may reflect not a firm's fair value but the strategic value to the acquiring firm.
- A drawback in valuing early-stage technology companies using the income method is that it fails to take into account the flexibility offered to management by technology platforms that have not been commercialized. Even for those technology platforms that

have been applied to a few applications, the income method is inadequate because it fails to consider the venture's opportunity to expand into different areas.

- An approach to quantifying a company's valuation by taking into account the flexibility or option available to management is real options valuation, and it is based on option theory in finance.

- Four methods used to value pre-revenue and positive earnings startup firms used as starting points for negotiations between founders and angel groups and venture capitalists are the venture capital method, the scorecard method, the Berkus method, and the risk factor summation method.

- The venture capital (VC) method, one of the more popular methods for the valuation of pre-revenue startup companies, assumes that no additional equity financing will occur in the future.

- The application of the VC method involves forecasting the earnings at the exit date and then applying the market method to get the forecasted terminal value at the exit date by identifying comparable companies or comparable transactions.

- Since the equity of a privately held company does not freely trade in a market, a liquidity discount must be applied in valuing a private company.

- Values for the liquidity discount range from a low of 6.5% to more than 40%.

FURTHER READINGS

Damodaran, Aswath, *Investment Valuation: Tools and Techniques for Determining the Value of Any Asset,* 3rd ed. (Hoboken, NJ: John Wiley & Sons, 2012).

Feldman, Stanley J., "Business Valuation 101: The Five Myths of Valuing a Private Business," http://www.score.org.

Feldman, Stanley J., "A Note on Using Regression Models to Predict the Marketability Discount," *Business Valuation Review*, September 2002, 145–151.

Feldman, Stanley J., "Overcoming IRS Challenges to the Amount of Marketability Discount," *Estate Planning*, January 2005, 33–35.

Feldman, Stanley J., *Principles of Private Firm Valuation* (Hoboken, NJ John Wiley & Sons, 2005).

Feldman, Stanley J., "The Valuation of Private Firms," in *Handbook of Finance*, ed. Frank J. Fabozzi (Hoboken, NJ: John Wiley & Sons, 2008).

Feldman, Stanley J., Tim Sullivan, and Roger Winsby, *What Every Business Owner Should Know about Valuing Their Business* (New York: McGraw-Hill Professional Books, 2002).

Koller, Tim, Marc Goedhart, and David Wessels, *Valuation: Measuring and Managing the Value of Companies,* 5th ed. (Hoboken, NJ: John Wiley & Sons, 2010).

Pratt, Shannon, and Roger J. Grabowski, *Cost of Capital, + Website: Applications and Examples* (Hoboken, NJ: John Wiley & Sons, 2014).

Pratt, Shannon, and John Lifflander, *Analyzing Complex Appraisals for Business Professionals* (New York: McGraw-Hill Education, 2016).

17

VALUING CAPITAL PROJECTS

The founders of a company are continually evaluating potential investment projects to determine which projects are worthwhile pursuing, which projects are unattractive from an economic perspective, and which projects may potentially offer an attractive return but should be postponed for the time being. The decisions regarding the investment projects in which the founders will invest are referred to as *capital budgeting decisions*. Though some capital budgeting decisions may be routine decisions that do not have a major impact on the potential success of a startup company, other decisions either will have an impact on the company's future market position in its current offerings of goods and services or will permit it to expand into new product lines in the future.

The economic assessment of a potential investment project is based on a proposed project's value. How does one determine the potential value of a project? As we will see in this chapter, the valuation of proposed investment projects applies the same principles described in chapter 16 using the discounted cash flow (DCF) method for valuing a company.

There is a drawback to valuation using the DCF method, as noted in that chapter: it tends to underestimate the enterprise value and the equity value. The same drawback applies to the valuation of proposed investment projects, particularly for high-tech firms. As explained in chapter 16, the way to handle this problem is to use the real options method to valuation, which we describe in the next chapter. This also applies to the valuation of investment projects.

The DCF method and the real options method are only two of several methods for valuing proposed investment projects. We will explain these other methods in this chapter and their limitations.

CLASSIFYING INVESTMENT PROJECTS

There are various ways of classifying proposed investment projects: by the economic life of a project, by the degree of risk associated with a project, and by the relationship of a project to other projects.[1]

---

1. When we discuss the real options approach in the next chapter, we will provide another way to classify proposed investment projects.

Classification by Economic Life

The *economic life* is the period of time over which the cash flow of a proposed investment project is expected to last. It is not necessarily the legal life of an asset because the economic life can be quite different from the legal life granted under the law. In the case of a physical asset such as a plant or equipment, the economic life is determined by physical deterioration, obsolescence, or the degree of competition in the market for a product.

What distinguishes a capital project from an investment that is considered to be a current asset (which is part of working capital) is its economic life. A current asset is expected to have an economic life of less than one year.

Classification by the Nature of Risk

There is risk associated with investing in any proposed capital project. However, the degree of risk varies with the type of capital project. Capital projects can be classified as replacement projects, expansion projects, and new product or service projects.

In the category of replacement projects are capital projects that involve the maintenance of existing capital projects needed to maintain production at the current operating level or to replace existing equipment with more efficient equipment. Typically, replacement projects expose a startup to less risk than the two other types of projects to be discussed. This does not mean there is no risk because even replacement projects expose a company to business risk—the risk that future sales or revenue will decline so as to not justify the expenditure.

Capital projects that seek to augment a startup company to increase its market share of existing products and services are referred to as expansion projects. This type of capital project exposes a company to the risk that the expenditure does not pay off because the market penetration sought is insufficient to justify the expenditure. So there is greater business risk with such capital projects than with replacement projects.

The greatest risk exposure is for capital projects that involve the introduction of new products or entering into new markets. The greater risk compared to replacement and expansion projects is because the founders may have little or no experience in the new product or market. Within this category of capital projects the risk can vary greatly depending on how closely the new product or market is related to the company's current products and markets.

Classification by the Capital Project's Relationship to Other Projects

A company has a portfolio of capital projects. The decision whether or not to adopt a proposed capital project must be considered in light of its relationship to both existing capital projects and other proposed capital projects. Proposed capital projects can be classified according to their relationship to existing and other proposed capital projects as independent projects, mutually exclusive projects, and complementary projects. This categorization depends on how the projected cash flows of a proposed capital project affect the cash flows of other capital projects.

When the projected cash flow of a proposed capital project has no impact on other capital projects, it is said to be an ***independent project***. Holding aside the amount budgeted for capital projects, when evaluating an independent project the decision to undertake it does not affect the decision whether or not to adopt other proposed capital projects. A good example is a proposed replacement project that involves replacing current equipment with equipment that embodies state-of-the-art technology.

Suppose that in the example of a replacement project there are three alternative proposed capital projects for replacing existing equipment. The founders must decide which of the three (if any) should be accepted. That is, the acceptance of one of the proposed replacement projects means that the other two will be rejected. Proposed capital projects where the acceptance of one capital project means the rejection of other proposed capital projects are said to be ***mutually exclusive projects***.

For some capital projects the acceptance of one project enhances the projected cash flow of other proposed capital projects. Such projects are referred to as ***complementary projects***.

ESTIMATING CASH FLOWS OF CAPITAL PROJECTS

As explained in chapter 16, in the valuation of a company it is necessary to project a cash flow—free cash flow to the firm to estimate enterprise value and free cash flow to equity to estimate the equity value. When evaluating proposed capital projects, the relevant cash flow is the projected change in the cash flow should the proposed capital project be undertaken. What is relevant for the valuation is therefore the projected ***incremental cash flow*** from adopting a proposed capital project. The underlying principle is that in the absence of the proposed capital project, a firm will have a cash flow as a result of its current operations. By adopting a proposed capital project, a firm will see a change in its cash flow. It is that change in the cash flow (i.e., incremental cash flow) that is relevant in valuing proposed capital projects. The value of a proposed capital project is then the present value of the projected incremental cash flow.

The incremental cash flow is composed of two components: operating cash flows and investment cash flows. The ***operating cash flows*** are the incremental after-tax cash flows projected for proposed capital projects as a result of operating activities. These cash flows are the result of a difference in the incremental revenue generated by a proposed capital project and the incremental operating expenses associated with that capital project.

The ***investment cash flows*** are the capital expenditures that are required to acquire the capital project that will generate the operating cash flows. These expenditures would include, in addition to the cost of the asset, any setup expenditures, shipping costs, and installation costs. A proposed capital project may require that all of the cash outlay be made before the capital project is placed in operation. Some proposed capital projects may require capital expenditures over time. There are capital projects that may involve expenditures for the disposal of the asset at the end of its economic life. Moreover, tax considerations must be taken into account in estimating investment cash flows. At the time of acquisition of a capital project, there may be a tax credit associated with the adoption of a capital project.[2] Tax considerations are also important when an asset is eventually disposed of. The impact on the investment cash flow depends on whether there is a capital gain when the asset is disposed of. Therefore, the projected incremental cash flow for a proposed capital project for any year is obtained by the following calculation:

Projected incremental operating cash flows − Projected investment cash flow.

Cash Flow Patterns

The pattern of the incremental cash flow over time in terms of positive and negative values varies by the type of capital project. For example, a common cash flow pattern is one in which the initial cash flows are negative (i.e., outlays), followed by positive cash flows. The reason why there might be several negative cash flows in more than one of the initial years is because it may take several years to develop a product or construct a facility. A pattern of cash flows that exhibits this attribute is referred to as a ***normal cash flow pattern*** or ***conventional cash flow pattern***. Basically, the sign of the cash flow changes from negative to positive only once.

Not all proposed capital projects exhibit this cash flow pattern. For example, a proposed capital project may have several early years with negative cash flows followed by years of positive cash flows, and then in the last year or years a negative cash flow again. The negative cash flows in the later years reflect the cost of closing a facility or disposing of an asset. Such a pattern is referred to as a ***non-normal cash flow pattern*** or an ***unconventional cash flow pattern***. That is, in a non-normal cash flow pattern, the sign of the cash flow changes more than once.

There relevance of the pattern of cash flows in valuing proposed capital projects will be clear later in this chapter.

CAPITAL PROJECT VALUATION METHODS

Once the projected incremental cash flows for a proposed project are determined, the next step is valuation to determine whether the candidate project merits adoption. Three valuation methods are used for this purpose: the net present value method, the internal rate of return method, and the real options method. We discuss the first two methods below, and in the next chapter we discuss the real options method. For both methods, we discuss the

---

2. A tax credit differs from a tax deduction in that a tax credit is a dollar-for-dollar reduction in a company's tax liability. The federal government provides such credits at times to encourage capital expenditure to promote economic growth. The most common type of tax credit that the federal government has instituted at various times is the investment tax credit.

decision rule as to whether a proposed capital should be considered a candidate for adoption and the rule for ranking projects based on relative attractiveness.

Net Present Value Method

The net present value method is an application of the DCF method described in chapter 16 to value a company. The procedure is as follows:

Step 1: Project the proposed capital project's incremental cash flow for each year.

Step 2: Determine a suitable discount rate at which to calculate the present value of the capital project's incremental cash flow each year.

Step 3: Sum the present value of the capital project's incremental cash flow for all the years.

The value computed in step 3 is said to be the *net present value* (NPV) for the proposed capital project. It is referred to as a "net" present value because it takes into account the investment cost of the proposed capital project.

For example, let's consider a proposed capital project that we will identify as project A, whose incremental cash flows are projected to be as follows (and which give us step 1 of the NPV method):

Year	Incremental cash flow
0	−$10,000,000
1	0
2	2,000,000
3	3,000,000
4	9,000,000

Suppose that appropriate discount rate for this project is 10%. The present value of each cash flow is shown below (step 2 of the NPV method):[3]

Year	Incremental cash flow	Discounted incremental cash flow at 10%
0	−$10,000,000	−$10,000,000
1	0	0
2	2,000,000	1,652,893
3	3,000,000	2,253,944
4	9,000,000	6,147,121

3. Note that in the illustrations in this chapter we do not use the midyear convention described in chapter 16.

Adding the last column of the above table gives an NPV of $53,958 (step 3 in the NPV method).

As a second illustration, consider project B, which has the following incremental cash flows with the same perceived risk as project A:

Year	Incremental cash flow
0	−$10,000,000
1	3,250,000
2	3,250,000
3	3,250,000
4	3,250,000

Notice that the cash flow pattern (i.e., the timing of the cash flows) of project B is quite different from that of project A. Assuming again a discount rate of 10%, it can be shown that the NPV of project B is $302,063.

Determining a suitable discount rate follows much the same procedure as determining the weighted average cost of capital (WACC) for a company, as explained in chapter 16. The discount rate used in step 2 is referred to as the ***required rate of return*** (RRR) or the ***hurdle rate***. The WACC is a starting point in the determination of the RRR for a project. The reason for this is that the risk of the proposed capital project must be taken into account. If a proposed project has the same risk as the company, then the WACC can be used as the RRR for discounting the incremental cash flows. However, if the proposed project has greater risk, then a discount rate greater than the WACC should be used. The challenge is estimating the risk and adjusting the WACC accordingly.

The decision rule as to whether or not to accept a proposed capital project based on the NPV method is that the NPV indicates whether the project is increasing or reducing value to the founders. That is, a positive NPV for a proposed capital project means that based on the projected incremental cash flows and the RRR, the project should add value to the company and therefore for its founders. Such projects should be accepted assuming there are no capital constraints (i.e., unlimited capital). At a minimum, positive NPV projects are those that are candidates for adoption subject to other constraints. A negative NPV for a proposed capital project means that the project at this time should not be considered for adoption. An NPV of zero means that the founders should be indifferent to adopting the proposed capital project. For project A and project B the NPV is positive. Therefore, both would be adding value for the founders and are acceptable investments.

With respect to ranking a list of proposed capital projects, the rule is simple. The higher the NPV, the more attractive is the proposed capital project (ignoring other constraints). If the founders had a capital expenditure budget that allowed for investment in both capital projects (i.e., $20 million in Year 0), then the founders would invest in both, assuming that the two projects are independent projects. If the two projects are mutually exclusive projects, project B, with the higher NPV, would be the capital project selected because of its higher NPV. If the founders had a limited capital expenditure budget in Year 0 of $10 million, then only one capital project could be selected and that would again be project B because of its higher NPV.

Internal Rate of Return Method

Another method that takes into consideration the time value of money (i.e., discounting projected cash flows) is the **internal rate of return method**. The internal rate of return (IRR) of a proposed capital project is also called the *yield* of a proposed capital project. The IRR of a proposed capital project is computed as follows:

Step 1: Project the proposed capital project's incremental cash flow for each year.

Step 2: Find the discount rate that will make the present value of the project's incremental cash flows equal to zero.

Step 2 involves an iterative process (i.e., trial and error).

As an illustration, consider project A, whose projected incremental cash flows were given earlier. Alternative discount rates for calculating the present value must be tried to obtain the IRR. If a discount rate of 10.17% is used, the NPV is zero and therefore the IRR is 10.17%. For project B it can be shown that the IRR is 11.39%.

The decision rule as to whether or not a candidate capital project warrants adoption (assuming no other constraints) is based on a comparison of the IRR and the RRR. If the IRR exceeds the RRR, then the proposed capital project is a candidate for adoption; if the IRR is less than the RRR, the proposed capital project should be rejected. If the candidate project has an IRR equal to zero, the founders would be indifferent to the project. In our illustration, project A and project B both have an IRR that exceeds their RRR. Hence, both are acceptable capital projects.

The ranking rule is that the higher the IRR, the more attractive is the proposed capital project (ignoring other constraints). Project B has a higher IRR than project A and is therefore ranked higher. A choice between project A and project B if they are mutually exclusive capital projects would result in the selection of the one with the higher IRR, project B. If there are no capital expenditure budget constraints, both could be undertaken. In the presence of a budget constraint, project B would be selected.

Why the NPV and IRR Methods May Yield Conflicting Rankings In our illustration, there was no conflict in terms of ranking of projects. However, that is not always the case. There are situations in which the NPV might give a different ranking of projects than the IRR. Let's consider once again project A and project B. Suppose that instead of a 10% RRR, the RRR is 7%. It can be shown that in that case, the NPV of project A exceeds that of project B. Thus the NPV method would rank project A ahead of project B. However, according to the IRR method, project B would be preferred to project A. There is thus a conflict in the ranking of projects by the two methods.[4] Which of the two methods should a founder employ in the case of conflicting rankings? Both methods require a projection of the incremental cash flows of a proposed capital project. Both methods also take into consideration the time value of money since all cash flows are discounted. Both use the RRR in the valuation process. To understand which method should be used, we must look at the reasons why there could be conflicts, and this will help us understand which method the founders should utilize.

There are two reasons why conflicting results may occur. The first results from the reinvestment assumption about interim incremental cash flows and the second from the possibility of multiple IRRs for certain types of capital projects.

Reinvestment assumption Although we have not reviewed the two methods in detail, there are two well-known mathematical properties of the two methods regarding the reinvestment of interim cash flows. The NPV method assumes that the interim cash flows when received can be reinvested by the company so as to earn the RRR. So, if the RRR is 9%, the computation assumes that the interim cash flows can be reinvested at 9% each year. This is not an unreasonable assumption.

In contrast, the IRR method assumes that the interim cash flows when received can be reinvested at the computed IRR. That is, if the IRR of a proposed capital project is 25%, then the computation assumes that the interim cash flows can be reinvested to earn a 25% return each year. This not likely to occur, and therefore it is an unreasonable assumption.

This reinvestment assumption has an impact on the selection of mutually exclusive capital projects that can lead to conflicting results when (1) there are differences in the cash flow patterns (i.e., the timing of the cash flows), (2) projects have different economic lives, and (3) there are significant differences of scale (i.e., size of the cash flows).

Multiple IRRs With the projected incremental cash flows for a proposed capital project and the RRR determined, one NPV will be calculated. Once the projected incremental cash flows for a proposed capital project are established, how many IRRs can be computed? The answer is that more than one are possible. As an example, consider a proposed capital project with the following incremental cash flows where a founder for an investment of $2.4 million can invest in a capital project that results in a positive incremental cash flow at the end of the first year of $15 million and a negative cash flow at the end of the second year of $15 million. That is, for this capital project, the projected incremental cash flow is:

Year	Incremental cash flow
0	−$2,400,000
1	15,000,000
2	−15,000,000

4. In fact, it can be show that if the RRR is below 7.5%, there will be a conflict.

If we want to calculate the IRR, let's try a discount rate of 25%. By doing so we obtain the following:

Year	Incremental cash flow	Discounted incremental cash flow at 25%
0	−$2,400,000	−$2,400,000
1	15,000,000	12,000,000
2	−15,000,000	−9,600,000

Summing the present value of the cash flows in the last column gives an NPV of zero. Since the IRR is the discount rate that makes the sum of the discounted incremental cash flows equal to zero, then the IRR must be 25%.

Let's try another discount rate, 400%. Below are the discounted incremental cash flows using that discount rate:

Year	Incremental cash flow	Discounted incremental cash flow at 400%
0	−$2,400,000	−$2,400,000
1	15,000,000	3,000,000
2	−15,000,000	−600,000

Summing the values in the last column gives an NPV of zero. Hence, 400% is the IRR.

What is the IRR for this capital project? It is both 25% and 400%. (There is no other solution.) Suppose that the RRR is 28%: is this capital project acceptable based on the decision rule for the IRR method? If the lower IRR of 25% is used, then it is not. If the higher IRR used, it is an acceptable project. There is no issue if the NPV is used since for any RRR there is only one NPV.

Why did two solutions occur? This is because our hypothetical capital project is a nonnormal cash flow pattern as explained earlier in this chapter. When there is more than one change in the sign of a cash flow, then there can be more than one IRR. In fact, mathematically it can be demonstrated that the number of possible IRRs is equal to the number of times the sign changes for the cash flows.[5] For our hypothetical capital project, there were two sign changes (negative to positive to negative). In a normal cash flow pattern there is only one change in sign (negative to positive), so there is only one IRR. There are ways of resolving this problem, but with the limitation regarding the reinvestment assumption, there is no need to discuss such solutions.

5. Here is the mathematical explanation. The mathematical equation from which the IRR is being solved is a polynomial equation. That is, the IRR is the solution to a polynomial equation. In mathematics, the number of positive roots (i.e., solutions with a positive IRR) is determined by Descartes' rule of signs. This rule states that the number of positive roots of a polynomial is either equal to the number of changes of sign in its non-zero coefficients or is less by an equal number. The coefficients in the polynomial equation are the incremental cash flows for a capital project.

It is also possible that there is no IRR for a proposed capital project. For example, consider a proposed capital project with the followed projected incremental cash flows:

Year	Incremental cash flow
0	$2,800,000
1	−2,400,000
2	+4,000,000

This cash flow pattern would arise when a founder acquires an asset that provides positive cash flow immediately, a payment in the next year (a negative cash flow), and then a positive cash flow. If a founder attempts to calculate the IRR, it cannot be found. In contrast, the NPV is positive regardless of the RRR.

Capital Rationing and the IRR Method   Several times in our discussion of the decision rule for both methods we mentioned that there may be capital constraints that limit the number of projects that can be undertaken. This constraint, referred to as *capital rationing*, may be self-imposed or imposed by funding available from the capital markets. This means that if the founders have determined a list of all proposed independent capital projects that are acceptable using either the NPV or IRR method, not all of these projects will be accepted if their total cost exceeds the capital expenditure budget.

The problem with using the IRR method in ranking proposed capital projects when there is capital rationing can be illustrated using the following proposed independent capital projects which are acceptable using either the NPV or IRR methods, assuming that the RRR is less than 20%:

Proposed project	Capital expenditure	NPV	IRR
1	$5,000,000	$650,000	20%
2	2,500,000	250,000	21%
3	1,500,000	125,000	22%
4	1,000,000	75,000	23%

Note that the four capital projects when ranked by the NPV method have the opposite ranking than when they are ranked by the IRR method. The total capital expenditure if all four capital projects are accepted is $10 million. In the absence of capital rationing, all four capital projects are accepted and the total NPV is $1,100,000.

Let's assume that the founders have imposed a capital expenditure budget of $5 million. If the IRR method is used, projects 2, 3, and 4 would be selected by the founders since they have the highest NPV and the capital expenditure is $5 million. The question is whether the selection of the proposed capital projects will provide the maximum value, as measured by the NPV, to the founders. For projects 2, 3, and 4 the total NPV is $450,000. However, by selecting project 1, which would require a capital expenditure of $5 million and has the lowest IRR, the founders would have the potential to realize an NPV of $650,000, which is $200,000 more than could be realized by selecting the other three capital projects.

The reason why this occurs is that the capital projects are of different size (as measured by the amount of the capital expenditure). The size difference distorts the ranking. Although the larger capital project, project 1, has a lower IRR than the capital expenditure for the smallest capital project, project 4, the founder would be earning 20% on a $5 million expenditure rather than 23% on a capital expenditure one-fifth its size. To make this clearer with a more extreme example: If a founder had a choice of spending $10 million on a capital project with an IRR of 20%, assuming an RRR of less than 20%, or $10,000 on a capital project with an IRR of 50%, the founder would benefit from the larger expenditure. The message is therefore that founders should look at NPV when there is capital rationing, not IRR.

OTHER CONSIDERATIONS IN CAPITAL PROJECT SELECTION

There are other aspects of capital project selection that founders consider. They include

- the time needed to recover the investment outlay,
- incorporating differences in capital project risks, and
- the managerial flexibility offered by a capital project.

If founders believe that the time to recovery is an important factor to supplement their capital project selection decision based on the NPV method, a measure known as the payback period can be used. We describe it below. We also explain several ad hoc measures for incorporating risk into the capital project selection decision. The managerial flexibility that might be offered by a capital project is discussed in the next chapter when we discuss the real options method for evaluating capital projects.

Payback Period

A proposed capital project's *payback period* is the length of time it takes for the incremental cash flows to recover the initial capital expenditure. It is a simple calculation that involves accumulating a capital project's incremental cash flows until the accumulated incremental cash flow is equal to the capital project's initial capital expenditure. The method favors capital projects that are heavily front-loaded in their incremental cash flows.

Consider once again project A, whose incremental cash flows were given earlier in this chapter. By the end of Year 3, the entire $10 million is not paid back, but by Year 4 the accumulated incremental cash flow reaches (and exceeds) $10 million. Therefore, project A's payback period is between three and four years.

Founders concerned with limited capital may utilize this measure not for determining the relative attractiveness of capital projects but to supplement the NPV or IRR method. The shorter the payback period, the more favorable is the capital project. Some founders may view the payback period as an indication of a capital project's risk. This is because in some industries, capital projects such as equipment become obsolete rapidly, or else the competitive conditions may be such as to increase the risk of recovery the further into the future the incremental cash flows are received.

There are two problems with using the payback period in selecting among candidate capital projects. The first problem is that it ignores incremental cash flows beyond the payback period. The second problem is that it ignores the time value of money. To overcome the second problem, founders can use the present value of the incremental cash flows (discounted at the RRR) rather than the undiscounted cash flows to determine the payback period. The resulting payback period measure is called the *discounted payback period*.

Incorporating Risk

Founders do take into account risk in some manner in evaluating the merits of proposed capital projects. Although finance theory has developed several theoretical methods for taking risk into account, these methods are often too difficult to apply in practice. Some simple tools are, however, available for a founder to get a feel for the risk associated with a proposed capital project. The two most often suggested are scenario analysis and Monte Carlo simulation.

Scenario analysis simply involves changing various assumptions made in generating the incremental cash flows, such as the assumed growth in revenue and the assumed operating costs. Based on alternative assumptions (which are the scenarios), an NPV can be calculated. By looking at the NPV under different scenarios, founders can assess the critical assumptions that have an impact on the NPV.

A more sophisticated approach is Monte Carlo simulation. This technique involves assigning probability distributions to all the critical variables that affect the NPV, assigning numbers to each critical variable based on the probability distribution, drawing random numbers that then refer to some value for each critical variable, and using all of the values to obtain an NPV. The result of the simulation is a probability distribution for the NPV. Although Monte Carlo simulation is a wonderful tool, it is often difficult for a founder to implement because of the difficulty of generating a probability distribution for the critical variables.

Other methods for incorporating risk into the analysis involve either adjusting the IRR to reflect the perceived risk associated with a proposed capital project or adjusting the incremental cash flows.

Adjusting the WACC In describing the NPV method, the appropriate discount rate for computing the present value of the incremental cash flows expected to be generated by the proposed capital project is needed. The starting point is the company's WACC, whose calculation we described in chapter 16. The WACC is the appropriate RRR to use when the founders believe that the proposed capital project has the same average risk as the company. If there is greater perceived risk than the average risk for the company, a risk premium is added to the WACC to get the RRR. Just how that risk premium is determined varies. Financial theory suggests some complex analysis to do so. Some companies simply create risk buckets for capital projects and assign a risk premium to each risk bucket. The RRR is determined accordingly and then used to discount the incremental cash flows for the proposed capital project.

Adjusting the Incremental Cash Flows   An alternative to adjusting the WACC to obtain the RRR is adjusting the incremental cash flows to reflect a proposed capital project's perceived risk. This is accomplished by determining the certainty equivalent for each incremental cash flow. A *certainty equivalent* is the amount that the founders would be willing to receive in the future with certainty rather than take the risk of not realizing the projected incremental cash flow.

For example, consider project A, which we used in our earlier illustration. At the end of Year 4, the projected incremental cash flow is $9 million. The founders must then determine how much they would be willing to receive at the end of Year 4 with certainty rather than take the risk of not receiving $9 million. Suppose that the founders would be willing to accept $7.5 million at the end of Year 4. Then $7.5 million is the certainty equivalent of $9 million. The greater the perceived risk associated with a projected incremental cash flow, the lower is the certainty equivalent.

Once the risky incremental cash flows are determined by the founders, they are then used to compute the NPV. In calculating the NPV, the WACC is used to discount the certainty equivalent incremental cash flows.

KEY POINTS COVERED IN THIS CHAPTER

- Capital budgeting decisions involve the evaluation of potential investment projects to determine those that are worthwhile undertaking.

- While some capital budgeting decisions do not have a major impact on the potential success of a startup company, some will either have an impact on the company's future market position in its current offerings of goods and services or permit it to expand into new products in the future.

- The economic assessment of a potential investment project is based on a proposed project's value.

- The valuation of proposed investment projects applies the discounted cash flow (DCF) method that is used to value a private company.

- A drawback in using the DCF method for valuing capital projects is that it tends to underestimate the enterprise value and equity value, particularly for high-tech firms, which might be better valued using the real options method.
- Proposed investment projects can be classified based on a project's economic life, a project's risk, and a project's relation to other projects.
- A project's economic life is the period of time over which the cash flow of a proposed investment project is expected to last.
- The degree of risk associated with a capital project varies with the classification of such projects as either replacement projects (less risk), or expansion projects (moderate risk), or new product or service projects (more risk).
- Replacement projects, that is, projects that involve the maintenance of existing capital projects needed to maintain production at the current operating level or to replace existing equipment with more efficient equipment, typically expose a startup to less risk than expansion projects or new product or service projects.
- Expansion projects involve expanding a company's market share of existing products and expose a company to the risk that the expenditure will not pay off because the market penetration sought is insufficient to justify the expenditure.
- Producing new products or entering into new markets exposes a company to the greatest risk.
- Because a company has a portfolio of capital projects, the decision whether or not to adopt a proposed capital project must take into account the candidate project's relationship to both existing capital projects and other proposed capital projects.
- Proposed capital projects can be classified by their relationship to existing and other proposed capital projects as independent projects, mutually exclusive projects, and complementary projects, depending on how the projected cash flows of the proposed capital project will affect the cash flows of other capital projects.
- The evaluation of a proposed independent project, a capital project where the projected cash flow has no impact on the cash flows of other capital projects, does not affect the decision whether or not to adopt other proposed capital projects.
- Mutually exclusive projects are proposed capital projects where the acceptance of one capital project means the rejection of other proposed capital projects.
- With complementary projects, the acceptance of one project enhances the projected cash flow of other proposed capital projects.
- When proposed capital projects are evaluated, the relevant cash flow is the projected incremental cash flow should the proposed capital project be undertaken.
- The incremental cash flow is composed of two components: operating cash flows and investment cash flows.

- The operating cash flows are the incremental after-tax cash flows projected for the proposed capital project as a result of operating activities.
- The investment cash flows are the capital expenditures that are needed to acquire the capital project that will generate the operating cash flows.
- The projected incremental cash flow for a proposed capital project for any year is equal to the different between the projected incremental operating cash flow and the projected investment cash flow.
- A normal cash flow pattern or conventional cash flow pattern is one in which the initial cash flows are negative, followed by positive cash flows (i.e., the sign changes once).
- A non-normal cash flow pattern or an unconventional cash flow pattern is one in which a proposed capital project may have several early years with negative cash flows followed by years of positive cash flows, and then in the last year or years a negative cash flow again (i.e., the sign changes more than once).
- Once the projected incremental cash flows for a proposed project are estimated, it is necessary to value the project to determine whether the candidate project merits adoption.
- Three methods used for valuing candidate projects: the net present value (NPV) method, the internal rate of return method, and the real options method.
- The NPV method is an application of the DCF method that involves three steps: (1) the proposed capital project's incremental cash flow is projected for each year; (2) a suitable discount rate at which to calculate the present value of the capital project's incremental cash flow each year is determined; and (3) the present value of the capital project's incremental cash flow for all the years is summed to obtain an NPV for the project.
- Determining a suitable discount rate follows much the same procedure as determining the weighted average cost of capital (WACC) for a company. The discount rate is referred to as the required rate of return (RRR) or the hurdle rate.
- If a proposed project has the same risk as the company, then the WACC may be used as the RRR for discounting the incremental cash flows.
- For a proposed project that is perceived to have greater risk than the company, a discount rate greater than the WACC should be used, with the challenge being estimating the risk and adjusting the WACC accordingly.
- A proposed project's NPV is an estimate of how the value of the company will change if the project is accepted.
- The NPV method takes into account the time value of money.
- A project with a positive NPV that is a candidate for adoption should be accepted, assuming no capital constraints exist (i.e., capital is unlimited).

- A negative NPV for a proposed project means that the project should not be considered for adoption at this time, while an NPV of zero means that the founders should be indifferent to the proposed project.
- In ranking a list of proposed projects using the NPV method, the higher the NPV is, the more attractive the proposed capital project (ignoring other constraints) should be considered.
- The internal rate of return (IRR) or yield is another method for evaluating projects that takes into account the time value of money.
- The IRR of a proposed project is computed by (1) forecasting the project's incremental cash flow for each year and (2) using an iterative process to find the discount rate that will make the present value of the project's incremental cash flows equal to zero.
- The decision rule as to whether or not a candidate project warrants adoption (assuming no other constraints) is based on a comparison of the IRR and the RRR.
- If the IRR exceeds the RRR, then the proposed capital project is a candidate for adoption. If the IRR is less than the RRR, the proposed capital project should be rejected.
- The ranking rule is that the higher the IRR, the more attractive is the proposed project (ignoring other constraints).
- There are situations in which the NPV might give a different ranking of projects than the IRR owing to (1) the reinvestment assumption about interim incremental cash flows and (2) the possibility of multiple IRRs for certain types of projects.
- Capital rationing means that there is a limit on the amount of the capital expenditure budget and, as a result, not all proposed independent capital projects that are acceptable by either the NPV method or the IRR method can be accepted if their total cost exceeds the capital expenditure budget.
- Other aspects of capital project selection that must be considered are (1) the time needed to recover the investment outlay, (2) incorporating differences in project risks, and (3) the managerial flexibility offered by a project
- A proposed project's payback period, the length of time it takes for the incremental cash flows to recover the initial capital expenditure, may be used to supplement the NPV or IRR method for determining attractive capital projects in the presence of capital rationing.
- The payback period ignores incremental cash flows beyond the payback period and ignores the time value of money.
- The discounted payback period is computed by calculating the present value of the incremental cash flows and therefore overcomes the problem of the payback period not taking into account the time value of money.
- Risk must be taken into account in some manner in evaluating the merits of proposed projects.

- Two tools for incorporating risk into capital budgeting analysis are scenario analysis and Monte Carlo simulation.

- Other methods for incorporating risk into capital budgeting analysis involve either adjusting the IRR to reflect the perceived risk associated with a proposed capital project or adjusting the incremental cash flows.

FURTHER READINGS

Bierman, Harold Jr., and Seymour Smidt, *Advanced Capital Budgeting: Refinements in the Economic Analysis of Investment Projects* (New York: Routledge, 2006).

Bierman, Harold Jr., and Seymour Smidt, *The Capital Budgeting Decision: Economic Analysis of Investment Projects,* 9th ed. (New York: Routledge, 2007).

Pachmanova, Dessislava A., and Frank J. Fabozzi, *Simulation and Optimization in Finance* (Hoboken, NJ: John Wiley & Sons, 2010), chap. 17.

Peterson, Pamela, and Frank J. Fabozzi, *Capital Budgeting: Theory and Practice* (New York: John Wiley & Sons, 2002).

18

REAL OPTIONS ANALYSIS

In our discussion of valuation of a private company and capital projects under consideration by the founders of a company, we explained the importance of (1) incorporating risk into the analysis and (2) the value of managerial flexibility. Although two tools for considering risk, explained in chapter 17, are available to investors, sensitivity analysis and simulation analysis, these tools do not provide guidance regarding which proposed capital projects to accept or reject and how to rank the alternatives. Another approach is to use decision trees, as was also explained in the previous chapter. The discounted cash flow (DCF) method used in valuing a company and proposed investment projects falls short of dealing with the value of managerial flexibility.

The approach suggested for dealing with both risk and managerial flexibility is the real options approach or real options analysis. Basically, the underlying principle of this approach is that in estimating enterprise value and equity value, within a company's existing portfolio of assets (its "assets in place") options have been created that offer the founders flexibility in making managerial decisions to increase a firm's value. In the case of proposed capital projects, there are options that may be created by a proposed capital project that should be taken into consideration in evaluating whether the project should be accepted.

Assets that a firm has in place or that founders are considering investing in may give founders the flexibility to

- expand business activity,
- contract business activity,
- abandon a business activity,
- grow by entering into a related business activity, or
- suspend a business activity and then restart that same business activity at some future time.

Moreover, proposed capital projects may provide founders not only with flexibility to do one or more of the above but also the flexibility to defer the decision to invest in a business activity. It is these flexibilities that founders may benefit from in the future that should be accounted for in valuing an enterprise and in valuing a proposed capital project. Yet such manager flexibility is not recognized by the DCF method.

In practice, real options analysis has been used by management in two general ways. The first is by using real options in a conceptual way. That is, real options analysis provides a way of thinking about the flexibility that a capital project can provide founders without trying to quantify the value of the options that a capital project may create. One might refer to this use of the real options analysis as *real options reasoning*. The second way it is used is in trying to quantify the value of the real options that may be created from a capital project. This use of real options analysis can be thought of as *real options valuation*.

What is important in understanding real options for a founding team to be able to create an option with value and then to abstract that value is differentiating between what eventually the founders must do on a project and what it may do.[1] When there are things that founders must do once a capital project is adopted, then, by definition, there is no managerial flexibility. Consequently, DCF is an acceptable approach. When there are things that founders may do, then value can be created when the founders can actively structure those elements as an option.

In this chapter we discuss the real options approach. Although our principal focus is on real options reasoning, we conclude this chapter with a brief description of real options valuation. Real options valuation requires considerable knowledge of not only standard option pricing theory, as explained in chapter 15 for the valuation of financial options, but also of how the theory must be modified to deal with the unique attributes associated with valuing capital projects and companies.

TECHNOLOGY AND REAL OPTIONS

Despite the widespread use of the DCF approach, recognition of the importance of the real options approach has long been recognized by practitioners and researchers. The concept of real options dates back to Stewart Myers, who in 1977 wrote:

It is useful for expositional purposes to think of the firm as composed of two distinct asset types: (1) real assets, which have market values independent of the firm's investment strategy, and (2) real options, which are opportunities to purchase real assets on possibly favorable terms.[2]

Myers goes on to explain why real options can be viewed as a call or a put option on real assets.

---

1. See Robert G. Fichman, Mark Keil, and Amrit Tiwana, "Beyond Valuation: 'Options Thinking' in IT Project Management," *California Management Review* 47, no. 2 (2005): 74–100. Although the focus of their paper is on IT project management, the same reasoning applies to any high-tech entrepreneurial firm.
2. Stewart C. Myers, "Determinants of Corporate Borrowing," *Journal of Financial Economics* 5 (1977): 163.

With respect to enterprise valuation, early-stage high-tech companies typically have only a few assets in place. Those assets may carry a zero value on a company's balance sheet, yet those assets in place may have created valuable options or managerial flexibility in the future. Michael J. Brennan argues that approaches to enterprise valuation should incorporate characteristics of knowledge-based high-tech firms rather than rely solely on the traditional valuation approach that has been applied to manufacturing firms, for example.[3] It is those real options that characterize high-tech companies that result in their higher valuation than that obtained from traditional valuation methods. When venture capital firms invest in an early-stage company, it is based on what they view as an early-stage company's growth opportunities, which often involve the introduction of new products and therefore effectively acquiring real options.

As an example, we may consider early R&D programs. In 1988, Graham R. Mitchell and William F. Hamilton noted that because R&D programs that were directed toward strategic positioning of a firm granted the firm the right but not the obligation to introduce the new technology to market when conditions in the market were favorable to do so, they had the attributes of put and call options on stocks.[4] As such, any investment criteria that failed to recognize the R&D option was flawed. This insight has led to a body of work referred to as the "technology options approach" in the area of longer-term strategic R&D investments. Avinash K. Dixit and Robert S. Pindyck further developed this way of thinking of how R&D capital projects were similar to financial options.[5]

Let's look at proposals for early-stage R&D expenditures.[6] To see how managerial flexibility or real options are created with such proposed capital projects, we can start with the various stages of an R&D program. The outcome of each stage for new technology provides information that enters into the decision to continue, postpone, or abandon the development of the new technology. Without the early R&D capital expenditure to reduce future uncertainty, future options cannot be created.

In the mid-1990s, Terrence W. Faulkner explained the valuable insights afforded by the principles of real options when he considered R&D programs at Eastman Kodak, and also explained how this approach generates a higher valuation than the DCF method.[7] Further, he suggested how to fix the DCF method to recognize real options. Faulkner suggested decomposing a project R&D program into phases. Each phase then would have its own discount rate for determining the value of the projected cash flow—rather than one discount

---

3. Michael J. Brennan, "Corporate Finance over the Past 25 Years," *Financial Management* 24, no. 2 (1995): 9–22.

4. Graham R. Mitchell and William F. Hamilton, "Managing R&D as a Strategic Option," *Research Technology Management* 50, no. 2 (March–April 2007): 15–22.

5. Avinash K. Dixit and Robert S. Pindyck, *Investment Under Uncertainty* (Princeton, NJ: Princeton University Press, 1994), and Avinash K. Dixit and Robert S. Pindyck, "The Options Approach to Capital Investment," *Harvard Business Review* 77 (May–June 1995): 105–115.

6. Real options that create future opportunities resulting from an early-stage R&D project to invest subsequently in a new technological area are sometimes referred to as technological options.

7. Terrence W. Faulkner, "Applying 'Options Thinking' to R&D Valuation Options," *Research Management Technology* 39, no. 3 (1996): 50–56.

rate being used for all cash flows as in the DCF method—and the analysis of each phase would depend on the analysis performed in the previous phase. In this manner, all of the options created by the R&D program would have to be considered in each phase.

There are three reasons that have been suggested as to why the valuation of technology differs from the valuation of the typical physical asset or financial asset:[8]

1. Innovative technology is an intangible asset and financially invisible. Recall from our discussion of the financial accounting treatment for intangible assets in chapter 9 that intangibles are written off as expenditures and therefore on the balance sheet they are carried at zero value. The value of innovative technology resides in the talents, experiences, and records of the scientists and engineers involved in an R&D program.

2. The value of a technology is inextricably linked to other technology assets and/or physical assets. These linkages include past, current, and future developments in technology, and the rights to this technology may be those internally generated by the firm, by the firm's customers or vendors, or by some unrelated third party. Because of these linkages, one can think of technology assets in mathematical terms as nonlinear, and they should be valued accordingly. In contrast, the analysis for valuing a potential capital project for new technology based on cash flow analysis such as NPV is a linear way of thinking about its value.

3. In contrast to the unique risk faced by investors in financial assets in the financial markets, unique risk can be far greater when investing in R&D programs. Exposure to considerable unique risk in the financial markets does occur in highly leveraged financial products known as options.

Boer goes on to explain the pitfalls, beginning with confusion between the hurdle rate and the discount rate when applied to valuing technology assets. As explained at the end of chapter 17, risk is typically taken into account in the valuation analysis by increasing the hurdle rate (or required rate of return, RRR) for higher-risk projects. Often, a firm may classify proposed capital projects into risk buckets, such as low, medium, and high risk, for example, and assign to each classification a minimum RRR. Proposed capital projects that involve new technology development usually are placed in the high-risk category and thereby require the highest RRR. When discounted at very high discount rates, the long-term cash flows become negligible, as illustrated in chapter 17. In fact, many new products can take as long as ten years (ten to fifteen years in the case of new drug R&D) to bring in significant positive cash flows. This is a misapplication of the time value of money in the case of the development of technology assets via R&D programs because it fails to take into account that further investments in an R&D program occur in stages and are not made until key risks are better assessed from earlier stages of the R&D process.

The implication is that because R&D programs occur in stages, with later stages providing information that sheds light on risk that was high at earlier stages, the RRR should not be

---

8. These reasons are suggested in F. Peter Boer, "Traps, Pitfalls and Snares in the Valuation of Technology," *Research Technology Management* 41, no. 5 (1998): 46.

constant over time. For example, in the late stages of an R&D program where a prototype has been developed and there has been customer acceptance, the appropriate RRR should be close to the risk reflected in the typical business activity of the firm rather than being assigned a high rating that may have been appropriate at an earlier stage of an R&D program.

Another pitfall is in the calculation of the DCF method is the terminal value of a proposed capital project. As explained in chapter 17, the founders select the number of years of operations that the cash flows will be measured and then the remaining years into the future are projected assuming a constant growth rate in order to obtain the terminal value. However, for technology assets it is in those years where most of the cash flow benefits are typically expected to occur. Both this arbitrary assumption about when the terminal value should be calculated and its calculation based on the assumption of a constant growth rate are unsuitable for a growth company that relies on technological innovation.

Boer also notes that the mind-set of financial analysts and those familiar with the key role played by technology in a corporate strategy is different in terms of how they view the attractiveness of proposed capital projects. Assuming no capital or other constraints, financial analysts use as their decision-making criterion the acceptance of a package of proposed independent capital projects that will maximize the company's NPV. Technology specialists, in contrast, realize that there are those complex linkages mentioned earlier that result in proposed capital projects not being truly independent and that technology is indeed all about linkages. As Boer states:

In summary, financial analysts are analyzers—they are comfortable dissecting projects into their components. It is a narrow but useful discipline.

The best technologists are synthesizers. They think broadly, are often in a domain where there are no quantitative tools, and use the language of technology. In this game, gut feel and a sense of the future, and *connectedness to the larger technological community* count as much as technical competence.[9]

Boer suggests that in valuing the options created by a proposed new technology, the following four factors should be considered: (1) technology pairing, (2) the size of current and potential markets, (3) the strength of linkages, and (4) polarization of the linkages.

MOTIVATION FOR THE REAL OPTIONS APPROACH

At this point, the discussion about how assets in place or proposed capital projects can create options that offer managerial flexibility that increase value has been abstract. To motivate the importance of the real option analysis, let's use an example.

Consider a founding team that must decide on an early R&D capital expenditure for the development of product A. The capital expenditure would be for $21 million to determine the technical feasibility of the product. To make the illustration simple, suppose that the

9. Boer, "Traps, Pitfalls and Snares in the Valuation of Technology," 51.

timeframe over which the capital project is being considered is so short that the time value of money can be ignored (i.e., we can work with undiscounted cash flows). The founding team has estimated the costs to build product A and the revenues that can be generated from product A should the product be technically feasible.

Assume that the revenue projected by the founding team is either $70 million or $182 million; estimated costs are projected to be $50 million, $112 million, or $168 million. To simplify, we will assume that the founding team believes that the two scenarios for the projected revenue are equally likely to occur, and the same for the projected costs. Hence in the analysis we can work with averages of the projected values for revenues and costs.

The average projected revenue is $126 million and the average projected cost is $110 million. Using the DCF method, the net present value (NPV) is given by:

NPV = $126 million − $110 million − $21 million = −$5 million.

Hence, based on the NPV rule, the capital expenditure for early R&D to develop product A should not be undertaken since the NPV is negative.

It is important to bear in mind that the NPV analysis above uses values for the revenues and costs that are uncertain. Let's make two assumptions here. First, let's assume that the major source of uncertainty is the cost of producing product A. Second, let's assume that the $21 million spent on early R&D will be able to provide more information about what the costs will be at the end of one year. If it is determined that the projected cost to manufacture product A is the largest of the three costs ($168 million), the founding team will not undertake the R&D expenditure given the assumptions above. The profit (i.e., revenue minus costs) for each scenario for the costs assumed is then given by:

Profit (if cost is $50 million) = $126 million − $50 million = $76 million.

Profit (if cost is $112 million) = $126 million − $112 million = $14 million.

Profit (if cost is $168 million) = $0.

Notice in the last cost scenario there is no revenue and no cost, so the profit is zero. The average profit would be $30 million, and the NPV would then be $9 million (= $30 million − $21 million). Since the NPV is positive, the NPV rule indicates that the capital expenditure for R&D for product A should be made once the value of the option to not proceed further with the project is recognized

Thus, using the NPV approach, the early R&D capital expenditure should not be undertaken, but after allowing for the resolution of the uncertainty about the cost of product A, that expenditure becomes worthwhile. The reason is that the $21 million expenditure created for the founding team an option to obtain more information on the cost associated with manufacturing product A, an option that is not taken into consideration by NPV analysis.

In our illustration, the early R&D expenditure allows the founding team to avoid scenarios that may result in losses. Another way of interpreting what we have just observed is that the founding team was able to abandon (i.e., had the option to abandon) the development of product A if the unfavorable cost scenario was likely to occur after more information was obtained from the $21 million expenditure.

Although we have simplified the illustration by assuming that the time period is short so that we can work with undiscounted values, there is another way in which the real options approach is superior to the NPV approach. Recall that under the NPV approach it is common practice to account for risk by adjusting the NPV. For example, suppose that the founding team that is considering the development of product A classifies capital projects into two risk categories: "high," requiring a rate of return of 30%, and "average," requiring a rate of return of 20%. Suppose further that 20% is the firm's weighted average cost of capital (WACC), and therefore 20% reflects the risk associated with the firm's typical capital project or business activity. Under the NPV approach, the R&D capital expenditure would have all cash flows discounted at 30%. However, with real options analysis, the resolution of uncertainty occurring after the initial investment may result in the founding team reclassifying the risk as an average risk, which in turn can justify the use of a 20% RRR (i.e., the firm's WACC).

Although our illustration focused on valuing a proposed capital project, the same principle of real options value that is created by assets in place applies when valuing enterprise value or equity value.

Interpretation of Buying Call and Put Options in the Context of Capital Budgeting

In chapter 15, we explained financial options and the payoff for the buyer of a call and put options. Let's look at an alternative way to interpret financial options that might be more useful in understanding real options.

We'll consider first a call option. This option gives the decision maker at some time in the future the right to purchase the option's underlying asset at the exercise price. The cost of buying the option is the option price. By exercising the call option, the decision maker is entitled to receive the expected future cash flow of the option's underlying asset. For example, in the case of a financial option, the underlying asset might be a share of common stock. By exercising the option, the decision maker pays the exercise price and is entitled to receive the stock's expected future cash flows. By not exercising the option, the decision maker avoids paying the exercise price and gives up the stock's expected future cash flows. Whether the option is exercised or not, the decision maker forgoes the option price paid.

Now let's assume that the underlying asset is a capital project that involves early R&D that the founders are considering, as in our earlier illustration in this chapter. In assessing the proposed capital project in the context of an option, if the founders decide to go ahead with the project, an investment outlay of $21 million must be made. Using financial option terminology, the $21 million is the option price. We assumed in our illustration that the founder must make the decision whether or not to invest an additional amount one year later after the information is obtained from the $21 million outlay. Remember that the founders have the right but not the obligation to exercise the option. If the founders decide to exercise the option by proceeding with the development of product A, the company is entitled to receive the project's expected cash flow.

Real Options Analysis and the R&D Process for Pharmaceutical and Biotechnology Companies

One of the most common applications of real options analysis is to R&D programs for new drugs by pharmaceutical companies and biotech companies.[10] As noted by Stewart Myers, "DCF is no help at all for pure research and development. The value of R&D is almost all option value."[11]

Here we provide a brief description of the R&D process, referring to the pharmaceutical company or the biotech company as the sponsoring company. We will focus on the technical risk. The purpose of providing this description is to highlight why real options are more complex than standard financial options.

Each compound tested by a sponsoring company is essentially a capital project. The risks faced by the sponsoring company bringing an innovative drug to market are technical risks and market risks. Technical risks are the risk of failure resulting from scientific failures. Market risks are the risks associated with the commercial performance of the drug when it is introduced into the market. Some important statistics provided by the pharmaceutical industry that are important for understanding the risks associated with bringing a new drug to market are the following:[12]

- It takes ten to fifteen years to develop a drug.
- The average cost to research and develop a successful drug ranges from $800 million to $1 billion, a figure that includes the costs associated with failures.
- For every 5,000 to 10,000 compounds that are investigated to develop a drug, only one gets approved.

The R&D process involves a highly regulated, fixed sequence of R&D stages. The R&D process has two stages before a request is filed for regulatory approval from the Food and Drug Administration (FDA) in the United States (or the European Medicines Agency in the European Union): the prediscovery stage and clinical trial stage. In each stage there are phases.

10. The difference between pharmaceutical companies and biotech companies is that the former develop small compounds that are small molecules based on chemicals or plant synthesis while biotech companies use biotechnology to create large-scale molecule drugs to cure a specific disease or condition. Because of the time it takes to recreate and test those drugs, the R&D process tends to be longer for biotech companies seeking to obtain regulatory approval. Pharmaceutical companies often enter into partnerships with biotech companies to license approved drugs.

11. Stewart C. Myers, "Financial Theory and Financial Strategy," *Interfaces* 14 (1984): 135.

12. "Drug Discovery and Development: Understanding the R&D Process," Pharma, February 2007, http://www.phrma.org/sites/default/files/pdf/rd_brochure_022307.pdf. The description of the R&D process here draws from this publication.

The prediscovery stage comprises the following two phases:

- **Prediscovery phase:** In this phase, the purpose is to understand the disease for which a drug treatment is sought, select the lead compounds that offer the opportunity to create a new drug, confirm that the target drug can act on the disease, perform initial tests on the lead compounds identified, and modify the structure of those lead compounds to improve their properties so that they will effectively perform as desired.
- **Preclinical testing phase:** In this phase, lab testing and animal testing are undertaken to determine whether the lead compounds that are candidates for use in the drug are safe enough to be tested in humans.

The prediscovery stage takes three to six years. If the prediscovery stage is successful, the sponsoring company must do clinical testing on humans. However, permission to move on to the clinical trial stage requires regulatory approval. The sponsoring company must submit an Investigational New Drug application to regulators. If it is approved by regulators, the sponsoring company may move on to clinical trials in humans. The clinical trial stage has three phases:

- **Phase 1:** Testing of the target drug is performed on 20 to 100 healthy volunteers to determine how it is absorbed in the body, metabolized, and eliminated from the body; to identify any side effects; to determine a safe dosage; and to determine whether the drug can be improved by further altering the structure of the leading compounds.
- **Phase 2:** Testing of the target drug is performed on 100 to 500 patients who are afflicted by the disease or condition. The purpose here is to identify potential short-term side effects and other medical risks, assess whether the drug is performing as expected, and determine the optimal dosage and scheduling of drug administration.
- **Phase 3:** The last stage of clinical testing is the most costly and has the longest testing period. The drug is administered to a large group of patients (1,000 to 5,000) to generate data that would provide statistically meaningful conclusions regarding the safety and efficacy of the drug.

During the clinical trial stage, particularly Phase 3, the sponsoring company will plan for the large-scale production of the drug.

After a statistical analysis of the data generated from the clinical trials, the sponsoring company seeking to market the drug must file a New Drug application with the FDA requesting approval to do so. The application, which may be more than 100,000 pages long, is then reviewed by an advisory committee of experts convened by the FDA to determine the safety of the drug and its effectiveness. The FDA's review process may have one of three outcomes: (1) approval, (2) approval pending the receipt of more information, or (3) denial of approval.

From this brief description of the R&D process that a pharmaceutical company must go through, the following should be noted as it relates to real options. First, the option is not a standard financial option but a compound option (more technically a compound call option). As explained in chapter 15, a compound option is a combination of sequential options in which the exercise of one option allows the option buyer (management) the choice of entering into another option agreement.

Second, real options analysis assumes that the capital project's value changes over time based on some assumed random (i.e., stochastic) process. The random process is assumed to exhibit high volatility for the random variables that are believed to drive the capital project's value. The reason for applying the standard option pricing model for financial options, described in chapter 15, is that the option has some value during its life. This is not the case for some capital projects because a capital project may at some point become worthless as a result of some event. Such events might include a technological problem that cannot be overcome or a government regulation that makes the intended product or service impossible to market. This is particularly true for drug R&D programs. As explained in chapter 15, a financial option that has this characteristic is called a knock-out option. Applying the straightforward standard option pricing model, which ignores the knock-out feature, would result in the overvaluation of a capital project, so the real options approach is preferred in this situation.

CLASSIFICATION OF REAL OPTIONS

Real options are created in existing assets and proposed capital projects. The most commonly used classification is that suggested by Thomas E. Copeland and Philip T. Keenan and is referred to as the 7S framework.[13] Within this classification are three categories: growth options, abandonment options, and deferral options. Within each category are different types of options. The real options, created by an asset in place or a proposed capital project, may occur in combination; that is, there are complex options such as compound real options and knock-out options, as explained chapter 15.

Growth Options

There are three types of growth options: scale-up options, switch-up options, and scope-up options. A *scale-up option* created by a proposed capital project offers future value-creating opportunities. A proposed capital project that gives management the flexibility to upgrade technology during a project's life in order to produce a better product or reduce the cost of production is called a *switch-up option*. When a capital project in a proprietary asset in one industry enables management to enter another industry on a cost-effective basis, that real option is referred to as a *scope-up option.*

---

13. Thomas E. Copeland and Philip T. Keenan, "How Much Is Flexibility Worth?," *McKinsey Quarterly* 2 (1998): 38–49.

Abandonment (Shrink or Disinvest) Options

Whereas growth options afford managerial flexibility for scaling up, switching up, and scoping up operations, abandonment options provide management with the flexibility for scaling down, switching down, and scoping down operations.

A *scale-down option* is an option created that allows management to either close down a capital project or reduce its scale as more information about the factors that could affect the profitability of the project is obtained. When a proposed capital project allows management to switch to a more cost-effective method of production as more information becomes available or market conditions change (such as the relative costs of inputs), the option is said to be a *switch-down option*. Finally, a *scope-down option* is created by a proposed capital project that allows management the flexibility to limit the scope of options or completely abandon the project if no further profit potential may be provided by the proposed capital project.

Deferral Options

A *deferral option* is a created option that allows management to delay investment in a capital project until more information is acquired or more resources can be acquired. Because this type of real option allows management to obtain more information before making a subsequent investment, it is also referred to as a *learning option*.

PRACTITIONER USE OF REAL OPTIONS ANALYSIS

The original work on real options was set forth by Stewart Myers in 1977 when he stated that there are "opportunities to purchase real assets on possibly favorable terms," followed by an extension of this work in 1984.[14] Beginning in the last decade of the twentieth century, publications started appearing describing the use of real options analysis by major companies. As far back as 1993, Angelien Kemna provided three case studies of the use of the real options approach by Shell.[15] In 1994 the then CFO of Merck in an interview published in the *Harvard Business Review* mentioned the use of real options analysis.[16] In the last five years of the 1990s, researchers developed analytical methods for estimating the value of real options.

Reports that major companies such as Shell and Merck were using the real options approach led Peter Coy in a 1999 *Business Week* article to declare that there was a "real options revolution" that would dominate capital budget decision making. Thomas Copeland and Vladimir Antikarov in 2001 predicted that the real options approach would be the dominant tool for assessing capital projects by the end of the first decade of the twenty-first

---

14. Myers, "Determinants of Corporate Borrowing" and "Financial Theory and Financial Strategy."
15. Angelien G. Z. Kemna, "Case Studies on Real Options," *Financial Management*, Autumn 1993, 259–270.
16. Nancy A. Nichols, "Scientific Management at Merck: An Interview with CFO Judy Lewent," *Harvard Business Review* 72 (1994): 89–99.

century.[17] A survey on the use of real options analysis for R&D decision making in the pharmaceutical industry by Marcus Hartmann and Ali Hassa, conducted in February and October 2004, concluded that the application of real options analysis as a concept was "gaining favour, because it provides a more holistic project analysis without the necessity to change current valuation methods fundamentally."[18] Despite this finding and the occasional publication indicating the use of real options analysis by a major company,[19] survey studies did not find widespread acceptance of this approach for capital budgeting.[20]

The criticism of using real options reasoning is that it is unclear in terms of what decision makers should do.[21] Some hold that advocates of the real options approach provide vague analogies as to why the approach should be used rather than specific implementation methods.[22] Consequently, some practitioners view the real options approach as a theoretical-academic construct.

REAL OPTIONS VALUATION MODELS

As explained at the outset of this chapter, real options analysis can be used by management in two ways: real options reasoning and real options valuation. Our focus thus far has been on the former. We conclude this chapter with a discussion of real options valuation.

Initially, advocates of real options valuation illustrated how the most popular pricing model for financial options, the Black-Scholes model discussed in chapter 15, can be used. Despite the popularity of the model, it is based on assumptions that make it unsuitable for the valuation of complex financial options. As described earlier, the real options faced by managers are more aptly described as complex financial options (compound options with knock-out features) rather than as standard financial options. Hence, very few practitioners apply the Black-Scholes model to value early-stage companies.

Instead, a more popular approach has been to identify and then quantify the key drivers of a company's cash flows in obtaining a valuation. The relevant cash flows are projected

17. Peter Coy, "Exploiting Uncertainty: The Real-Options Revolution in Decision Making," *Business Week,* June 7, 1999, 118–124.

18. Marcus Hartmann and Ali Hassa, "Application of Real Options Analysis for Pharmaceutical R&D Project Valuation: Empirical Results from a Survey," *Research Policy* 35 (2006): 343–354.

19. See, for example, Martha Amram, Fanfu Li, and Cheryl A. Perkins, "How Kimberly-Clark Uses Real Options," *Journal of Applied Corporate Finance* 18 (2006): 40–47.

20. These surveys of companies since 2006 include Fadi Alkaraan and Deryl Northcott, "Strategic Capital Investment Decision-Making: A Role for Emergent Analysis Tools? A Study of Practice in Large UK Manufacturing Companies," *British Accounting Review* 38 (2006): 149–173, 2006; Stanley Block, "Are 'Real Options' Actually Used in the Real World?" *Engineering Economist* 52 (2007): 255–267, and Richard M. Burns and Joe Walker, "Capital Budgeting Surveys: The Future Is Now," *Journal of Applied Finance* 19 (2009): 78–90.

21. Ron Adner and Daniel A. Levinthal, "What is Not a Real Option: Considering Boundaries for the Application of Real Options to Business Strategy," *Academy of Management Review* 29 (2004): 74–85.

22. Michael L. Barnett and Roger L. M. Dunbar, "Making Sense of Real Options Reasoning: An Engine of Choice or Backfires?" in *Handbook of Organization Decision Making*, ed. Gerald P. Hodgkinson and William H. Starbuck (New York: Oxford University Press, 2008), 383–398. Barnett and Dunbar trace the development of real options reasoning and explain the difficulties associated implementing real options reasoning.

over time using statistical models, and those models allow managerial flexibility with respect to the assets that the company has in place in the case of enterprise valuation, and managerial flexibility provided by the proposed capital project in the case of project valuation. The approach involves considerable statistical and modeling skills.

Below we provide a sampling of the models for real options valuation for enterprise valuation and capital project valuation.

Enterprise Valuation Model for Early-Stage High-Tech Companies: The Moon-Schwartz Model

A complex real options valuation model for enterprise valuation was first used in valuing Internet companies by Eduardo S. Schwartz and Mark Moon in 2000. They then applied their model to the valuation of Amazon.com.[23] Although we will not provide the details of their enterprise valuation model for Internet companies, we will describe the key modeling aspects so that the complexities associated with such valuation approaches for estimating enterprise value can be appreciated.

Schwartz and Moon begin with a "continuous-time model" of the key drivers of an Internet company valuation. Continuous-time models are commonly used in finance for modeling variables.[24] The key drivers are those variables that affect the cash flows of the company whose valuation is sought, such as revenue and expenses (both fixed and variable, as explained in chapter 14). Although the valuation model is formulated as a continuous-time model, the data for a company whose valuation is sought are provided in discrete time, typically quarterly. Consequently, Schwartz and Moon had to obtain a "discrete-time model" that could approximate the continuous-time model.

To implement the model, they had to make numerous assumptions about possible future financing and about future cash distributions to both stockholders and bondholders. The implementation of the model to obtain the valuation required estimating the parameters of the model based on available data from the company. There were more than twenty parameters in the model. As Schwartz and Moon note, "The estimation of the parameters of the model is probably the most critical in the analysis—and the one that requires the most expertise about the particular Internet company being valued and its industry."[25] The problem is that for early-stage companies, the limited history in terms of financial information and operating performance means that the parameters estimated for the model are subject to considerable estimation error. For Amazon.com, Schwartz and Moon used quarterly sales and costs to obtain earnings before interest, taxes, depreciation, and amortization (EBITDA) for fifteen quarters, March 1996 to September 2009.

---

23. Eduardo S. Schwartz and Mark Moon, "Rational Pricing of Internet Companies," *Financial Analysts Journal,* May–June 2000, 62–74.
24. More specifically, the key variables are modeled in terms of a stochastic differential equation. For a comprehensive discussion of continuous-time models, see Robert C. Merton, *Continuous-Time Finance* (New York: Wiley-Blackwell, 1992).
25. Schwartz and Moon, "Rational Pricing of Internet Companies," 65.

Given the discrete-time model and the estimated parameters, the valuation is obtained using Monte Carlo simulation. Because the parameters of the model are subject to estimation error, scenario analysis using alternative estimates for the parameters was employed. In applying their valuation model to Amazon.com, Schwartz and Moon found that two sets of parameters had a significant impact on the firm's value. The first was the variable components of the cost function. The second was the stochastic process of the changes in the growth rate in revenues.

There are two interesting takeaways from the work by Schwartz and Moon. First, despite the statement that the model they present is simple, to those not trained in financial modeling the model is far from simple. What it does do in attempting to financially model the company—and this is the second takeaway—is that it makes the founders focus on the key drivers of their company's value. This gets us back to the use of real options analysis for real options reasoning purposes.

The Schwartz-Moon model was applied to the valuation of an Internet firm that is traded in the market. Its application to the valuation of an early-stage high-tech firm is much more difficult owing to the absence of a sufficient operating and financial history necessary to estimate the parameters required to implement a financial model. Subsequent researchers have proposed applying the real options method to early-stage companies.

Enterprise Valuation Model for R&D for Pharmaceutical and Biotechnology Companies

Evaluating R&D programs for drug development by pharmaceutical and biotechnology companies has been a principal focus of advocates of the real options approach. Several studies have shown how valuation using the real options approach is superior to the DCF approach for assessing R&D investment strategies in the pharmaceutical industry.[26] These studies show how the real options approach to valuing R&D projects can be formulated to allow for the possibility of permanent project failure. Schwartz and Moon, for example, developed a real options model to evaluate R&D projects when there is a possibility of a catastrophic event resulting in a project's value being zero.[27] Danny Cassimon, M. De Backer, Peter-Jan Engelen, Martine Van Wouwe, and V. Yordanov treated the problem as a compound options problem, using discrete success-failure probabilities at each stage of the project to reflect technical catastrophic failure to value R&D for a pharmaceutical licensing opportunity.[28]

The Schwartz-Moon model for enterprise valuation of Internet companies described earlier values an early-stage company in what might be aptly described as a "stand-alone"

26. See, for example, Rita Gunther McGrath and Atul Nerkar, "Real Options Reasoning and a New Look at the R&D Investment Strategies of Pharmaceutical Firms," *Strategic Management Journal* 25 (2004): 1–21.
27. Edwardo S. Schwartz and Mark Moon, "Evaluating R&D Investments," in Michael Brennan and Lenos Trigeorgis (eds), *Project Flexibility, Agency and Competition* (Oxford: Oxford University Press, 2000), 85–106. The stochastic process that Schwartz and Moon assume is the Poisson process.
28. Danny Cassimon, M. De Backer, Peter-Jan Engelen, Martino Van Wouwe, and V. Yordanov, "Incorporating Technical Risk into a Compound Option Model to Value a Pharma R&D Licensing Opportunity," *Research Policy* 40 (2011): 1200–1216.

model. That is, the company is valued by considering all of its business opportunities collectively. Another approach is to value a company by looking at it component businesses. David Kellogg and John M. Charnes used this type of approach to value biotechnology companies.[29] Their purpose was to produce a model that could be used by common stock analysts to value biotech companies that showed promise of developing a blockbuster drug. The valuation is equal to the sum of the values of its drug development projects. The model was applied to Agouron Pharmaceuticals, which was developing a drug to treat HIV-positive patients (Viracept).

Kellogg and Charnes added a growth option to the valuation model because the development of an initial new molecular entity is similar to buying a call option on the value of a subsequent new molecular entity. The method used to calculate the value of Agouron Pharmaceuticals was a binomial-lattice model, a common model for valuing financial options and one that allows inclusion of the growth option.

Because Agouron Pharmaceuticals was a publicly traded company since 1987, Kellogg and Charnes were able to compare their valuation to the traded stock price. The valuations were compared on five significant dates in the development of Viracept: the start of preclinical trials (June 1994), the announcement that the company would begin Phase 1 trials (October 20, 1994), fiscal year-ends 1995 and 1996, and the announcement that the company was filing a new drug application for Viracept (December 23, 1996). Kellogg and Charnes found the following:

The methods used here to find the value of Agouron worked best early in the life of the Viracept project, when the use of industry averages for completion time and revenue streams were more easily justified. As Viracept progressed, our use of averages did not work as well. A financial analyst closely following the stock would probably have had better estimates for the later stages of the important inputs. Using the real-options approach outlined here with better information could be a powerful addition to a security analyst's toolbox.[30]

Real Options Valuation for High-Tech Companies with Patents Pending

Because of the uncertainty that investors face as to whether a patent application will succeed, the valuation of an early-stage company that must include a technology that is as yet unpatented makes valuation difficult. J. Barry Lin and Anthony F. Herbst propose a real options model for the valuation of a company that has patents pending.[31] Effectively, such cases involve the valuation of an embedded growth option. Using a numerical example, Lin and Herbst demonstrate how the real options approach can be applied to an early-stage high-tech company to resolve the uncertainty associated with pending patents and how to

---

29. David Kellogg and John M. Charnes, "Real-Options Valuation for a Biotechnology Company," *Financial Analysts Journal,* May–June 2000, 76–84.
30. Kellogg and Charnes, "Real-Options Valuation for a Biotechnology Company," 84.
31. J. Barry Lin and Anthony F. Herbst, "Valuation of a Startup Business with Pending Patent Using Real Options," January 15, 2003, http://www.usapr.org/Papers_Source/37.pdf.

properly value an optimally exercised growth option. The optimal exercise is critical in the valuation. In addition, Lin and Herbst explain an important difference between the asset value-evolution type of uncertainty associated with the real options, and the business risk type of uncertainty associated with the patent application.

Commercial Software Models for Valuing Real Options

Several commercial vendors offer software that can be used for valuing real options. Consulting firms that specialize in real options valuation employ proprietary models. Real options valuation models should not be used blindly. Candidate models should be carefully evaluated for the underlying assumptions and framework. The assumptions and the estimates of the parameters are critical to the valuation. For example, a naïve application of the Black-Scholes model may produce valuations that are unrealistic for the valuation at hand.

KEY POINTS COVERED IN THIS CHAPTER

- A switch-up option created by a proposed capital project gives management the flexibility to upgrade technology during a project's life in order to produce a better product or reduce the cost of production.

- A scope-up option created by a proposed capital project in a proprietary asset in one industry enables management to enter another industry on a cost-effective basis.

- Abandonment options embedded in a proposed capital project provide management with the flexibility to scale down, switch down, and scope down operations.

- A scale-down option embedded in a proposed capital project allows management to either close down a capital project or reduce the scale of a capital project as more information about the factors that could affect the profitability of a project is obtained.

- A switch-down option in a proposed capital project allows management to switch to a more cost-effective method of production as more information becomes available or market conditions change.

- A scope-down option created by a proposed capital project allows management the flexibility to limit the scope of options or completely abandon the project if no further profit potential may be provided by the proposed capital project.

- A deferral option (or learning option) is an option that allows management to delay investment in a capital project until more information or more resources can be acquired.

- From an implementation perspective, the criticism of even the real options reasoning approach is that it is unclear in terms of what decision makers should do, providing only vague analogies as to why the approach should be used rather than specific implementation methods.

- With respect to using real options analysis for enterprise valuation, the real options faced by managers are complex financial options (compound options with knock-out features) rather than standard financial options.

- The assumptions required to apply the most popular option pricing model, the Black-Scholes model, to estimate the enterprise value of early-stage companies makes it difficult to use in practice.

- A popular approach to applying real options analysis has been to identify and then quantify the key drivers of a company's cash flows to determine a company's valuation.

- Several complex real options valuation models for enterprise valuation have been proposed.

- Implementation of models to use real options analysis requires considerable modeling and statistical skills, as well as the imposition of many assumptions about possible future financing and about future cash distributions to both stockholders and bondholders.

- Evaluating R&D programs for drug development by pharmaceutical and biotechnology companies has been a principal focus of advocates of the real options approach.

- Real options analysis has been used for the valuation of early-stage high-tech companies to resolve the uncertainty associated with pending patents and how to properly value an optimally exercised growth option.

- Several commercial vendors have developed software that can be used for valuing real options.

FURTHER READINGS

Real Options Reasoning

Dzyuma, Ulyana, "Real Options Compared to Traditional Company Valuation Methods: Possibilities and Constraints in Their Use," *e-Finanse: Financial Internet Quarterly* 8, no. 2 (2012): 51–68.

Feinstein, Steven P., and Diane M. Lander, "A Better Understanding of Why NPV Undervalues Managerial Flexibility," *Engineering Economist* 47 (2002): 418–435.

Goldberg, David H., and Michael D. Goldenberg, "Why Entrepreneurs and VCs Disagree in Valuing Start-up Firms: Imputing the Target Rate of Return using DCF vs. Option-Based Approaches," *Journal of Private Equity* 13, no. 1 (2009):73–79.

Guerrero, Raul, "The Case for Real Options Made Simple," *Journal of Applied Corporate Finance* 19 (2007): 38–49.

Kester, W. Carl, "Today's Options for Tomorrow's Growth," *Harvard Business Review* 62, no. 1 (1984): 153–160.

Kulatilaka, Nalin, "Operating Flexibilities in Capital Budgeting: Substitutability and Complementarity in Real Options," in *Real Options in Capital Investment: Models, Strategies and Applications,* ed. Lenos Trigeorgis (Westport, CT: Praeger, 1995).

Kulatilaka, Nalin, "The Value of Flexibility: A General Model of Real Options," in Trigeorgis, ed., *Real Options in Capital Investment: Models, Strategies and Applications.*

McGrath, Rita G., "Falling Forward: Real Options Reasoning and Entrepreneurial Failure," *Academy of Management Review* 24, no. 2(1999): 13–30.

McGrath, Rita G., "A Real Options Logic for Initiating Technology Positioning Investments," *Academy of Management Review* 22, no. 4 (1997): 974–996.

Mun, Johnathan, *Real Option Analysis: Tools and Techniques for Valuing Strategic Investments and Decisions* (New York: John Wiley & Sons, 2002).

Myers, Stewart, and Saman Majd, "Abandonment Value and Project Life," *Advances in Futures and Options Research* 4 (1990): 1–21.

van Putten, Alexander B., and Ian C. McMillian, "Making Real Options Really Work," *Harvard Business Review* 82, no. 12 (2005): 134–143.

Real Options Applications

Angelis, Diana I., "Capturing the Option Value of R&D," *Research Technology Management* 43, no. 4 (2000): 31–34.

Benaroch, Michele, Sandeep Shah, and Mark Jeffery, "On the Valuation of Multistage Information Technology Investments Embedding Nested Real Options," *Journal of Management Information Systems* 23, no. 1 (2006): 239–261.

Dai, Qizhi, Robert J. Kauffman, and Salvatore T. March, "Valuing Information Technology Infrastructures: A Growth Options Approach," *Information Technology and Management* 8 (2007): 1–17.

Hartmann, Marcus, and Ali Hassan, "Application of Real Options Analysis for Pharmaceutical R&D Project Valuation: Empirical Results from a Survey," *Research Policy* 35 (2006): 343–354.

Lia, Ye, Peter Jan Engelenab, and Clemens Koola, "A Barrier Options Approach to Modeling Project Failure: The Case of Hydrogen Fuel Infrastructure," Tjalling C. Koopmans Research Institute, Discussion Paper Series 13–01, December 2012.

Lint, Onno, and Enrico Pennings, "An Option Approach to the New Product Development Process: A Case Study at Philips Electronics," *R&D Management* 31, no. 2 (2001): 163–172.

Myneni, Ravi, David P. Newton, and Alan W. Pearson, "Managing Uncertainty in Research and Development," *Technovation* 21 (2001): 79–90.

Newton, David P., Dean A. Paxson, and Martin Widdicks, "Real R&D Options," *International Journal of Management Reviews* 5/6, no. 2 (2004): 113–130.

Newton, David P., and Alan W. Pearson, "Application of Option Pricing Theory to R&D," *R&D Management* 24 (1994): 83–89.

Pachamanova, Dessislava A., and Frank J. Fabozzi, *Simulation and Optimization in Finance* (Hoboken, NJ: John Wiley & Sons, 2010), chap. 18.

Sereno, Luigi, "Real Options Valuation of Pharmaceutical Patents: A Case Study," *SSRN Electronic Journal,* 2/2010, doi: 10.2139/ssrn.1547185.

Shockley, Richard L., Staci Curtis, Jonathan Jafari, and Kristopher Tibbs, "The Option Value of an Early-Stage Biotechnology Investment," *Journal of Applied Corporate Finance* 15, no. 2 (2003): 44–55.

Appendix A

CASE: UBER (2014)

In 2010 the founders of StumbleUpon (Garrett Camp) and Red Swoosh (Travis Kalanick) revolutionized the ride-sharing and taxi industries with their next big thing: Uber, a transportation network startup that connects passengers with nearby drivers through a mobile application. The entrepreneurs began by identifying a clear problem: the near impossibility of hailing a cab in San Francisco. They wanted to find a solution that would allow "style, comfort and convenience." Thus Uber emerged as a limo time-share service company, using an iPhone app for transporting customers around San Francisco on demand. By its third year, Uber was generating $125 million in annual revenue.

However, this on-demand transportation service has not faced the warmest reception from some competitors and customers alike. Uber has been the defendant in many lawsuits and considerable litigation, in addition to public protests, from the taxi unions, Uber drivers, and the victims "its drivers" have injured. It has also faced backlash for its price surges and is currently banned in many cities.

Despite these speed bumps, Uber continued to look forward, growing at 20% a month and adding nearly 80,000 new clients a week, with a presence in over 100 cities as of May 2014. Uber also offered a variety of brands, such as UberX and UberTaxi, allowing it to appeal to customers in all price ranges. Furthermore, its management does not seem to be thinking of stopping any time soon. According to Uber CEO Travis Kalanick, there was a lot more in store beyond the taxi industry. For example, as of May 2014 Uber had tested other forms of transportation, such as helicopters between New York City and the Hamptons on Long Island, New York.

In this case study we describe Uber's business model, the milestones it achieved on its way to becoming the huge international brand it is today, and its financing over various stages of its startup cycle.

This case was prepared in May 2014 by Dalia Katan, Joseph Saitta, Thomas Hopkins, David Coneway, Joseph Cloud, Amanda Bird, and Brett Geren as part of a course project (Entrepreneurial Finance) at Princeton University. Subsequently one of the co-authors, Joseph Saitta, joined the staff of Uber and received permission from the firm to remain a co-author.

Company Background

With a prototype developed in 2009 and a first test run in January 2010, Uber was ready for its official launch in San Francisco in June 2010. By August 2010 Uber had its first CEO, Ryan Graves, and had caught the eye of customers, competitors, and investors alike. Gone were the days of hailing cabs or calling a dispatcher, for Uber had found a way to "fix bad taxis forever"[1] through its luxury on-demand car service.

Camp and Kalanick definitely had a knack for spotting opportunities from the start. In many ways, San Francisco was the perfect incubator for Uber's launch. Not only was San Francisco known for its poor cab service, but it was (and is) also known for its large technology community, which is "continually looking for new tools and services that improve their quality of life" and ready to talk about these services on a moment's notice.[2] Customers loved the simplicity of Uber: iPhone and Android users merely had to download the app, enter their payment information, and request a car. Through Uber's sponsorship of local technology events and free rides, the technology community was quickly abuzz about the new app that had completely changed their commute home. After its success in San Francisco, Uber expanded to nearly ten cities the following year, and in April 2012 it launched its taxilike service in Chicago, when the new CEO, Kalanick, caught on to the city's high capacity of cabs (50% more per capita than New York City)[3] and low prices. Camp and Kalanick also quickly caught on to what customers wanted, holding a wide array of promotions from on-demand ice cream trucks in the summer of 2012 (Uber Ice Cream) to helicopter rides from New York City to the Hamptons the following July.

Funding came quickly too, with venture funding in late 2010 from super angel investors in Silicon Valley and more than $11.5 million in Series A funding by 2011. Not long thereafter, Uber raised another $32 million from several companies, including Goldman Sachs, Menlo Ventures, and Bezos Expeditions. By August 2013 Uber had closed $361.2 million in its latest round of funding, with nearly $268 million from Google Ventures, valuing the company at $3.76 billion post-money.

Business Model

In discussing business models in their book *Business Model Generation*, Alexander Osterwalder and Yves Pigneur state, "Business models describe the rationale of how an organization creates, delivers and captures value."[4] They list nine building blocks that should make up a business model, and together these nine elements form the Business Model Canvas. The business model for Uber will be discussed using this established template.

---

1. See the web page http://www.businessinsider.com/uber-has-changed-my-life-and-as-god-is-my-witness-i-will-never-take-a-taxi-again-where-available-2014-1.
2. See the web page http://growthhackers.com/companies/uber.
3. See the web page http://techcrunch.com/2012/04/18/uber-experiments-with-lower-priced-taxis-in-chicago-through-newly-launched-labs-group-garage.
4. Alexander Osterwalder and Yves Pigneur, *Business Model Generation* (Hoboken, NJ: John Wiley & Sons, 2010). For a further description of the Business Model Canvas, see chapter 2 in this book.

The first part of the Business Model Canvas is a company's key partners. Uber's main partnerships are local limousine companies. Uber works with many local limousine companies in each city in which it operates to acquire a steady stream of drivers. These drivers are able to keep around 80% of the fares from their trips while Uber receives the other 20%.[5] In addition to partnering with local limousine companies, Uber partnered with Google in May 2014. On May 6, 2014, Google updated its Google Maps app to include Uber integration. With this new feature, users of Google Maps can immediately hire an Uber car when searching for locations on the map.[6] Finally, Uber has also partnered with the NFL Players Association to encourage users to hire a Uber ride after a night out.[7]

The next building block is key activities. The first key activity that is part of Uber's business model is mobile app creation and maintenance. Uber is an app that operates on smartphones, and the app must remain problem free for Uber to be successful. The second key activity in Uber's business model is hiring drivers. As described earlier, Uber contracts with local limousine companies to maintain a steady supply of drivers in every city.

The next important building block is the value proposition. A value proposition describes the unique benefit that a firm offers to its customers. Uber's value proposition is simple: the service allows users to remotely call for a ride that Uber guarantees to be clean, professional, safe, and on time.[8] In large cities, where hailing a taxi from the street can often be extremely difficult, Uber offers the convenience of a scheduled ride for an affordable price and connects its customers with a reliable source of transportation at the click of a button on a phone.

Another building block in the Business Model Canvas is customer relationships. For Uber, this is one of the most important parts of the company's business model. Uber establishes relationships with its customers through personal assistance. An Uber employee directly picks up customers and drives them to their destination. Uber also interacts with customers through its automated services as Uber customers order their rides through a mobile app. To build positive customer relationships, Uber must do two things. First, it must ensure that its automated services (the mobile app) are working properly. Second and must ensure that customers are receiving the clean, professional, safe, and prompt ride that they are promised. These two areas capture the core of Uber's customer relationships under their business plan.

The next part of the Business Model Canvas is the customer segment. Uber creates value for consumers in the mass transportation market. Anyone who has a smartphone has access to a ride provided by Uber that would cost an amount comparable to that charged by most

---

5. See the web page http://www.huffingtonpost.com/david-fagin/life-as-an-uber-driver_b_4698299.html.
6. See the web page http://techcrunch.com/2014/05/06/google-maps-on-mobile-gets-uber-integration-and-more.
7. See the web page http://techcrunch.com/2013/09/04/uber-inks-its-first-sports-deal-partners-with-the-nfl-to-promote-safe-rides-for-pro-footballers.
8. See the web page http://www.businessinsider.com/uber-has-changed-my-life-and-as-god-is-my-witness-i-will-never-take-a-taxi-again-where-available-2014-1.

taxi services. Because of the ease of use and pricing similar to those of taxi rides, Uber can reach a large customer segment and increase its revenue stream.

Key resources are the next building block. Uber has two key resources: its drivers and its mobile application. Both the app and the Uber drivers are needed to set up rides for customers and to generate revenue.

The next building block of the Business Model Canvas is the distribution channels. Again, Uber reaches its customers through two primary distribution channels. The first channel is the Uber mobile app. As stated previously, Uber customers use the mobile app to schedule and pay for their rides. The second channel is the actual driving of customers by Uber employees. This is the channel through which customers receive the value paid for on the mobile app.

Another building block is the cost structure. Uber employs a cost-driven cost structure. Uber minimizes its costs by not owning any of the cars used by the drivers. Because of this, Uber does not need to fund the up-front costs for a fleet of cars or any additional maintenance fees that are associated with car ownership. The only costs for Uber are a fixed percentage of all ride fares being paid to Uber drivers and all costs associated with building and maintaining the Uber mobile app, including customer service, overhead, and the like.

The final building block in the Business Model Canvas is the revenue stream. This is discussed in more detail later in this case study. Uber's stream of revenue comes from fares collected by Uber drivers. As previously mentioned, Uber collects around 20% of all fares, with the remaining balance going to the Uber driver.[9] Uber has also introduced a way to increase revenue through surge pricing. Uber has found that demand for transportation during rush hours will still exist even if prices are raised to a premium rate.[10] Because of this, Uber now charges higher rates during the busiest hours of the day. In addition to this surge charge during rush hour, Uber introduced a safety fee in response to criticism from insurance companies.[11] This increased fee serves as another stream of revenue to combat any regulatory fees that Uber has to pay.

Expansion, Innovation, and Funding
As of this writing, Uber operates in more than 100 cities and towns worldwide. Since the company's official launch in 2010, Uber's rapid rate of growth has allowed the company to standardize and streamline its expansion process. With each new city in which Uber launches a fleet of drivers, the company first tests prospect areas with "secret launches" approximately one month prior to the official launch.

---

9. See the web page http://www.huffingtonpost.com/david-fagin/life-as-an-uber-driver_b_4698299.html.
10. See the web page http://pando.com/2013/12/17/the-problem-with-ubers-surge-pricing-isnt-the-money-its-an-increasing-lack-of-trust.
11. See the web page http://www.bizjournals.com/cincinnati/news/2014/04/21/uber-adds-new-fee-to-cover-safety-costs.html.

The reason for these secret launches is threefold. First, Uber tests its software and its vehicles in the city in question, allowing drivers to familiarize themselves with the area. Uber's blog explains that each city is unique in its transportation pain points, density, transportation alternatives, and transportation culture. Second, the "secret" Uber vehicles act as mobile marketing agents by driving through densely populated areas while promoting the Uber brand. This marketing technique is facilitated by the use of "rider zeroes," the initial wave of celebrity riders of the Uber city service (TV celebrities, Olympians, and the like). Third, Uber uses this opportunity to finalize legislative obligations with municipal government bodies.

To further its expansion, Uber began to employ a loss-leading strategy in U.S. cities to attract a new customer base comprising more than early adopters. So far, Uber has announced that it will give two weeks of free rides to residents of Cincinnati, Cleveland, Ann Arbor, and Memphis.

Milestones

To better understand the growth that Uber has enjoyed since its founding, the milestones that Uber has hit since 2010 are parsed in three discrete categories: expansion milestones, innovation milestones, and funding milestones. The events in these three categories tell the story behind the monumental success of this technology/transportation startup.

Expansion Milestones   Since the company's founding and initial launch in San Francisco in June 2010, Uber has expanded to most of the major metropolitan regions in the world. Following is a short list of international expansion milestones that the company has hit to boost its revenue stream and publicity:

- *December 7, 2011:* Uber launched its UberEurope and UberParis brands, which opened the Uber app software and transportation service to European residents.
- *November 29, 2012:* Uber launched in Sydney, its first Australian city.
- *February 22, 2013:* Uber launched in Singapore, its first Asian territory.
- *August 2, 2013:* Uber declared its first multicity launch in Taipei, Seoul, and Mexico City. Since then, Uber has initiated seven other multicity launches in clusters ranging from two to four cities.
- *August 7, 2013:* Uber launched in Johannesburg, its first African city.
- *August 27, 2013:* Uber launched in Dubai, its first Middle Eastern city.
- *October 24, 2013:* Uber launched in Bogota, its first South American city.
- *April 23, 2014:* Uber offers its general service and software platform in more than 100 cities.

Innovation Milestones   Uber has quickly diversified its product and services to expand into and to disrupt multiple transportation industries. With each financial milestone, it has hit, the company has quickly innovated its marketing strategies to give it a competitive edge against other entrants into the tech/transportation industry. Here are some of Uber's most popular innovations:

- *UberX:* On October 30, 2013, Uber launched its low-end ride-sharing UberX service in Oklahoma City. The UberX service is a low-cost version of the standard Uber service that partners a city's own drivers with the Uber service. By coupling local drivers with the Uber software platform, this ride-sharing plan made efficient use of the existing cars in "Uberized" cities. Uber claims that the benefits of such a service include fewer cars on the road (helping to ease the traffic and environmental strains of cities) and job opportunities for local drivers. Applicant drivers undergo an arduous screening process that includes (1) a stringent background check, (2) a driving history check, (3) an in-person interview, (4) a city knowledge exam, and (5) a series of ongoing quality control assessments.[12]

- *UberBLACK:* UberBLACK is a premium service running parallel to the low-cost UberX option. In this luxury version of the Uber service, riders are conveyed by licensed chauffeurs in black luxury sedans or SUVs. Like the UberX plan, the chauffeurs undergo a thorough screening process and are covered by $1 million in liability insurance.[13]

- *UberRUSH:* UberRUSH represents Uber's disruption of the mail delivery industry. Currently operating in Manhattan, UberRUSH allows for fast messenger pickups and immediate deliveries of mail within a predetermined delivery sector. Regarding the pricing of Uber's delivery service, the company states that "Rates are calculated based on zone pricing. If a delivery begins and ends within the same zone, it's a flat $15. Each zone crossed during delivery is an additional $5. Additional stops may result in a higher fare."[14]

Funding Milestones   Uber has realized tremendous success in raising capital throughout the various stages of its startup cycle, as reported by *CrunchBase*:[15]

- *Seed financing:* With the conception of a working software prototype, in August 2009 Uber cofounders Garrett Camp and Travis Kalanick raised $200,000 in seed funding to initiate the UberCab taxi service in San Francisco.[16]

---

12. "Ridesharing: A Slam Dunk for the 'Big Friendly,'" blog post, October 30, 2013, http://blog.uber.com/LaunchOKC.

13. Steven Gursten, "What's the Difference between Uber Black and UberX, and What Are My Rights If I Am Injured in an Uber Car Crash?," *Detroit Legal Examiner,* Detroit Michigan Personal Injury Lawyer, 2014, http://detroit.legalexaminer.com/automobile-accidents/uber-black-uberx-rights-if-injured.

14. "A Reliable Ride for Your Deliveries," blog post, April 7, 2014, http://blog.uber.com/RUSH.

15. CrunchBase, "Company Overview: Uber," CrunchBase.com, http://www.crunchbase.com/organization/uber. The information on this web page was compiled by one of the authors.

16. First Round Capital, "Uber—Capital," FirstRound.com, http://firstround.com/company/uber.

- *Angel financing:* After establishing itself under the company name, UberCab in October 2010, the Uber team raised $1.25 million in an angel investor round led by First Round Capital and the "super angel" investor Chris Sacca.[17]

- *Venture capital (Series A):* In a fundraising round intended to expand Uber to areas outside San Francisco, the company closed an $11 million investment round led by Benchmark Capital in February 2011, which valued the company at $49 million pre-money valuation ($60 million post-money).[18]

- *Series B:* To fund the December 2011 Europe expansion, Uber raised $32 million in its Series B financing from an array of high-profile investors. New investors included Menlo Ventures, Goldman Sachs, and Bezos Expeditions. Other significant participating investors included Benchmark Capital, and Lowercase Capital.[19]

- *Series C:* In August 2013, Google instigated a massive funding round for Uber with its venture capital arm. With this round of funding, Uber received $258 million on a company valuation of around $3.5 billion. With speculation of Uber becoming the next big tech IPO, Google's noteworthy investment was motivated not just by Uber's potential but also by the potential for the two companies to work together on projects. David Krane, the Google Ventures partner who orchestrated the investment, mentioned that projects involving Google's software (namely, Google Maps) and Google's self-driving cars are among the future collaborations between the two tech companies.[20]

17. First Round Capital, "Uber—Capital."
18. Michael Arrington, "Huge Vote of Confidence: Uber Raises $11 Million from Benchmark Capital," *TechCrunch,* February 14, 2011, http://techcrunch.com/2011/02/14/huge-vote-of-confidence-uber-raises-11-million-from-benchmark-capital.
19. Arrington, "Huge Vote of Confidence."
20. Marcus Wohlsen, "What Uber Will Do with All That Money from Google," *Wired,* January 3, 2014, http://www.wired.com/2014/01/uber-travis-kalanick.

APPENDIX B

CASE: VALUATION OF TENTEX

In chapter 16, we described four valuation methods. In this chapter we apply two of the methods, the income method and the market method, to the valuation of a private company, Tentex, to estimate its enterprise value and equity value. As will be evident, in practice the application requires a considerable number of assumptions and the use of financial models whose parameters/inputs must be estimated. The valuation date is year-end 2006.

About Tentex

Tentex, a C corporation, is a family-owned business located in the midwestern United States. Tentex had been operating profitably for more than ten years at the time of the valuation. It was founded with the mission to develop ultraviolet (UV) technology, as is used in municipal water treatment plants, for use in a personal, portable device that would provide the user with safe drinking water anywhere. The company's flagship product, Tester, purifies water using UV light and destroys viruses, bacteria, and protozoa, including *Giardia* and *Cryptosporidium*, in seconds. The product can purify water from such sources as a clear running brook or a hotel tap. Tentex is a stage 6 company[1] operating in North American Industry Standard Classification System (NAICS) 333319 (Other Commercial and Service Industry Machinery Manufacturing). Since this company at the time of valuation was in stage 6 in its life cycle, then, as suggested by the AICPA guidelines, we will not use the asset-based method.

The Income Statement and Required Adjustments

Tentex's reported earnings before interest and taxes (EBIT) were positive and relatively small. Its cash flow after required adjustments was significantly positive. To arrive at cash flow for valuation purposes, several sets of adjustments to Tentex's reported income

---

1. According to the AICPA Practice Guide, a stage 6 company means that the "enterprise has an established financial history of profitable operation or generation of positive cash flows. An IPO could also occur during this stage."

This appendix is co-authored with Dr. Stanley Jay Feldman, chairman of Axiom Valuation Solutions.

statement were made. To demonstrate these adjustments, we start with table B.1, which shows Tentex's latest income statement. The column labeled "Reported Value" in the table shows that Tentex reported a positive EBIT in its most current year, which we have called Year 0. After making the adjustments, Tentex's adjusted EBIT significantly increases above its reported level. The adjustments made to the reported income statement are of two types: (1) adjustments related to the compensation of officers and other personnel related to the owners and (2) adjustments related to discretionary expenses or expenses that are made but are not necessarily business-related.

Adjustments   The reported compensation per owner/officer of $370,000 can be conceptually divided into two components: (1) a wage and (2) a dividend equivalent each owner/ officer receives. To estimate the true cost of labor, it is necessary to determine the market wage (including benefits) the company would have to pay to acquire the same services each owner/officer currently provides. Compensation less the market wage (including benefits) equals the dividend equivalent each owner/officer receives.

Table B.1 also shows the "benchmark wage" for each owner/officer, labeled "Benchmark Value" in the table. This benchmark is based on the company's industry, asset size class, and geographic location, as shown in table B.2. Tentex's asset size is $5 million and the company is located in the state of Illinois. The benchmark wage (by state) for each owner/officer is $129,287. The difference between compensation paid per owner/officer and this benchmark wage is $240,713. This $240,713 dividend equivalent is added back to the reported EBIT. The total add-back from this source is $481,426.

The same adjustments for owners/officers are made for owners' family members employed by the company. It is not uncommon for owners to compensate family members in excess of what the company would pay if the company hired equivalently skilled third parties to do the same job. Like officer compensation, occupation wage levels vary by industry and geographic location. Based on the data from the Bureau of Labor Statistics, Tentex pays owners' family members close to twice their market wages. Based on these adjustments, the reported EBIT increases by $81,190.

Discretionary expenses are incurred but are not necessary for the normal functioning of the business. A database of discretionary expense percentages by industry is used. The second panel in table B.2 shows the discretionary expense ratios applied to Tentex. A discretionary expense benchmark is obtained by multiplying each discretionary expense ratio by Tentex's total revenue. These benchmark values are then compared to the actual discretionary expenses, with the adjustments to EBIT being as follows:

- If the actual expense exceeds its benchmark, the cost is reduced by the amount of the difference, and the adjusted EBIT is correspondingly increased.
- If the company does not spend enough in a particular category, the expense level is raised and the adjusted EBIT declines.

Table B.1
Tentex's Income Statement and Adjustments to Reported Income Statement for Valuation Purposes at Year 0

	Concept	Reported Value	Benchmark Value	Adjustment to Total Costs	Adjusted Value
1	Gross receipts less returns and allowances	$4,526,341	N/A	$0	$4,526,341
2	Cost of goods sold	2,444,000	N/A	2,444,000	
3	Depreciation	300,000	N/A	0	300,000
4	Compensation of owners/officers	740,000	258,574	(481,426)	258,574
5	Compensation of owner/officer 1	370,000	129,287	(240,713)	129,287
6	Compensation of owner/officer 2	370,000	129,287	(240,713)	129,287
7	Salaries and wages	350,000	268,810	(81,190)	268,810
8	Bookkeeping clerk (wife)	50,000	28,650	(21,350)	28,650
9	Secretary (son)	45,000	26,390	(18,610)	26,390
10	Product promoter (brother)	55,000	25,360	(29,640)	25,360
11	Machinist (daughter)	45,000	33,410	(11,590)	33,410
12	Other	155,000	N/A	0	155,000
13	Repairs and maintenance	250,000	N/A	0	250,000
14	Rents	67,000	N/A	0	67,000
15	Interest	55,800	N/A	0	55,800
16	Other deductions	175,000	48,622	(126,378)	48,622
17	Travel expenses	75,000	28,009	(46,991)	28,009
18	Family vacation	25,000			
19	Trip to Super Bowl	10,000			
20	Family automobile	35,000			
21	Fuel for family vehicles	5,000			
22	Entertainment expenses	45,000	3,331	(41,669)	3,331
23	Company parties	20,000			
24	Televisions	15,000			
25	Season tickets to sports teams	10,000			
26	Meal expenses	50,000	13,534	(36,466)	13,534
27	Family dinners	35,000			
28	Sales dinners	15,000			
29	Club expenses	5,000	3,748	(1,252)	3,748
30	Operating income	144,541			833,535
31	Earnings before interest and taxes (EBIT)	200,341			899,335
32	Tax rate	40%			40%
33	Net operating profit after tax (NOPAT)	$120,205			$533,601

Table B.2
Inputs for Benchmark Value

A. Benchmark Values for NAICS for Officer Compensation

			Asset Size			
	$100,000	$500,000	$1,000,000	$5,000,000	$25,000,000	$250,000,000
National	59,870	97,870	133,818	133,818	182,970	299,103
Illinois	57,843	94,556	129,287	129,287	176,774	288,974

B. Benchmark Values for NAICS for Discretionary Expenses

Expense	Expense Benchmark (as percentage of total revenue)
Travel	0.6188
Entertainment	0.0736
Meals	0.2990
Club Fee	0.0828

C. Benchmark Value from Bureau of Labor Statistics for Worker Compensation

Occupation	Value
Bookkeeping clerk	$28,650
Secretary	26,390
Product promoters	25,360
Machinist	33,410

Sources: Axiom Valuation Solutions Compensation Database (panel A), Axiom Valuation Solutions Discretionary Expense Database (panel B), Bureau of Labor Statistics (panel C).

An investor should adjust the reported value based on an appropriate benchmark. At a minimum, criteria should be developed based on the facts and circumstances that characterize the business being valued, and where possible, data should be employed that would offer guidance as to how to adjust the reported value.

Net operating profit after tax (NOPAT) is equal to EBIT multiplied by one minus the combined marginal federal, state, and local tax rates. For Tentex, a 40% tax rate has been assumed in the calculations. Tentex's NOPAT as reported is $120,205. After the adjustments, the adjusted NOPAT is $533,601.

As a result, the last column of table B.1 shows that the adjusted value is significantly greater than the reported value, which yields a higher enterprise value and equity value than if the adjustments were not made. The details are shown in the following paragraphs.

For all the adjustments to Tentex shown above, we rely on industry benchmark values for officer compensation to revenue, which is part of the Axiom Valuation Solution database, which in turn uses compensation and related expense data from the Bureau of Labor Statistics and the Bureau of Economic Analysis. While we did not use Robert Morris Associates' data at the time of this valuation, they are nevertheless another source for officer's compensation data by industry.[2] The analysis involves multiplying the officer compensation to revenue ratio by the revenue of the company whose valuation is sought. The difference between the reported compensation and this benchmark compensation value is treated as excess (shortage) compensation, if this difference is positive (negative), which means that the officer's compensation should be adjusted downward (upward). As can be seen in table B.1, the adjusted value is significantly greater than the reported value. As demonstrated below, the adjustments result in a higher valuation for the company.

Computing the Free Cash Flow

Table B.3 shows how to calculate the free cash flow for Tentex step by step, based on six years of data. The first year is the current year (Year 0) and there are six years shown beyond the current year. The last column represents the aggregate of all the years beyond Year 6. The Year 0 information is taken from table B.1, Tentex's income statement, "Adjusted Value" column. The adjusted EBIT ($889,335) and adjusted NOPAT ($533,601) are shown in table B.3, rows 3 and 6, respectively.

Rows 8 through 12 provide information based on the balance sheet and cover changes in net fixed capital and net working capital. The changes in net fixed capital and net working capital are adjustments made to NOPAT to obtain free cash flow (FCF). To get the FCF, it is necessary to adjust NOPAT by subtracting changes in net fixed capital and net working capital since these capital additions are needed to support firm growth.

Table B.4 shows Tentex's balance sheet in Year 0. Net fixed capital is calculated by adding row 8, $6,789,512, gross plant and equipment, and row 9, −$5,513,731, accumulated depreciation. The $1,275,781 net fixed capital for Year 0 is shown in row 9 of table B.3. Net working capital is equal to current assets minus current liabilities. Tentex's current assets include cash, accounts receivable, inventories, and other current assets, as shown in table B.4. Some adjustments should be made to the values on the balance sheet to obtain the figure we will need to compute the free cash flow. More specifically, in the case of cash an adjustment is needed because it is not unusual for private companies to have excess cash buildup on the balance sheet. This is particularly the case for C corporations, whose excess cash is taxed at the stockholder level if the excess cash is distributed. There are various ways to determine the appropriate level of cash needed to operate the firm and make the adjustment thereafter. For Tentex, cash in excess of 5% revenue is assumed to be excessive. Taking Year 0 as an example, as shown in table B.1, the Year 0 revenue is $4,526,341. Under the assumption, $226,317 (5% × $4,526,341) is sufficient for Tentex's operation. This amount is shown in row 2 of table B.4 and it is to be used in calculating the adjusted current assets. The adjustments must also be made to the current liabilities. Adjusted current liabilities include only the liabilities that emerge from operating the business. The short-term debt and current portion of long-term debt are part of the overall debt level. Therefore they are not included in the adjusted current liabilities. The Year 0 adjusted

---

2. Robert Morris Associates, *Annual Statement Studies* (Philadelphia: RMA, 2006).

Table B.3
Calculation of Tentex's Free Cash Flows

Inputs:
Perpetuity growth rate = 2.00%.
Weighted average cost of capital (WACC) = 25.25%.

	Concept	Time Period							Value in Perpetuity
		0	1	2	3	4	5	6	
1	Revenue	$4,526,341	$5,205,292	$5,829,927	$4,354,621	$6,799,444	$7,003,427	$7,213,530	
2	Revenue growth		15%	12%	9%	7%	3%	3%	
3	EBIT	899,335	1,004,949	1,105,443	1,271,260	1,398,384	1,482,288	1,526,757	
4	EBIT growth		13%	10%	15%	10%	6%	3%	
5	Tax at 40%	355,734	401,979	442,177	508,504	559,354	592,915	610,703	
6	NOPAT	533,601	602,969	663,266	762,756	839,031	889,373	916,054	
7	NOPAT growth		13%	10%	15%	10%	6%	3%	
8	Net capital expenditure growth		7%	7%	7%	7%	7%	7%	
9	Net fixed capital	1,275,781	1,365,086	1,460,642	1,562,887	1,672,289	1,789,349	1,914,603	
10	Change in net fixed capital		89,305	95,556	102,245	109,402	117,060	125,254	
11	Net working capital	677,536	724,964	775,711	830,011	888,111	950,279	1,016,799	
12	Change in net working capital		47,428	50,747	54,300	58,101	62,168	66,520	
13	Free cash flow		$466,237	$516,963	$606,211	$671,528	$710,145	$724,280	$4,018,818

current liabilities for Tentex exclude the $200,000 short-term debt and the current portion of long-term debt shown in row 12 of table B.4. For Tentex at Year 0, the $677,536 adjusted working capital is equal to the $1,850,536 adjusted current assets minus the $1,173,000 adjusted current liabilities shown in row 22 of table B.4.

For Year 1 to Year 6, the following assumptions are made in the analysis:

- the growth in revenue each year;
- the growth in net fixed capital and net working capital each year.

The calculations for changes in net fixed capital and net working capital for Year 1 are explained below. The net fixed capital and net working capital are assumed to grow 7% from Year 0 to Year 1. Year 0's net fixed capital is $1,275,781, based on table B.4. Year 1's net fixed capital is calculated to be $1,365,086 ($1,275,781 × (1 + 7%)). The amount for the change in net fixed capital is equal to $89,305 ($1,365,086 – $1,275,781). It is the amount shown in row 10 of table B.3. A similar calculation is done to obtain the change in net working capital for Year 1 ($47,428). The free cash flow for Year 1 ($466,237) is obtained by deducting from the Year 1 NOPAT ($602,969) the changes in net fixed capital ($89,305) and net working capital ($47,428), with the result shown in row 13 of table B.3. The calculations of the free cash flow for the next five years follow the same procedure.

The final free cash flow to be determined is the perpetuity or terminal value. This value is the present value of all the future cash flows beyond Year 6. The terminal value is calculated based on the Gordon-Shapiro constant growth model, explained in chapter 16. In applying the Gordon-Shapiro constant growth valuation model, beyond Year 6, the assumptions are a 2% perpetuity growth rate, since Tentex no longer has a sustainable competitive advantage; a 25.25% cost of capital (WACC—weighted average cost of capital); and no further changes for both net fixed capital and net working capital.

Calculating the WACC

Given Tentex's free cash flows as shown in row 13 of table B.3, discounting these free cash flows requires determining the firm's cost of capital, WACC. The WACC equals the sum of the costs of the equity and debt components. The equity cost component is calculated by multiplying the percentage of equity to overall capital and the cost of equity. The debt cost component is calculated by multiplying the percentage of debt to overall capital and the after-tax cost of debt.

The calculation of WACC requires an assumption about what the capital structure is expected to be. Tentex's capital structure at the time of the valuation was 67.56% equity and 32.44% debt. This capital structure is used to compute Tentex's WACC.[3] Later on the equity model used to determine the cost of equity is described. The equity model is based

3. The firm's optimal capital structure is used when valuing a firm. Though there are methods to calculate it, it is generally assumed that the average or median capital structure of the set of public firm comparables approximates the optimal capital structure. In this case, the facts and circumstances were such that this rule of thumb was not appropriate.

Table B.4

Tentex's Balance Sheet and Calculation of Net Fixed Capital and Net Working Capital at Year 0

	Concept	Year 0
	Assets:	
1	Cash	$400,000
2	Cash required for operations	266,317
3	Excess cash	173,683
4	Accounts receivable	452,634
5	Inventories	1,131,585
6	Other current assets	40,000
7	Total current assets	2,024,219
8	Gross plant and equipment	6,789,512
9	Accumulated depreciation	(5,513,731)
10	Net fixed capital	1,275,781
11	Total assets	$3,300,000
	Liabilities and equity:	
12	Short-term debt and current portion of long-term debt	$200,000
13	Accounts payable	1,123,000
14	Accrued liabilities	50,000
15	Total current liabilities	1,373,000
16	Long-term debt	490,000
17	Other long-term liabilities	0
18	Deferred income taxes	0
19	Total shareholder equity	1,437,000
20	Total liabilities and equity	3,300,000
21	Net fixed capital	$1,275,781
22	Net working capital: (R7:R3) − (R15 − R12)	$677,536
23	Book value of debt/equity	48%

on four risk factors—business risk, financial risk, size risk, and firm-specific risk. The cost of equity based on the equity model is estimated to be 33.79%. The cost of debt calculation is explained in the financial models section later in this appendix. Based on the statistical model, the pre-tax cost of debt is estimated to be 12.46%. Factoring in the assumed 40% tax rate, the after-tax cost of debt after adjusting for the tax deductibility of interest is 7.48% (12.46% × (1 − 40%)).

Tentex's WACC = 67.56% × 33.79% + 32.44% × 7.48% = 25.25%.

Tentex's 25.25% WACC will be used to discount the free cash flows.

Market Value of Debt

Another value that must be estimated to obtain the equity value of Tentex is the market value of debt. As noted earlier, the equity value is the enterprise value minus the market value of debt. The market value of debt for Tentex is calculated using the four steps described below.

Step 1: Estimate the credit rating of the debt. The statistical credit scoring model is explained later and applied to Tentex. The credit rating for Tentex based on the statistical model is B3/B–. This B3/B– rating can be used to determine the credit spread for Tentex.

Step 2: Estimate the maturity of the current debt on the firm's balance sheet. The weighted average maturity of the debt is six years for Tentex's debt.

Step 3: Based on the maturity of the debt and the credit spread corresponding to Tentex's credit rating at the valuation date, the pre-tax cost of debt is estimated as the sum of the risk-free rate for the given maturity plus the credit spread for that maturity. The six-year risk-free rate is 4.71%, and for a B3/B– credit rating, the credit spread for debt of six-year maturity is 7.75%. Thus the pre-tax cost of debt is 12.46% (4.71% + 7.75%).[4]

Step 4: Based on the 12.46% pre-tax cost of debt from step 3, discount the interest expenses and principal repayments over the maturity of the debt. For Tentex, the book value of the debt at the valuation date was $690,000. The interest expenses were $27,900 every six months. The market value of the debt is the present (discounted) value of the debt's cash flows. The cash flows are the twelve semiannual interest payments ($27,000) and the principal repayment ($690,000) at Year 6. The discount rate used to determine the present value of the cash flows is the estimated 12.46% pre-tax cost of debt. Table B.5 shows the calculation of the market value of debt.

Valuing Tentex's Enterprise Using the Income Method

Given the free cash flows for Tentex as shown in table B.3, row 13, and the discount rate (25.25% WACC), the enterprise value can be estimated. Table 16.1 in chapter 16, which illustrated how to compute the present value of a series of future values, has the free cash flows from table B.3. One of the two discount rates used in that illustration is 25.25%, Tentex's WACC. The present values given in table 16.2 in chapter 16 were computed using the midyear convention. Hence the $3,068,848 sum of the present values shown in the last column of table 16.2 is the enterprise value.

The potential buyer of Tentex would also be receiving the excess cash of $173,683 (row 3 in table B.4) described earlier in the discussion of how to adjust the working capital reported on the balance sheet. This amount must be added to the enterprise value. Thus the enterprise value with excess cash is $3,242,531 ($3,068,848 + $173,683).

---

4. The spread between six and ten years varies between 7.25% and 7.75%. We have used the higher spread here to reflect the fact that Tentex is a small firm and the spread is likely to be somewhat higher than a six-year spread would suggest.

Table B.5
Calculation of the Market Value of Tentex's Debt

Year	Future Value of Cash Flows	Present Value of $1 at 12.46%	Present Value of Cash Flows
0.0	$0	$1.0000	$0
0.5	27,900	0.9430	26,309
1.0	27,900	0.8892	24,809
1.5	27,900	0.8385	23,394
2.0	27,900	0.7907	22,060
2.5	27,900	0.7456	20,802
3.0	27,900	0.7031	19,616
3.5	27,900	0.6630	18,497
4.0	27,900	0.6252	17,443
4.5	27,900	0.5895	16,448
5.0	27,900	0.5559	15,510
5.5	27,900	0.5242	14,626
6.0	717,900	0.4943	354,875
		Sum	574,389

   The equity value of Tentex is found by reducing the enterprise value with excess cash by the $574,389 market value of debt. The calculated equity value is $2,668,142 ($3,242,531 − $574,389).

   Finally, as explained in chapter 16, an adjustment for the lack of liquidity is applied. A 20% liquidity discount is assumed. An assumed 20% liquidity discount of the equity value gives the liquidity discount dollar value of $533,628. Subtracting this liquidity discount from the $2,668,142 equity value gives the liquidity-adjusted equity value of $2,134,514.

   To summarize,

	Enterprise value (Sum of present value of free cash flows) $3,068,848
+	Excess cash $173,683
=	Enterprise value, including excess cash, $3,242,531
−	Market value of debt $574,389
=	Equity value $2,668,142
−	Liquidity discount (20%) $533,628
=	Liquidity-adjusted equity value $2,134,514

Table B.6
Comparison of Tentex to Selected Peer Firms

Dimension	Basin Water	Seychelle Environmental Technologies	Tentex
Revenue	$12,231,000	$684,000	$4,526,341
NOPAT/revenue	5.81%	−91.81%	11.79%
Debt/revenue	62.19%	71.05%	15.24%
Debt/equity	0.057	0.042	0.48
WACC	19.12%	29.99%	25.25%
Enterprise value/revenue	11.51×	17.46×	—

The liquidity-adjusted enterprise value including excess cash is $2,708,903 ($3,242,531 − $533,628), found by subtracting the liquidity discount from the enterprise value including excess cash.[5]

Valuing Tentex Using the Market Method: Guideline Public Company Analysis

In chapter 16 we explained how to use the income method, more specifically, the discounted cash flow method, to value Tentex. The management of Tentex identified two public firms that are direct competitors. Though several private firms compete with Tentex, there were no recent private firm transactions in Tentex's space that could be used as valuation comparables for the guideline transactions analysis. Though several transactions had taken place more than a year before the analysis, the economic and industry conditions had changed enough to indicate that these transactions could not be used as comparables to value Tentex. Thus, we use only public firm comparables and make adjustments to the valuation metric to account for differences between the two public firms that management identified and Tentex.

Table B.6 shows the data for the two public firms that are comparable to Tentex. Both firms operate in Tentex's segment. Basin Water is far larger than Tentex, while Seychelle Environmental Technologies is far smaller and also had a negative NOPAT margin. It appears that Tentex does not compare exactly to selected peer firms across a number of important dimensions that affect a firm's value. Therefore, the peer firm multiples are not used directly to develop a multiple for Tentex.

As noted earlier in the discussion of the valuation method, even within the same industry, there is often a wide variation in firm size and in the values of relevant financial variables across firms. One may use the Gordon-Shapiro constant growth model as given by equation (16.6) in chapter 16 to derive a "shadow" multiple for the enterprise valuation to revenue ratio as shown in equation (16.7) in chapter 16.

5. In cases where excess cash is not distributed, as is assumed here, excess cash is subjected to a liquidity discount. When the firm is sold in the form of its stock, excess cash is distributed to shareholders prior to the transaction so the liquidity-adjusted equity value does not include excess cash.

Since the NOPAT margin for Seychelle Environmental Technologies is negative, it is removed from the analysis. Basin Water's WACC is calculated and the growth rate g (the implied growth in NOPAT) is solved using equation (16.8) in chapter 16. Based on the calculation, Basin Water's implied growth rate g is 18.52%. Assuming that the growth potential of Tentex is equal to Basin Water's calculated growth rate g, the implied multiple for Tentex is then calculated. The information for Basin Water is the same as used earlier to illustrate the calculation in equation (16.8) in chapter 16.

In the Gordon-Shapiro model as used in this analysis, g represents the average long-term growth rate in NOPAT. This g is the geometric average of the projected NOPAT growth rates over a long period of time, such as ten years from the valuation date. Hence g incorporates near-term growth, whereas NOPAT growth can be expected to be quite high and to exhibit far more modest growth during the perpetuity period. For Tentex, using the Gordon-Shapiro model combines the implied market assumptions about the growth rate and the unique characteristics of Tentex in calculating the implied target trading multiple. When this type of analysis is undertaken, more than one implied growth rate from peer firms can be employed. The implied g for each comparable public trading company is calculated and the median of all the growth rates is used in calculating the implied trading multiple for the target firm. In some cases the median growth rate from the peer firms might be too large or too small, requiring some adjustments to reflect these judgments.

Since the multiple is highly sensitive to changes in g, any adjustment made relative to the median value for a peer group should be based on a knowledge base that reflects the dynamics of the target firm's market segment or strategic considerations of management. In the case of Tentex, the expected long-term growth for Tentex at the valuation date was 8%, far lower than Basin Water's implied growth rate of 18.52%. The predominant reason is that Tentex has a regional rather than a national footprint. Since market buyers are expected to manage the firm in much the same way as current ownership, the growth rate used to calculate the trading multiple is expected to be well below that of Basin Water.

The NOPAT/revenue ratio is equal to 11.79% ($533,601/$4,526,341) and WACC is equal to 25.25%. Substituting these values into equation (16.7) in chapter 16, we obtain

$$\frac{\text{Enterprise value}}{\text{Revenue}} = \frac{0.1179 \times (1+g)}{0.2525-g}.$$

Since the expected growth rate for Tentex at the time of the analysis was 8%, substituting this value for g in the above equation yields the following:

$$\frac{\text{Enterprise value}}{\text{Revenue}} = \frac{0.1179 \times (1.08)}{0.2525-0.08} = 0.74.$$

Multiplying this 0.74 estimated trading multiple by the $4,526,341 for Tentex's revenue, Tentex's enterprise value based on the trading multiple is $3,340,806 (0.74 × $4,526,341).

As explained in the chapter 16, Tentex's excess cash of $173,683 must be added. Based on the calculated trading multiple, Tentex's enterprise value, including the excess cash, is $3,514,489 ($3,340,806 + $173,683).

Combining Valuations from Discounted Cash Flow Analysis and Guideline Public Company Analysis It is common to utilize information from both valuation methods to obtain an estimate of enterprise value. A weight can be applied to each method's enterprise value to obtain a weighted average enterprise value. These weights are subjective based on the fact that the discounted cash flow (DCF) method often contains more accurate information about the company whose valuation is sought than the market method does. As Steven N. Kaplan and Richard Ruback have shown, the DCF method yields a more accurate valuation than the method of comparables when the comparable firms are not clones of the target company whose valuation is sought.[6]

Suppose that the DCF method's valuation receives a weight of 70% and the market method a weight of 30%. As explained in chapter 16, using the DCF method, the enterprise value including excess cash is estimated to be $3,242,531. As shown in this chapter, using the market method, the enterprise value including excess cash is estimated to be $3,514,489.

Weighted enterprise value including excess cash = 70% × $3,242,531 + 30% × $3,514,489,

   = $3,324,118.

Given the weighted enterprise value including excess cash and the information provided earlier, the equity value can be calculated as follows:

Equity value = Weighted enterprise value including excess cash − Market value of debt,

   = $3,324,118 − $574,389,

   = $2,749,729.

The same 20% liquidity discount is applied as shown in chapter 16. Applying this discount to the above equity value, the liquidity discount is $549,946. Based on this weighting method, the equity value adjusted for liquidity is $2,199,784.

Financial Models to Estimate the WACC
The cost of debt and the cost of equity are estimated from financial models. Our discussion of the Tentex case concludes with a description of the two models used.

---

6. Steven N. Kaplan and Richard Ruback, "The Market Pricing of Cash Flow Forecasts: Discounted Cash Flows vs. The Method of Comparables," *Journal of Applied Corporate Finance* 8, no. 4 (1996): 45–60.

Estimating the Cost of Equity   To estimate the cost of equity, various financial models have been used. Two of the commonly used models, the capital asset pricing model and the factor model, are discussed below.

Capital Asset Pricing Model   The **capital asset pricing model** (CAPM) is a commonly used model for estimating the cost of equity. The assumption for CAPM is that all investors will hold a combination of two assets: a well-diversified portfolio that consists of all assets in the market and a risk-free asset. The well-diversified portfolio of all assets in the market is referred to as the **market portfolio**. The market portfolio is a theoretical bundle of investments that includes every type of asset available in the world financial market, with each asset weighted in proportion to its total presence in the market. The expected return of a market portfolio is identical to the expected return of the market as a whole. Because a completely diversified portfolio is exposed only to systematic risk (risk that impacts the overall market) and not to unsystematic or nondiversifiable risk (the risk that cannot be diversified away). In practice, the proxy for the market portfolio (which is supposed to consist of all assets) is normally a stock market index, such as the S&P 500. The risk-free asset is assumed to be the interest rate available on a long-dated investment in U.S. Treasury securities, such as the interest rate on a twenty-year Treasury Bond.

The CAPM recognizes that all assets have unique risks. However, according to the theory, the only risk that is priced by investors is market risk because when investors hold the market portfolio, which is the portfolio of all traded assets, the unique risks of each asset are diversified away and therefore the returns from these assets are determined by their nondiversifiable characteristics and hence their market or nondiversifiable risk. Put differently, CAPM theory concludes that firm-specific risks, while real, are not rewarded by the market because an investor can protect himself by owning the market portfolio and being fully diversified. Hence the market does not reward investors for taking risk they do not have to take. As far as diversification is concerned, the market portfolio is the least risky portfolio that an investor can expect to construct. Assuming that investors hold well-diversified portfolios (approximating the market portfolio), the only risk they have is nondiversifiable risk.

There are other terms used to describe nondiversifiable risk or market risk. Because each asset possesses some degree of market risk, insofar as market risk is systematic across assets, nondiversifiable risk or market risk is often referred to as **systematic risk**. In contrast, diversifiable risk is referred to as **unsystematic risk**. Other terms used to describe diversifiable risk are **company-specific risk**, **idiosyncratic risk**, and **unique risk**. Unsystematic risk arises because there is risk that is specific to the company's own situation—such as the risk of lawsuits and labor strikes—and is not part of the risk that pervades all assets in the market.

The measure of the sensitivity of an asset's return to the market's return (corresponding to bearing market risk) is referred to as that asset's **beta**, denoted by the Greek letter ß. The details for calculating beta are not the focus of this chapter. In brief, the calculations for beta involve the application of statistical tools for regression analyses. For publicly traded companies, there are Internet resources that provide this information (i.e., Yahoo! Finance).

In general, beta is the approximate percentage change in an asset's expected return relative to the return realized by a market portfolio. A beta of one means that if the market portfolio's return increases by 1%, the asset's expected turn is expected to increase by 1%. Assets that have a beta greater than one are said to have greater expected return volatility relative to the market. A beta of less than one means that the asset has less volatility relative to the market's volatility.

According to the CAPM, the company's cost of equity can be estimated as follows, given a company's beta:

Cost of equity = Risk-free rate + beta × (Expected market return − Risk-free rate).

To apply the CAPM model shown above, two additional pieces of information are needed other than beta: the risk-free rate and the expected market return. The CAPM model provides general guidance in selecting the risk-free rate. In practice, a Treasury rate is used. A more challenging task is estimating the expected market return. There are institutes that will provide the expected market return each year (e.g., Ibbotson Associates). The CAPM model is derived from a specified set of assumptions that are assumed to reflect market realities. Numerous empirical studies have sought to validate the CAPM model. Although the CAPM model is often used in practice in valuation applications, there is a paucity of empirical supporting the CAPM model.

Risk Factor Models   Empirical studies have shown that the simple CAPM model does not fully explain stock returns. As a result, academics and practitioners have developed a series of risk factor models that have been more successful in explaining stock returns. These risk factor models replace the CAPM model's "market portfolio" concept with a series of risk factors that better explain the stock returns.[7] The set of factors often includes a diversified portfolio like the S&P 500 in addition to other variables. In this context, as with the simple CAPM model, the factors identified are systematic. The central characteristic of these variables is that the risks they reflect affect all risky assets to one degree or another and hence they cannot be removed, or, in the language of finance, an investor in risky assets cannot escape (i.e., diversify away from) these risks. Although the risks can be minimized, they cannot be fully diversified away. Since the risks cannot be removed, investors require an incremental return for each identified risk undertaken. The incremental return required is known as the risk premium for the identified risk in question or the market risk premium for the identified risk. In the simple CAPM model, the risk premium is measured as the

7. The CAPM model is often referred to as a one-factor model, with the market portfolio being the factor. Risk factor models are obtained through empirical analysis, with the first step being the identification of the risk factors. When a risk factor model uses only one factor, a general stock market index, it is said to be a "single factor model" or a "single index market model."

difference between the expected rate of return on the market portfolio and the risk-free rate. In a risk factor model, each identified risk, as represented by its beta (the sensitivity of an asset's return to change in the systematic risk factor), is multiplied by its risk premium, also referred to as the price of risk.

It is important to understand that these risk factor models, though empirically more robust than the simple CAPM model, are also less transparent since they do not specify the risk factors but treat them as an issue better left to empirical researchers to determine. The beauty of the CAPM model lies in its simplicity and its dependence on only the market portfolio. Because constructing the market portfolio identified in the theory has been virtually impossible, and hence there is no way to simply test the simple CAPM theory with any degree of preciseness, researchers have opted for models that can be realistically implemented in practice, but they have done so at a cost of not being able to specify the unique factors that drive stock returns. As a result, a number of risk factor models have been developed and tested, including various versions of the multifactor CAPM. A detailed description of these models is beyond the scope of this book.

In equation form, risk factor models are represented by the following equation.

Expected equity return = risk-free rate + β_1 (market risk premium for risk factor 1) + ... + β_K (market risk premium for risk factor K),

where β_i is the factor sensitivity of the stock's return with respect to risk factor i and K is the number of risk factors. The market risk premium is the required compensation for accepting the risk of the identified factor.

One example of a basic factor model, and the one we used in the Tentex case study, uses the following four risk factors and their associated risk premiums: business risk, financial risk, size risk, and firm-specific risk. Although the firm-specific risk is not systematic, for the reasons noted above, we'll explain why it is included as a risk factor in our case study. A metric is needed to proxy for each of these risk factors. We will explain how this is done for each risk factor.

The core systematic risks that have an impact on the firm's business are referred to as its ***business risk***. This risk is quantified by measuring the sensitivity of the firm's common stock return to changes in the return for the overall stock market as proxied by a broadly diversified stock market index such as the S&P 500 index. This is also referred to as ***market risk***. To account for differences in the capital structure of firms, an additional adjustment is made. This adjustment reflects the ***financial risk*** of the firm. The higher the debt-to-equity ratio, the more debt the firm is using relative to equity and hence the greater the risk to equity holders from the firm having too much leverage. The final systematic risk is ***size risk***. Empirical work indicates that when two firms are equivalent in every way except size, investors require an incremental return to compensate them for investing in the smaller firm rather than its larger counterpart. Size is measured by a firm's market capitalization.

Firm-specific risk is the risk that is unique to the firm. In theory, this unique risk can be fully diversified away by allocating funds to competitor firms in the industry, as well as firms outside the industry. Investors in private firms, such as firm owners, for example, typically have a substantial amount of their wealth tied up in the business and so their ability to diversify is limited. Hence even large institutional investors in private firms take on firm-specific risk and want to be compensated appropriately for taking it.

All of the measures for risk factors are available for private firms except the unlevered beta, which is a measure of the firm's systematic risk, and we only describe the steps in measuring the unlevered beta. These steps are summarized as follows:

1. Select a set of publicly traded guideline companies that are equivalent to the private firm with respect to industry, product or service offered, and general business model.
2. Calculate the monthly stock returns for each firm and the S&P 500 index for the latest sixty months.[8]
3. Using the statistical tool of regression analysis, regress guideline returns against the index returns. The slope coefficient of this regression is the levered beta.
4. For each firm, delever the beta using the following formula to compute the unlevered beta:[9]

$$\text{Unlevered beta} = \frac{\text{Estimated levered beta}}{1 + (\text{Debt / Equity}) \times (1 - \text{Marginal tax rate})}.$$

5. Calculate the median unlevered beta from the guideline firms and use it as the beta for the private firm.

Using the above discussion as guidance, one can calculate the cost of equity for a private firm using four risk premiums:

Cost of equity = Risk-free rate + Unlevered beta × Business risk premium + Financial risk premium

+ Size premium + Firm-specific risk premium,

where

Financial risk premium = Unlevered beta × (Debt/Equity) × (1 − Marginal tax rate) × Business risk premium.

Note that in standard finance theory, the equity cost of capital does not reflect firm-specific risk since it is assumed that the risk that is unique to the firm can be diversified

---

8. While five years is typical, in cases in which the firm's characteristics have changed—for example, through acquisitions outside the predominant industry of the firm being valued—the data set used should only reflect the period when the peer and the firm being valued are sufficiently similar.

9. This formula was developed in Robert S. Hamada, "The Effect of the Firm's Capital Structure on the Systematic Risk of Common Stocks," *Journal of Finance* 27 (1972): 435–452.

away. Thus, if the investor does not have to bear unique risk, then the financial markets will not reward the investor for taking it. In estimating the cost of equity capital for a private firm, it is generally assumed that the owners and market participants that might purchase the firm or the firm's equity cannot diversify away the unique risk that the firm represents, and therefore they would incorporate a premium to reflect this fact. If the acquirers are large institutional investors, such as private equity firms, the case for a firm-specific risk premium is conceptually less compelling since these acquirers can more or less diversify this risk away. However, one study suggests that the alphas on venture capital investments are unusually large, suggesting that these investors require an additional return for accepting firm-specific risk.

Below we explain each component of the cost of equity for Tentex.

- **Risk-free rate**: The risk-free rate used is the ten-year Treasury rate. This information is obtained from the publications of the Federal Reserve Board. At the time of the valuation, this rate was 4.71%.
- **Marginal tax rate**: The rate is assumed to be 40%.
- **Debt/Equity**: Based on Tentex's balance sheet, the debt/equity ratio was 0.4802.[10]
- **Unlevered beta**: The estimated median unlevered beta based on the guideline companies was 1.562.
- **Levered beta**: Given the median unlevered beta, Tentex's levered beta is found by solving

$$\text{Unlevered beta} = \frac{\text{Estimated levered beta}}{1 + (\text{Debt} / \text{Equity}) \times (1 - \text{Marginal tax rate})}.$$

$$\text{Estimated levered beta} = \text{Unlevered beta} \times [1 + (\text{Debt} / \text{Equity}) \times (1 - \text{Marginal tax rate})].$$

Therefore, Tentex's estimated levered beta is

$$= 1.562 \times [1 + 0.482 \times (1 - 0.40)] = 2.0127.$$

- **Business risk premium:** This is equal to the unlevered beta of $1.562 \times 7.08\%$ (Market risk premium) = 11.06%
- **Financial risk premium:** This is based on the unlevered beta, a debt/equity ratio of 0.4802, a marginal tax rate of 40%, and a market risk premium of 7.08%:[11]

---

10. In general, the average of the debt-to-equity ratios of the comparable firms is assumed to be the capital structure that would be used to finance the asset base of the firm. In this case, based on facts and circumstances facing the firm, it was concluded that a market participant considering buying the firm would do so at Tentex's capital structure.

11. There are slight rounding differences depending on how the calculation is done. We have benchmarked to 14.25% and forced the components to add to this total.

Financial risk premium = Unlevered beta × [(Debt/Equity) × (1 − Marginal tax rate)] × Market risk premium

$$= 1.562 \times 0.482 \times (1 - 0.4) \times 7.08\% = 3.20\%.$$

Business risk premium + Financial risk premium = Levered beta × Market risk premium

$$= 11.05\% + 3.20\% = 2.017 \times 7.08\% = 14.25\%.$$

- *Market risk premium:* The market premium used is 7.08%, a value developed by Ibbotson Associates,[12] and reflects a historical measure of systematic risk, namely, what the return on a diversified portfolio of stocks has been in excess of the yield offered on long-dated Treasury bonds. Several financial economists argue that the market risk premium is too large relative to an assumed measure of market participant risk aversion.[13]
- *Size premium:* The value used of 9.83% is a value developed by Ibbotson Associates.[14]
- *Firm-specific risk premium:* Table B.7 shows factors that are ordinarily considered when assessing the magnitude of firm-specific risk. In this example, high risk, moderate risk, and low risk are assigned five points, three points, and one point respectively. The weights given to each of the factors are arbitrary, although their relative values generally conform to the relative importance of the factors that have the greatest impact on the expected performance of private firms. Based on the analysis shown in table B.7, Tentex's specific risk premium was 5%.

Based on the above, Tentex's cost of equity is

Cost of Equity = Risk free rate + Financial risk premium + Size premium + Firm-specific risk premium,

$$= 4.71\% + 14.25\% + 9.83\% + 5.00\% = 33.79\%.$$

Tentex's cost of equity exceeds 30%, which is primarily the result of two components, the size premium and the firm-specific risk premium. The size premium emerges because all else equal, smaller firms have a higher cost of capital than larger firms and the increment in capital cost is nonlinearly related to size decrements. Firms with market capitalizations below $50 million have very large size premiums. The second component is the firm-specific risk premium.

---

12. Table 5–6 in Ibbotson Associates, *Stocks, Bonds, Bills and Inflation: Valuation Edition* (Chicago: Ibbotson Associates, 2006).
13. Several financial economists argue that the market risk premium is too large relative to an assumed measure of market participant risk aversion. See, for example, Jeremy Siegel and Richard Thaler, "Anomalies: The Equity Risk Premium Puzzle," *Journal of Economic Perspectives* 11, no. 1 (1997): 191–200. On a going forward basis, using the historical market risk premium assumes that multiple expansions will continue, and some investors believe there is little basis to expect this not to occur. Unfortunately, addressing the complexity of this issue is beyond the scope of this book, but the research does suggest that using the historical risk premium as a measure of the incremental return expected for accepting business risk will result in a cost of capital that is too high, all else held equal. Nevertheless, for most private firms the differential size of the equity risk premium, while important, is not the most important contributor to the size of the equity cost of capital.
14. Table 7–7 in Ibbotson Associates, *Stocks, Bonds, Bills and Inflation.*

The relationship between the point total and the size of the firm-specific risk premium is based on research and investor judgment. As a matter of practice, in valuing a firm, an investor may have a rule that says if the point total is greater than 4, then the firm-specific risk premium is 5%. If the point total is between 3.1 and 3.9, then the risk premium would be set at 4%, and so on. To get an idea of the size of the firm-specific risk premium, one can review the returns earned on venture capital (VC) funds. Venture capitalists raise money from diversified investors, paying a return consistent with the investment's systematic risk and capturing the resulting excess return. This additional return is what venture capitalists require to accept the firm-specific risk of the firms in their funds. Part of these excess returns will reflect substantial size premiums, so they are not equivalent to what traditional financial theory based on the CAPM alphas would indicate but they are nevertheless suggestive of the magnitude of the size premium.

Paul A. Gompers and Josh Lerner measured returns for a single private equity group from 1972 to 1997.[15] Using a version of the CAPM model, they found that the additional return earned above the CAPM return was about 8%. John H. Cochrane studied all VC investments by investment round in the VentureOne database from 1987 through June 2000.[16] After adjusting the data for selection bias, he estimated an arithmetic average annualized return of 59%, with an arithmetic standard deviation of 119%. The alpha, the return in excess of that predicted by the CAPM, is 32%. As Cochrane notes, the reported alpha reflects both the size and the illiquidity of VC investments, and so it is not a pure alpha in the CAPM sense. However, if this value is reduced for size (9%, as reported by Ibbotson Associates) and illiquidity (13%, based on Axiom Valuation Solutions research), the resulting adjusted alpha is in the neighborhood of 10%, which is far closer to the value reported by Gompers and Lerner. Despite the difficulty in determining the appropriate size of the firm-specific risk premium, an estimate of it needs to be considered when calculating a private firm's cost of capital. In the Tentex case, firm-specific risk is determined to be 5%.[17]

Estimating the Cost of Debt   There are various approaches to estimate the cost of debt. In financial modeling, there are various statistical models that have been proposed for doing so. The statistical model we describe here and applied in our Tentex case study is the line discriminate model. This statistical model seeks to identify the relative important risk factors that can be used to derive a credit score or equivalently a credit rating for the debt that would be issued by the firm.

---

15. Paul A. Gompers and Josh Lerner, "Risk Reward and Private Equity Investments: The Challenge of Performance Assessment," *Journal of Private Equity* 1 (1997): 5–12.

16. John H. Cochrane, "The Risk and Return of Venture Capital," *Journal of Financial Economics* 75 (2005): 3–52.

17. Note that 5% is not necessarily the maximum value for the firm-specific risk premium as the comments in the text suggest. However, for a firm that has an operating history, it is a good first approximation. In the case of startups, the firm-specific risk may well be greater than 5%.

Table B.7
Calculating Tentex's Firm-Specific Risk

| Risk Concept | Firm-Specific Risk Matrix | | | |
	Measurement	Assessment	Factor Weight (%)	Weighted Assessment
Business stability	How long has the company been profitable? 1–3 yrs—high risk: 5; 4–6 yrs—moderate risk: 3; More than 6 yrs—low risk: 1	High risk: 5	10	0.50
Business transparency	Does the firm produce an audited financial statement at least once a year? Yes—low risk: 1; No—high risk: 5	High risk: 5	10	0.50
Customer concentration	Does the firm receive more than 30% of its revenue from less than 5 customers? Yes—high risk: 5; No—low risk: 1	High risk: 5	25	1.25
Supplier reliance	Can the firm change suppliers without sacrificing product/ service quality or increasing costs? Yes—low risk: 1; No— high risk: 5	High risk: 5	10	0.50
Reliance on key people	Are there any personnel critical to the success of the business who cannot be replaced in a timely way at the current market wage? Yes—high risk: 5; No— low risk: 1	High risk: 5	20	1.00
Intensity of Competition	What is the intensity of firm competition? Very intense— high risk: 5; Modestly intense— moderate risk: 3; Not very intense—low risk: 1	High risk: 5	25	1.24
Sum			100%	5.00

The most popular linear discriminant model used in credit scoring is that developed by Edward I. Altman and referred to as the *z-score model*.[18] The steps in determining the cost of a private firm's debt using this model are the following:

Step 1: Estimate the firm's z-score using the model.

Step 2: Convert the z-score to a credit rating.

Step 3: Determine the cost of debt for a given maturity as the rate on a Treasury security of equivalent maturity plus the expected yield spread associated with the credit rating.

---

18. The original model appeared in Edward I. Altman, "Financial Ratios, Discriminant Analysis and the Prediction of Corporate Bankruptcy," *Journal of Finance*, 1968, 189–209.

The z-score model for manufacturers, nonmanufacturer industrials, and emerging market credits as estimated by Altman[19] is given by

$$Z = 0.717 * X_1 + 0.847 * X_2 + 3.107 * X_3 + 0.42 * X_4 + 0.998 * X_5,$$

where

X_1 = (Current assets − Current liabilities)/Total assets,

X_2 = Retained earnings/Total assets,

X_3 = EBIT/Total assets,

X_4 = Book value of equity/Total liabilities, and

X_5 = Sales/Total assets.

Altman suggests that the above model is appropriate for calculating the credit risk of private firms. Each of these financial accounting measures and financial ratios are described in chapter 12.

The z-score model compares firms that defaulted and their financial characteristics to similar firms that did not default. The coefficients in the above equation relate the size of each financial metric to its contribution to the z-score. The higher a firm's z-score, the lower its credit risk. The crosswalk between the z-score and the S&P credit rating was developed by Altman. The credit spreads for each credit rating were developed by Axiom Valuation Solutions using Reuter financial spread data.

Table B.8 shows the relationship between a firm's debt rating and its z-score by maturity of debt at approximately the same time as the Tentex case study discussed earlier. The first column in the table shows the credit rating used by the credit rating agency. The second column shows the z-score that corresponds to the credit rating in the first column. The last seven columns correspond to the maturity of the debt and the credit spread to be added to the Treasury security with that maturity.

Now let's see how the linear discriminant model above was used to estimate the cost of debt for Tentex. For Tentex, the value of the variables in the z-score model is given by

X_1 = (Current assets − Current liabilities)/Total assets = 0.20,

X_2 = Retained earnings/Total assets = 0.44,

X_3 = EBIT/Total assets = 0.27,

X_4 = Book value of equity/Total liabilities = 0.77, and

X_5 = Sales/Total assets = 1.37.

Substituting these values into the linear discriminant model, we get:

$$z = 0.717 \times 0.20 + 0.847 \times 0.44 + 3.107 \times 0.27 + 0.42 \times 0.77 + 0.998 \times 1.37 = 3.04.$$

---

19. An updated version of the model appears in Edward I. Altman, "Predicting Financial Stress of Companies: Revisiting the Z Score and Zeta Models," Stern School of Business Working Paper, 2000.

Table B.8
Relationships between Z-Score and Credit Rating by Maturity of Debt

Credit Rating	Z-Score	Yield Spreads over Like Maturity Treasuries: Basis Points						
		1	2	3	5	7	10	30
Aaa/AAA	8.15	5	10	15	22	27	30	55
Aa1/AA+	7.60	10	15	20	32	37	40	60
Aa2/AA	7.30	15	25	30	37	44	50	65
Aa3/AA−	7.00	20	30	35	45	54	60	70
A1/A+	6.85	30	40	45	60	65	70	85
A2/A	6.65	40	50	57	67	75	82	89
A3/A−	6.40	50	65	70	80	90	96	116
Baa1/BBB+	6.25	60	75	90	100	105	114	135
Baa2/BBB	5.85	75	90	105	115	120	129	155
Baa3/BBB−	5.65	85	100	115	125	133	139	175
Ba1/BB+	5.25	300	300	275	250	275	225	250
Ba2/BB	4.95	3.25	400	425	375	325	300	300
Ba3/BB−	4.75	350	450	475	400	350	325	400
B1/B+	4.50	500	525	600	425	425	375	450
B2B	4.15	525	550	600	500	450	450	725
B3/B−	3.75	725	800	775	750	725	775	850
Caa/CCC	2.50	1,500	1,600	1,550	1,400	1,300	1,375	1,500

The following table indicates that a z-score of 3.04 is between a B3/B− and CCC. Based on the facts and circumstances of the valuation and Tentex's business performance, we have concluded that the credit rating is closer to B− than CCC and have also concluded that the proper spread is 775 basis points or 7.75%.

Credit rating	Z-score
Aaa/AAA	8.15
Aa1/AA+	7.60
Aa2/AA	7.30
Aa3/AA−	7.00
A1/A+	6.85
A2/A	6.65
A3/A−	6.40
Baa1/BBB+	6.25
Baa2/BBB	5.85

Credit rating	Z-score
Baa3/BBB–	5.65
Ba1/BB+	5.25
Ba2/BB	4.95
Ba3/BB–	4.75
B1/B+	4.50
B2/B	4.15
B3/B–	3.75
Caa/CCC	2.50

With the credit rating and the average maturity of the debt known, the cost of debt is determined as the sum of the risk-free rate plus a suitable credit spread. The risk-free rate is the yield on U.S. Treasury securities with a maturity that approximates the maturity of Tentex's debt. For this exercise the ten-year Treasury rate was used since this security is actively traded and highly liquid and therefore is a better measure of the yield on the risk-free asset. Based on the above, the cost of Tentex debt is estimated to be 12.46%:

	Risk-free rate	4.71%
+	Credit risk premium based on z-score	7.75%
=	Pre-tax cost of debt	12.46%

This is the interest rate used in the case study, which was then adjusted for the tax deductibility of the interest expense. Recall that the estimation does not assume that debt obligations are collateralized with business or personal assets. If owners personally guaranteed business debt obligations in whole or in part, then the rate on these financial liabilities would be lower than shown here.

Index